The
Wenner-Gren
Foundation
For Anthropological Research, Inc.

Indigenous Experience Today

WENNER-GREN INTERNATIONAL SYMPOSIUM SERIES

. . . .

Series Editor: Leslie C. Aiello, President, Wenner-Gren Foundation for Anthropological Research, New York.

ISSN: 1475-536X

Previous titles in this series:

Anthropology Beyond Culture
Edited by Richard G. Fox & Barbara J. King, 2002

Property in Question: Value Transformation in the Global Economy
Edited by Katherine Verdery & Caroline Humphrey, 2004

Hearing Cultures: Essays on Sound, Listening and Modernity
Edited by Veit Erlmann, 2004

Embedding Ethics
Edited by Lynn Meskell & Peter Pels, 2005

World Anthropologies: Disciplinary Transformations within Systems of Power
Edited by Gustavo Lins Ribeiro and Arturo Escobar, 2006

Sensible Objects: Colonialisms, Museums and Material Culture
Edited by Elizabeth Edwards, Chris Gosden and Ruth B. Phillips, 2006

Roots of Human Sociality: Culture, Cognition and Interaction
Edited by N. J. Enfield and Stephen C. Levinson, 2006

Where the Wild Things Are Now: Domestication Reconsidered
Edited by Rebecca Cassidy and Molly Mullin, 2007

Anthropology Put to Work
Edited by Les W. Field and Richard G. Fox, 2007

Since its inception in 1941, the Wenner-Gren Foundation has convened more than 125 international symposia on pressing issues in anthropology. These symposia affirm the worth of anthropology and its capacity to address the nature of humankind from a wide variety of perspectives. Each symposium brings together participants from around the world, representing different theoretical disciplines and traditions, for a week-long engagement on a specific issue. The Wenner-Gren International Symposium Series was initiated in 2000 to ensure the publication and distribution of the results of the foundation's International Symposium Program.

Prior to this series, some landmark Wenner-Gren volumes include: *Man's Role in Changing the Face of the Earth* (1956), ed. William L. Thomas; *Man the Hunter* (1968), eds Irv DeVore and Richard B. Lee; *Cloth and Human Experience* (1989), eds Jane Schneider and Annette Weiner; and *Tools, Language and Cognition in Human Evolution* (1993), eds Kathleen Gibson and Tim Ingold. Reports on recent symposia and further information can be found on the foundation's website at www.wennergren.org.

The
Wenner-Gren
Foundation
For Anthropological Research, Inc.

Indigenous Experience Today

Edited by

MARISOL DE LA CADENA AND ORIN STARN

WITHDRAWN

Oxford · New York

First published in 2007 by
Berg
Editorial offices:
1st Floor, Angel Court, 81 St Clements Street, Oxford, OX4 1AW, UK
175 Fifth Avenue, New York, NY 10010, USA

Berg is the imprint of Oxford International Publishers Ltd.

Library of Congress Cataloguing-in-Publication Data

Indigenous experience today / edited by Marisol de la Cadena and
Orin Starn.
     p. cm. — (Wenner-Gren International Symposium series)
    Includes bibliographical references and index.
    ISBN-13: 978-1-84520-518-8 (cloth)
    ISBN-10: 1-84520-518-9 (cloth)
    ISBN-13: 978-1-84520-519-5 (pbk.)
    ISBN-10: 1-84520-519-7 (pbk.)
  1. Indigenous peoples—Social conditions. 2. Indigenous peoples—
Government relations. 3. Culture and globalization. I. Cadena,
Marisol de la. II. Starn, Orin.

  GN380.I523 2007
  305.8—dc22

                          2007012821

British Library Cataloguing-in-Publication Data

A catalogue record for this book is available from the British Library.

ISBN 978 1 84520 518 8 (Cloth)
ISBN 978 1 84520 519 5 (Paper)

Typeset by JS Typesetting Ltd, Porthcawl, Mid Glamorgan
Printed in the United Kingdom by Biddles Ltd, King's Lynn

www.bergpublishers.com

Contents

Participants at the Wenner-Gren Foundation International Symposium "Indigenous Experience Today"

Amita Baviskar, Institute of Economic Growth, Delhi
Michelle Bigenho, Hampshire College
Claudia Briones, University of Buenos Aires
Michael F. Brown, Williams College
James Clifford, University of California, Santa Cruz
Julie Cruikshank, University of British Columbia
Marisol de la Cadena (Organizer), University of California, Davis
Kregg Hetherington (Monitor), University of California, Davis
Valerie Lambert, University of North Carolina
Francesca Merlan, Australia National University
Francis B. Nyamnjoh, CODESRIA, Dakar, Senegal
Mary Louise Pratt, New York University
Louisa Schein, Rutgers University
Paul Chaat Smith, National Museum of the American Indian
Orin Starn (Organizer), Duke University
Anna Tsing, University of California, Santa Cruz
Linda Tuhiwai Smith, University of Auckland
Emily T. Yeh, University of Colorado, Boulder

Introduction

Marisol de la Cadena and Orin Starn

A century ago, the idea of indigenous people as an active force in the contemporary world was unthinkable. According to most Western thinkers, native societies belonged to an earlier, inferior stage of human history doomed to extinction by the forward march of progress and history. Even those sympathetic with indigenous peoples—whether Maori in New Zealand, San in South Africa, or Miskitu in Nicaragua—felt little could be done to prevent their destruction or at least assimilation into the mainstream. The U.S. poet Henry Wadsworth Longfellow described Native Americans as "the red sun descending" in *The Song of Hiawatha,* an immensely popular and by turns maudlin, mesmerizing, and romantic 1855 epic poem. As forward-looking as he was in some respects, an icon of anti-imperialist Latin American nationalism, Augusto César Sandino, longed for the day when Nicaraguan Indians would be absorbed into a single mestizo, or mixed nation. The future of the world, it seemed, belonged everywhere to the West and its own peculiar brand of progress and civilization.

History has not turned out that way at all. Many tribal societies have indeed been wiped out by war, disease, exploitation, and cultural assimilation over these last centuries.[1] But far from vanishing as the confident predictions once had it, native peoples today show demographic strength, even growth. More than four million people in the United States now classify themselves as "Native American." Many times more claim indigenous membership globally from the BaSarwa in Botswana to New Caledonians in Oceania and the Ainu of northern Japan. One recent estimate puts the number at over 250 million worldwide spread across more than 4,000 different groups.[2] Just as importantly, indigenous peoples have asserted their place in 21st-century global culture, economy, and politics. New Zealand Maori have become a force to be reckoned with in the arts, sports, music, and national life with Maori actors starring in the box-office hits *Once Were Warriors* (1994) and *The Whale Rider* (2003). In Ecuador, newly elected Quichua mayors have transformed local government. And although poverty, discrimination and second-class citizenship very often shape indigenous lives today, notable exceptions also undercut any simple association of indigeneity with misery and marginalization—and the status of indigenous peoples as objects of sometimes condescending pity. In the especially dramatic case of the United States, once impoverished tribes like the Pequot, Kumeyaay, and Umatilla have built casino complexes complete with golf courses, luxury hotels, tribal museums, and giant parking lots for visitors bused in from big cities. These groups have gone from poor, forgotten, and virtually invisible to a formidable force in less than a generation.

Equally evident is that indigenous peoples are highly heterogeneous in their views and agendas. Consider two contrasting examples. In Alaska, the Kaktovik Inupiat Corporation—an organization made up of Kaktovikmiut and local whaling captains—supports oil development in the Arctic National Wildlife Refuge (ANWR), which some native people feel was created without adequate consultation in the first place. This group has clashed with environmentalists, and wants to work with the Shell Oil Company.[3] By contrast, Bolivian President Evo Morales, the first self-declared indigenous president in modern Andean history, ordered troops to occupy his country's oil and gas fields ceded earlier to multinational corporations. "Capitalism is the worst enemy of humanity," he announced together with his intention to renegotiate all contracts. If most talk about "diversity" and indigenous peoples concentrates on culture and language, the variety of their sometimes conflicting economic and political viewpoints prove just as pronounced.

This book examines the varied faces of indigenous experience today. By contrast with the image of natives rooted always to their original territories, the chapters collected here chart diasporic indigenous experiences, and the global circulation of the discourse and politics of indigeneity. Rather than relying on shopworn notions of unchanging "native tradition," our contributors show indigenous people dealing with the tense dynamics of being categorized by others and seeking to define themselves within and against indigeneity's dense web of symbols, fantasies, and meanings. None of these chapters assume that the criteria for indigeneity are ever self-evident or intrinsic; they examine instead the changing boundary politics and epistemologies of blood and culture, time, and place that define who will or will not count as indigenous in the first place. We share a view of mixture, eclecticism, and dynamism as the essence of indigeneity as opposed to a falling off or "corruption" of some original state of purity. A further common thread is our desire to historicize indigeneity so as to expose its lack of preestablished, "natural" boundaries of any sort. We believe this the only way to undo thickly sedimented stereotypes about timeless "tribal cultures" that materialize in everything from glossy travel magazines to Hollywood movies and state policies—and sometimes in the declarations of activists and advocates themselves. Reckoning with indigeneity demands recognizing it as a relational field of governance, subjectivities, and knowledges that involves us all—indigenous and nonindigenous—in the making and remaking of its structures of power and imagination.

Reconceptualizing Indigeneity

In the last decades the public presence of indigenous intellectuals has successfully undermined evolutionary historicism's authority to force a rethinking of the notion of indigeneity itself. One thinks of the short stories of Coeur D'Alene writer Sherman Alexie, the painting of Australian aboriginal artist Emily Kngwarreye, or the filmmaking of Inuit director Zacharias Kunuk. Maori educators have influenced national social policy in New Zealand, while Aymara historians and Maya linguists have had a strong hand in constitutional reforms in Bolivia and Guatemala. The very idea of such interventions would have been unimaginable within older modernist teleologies that had no place for indigenous agency or futures.

But, as a number of indigenous critics have themselves insisted, recent achievements do not mean that indigenous individuals have somehow suddenly found deliverance in a happily multicultural world. Neither does it mean that in its new public presence, indigeneity is peopled by instinctive environmentalists, spiritual do-gooders averse to material things, and naturally communitarian leftists always aligned against capitalist interests and the status quo. These views too often express what Ramachandra Guha (1989) has called "reverse Orientalism" a discourse that precludes an understanding of indigeneity as an open-ended historical process, inevitably marked by past and present colonialisms and yet also unfolding along as yet undetermined pathways. By contrast, we borrow from Stuart Hall's (1996) influential conception of black cultural politics to propose that indigenous activism is "without guarantees." Indigenism has never been a singular ideology, program, or movement, and its politics resist closure. To assume that it possesses a unified much less predetermined trajectory is historically inaccurate, conceptually flawed, and simplistic. Although indigenous activism can well be linked to social justice and inspire transformative visions, as a political order it can be motivated by different ideological positions, all of them able to effect exclusions and forced inclusions (Mouffe 2005).

But how, then, might indigeneity be reconceptualized? A vital starting point is to recognize that indigeneity emerges only within larger social fields of difference and sameness; it acquires its "positive" meaning not from some essential properties of its own, but through its relation to what it is not, to what it exceeds or lacks. (Butler 1993; Hall 1996). This is not to say that the indigenous condition is somehow derivative or without powerful visions and directions of its own. What it does mean is that indigenous cultural practices, institutions, and politics *become such* in articulation with what is not considered indigenous within the particular social formation where they exist. Indigeneity, in other words, is at once historically contingent and encompassing of the nonindigenous—and thus never about untouched reality. "Settler and native go together," as political theorist Mahmood Mamdani (2004: 10) concludes, and "there can be no settler without a native, and vice versa."

As Mary Louise Pratt writes in her contribution to this volume, indigeneity names a relationship based on a conception of time and space that differentiates among groups of people. Words like *Indian* in the Americas and *Aborigine* in Australia were European inventions for peoples already there, *prior* to the arrival of the colonizers; and for its part *indigenous* derives from the French *indigene* and the Latin *indigena*. The label *indigenous* further disclosed a relationship with other non-Europeans: The first English usage comes in a 1598 report about the discovery of America to distinguish between "indigenes" (defined as "people bred upon that very soyle") and the people that Spaniards and Portuguese brought from Africa as slaves.[4] Not surprisingly, these forms of relationality expressed European superiority insofar as "indigenous" was synonymous with "pagan," heathen souls to be saved through Christianity. Later, as reason displaced faith as authority's foundation, "the pagan" was renamed "the primitive" (as opposed to "civilized") including those classified as "tribal," "native" and "aborigine" in colonial administrative lexicons.

Tensions between difference and sameness also characterized colonial articulations of indigeneity. Although it would be hard to imagine groups more unlike each other than, say, the small-scale, egalitarian bands of the Kalahari Desert and, at another extreme, the vast, highly stratified, militaristic empires of the Incas and Aztecs in the Americas; to colonial administrators and their sciences, the differences only reflected stages in the evolution of human societies. And yet, measuring native societies with evolutionary yardsticks also yielded differences that, notwithstanding the ahistorical imagination that conceived of them, became material practice as they shaped colonial policies that influenced postcolonial relations to our days. Take the West African case of Togo. Kabre villagers in the mountainous North seemed to French colonizers to be more intractably "savage" and "uncivilized" than the more urban, politically centralized Ewe in the coastal south, who had experience with earlier European slavers and traders. Thus, the French concentrated missionary and educational efforts with the Ewe, enabling them to become teachers, priests, and civil servants. The Kabre were instead conscripted as forced laborers to build roads and railroads for their French and then German masters. These colonial policies fed a dynamic in which the southern Ewe regarded the northern Kabre as backward and brutish and the Kabre, in turn, resented the southerners that the European colonizers favored. The resulting divisions shape Togo's fraught postcolonial politics even today (Piot 1999; Toulabor 1985).

If differences among local societies were important, the policies of different colonial powers were also varied and changeable across time, with still further consequences for indigeneity's divergent pathways. For example, the 16th-century Iberian conquerors of Mexico intermarried with Indians enabling the later invention of the mestizo, the racial category made emblematic in modern Mexican nationalism of the supposed reconciliation between the Spanish and Indian worlds. By contrast, the Dutch colonizers of 19th-century Indonesia adhered to dogmas about "racial degeneration" then dominant in scientific discourse; they choose to enforce white endogamy to try to prevent "dangerous mixtures" between Europeans and natives (Stoler 2002). The same imperial epistemology of native original sameness—and the disavowal of local ethnicities and their mixtures—underlay Indonesian elite nationalism years later, this time with nativeness positively recoded as the touchstone of a homogenized vision of national citizenship. These contrasting colonial histories manifest themselves in conditions of indigeneity today. Although in Mexico being indigenous is an old and unchallenged image, convenient and even necessary for the constant production of the mestizo, in Indonesia claiming to be indigenous is a new and highly controversial step for poor and rural minorities in their challenge to elite nationalist claims of native sameness. The diversity of indigenous histories is yet more evident when one considers non-European forms of colonialism. The Ami, Atayal, and other aboriginal peoples in present-day Taiwan suffered multiple colonizations: first by 17th-century Fulao and Hakka farmers from mainland China; second by the Japanese following the Sino-Japanese War in 1894; and finally by Chinese nationalist forces fleeing Mao's Communist revolution in 1949. These native groups must seek cultural and political rights in a society where the more numerous Fulao and Hakka now claim to be "indigenous Taiwanese" for having predated the massive Kuomintang landing (Chung-min et al. 1994; Wachman 1994).

All this heterogeneity has been at uneasy odds with visions of indigeneity as a unitary category occupied by those imagined at humanity's "lowest" rung. Whether Indians in Ibero-America or "tribals" in Africa, India, or North America, these labels described mostly rural populations ("hunter-gatherers" or "cultivators") uniformly imagined as close to "nature" (the beginning of the world) and far-off from "civilization" (the goal of History). Denied were the manifold particular histories of interaction among natives, settlers, and other groups (like the African slaves who arrived to the Americas with the Spanish or the indentured Indian laborers brought to Fiji by the British). Canonical Western philosophers—most notably Immanuel Kant and Georg Wilhelm Friedrich Hegel—used linear time and proximity to nature to explain cultural (and racial) difference between "non-civilized" peoples and Europeans. In the social sciences, Emile Durkheim, Lucien Lévy-Bruhl, and other prominent scholars would have agreed with E. B. Tylor, a founding figure in anthropology, that "one set of savages is like the other" (1903: 6). Even if scholars granted importance to local specificities, these would always fit the evolutionary epistemology that Universal History had popularized. Rome was "the embryo of human civilization" claimed James Frazer (1931 [1888]) and primitive cultures were survivals;[5] differences among them represented different moments of the past. What Michel-Rolph Trouillot (1991) calls the "savage slot" further materialized with the new disciplinary field of anthropology taking indigenous peoples for its object of study and, at times, advocacy.

Yet Western scholars and bureaucrats were never alone in crafting indigeneity. This formation also owes its complex genealogy precisely to those intellectuals, politicians, and common people classified by colonial knowledge as "natives" (in its multiple synonyms) who challenged their alleged anachronism, denounced European ignorance and inhumanity; in so doing, they contributed to alternative, often disparate, representations of indigeneity. For example, Guamán Poma de Ayala, a Quechua Indian, took up his pen in 1585 to detail the abuses of Spanish priests, judges, and soldiers in a 1,200 page letter to King Phillip III. In the 1780s, as the Iroquois Confederation came under attack following the American Revolution, Thayeendanegea, a Mohawk leader (whose Christian name was Joseph Brandt, and who had been educated in the classics at Moor's Charity School, now Dartmouth College) wrote to George Washington's new government. Thayeendanegea reminded the U.S. authorities that he was born and raised "among those whom you are pleased to call savages," that he had traveled extensively in North America and Europe meeting great leaders. "Nevertheless," he continued, "after all this experience and after every exertion to divest myself of prejudice, I am obliged to give my opinion in favour of my own people" because "in the government you call civilized, the happiness of the people is constantly sacrificed to the splendor of empire." (Tully 1995: 95)

Similar concerns triggered minor acts of resistance, small-scale uprisings, and sometimes massive rebellions. Contemporaries of Thayeendanegea, Túpac Amaru and Túpac Katari (Quechua and Aymara indigenous leaders, respectively) mounted massive insurrections reaching hundreds of miles across the Andes (Thomson 2003). In the 19th century (at the time when Ibero-America severed colonial ties with the Spanish and Portuguese Crowns) Maoris protesting British rule of their island—Aotearoa, or New Zealand in English—joined the Pai Maire revolt led by Te Ua Haumene, a politician who subscribed to millenarian ideologies of European expulsion and the restoration of native rule. Like Guamán Poma, Maori also addressed the ruling monarch, this time the British Queen, denouncing settler ignorance and abuse (Adas 1979). These often very cosmopolitan indigenous activists contributed to the dense dialogic formation we are calling "indigenity," in which groups and individuals occupying nonindigenous subject positions also participated.

This activism, however, did not undo the opposition between the "primitive" and the "civilized," which remained pivotal in indigeneity's intricate field of meanings, practices, and politics, and was sometimes adopted by indigenous leaders themselves. A grammar of analogous contrasts has further linked indigeneity to the backward, rural, and illiterate as against the goals of modernity, urbanization, and literacy enshrined as the desired endpoints of development and progress. As the project of assimilation gained currency in the early 20th century, the aim of absorbing indigenous people into homogenized modern nation-states found expression in the Latin American ideology of mestizaje; the U.S. policy of so-called "termination and relocation" during the Eisenhower years; and in France's *mission civilizatrice* (civilizing mission) in its African colonies. Assimilation was sanctioned by the UN International Labor Organization (ILO) in 1957: it encouraged member states to "integrate" the "tribal" and "semi-tribal" populations who occupied "a less advanced stage than the average in their country."[6] Meanwhile, many Marxist groups dismissed indigenous practices as an "archaic" brand of "false consciousness" that obstructed class unity and revolution. And far from exclusive to the West, Muslim and Hindu intellectuals also imagined a backward population of their own, which they identified as lacking a world religion; classified as "animists," these groups, mostly rural and peasants, were labeled as tribal and traditional, a backward Other assumed to be "behind" civilization's curve (see Baviskar this volume).

But by the late 20th century, indigenous political movements worldwide were forcefully questioning assimilationism. The ILO reversed field in 1989 to recognize "the aspirations of these peoples to exercise control over their own institutions, ways of life and economic development ... and to maintain and develop their identities, languages and religions, within the framework of the States in which they live."[7] The gradual discrediting of assimilationist agendas and their replacement with diversity as the putative goal of social policy—coinciding with the Cold War's end and the seeming triumph of the so-called neoliberal model of capitalism and democracy—accompanied the ascendance of various forms of multiculturalism (Kymlicka 2001; Van Cott 2000). Although embracing the credo of cultural pluralism and equality, multiculturalism has posed new dilemmas and constraints of its own. Critics worry that "multicultural neoliberalism" incorporates "diversity" as little more than a strategy of management, containment, and global capitalist expansion without any real change to structures of racial hierarchy and economic inequality (Hale 2006; Postero and Zamosc 2004). And even in cases in which multiculturalism has sparked genuine talk about dignity and respect for native cultures, it has not done away with the compulsion to equate indigeneity, or at least authentic indigeneity, with autocthony and the premodern.

Emerging from, along with, and against these political and academic practices contemporary indigenous experiences are marked by inconsistent expectations underpinned by fantasies of indigeneity as exterior to history and uniquely nonmodern. On the one hand, those who dress in feathers, face paint, "native costume" or otherwise publicly embrace their traditions risk self-positioning in the semantic extremes of exotic primitivism, what Ramos (1998) calls "the hyperreal Indian." On the other hand, those who do not seem to measure up to stereotypical "feathers-and-beads" expectations often find themselves stigmatized as "half-breeds," "assimilated," or even imposters; wearing suit and tie risks accusations of false indigenousness. Recently for example, the acclaimed Peruvian writer Mario Vargas Llosa, dismissed Bolivian Aymara President Evo Morales as a "fake" Indian—in spite of the fact that Morales speaks the indigenous language and grew up in a poor mountain village. "Evo," Vargas Llosa asserts, is "the emblematic Latin American criollo, cunning as a squirrel, a political climber and charlatan, with a vast experience as a manipulator of men and women acquired in his long trajectory as leader of *coca* leaf growers and member of the labor union aristocracy."[8] The spurious calculus of authenticity and cultural purity here at work assumes that "genuine" indigenous intellectuals, businessmen, filmmakers, sports stars, and politicians do not, indeed cannot, exist—or are rare, oxymoronic exceptions, at best.

That the same Mario Vargas Llosa had, some years earlier, approvingly identified the new Peruvian president Alejandro Toledo as an Indian only underlines the fickle, sometimes contradictory expectations surrounding indigeneity.[9] Besides Toledo not speaking Quechua, the main difference between him and Morales is ideological: the Bolivian opposes neoliberalism, the Peruvian embraces it—as does Vargas Llosa. The famous writer's selective willingness to grant Indian authenticity to one and not the other might be labeled politically motivated; some might claim the same about Morales's or Toledo's self-positioning as indigenous. More deeply, it becomes evident that very different notions of "indigenous identity" can coexist in the mind of one and the same person (in this case an internationally acclaimed novelist): as an evolutionary narrative according to which no modern politician can really be indigenous, or by contrast as a fixed subject position deriving from "blood," "heritage," and social background in which current occupation is irrelevant. Both interpretations are part of indigeneity as a social formation—although neither is more real than the other one, their respective truth claims have different political and economic consequences.

Indigeneity Beyond Ethnicity?

The last few decades have witnessed the convergence of indigenous activists in what some have called a global indigenous movement (Niezen 2000). The most immediate roots of this new organizing date to the protest years of the 1960s and 1970s and the indigenous groups that emerged in that period of decolonization and social upheaval. The U.S. Red Power movement—which joined elements of Marxist and Indian pride ideologies—was one especially important influence (Smith and Warrior 1996). Extensive media coverage of protests like the takeover of Alcatraz Island and the Trail of Broken Treaties broadcast indigenous concerns worldwide. But even within the United States, this activism was never neatly unified in ideology or aims; on the contrary, tensions and antagonisms were part of the indigenous political sphere. Some older Native American activists disliked the Red Power radicalism of the American Indian Movement—and some women found its male-dominated "warrior" ethos to be oppressively patriarchal. In New Zealand, the Marxist-inspired Polynesian Panther Movement (with ties to the Black Panthers in the United States) squared off against the Nga Tamatoa, a non-Marxist, antiracist, and more culturally minded group led by university-trained Maori intellectuals.[10] In Latin America, indigenous groups ranged from militant ethnic nationalist groups that rejected any outsider involvement—like some early Bolivian Aymara organizations—to organizations working for modest state reforms, while promoting indigenous integration into capitalist markets. Indigenous organizations multiplied in the 1980s and 1990s with important support from NGOs with indigenous concerns acquiring unprecedented political visibility in Latin America, the United States, Canada, New Zealand, and Australia.

Varied demands found vigorous expression. They included land claims, control over cultural heritage, bilingual education, the inclusion and commemoration of indigenous histories in national imaginaries, and the rights of indigenous peoples to speak for and represent themselves as opposed to being "spoken for" by nonindigenous experts, bureaucrats, and policymakers. The increasing visibility of this activism—aided by multiculturalism's new ascendancy in global political discourse—led the United Nations to declare 1993 the "Year of the World's Indigenous Peoples." A Maya woman, Rigoberta Menchú, won the Nobel Peace prize and became a lightning rod for controversy about the brutal counterinsurgency campaign of the Guatemalan army against Indian villagers.[11] The concept of indigenous rights traveled to new parts of the world with varying results (Brysk 2000; García 2005; Hodgson 2001; Tsing 2005).

Contemporary indigenous political activism raises fundamental issues, some familiar and others less so. Current indigenism continues to challenge the Western model of civilization and progress by insisting that Euroamerican colonialism and capitalist expansion have been a misadventure of violence, destruction and the trampling of non-Western peoples. New attempts have also been made to decolonize the categories of "Indian" and "native," undoing evolutionary viewpoints and recovering the historical local distinctiveness of marginalized groups. Moreover, in some emergent versions a concerted effort has occurred to connect indigenous and nonindigenous subaltern groups that share relatively similar political interests. This strategy—at least in theory—would yield a broad coalition of subaltern organizations underpinned by a flexible notion of demands for "cultural rights" including claims for the political self-representation of marginalized groups. Such indigenous activism thus may serve to articulate projects for social justice beyond exclusive notions of ethnic identity. In this vein, Peruvian sociologist Aníbal Quijano perceives a trend among Andean activists toward "subalternizing indigenous politics and indigenizing subaltern politics" to generate an organic link among political organizations representing ethnic *and* non-ethnic subaltern interests (Quijano 2006).[12] The Zapatista movement originating in Mexico's impoverished Mayan-dominated Lacandon jungle region is one tangible example of such new expressions of indigeneity.

The resulting new mixed forms of indigenous identity and politics involve what anthropologist Tania Li calls "positionings" historically enabled by "sedimented practices, landscapes, and repertoires of meaning" and brought about through "particular patterns of engagement and struggle" (2000: 151). As it always has been, indigenism today is a process; a series of encounters; a structure of power; a set of relationships; a matter of becoming, in short, and not a fixed state of being. In its most ambitious expressions, and articulated to alter-globalization processes, the new indigenism seeks to undo hegemonic signifiers, affect their usual semantic chemistry to produce new valences, and thus reconfigure indigeneity itself opening it up to the acknowledgement of historical contemporaneity and radical social justice. Obviously, because indigenous activism is not a monolithic entity but, on the contrary, a necessarily fragmented process, some of its fractions are included in the dominant and the hegemonic (Hall 1996; Williams 1977), whereas others emerge as counterhegemonic formations—and still others straddle both, or move from one to the other. Moreover, we have to remember that indigeneity encompasses much more than identities or social movements. It is a worldwide field of governance, subjectivities, and knowledges involving both indigenous and nonindigenous peoples in their own different ways. Indigeneity itself materializes in an intricate dynamic among converging and competing agendas, visions, and interests that transpire at local, national, and global levels.

The chapters in this volume show the immense variation in the processes of localization (or rejection) of indigenous identities and the diverging national and regional forms they can assume. Together they seek to contribute to what James Clifford (this volume) calls "an interactive, dynamic process of shifting scales and affiliations, uprooting and rerooting, the waxing and waning of identities" that has historically characterized indigenous experiences. The histories described in the chapters that follow are not deviations from some baseline, "normative" checklist of expectations for indigenous culture and politics. They aim instead to release indigeneity from the flattening epistemologies that overlook that any attempt to define what is indigenous and what is not is necessarily relational and historical—and therefore provisional and context related.

Indigenous Identities, Old and New

The globalization of the concept of indigenous rights has been by turns powerful, uneven, and unpredictable. As it has traveled from familiar contexts like Canada, the United States, and Brazil to newer ones like India and Indonesia, the discourse of indigeneity has encountered interlocutors among marginalized, usually rural populations. Here nationalist policies have very often classified villagers as "backward" and "in need of improvement" while simultaneously declaring the entire national citizenry to be "indigenous" and thus obscuring the cultural singularity of local minority groups (usually non-Muslim, or non-Hindu). In Indonesia, for example, Anna Tsing (this volume) describes how young environmental activists carved a national space for indigeneity by articulating it to *adat,* a local idiom with long historical semantics, and therefore local leverage, but that had to be resignified in the process of political activism. By contrast with North America, where a racialized biopolitics of white supremacy and brown subalternity has imprinted the dynamics of indigeneity, in Indonesia or India, caste or religion mark the difference between those potentially considered indigenous or nonindigenous, which therefore do not necessarily "look" different as usually imagined in Canada or the United States. Tsing insists that any assessment of the "powerful traveling axes of indigenous concern" must attend to the "concrete history of divergent indigeneities" and trace "links without subsuming them to universals."

And, in fact, given the weight of local histories, the spread of these emergent forms of indigeneity has met with opposition or at least indifference in some places—even where indigenous peoples have had a long-established marginal presence. For example, by contrast to vigorous activism in neighboring Bolivia and Ecuador, Peruvian Aymaras and Quechuas have been relatively unresponsive to social movements organized under the banner of indigenous cultural rights.[13] Emily Yeh (this volume) examines the case of Tibet as an example of indigenism disavowed. Although they might seem to fit the archetypal formula of inhabiting an ancestral homeland, possessing a distinctive language and culture, and being colonized by outsiders, Tibetans seldom call themselves "indigenous," and more often use as "sa skye rdo skyes (lit., 'born of this soil and rock')." Yeh traces this lack of "uptake" of the widely circulating global category of "indigenous peoples" partly to official Chinese policy. State insistence that everyone in China is "indigenous" has effectively stripped the category of its power to convey Tibetan feelings of occupation and domination by Beijing. Many Tibetan exiles also find the idiom of indigenous rights—and its association with a claim of sovereignty as opposed to secession—too weak to express their desire for independence from China. Becoming indigenous is always only a *possibility* negotiated within political fields of culture and history.

Every generation, too, may seek to redefine indigenous identities. Claudia Briones (this volume) finds young Argentine Mapuches less interested in older Mapuche agendas of land rights and traditional political organizing than in asserting their Mapucheness while establishing identities as punk rock and heavy metal fans and musicians. These self-announced "Mapunkies" and "Maheavies" embrace the rebelliousness of global youth culture and, at the same time, add a new dimension as in lyrics about the travails of Mapuche history. An older, more organized politics aiming to transform or even sever relations between Mapuches and the Argentine state gives way to a new cultural politics that focuses on the body, material culture, and the politics of style and mass media—while at the same time asserting their right to a place as Mapuches in Argentina as a nation. These younger Mapuche with their tatoos, piercings, and black leather jackets define a new urban indigenous identity. Their presence undercuts standard views of Argentina as a homogeneously white nation while underscoring the absurdity of persisting mythologies about Indians as still somehow belonging to a premodern world of the grass hut and the bow and arrow.

Territory and the Question of Sovereignty

The more familiar matters of territory and sovereignty remain very much of concern to indigenous peoples in many parts of the world. Many groups possess a sense of rootedness to the land—and of prior occupation to foreign invaders—characterized by distinctive historically and culturally shaped understandings and connections to an intimately known landscape (Kirsch 2001). This is the case of First Nation individuals, in Northern Yukon Territories, whose oral traditions, according to Julie Cruikshank (this volume), reveal a "dwelling perspective" derived from "intense engagement with environment maintained through millennia."[14] Land and water were the basis of indigenous life in an older day, and remain so in some cases today. Because colonization by outsiders so often went along with the traumatic breakdown of precolonial ways of being, the defense or recovery of territory has very often become more than just a matter of economic survival, but also connected to the dream of revitalization, homeland, and restored dignity. At the same time, struggles over territory are seldom neatly cohesive or driven by noble or utopian ideals alone. Money and corporate appetites can enter the mix, creating dissension within native groups or pitting them against one another. A well-known example is the long-running, sometimes fierce dispute between Navajo and Hopi over Arizona land claimed by both tribes exacerbated by the involvement of the giant Peabody Coal Company and the lucrative mineral leasing rights involved.

Anthropologist Francesca Merlan (this volume) considers the case of Australia. She scrutinizes the key role that land has taken in aboriginal political mobilization there over the last three decades. As Merlan sees it, privileging land as an object of struggle assumes a kind of uniformity of native interest in defense of the land and environment that belies that some aboriginal groups have supported mining and other development with hopes for employment and economic opportunity. To stress native links to a fixed territory can also inadvertently reinforce a dominant Australian vision of aborigines as "undomesticated" and "wild"—and a corresponding view of those who live in cities as "inauthentic" and not "real" native people. Most aborigines make their homes now in Sydney and other big cities. Their social needs, Merlan notes, revolve around the educational system, access to health care and good jobs for these families that have not lived off the land in any traditional sense for generations. Merlan suggests that aboriginal political activism might be recalibrated so as to address territorial rights in conjunction with more encompassing agendas of social welfare and economic opportunity.

The concern for territory links to broader demands for sovereignty. Anthropologist Valerie Lambert (this volume) examines the accomplishments and challenges for the Choctaw in the United States in their quest for a measure of real tribal power over their own lives and land. As victims of violent removal to Oklahoma under Andrew Jackson's hard-line Indian policy in the early 19th century, the Choctaw were devastated by the march of white conquest. Now the tribe has managed to win a hard-earned measure of prosperity through its tribal gas stations, casinos, and other business ventures bringing in several hundred million dollars a year through an entrepreneurial brand of "reservation capitalism." But Lambert, Choctaw herself, also points to limits in this native success story. U.S. Indian policy draws a strict, sometime arbitrary line between federally "recognized" and "unrecognized" tribes, the latter without any rights to land or sovereignty. Even "recognized" tribes like the Choctaw find their authority far more restricted than the official government rhetoric of Indian sovereignty and self-determination allows. The Choctaw have been unable even to secure complete recognition of water rights within their own tribal territorial boundaries. Choctaw poverty and unemployment rates remain higher than the national average despite the major recent advances (and in contrast to mistaken assumptions that most or all of the more than 400 casino-owning tribes in the United States have somehow become flush overnight with glitzy gambling cash).

Michael Brown (this volume) observes that sovereignty has become a crucial watchword in indigenous activism worldwide. But Brown questions this broad trend and its possible negative consequences for social change and justice. He points to the danger of "native sovereignty" being invoked by tribes to justify discriminatory policies as in one New Mexico pueblo's policy of denying tribal citizenship to the children of women with nontribal members but granting it to those of men who marry outside the tribe. That tribes may be exempted from federal labor laws also raises potential for abuses of worker's rights at casinos and other reservation businesses. Brown also argues that the very concept of sovereignty fails to admit the fluid, multiplex realities of native mobility and cultural intermixture; it rests instead on the misleading premise of stable, clear-cut cultural, ethnic, and territorial boundaries and fixed, singular identities. Such assumptions overlook that many non-natives live on reservations or other tribally controlled territories, among other potential complications to simple visions of indigenous autonomy and self-determination (Valerie Lambert notes that roughly 90 percent of those living within Choctaw tribal boundaries are non-Indian, having married in or from white or African American families who have long resided there). Brown reminds us that the idea of sovereignty derives in the first place from Western and not any native political philosophy. Perhaps, he concludes, it should "wing its way back to its birthplace in the cheerless castles of Europe."[15]

It may be useful to think of indigenous sovereignty as a hard-won political feat, and yet also as a set of questions. Is the problem the lack of respect for native sovereignty as the Choctaw experience suggests? Or is the very concept so flawed as to be more obstacle than help to indigenous struggles for dignity and justice? What alternative forms of political imagination and organization might be worth considering? The Mohawk political scientist Taiaiake Alfred suggests, albeit very schematically, drawing on older indigenous traditions that rejected "absolute authority," "coercive enforcement decisions," and the separation of political rule from other aspects of everyday life (2001: 27). Others have called for a "decentered diverse democratic federalism" allowing for real native autonomy and self-government yet without any rigid separatist agenda (Young 2000: 253).[16] As much as indigeneity itself, the debate about sovereignty is linked to social context and political dynamics, and there is no "disinterested" position about its content and limits. The complex, contested, and often powerfully emotional questions at stake guarantee that sovereignty will continue to be applied and reworked in multiple, tense, and sometimes contradictory ways.

Indigeneity Beyond Borders

Conventional thinking about indigenous groups still often assumes the stable, continuous occupation of a single territory. What Donald Moore (2004) calls "the ethnospatial fix" can occlude the centrality of uprooting and displacement in indigenous experience, and the vicissitudes of being rounded up, confined, and marched to new, less desirable corners of the earth. The Cherokee were driven from the southeastern United States to Oklahoma on the Trail of Tears (Ehle 1988); the Australian government shipped aboriginal children to boarding schools halfway across the country to learn "civilized" ways (Human Rights and Equal Opportunity Commission 1997); the authoritarian postcolonial regime in Zimbabwe "resettled" rebellious tribal groups in new "model" villages (Moore 2004). Even earlier, chronologically speaking, *forastero* (foreigner) was a Spanish colonial label for indigenous Andean villagers who left home to avoid tribute and forced labor obligations; but these migrants very often maintained connections with their rural kin, or *ayllu,* and periodically returned to tend land and animals. These migrations, forced or voluntary, sometimes achieved intended ends of assimilation and control, but they could also fortify oppositional feelings of victimization and solidarity or even generate new forms of indigeneity. "What made us one people is the common legacy of colonialism and diaspora" writes cultural critic Paul Chaat Smith (1994: 38) in describing how "Indian" became a shared identity for diverse, widely scattered Native North American tribes only in the aftermath of European conquest.

James Clifford (this volume) speaks of "indigenous diasporas." He underlines that native peoples today are rarely bound to any one place and that geographic mobility whether forced or chosen is not a recent feature of indigeneity. Indigenous cosmopolitanism has only increased with the borders between tribal "homeland" and urban center, home and away, here and there now crisscrossed everywhere by frequent travel, family visits, e-mail, text messages, and phone calls. "Across the current range of indigenous experiences," Clifford says, "identifications are seldom exclusively local or inward looking but, rather, work at multiple scales of interaction."

As Louisa Schein (this volume) shows for the Hmong/Miao, the trials of trasnationality can power nostalgia for lost homelands. The Hmong/Miao diaspora stretches from China to Laos, Thailand, Vietnam and overseas to North America, including some 200,000 refugees arriving to California, Minnesota, and other parts of the United States following the Vietnam War. Their condition of what Schein calls "chronic statelessness" and minoritization is transected today by return visits and business ventures, remittances to poor kin back in Asia, and other forms of trans-Pacific interconnectedness. A thriving Hmong/Miao video-making business now produces historical epics about the trauma of the Vietnam War and the longer history of Hmong/Miao loss and displacement. These videos also cater to and strengthen migrant desires for an often idealized traditional past. Foklorized images of country festivals, cherry blossoms and gurgling brooks, and costumed protagonists enact a "virtual or remote place-making" that answers to these longings for "cultural continuity" and "fixed significance" (and sometimes play to patriarchal male fantasies about a "virginal," "pure," and "loyal" village femininity). Like Tibetans, the Miao-Hmong have not embraced the discourse of indigeneity for reasons of their own. But Schein argues that those "diasporic longing and those championing preservation of indigenous lifeways are not so far apart." Diasporic identity, indigenous or not, entails a measure of marginality or at least off-centeredness in relationship to ruling states. Schein suggests a "worldwide malaise that prompts those with the means of representation to offer recuperations of the traditional, the untouched, and the timeless alongside cautionary tales about too much intercourse with the outside."

Michelle Bigenho (this volume) explores music's role in the transnational cultural politics of indigeneity. She focuses on Andean music as it travels from Bolivia and Peru to Tokyo and back home. A nonindigenous Peruvian folklorist composed the famous, seemingly "indigenous" Andean anthem, *El Cóndor Pasa*; the U.S. megastars Paul Simon and Art Garfunkel made it into a worldwide folk hit later in the 20th century. That rendition piqued the interest of Japanese musicians in Andean folk music in these zig-zagging global circuits in which new interest in "indigenous cultural references" came about partly "through a circuitous route of foreign associations." Although donning ponchos, woven belts, and other "Indian" garb for their performances, the majority of the touring Bolivian musicians Bigenho describes would not themselves identify as indigenous at home (and she, a North American, played violin in this group). A mix of essentialism and nostalgia for its own imagined "non-Western" past heightens Japanese feelings of "intimate distance" with Andean music. Bigenho believes the multiplex desires, interests, and contexts in such global circulations of indigeneity warn against simple dismissals of the phenomenon as the "mere commodification of the exotic." She worries nonetheless that Japanese interest in Bolivian music remains at best "disjointed" from any real engagement with Bolivia's fraught history of poverty, discrimination, and struggle.

The Boundary Politics of Indigeneity

It should be evident that the boundaries between indigenous and nonindigenous spheres are a matter of history and politics. Consider the United States. In recent decades, various factors have made it more acceptable, even glamorous and exotic, to be Indian. In what Circe Sturm calls "race-shifting" (2002), Americans have begun to claim tribal heritage in a "migration from whiteness to redness." The increasing numbers of those checking "American Indian/Alaska Native" on the census box is one reason for strong Native American demographic growth in the late 20th century. Are these "race-shifters" little more than "wannabes" without any real claim to indigenous identity? Or does the turn to embrace Indianness measure recognition of native genealogies that earlier generations chose or were forced to deny in the age of assimilationism? The sometimes vitriolic debate about these questions underlines the volatility of the changing boundary politics of belonging and exclusion.

We should also recall that indigeneity operates within larger structures of ethnicity and identification. "National formations of alterity," as Claudia Briones (this volume) calls them, position native peoples within hierarchies of color, gender, generation, geography and class that operate to differentiate between *and within* groups. The structure of society seldom, if ever, involves a neat binary between indigenous people and colonizers or their descendants—and even less so given the frequent lines of tension and cleavage that often exist among different groups in any particular place.[17] Forming political alliances within and across multiple divides can be a difficult endeavor with unpredictable outcomes.

The example of India illustrates the pitfalls, dilemmas, and varied valences of indigenous mobilization. Here the influence of the global discourse of indigeneity has helped to give the category of *adivasi*, or tribal people, a growing visibility in recent years. As Amita Baviskar (this volume) shows, the new politics of *adivasi* identity invokes aspects of old colonial visions of them as "uncivilized" exotic, loincloth-wearing forest peoples (and overlooks that many *adivasi* live now in cities and towns). The trajectory of *adivasi* organizing has also been shaped by the changing dynamics of caste and modern state classificatory schemes as well as the powerful sometimes deadly religious violence and hatred pitting Hindus against Muslim. Baviskar shows how the image of "natural," "ancestral" *adivasi* ties to the earth became a powerful rallying point in the courageous fight against the destructive Narmada Valley dam project. But she also notes the more problematic pathways of indigenous claims, and, in particular, how *adivasis* have sometimes joined Hindu supremacists in hate politics and mass violence against Muslim minorities. Baviskar further worries that drawing lines between "tribal" peoples and other poor Indians—a legacy of colonial British social classification—may obstruct efforts to mobilize a more common front for change in India. "We cannot assume," she underlines, "that indigeneity is intrinsically a sign of subalternity or a mode of resistance."

The politics of indigeneity in parts of Africa also raises very difficult, critical questions about exclusion and inclusion, and the perils of social boundary drawing gone awry. Colonialism and its strategies of governance and classification imposed strict divisions both between Europeans and Africans and various "tribal" groups. The notorious case of apartheid South Africa involved an ideology of ethnic belonging that linked particular groups to strictly circumscribed, supposedly partly autonomous "homelands," or "Bantutustans." This Afrikaner social engineering restricted the mobility of black South Africans, kept them in marginal areas, and denied them the vote and full national citizenship. The 1994 Rwandan genocide points to the most extreme and perilous potential deployments of the idiom of indigeneity. There, Belgian colonizers had helped to foster a so-called "Hamitic hypothesis" asserting Tutsis to have migrated to Rwanda from northern Africa with Hutu as the real "autocthonous" inhabitants of the country. A view of the Tutsi as foreign usurpers underlay Hutu hatred that led to the slaughter of several hundred thousand Tutsi with the United States and the rest of the international community failing to intervene to stop the violence (Mamdani 2002).

Anthropologist Francis Nyamnjoh (this volume) examines competing nativist claims in Botswana. Although its economy has prospered in recent decades, the country has witnessed growing tensions with competing tribal claims to "indigenous" occupation of the land. Thus, the Batswana majority distinguish between themselves as fully entitled "owners of the home *(beng gae)*" in relation to other tribal identities labeled as "close *(Ba tswa ka)*" all the way to putatively more recently arrived "outsiders *(Makwerekwere)*." Here the claim of firstness is deployed to legitimate stratification, exclusion, and ethnic domination, no matter that it has no real historical basis of any kind. The most "indigenous" Botswanans by longevity of occupation would be the so-called "Bushmen," more properly called the BaSarwa. These traditionally hunter-gatherer people have inhabited the country's deserts for at least 2,000 years. But the BaSarwa have virtually no voice under a calculus of backwardness and advancement that allows for "rightful ownership" only by settled farmers. Nyamnjoh argues that this particular brand of indigeneity and nativism denies the hybrid, heterogeneous, and shifting realities of Botswanan experience. Prevailing instead are what he calls "ever-diminishing circles of inclusion." Nymanjoh suggests the need for a "flexible indigeneity" that would recognize and even embrace the fact of multiple allegiances, geographical mobility, and entangled histories.

Linda Tuhiwai Smith (this volume) explores the more hopeful history of New Zealand. The Thatcheresque neoliberal model first implemented in the mid–1980s dismantled New Zealand's welfare state in favor of privatization, deregulation, and the slashing of government programs. These measures threatened to undermine Maori organizing that had been gathering strength around protecting native rights accorded by the 1840 Treaty of Waitangi and Maori language revitalization. But many Maori had no love lost for the old welfare state with its dimensions of paternalism, condescension, and insensitivity to native concerns. As Tuhiwai Smith shows, they took advantage of "pauses" and "spaces" in the emerging neoliberal order to further their own decolonizing agendas, especially in educational reform. New state policy promoted a more entrepreneurial, market-based model of school-ing that foregrounded "school choice" and "parental control." Native activists adopted this language to press successfully for Kara Kaupapa Maori, or Maori language immersion schools, and other at least partial reforms to a formerly white-controlled, assimilation-minded educa-tional system.

Tuhiwai Smith draws lessons from New Zealand for thinking about indigeneity in the age of advanced global capitalism. If an uneasy kind of multicultural neoliberalism has developed there, it has done so in the push and pull of familiar dominant ideologies of free markets and individual entrepreneurship and the struggle of Maori activists for a measure of group rights and recognition. Multicultural neoliberal regimes have themselves encouraged forms of collective indigenous subjectivity in other parts of the world. One notable example is Brazil, where new state policies granting land rights to indigenous and slave descendant groups have given new incentive for community identification and organizing (French 2004). As Brazilian analyst Evelina Dagnino (2002) puts it, current political processes are marked by "perverse confluences" between neoliberalism and social justice activism. The relationship between neoliberal modes of governmentality and indigenous activism is indeed at once deeply intertwined and marked by fissures, disjunctures, and confrontations of various kinds. Tuhiwai Smith notes varied obstacles in the Maori case including activist "burn out," the temptations of assimilationism, and internal divisions. She finds evidence even so in New Zealand for how marginalized groups may be able to find "aspects of neoliberal reform with which communities can engage and can find ground to shift the agenda."

Indigenous Self-Representation, Nonindigenous Collaborators, and the Politics of Knowledge

We have heard recent warnings about the dangers of cultural criticism and postcolonial theory. "Is it the duty of intellectuals to add fresh ruins to the field of ruins?" asks Bruno Latour (2004: 225). It should be obvious enough that this book's sensibilities bear the imprint of the antifoundationalist agendas of various brands of poststructural and postcolonial theory with their suspicion of purity claims, fixed borders, and singular narratives. But our purpose is not to debunk, disable, or to play the tired role of the all-seeing critic who claims to see truth uncontaminated by illusion. Tracing the trajectories of indigeneity should be about enablement and not endless deconstruction. We are motivated by an ethics of concern, care, and accountability to forms of vision and organizing that embrace a situated interconnectivity in any work toward sustainable futures and new horizons of hope (Braidotti 2006). A role for careful, engaged scholarship can be to contribute to understanding and activism that recognizes the paradoxes, limits, and possibilities of indigeneity's varied vectors instead of falling back into tired, monological brands of essentialized analysis and judgment.

The very ground of research, scholarship and the politics of knowledge has been shifting in other ways. Indigenous activism has broken up the old monopoly of outside "experts" on explicating the "reality" about native life. Perhaps the single most publicized example of growing demands for native self-representation has been the big new National Museum of the American Indian (NMAI) of the Smithsonian Institution. As a curator at this newest museum on the mall in Washington, D.C., Paul Chaat Smith (this volume) offers an insider's view of the challenges of putting together the exhibits in time for its 2004 opening. In an older day, anthropologists and other whites ran museums with their dioramas and exhibits about native life. The native-curated, native-directed NMAI reflects a changing economy of visibility, money, and representation. Chaat Smith underlines that these changes bring a whole new set of uncertainties and dilemmas into play—and that the stakes were heightened at the NMAI by the $300 million budget and equally large expectations. What about "essentialist Indian gatekeepers" who might want the museum to avoid history's complexities? Could the NMAI develop a "*Simpsons* model" to make the museum appealing to children while at the same time to adults through other, more sophisticated references, layers, and double meanings? And how would the curators deal with so many stories, languages, and ways of being that were lost for good in the storm of conquest? Chaat Smith describes the final product as a matter of "brilliant mistakes," "realized dreams," and limiting constraints. Self-representation, as the NMAI shows, is never simple or straightforward—and even less so when that "self" is a group that has always been internally differentiated culturally, politically, and economically.

Moreover, indigenous self-representation involves broad networks of collaboration that include peoples from many walks of life. Chaat Smith notes that non-native museum specialists and others were important collaborators at the NMAI, and, more broadly, indigeneity has always involved enunciation, both conflicting and harmonizing, from indigenous and nonindigenous subject positions. This volume itself involves the collaboration of contributors writing from varied standpoints, indigenous and not. Although sharing common training in academic idioms and epistemologies, we also come from different disciplinary traditions: anthropology, geography, history, literature, and sociology. If economists, political scientists, or demographers had been involved, this project would doubtless have had another cast. As annoying a buzzword as *interdisciplinarity* can sometimes be, the project of working across and beyond established academic boundaries remains full of potential. The larger promise lies in generating new, "undisciplined" forms of understanding and knowledge in the best sense of the word (Escobar in press).

Thus, while recognizing that all knowledge is produced through vast collaborative networks, it is vital to remember that political narratives—embedded in discourses of universal knowledge—work to make some actors and their practices more visible than others (Latour 1993). In her chapter in this volume, Julie Cruikshank analyzes the collaboration between First Nation individuals in the Yukon Territory and archaeologists, climatologists, physicists, and environmentalists—and herself, a cultural anthropologist—arising from converging interests in histories and facts around the melting glaciers of Canada's Saint Elias Mountains. This work, Cruikshank observed, although amicable, and indeed respectful of all parts involved, was entangled in the complex hegemony of scientific knowledge even as its practitioners were aware of the need, and willing, to take local stories into consideration. For example, in local Atapashkan and Tinglit narratives, glaciers figure as sentient actors in a relational cosmology that explains weather change and colonial encounters, natural and social history, in one and the same stream of thought. Of significance, these narratives, notes Cruikshank, "are continuously made in situations of human encounter: between coastal and interior neighbors, between colonial visitors and residents, and among contemporary scientists, managers, environmentalists, and First Nations." Included in the collaboration are well-meaning definitions of *indigenous knowledge* that imagine these local stories as a bundle of myth and wisdom handed down unchanged across the generations. The task of Western scientists (of any sort) then becomes to "discover" such knowledge, extricating it as "information" and thus disregarding storytelling as a historical form of knowledge that changes—just as science does—with the circumstances. Such problematic treatment of storytelling transmogrifies completely contemporary interpretations into fixed, dehistoricized cultural "data" putatively transmitted by "the vessel of culture" to present day people—who therefore belong to *our* past. The coloniality of indigeneity, Cruikshank reminds us, may be reinforced by hierarchies of knowledge even in seemingly progressive contexts.

Like Cruikshank, many of us have also been involved in forms of collaboration involving both academic and nonacademic intellectuals (e.g., de la Cadena 2006; Tuhiwai Smith 1999). We want to call attention to the profound asymmetries organizing such collaboration—which start with inequalities of geography, economy, race, and gender but go far beyond, right into the heart of the knowledge-production venture itself. As Talal Asad wrote more than 20 years ago, languages are structurally imbued with differentiated power, and this affects the production of knowledge. "Western languages," he wrote, "produce and deploy *desired* knowledge more readily than Third World languages do." Conversely, "the knowledge that Third World languages deploy more easily is not sought by Western societies in quite the same way, or for the same reason" (Asad 1986: 162).

More recently, Dipesh Chakrabarty has called this condition one of "asymmetric ignorance." Speaking about his discipline, history, he writes: "Third world historians feel a need to refer to works in European history; historians of Europe do not feel any need to reciprocate" (Chakrabarty 2000: 28). An analogy can be drawn with almost any discipline—anthropology obviously included. Ideological coincidences, although helpful in joint political ventures, do not alter the structural and historical asymmetries that organize collaborative efforts among "Europeans" and "non-Europeans" broadly understood. Images of smooth, equal participation in research ventures, as comforting as they be, are hard to achieve and as often as not a well-intended academic illusion. Collaborations wanting to undo preexisting epistemic institutions and hierarchies—including those that have historically separated

Western and non-Western spheres of knowledge and their languages —require more than desire for horizontal work relations; it requires awareness of the hegemony of established epistemologies, and the need at least to question them. It also demands constant multidirectional negotiation as well as recognition and inspection of the conflicts that give raise to such negotiation. Last, although this should be the starting point as well, collaboration also requires the acceptance that complex entanglements of power will always structure the relationship— although, of course, the entanglement will constantly shift forms and connections. In all these may lie potential for a different way of laboring, which could produce news visions of reality, new concepts emerging from those visions—in which "new" does not mean "moving forward," but moving in any direction, differently. Such work would seek to change knowledge production through, for example, hybrid genres simultaneously academic and nonacademic, local and universal, and committed to blurring the boundaries between these spheres while intervening in them all.

But these remain fragile emergent ideas and heterotopias, available for exploration. The chapters that follow explore indigeneity's lines of containment and flight into this early 21st century present. We hope they may also be of some value in thinking toward the future and its limits and possibilities.

Notes

Acknowledgments. We are deeply grateful for the extensive, insightful comments of Claudia Briones, Arturo Escobar, Richard Fox, Charles Hale, Donald Moore, Ben Orlove, Eduardo Restrepo, and Randolph Starn on earlier drafts of this introduction. Kristina Lyons, an anthropology student at the University of California, Davis, shared her insights about this volume, translated from Spanish, and helped us put this manuscript in order. Two anonymous readers for the Wenner-Gren Foundation also provided useful feedback. Ya Chung-Chuang, Valerie Lambert, Francesca Merlan, and Linda Rupert made important suggestions; so did members of the "Diaspora and Indigeneity" Franklin Humanities Institute seminar at Duke University. We also thank our colleagues at the "Indigenous Experience Today" symposium in Rivarotta di Pasiano, Italy, March 18–25, 2005. Responsibility for the arguments and any errors in what follows is entirely our own.

1. Starn (2004) explores the brutal extermination of one native society, California's Yahi, and the story of its last survivor, Ishi.

2. See the website of Survival International (www.survival-international. org) for more on these figures. Of course, calculating any total depends very much on the tricky question of who should be counted as "indigenous" in the first place, a question taken up in this introduction and throughout the volume.

3. Other Kaktovikmiut oppose oil drilling in ANWR.

4. See the Oxford English Dictionary (n.d.) for indigenous.

5. The Frazer quote appears in Stocking 1995.

6. These populations were regarded as "indigenous" following their occupation of the country prior to the time "of conquest or colonization" (Thornberry 2003).

7. See Office of the High Commissioner for Human Rights 1989.

8. See BBC World 2006.

9. The writer said: "It is very interesting for an Indian without resentments, without complexes, without scornfulness to occupy the Presidency [of Peru]." Interview by Joaquín Ibarz, *Diario La Vanguardia*, Barcelona, April, 6, 2001.

10. See Ahu n.d.

11. Stoll (1999) charged Menchú with making up part of her story; for a wide range of views on the controversy, see Arias (2001).

12. This is the translation we believe best captures Quijano's original phrasing in Spanish—"popularizar lo indígena e indigineizar lo popular." See also García Linera (2006).

13. De la Cadena (2000) explores the politics of indigeneity, race, and culture in the Cuzco region of Peru; Starn (1999) does so in the context of northern Peru.

14. Cruikshank takes the phrase "dwelling perspective" from the work of Timothy Ingold (2000).

15. Sheehan (2006) offers a useful overview of the question of sovereignty in European history.

16. We are grateful to Michael Brown for the citations here, and he discusses the work of Alfred and Young more extensively in his chapter in this volume.

17. Only quite recently have scholars begun to examine in the interlocking forms of discrimination and intimate connection among African Americans, Indians, and whites in the United States (Brooks 2002). New work about the sometimes-tense relationships between Chinese and Sikh migrants and Aborigines has added another level of complexity to ways of narrating Australian history as just a matter of white conquest (De Lepervanche 1984; Reynolds 2003).

References

Adas, Michael. 1979. *Prophets of Rebellion: Millenarian protest movements against the European order.* Chapel Hill: University of North Carolina Press.

Ahu, Te. n.d. The evolution of contemporary Maori Protest. Electronic document, http://aotearoa.wellington.net.nz/back/tumoana, accessed July 27, 2005.

Alfred, Taiaiake. 2001. From sovereignty to freedom: Towards an Indigenous political discourse. *Indigenous Affairs* 3: 22–34.

Arias, Arturo, ed. 2001. *The Rigoberta Menchú controversy.* Minneapolis: University of Minnesota Press.

Asad, Talal. 1986. The Concept of Cultural Translation in British Social Anthropology. In *Writing culture: The poetics and politics of ethnography,* edited by James Clifford and George E. Marcus, 141–164. Berkeley: University of California Press.

BBC World. 2006. Vargas Llosa: "Un nuevo racismo." Electronic document, http://news.bbc.co.uk/hi/spanish/latin_america/newsid_4633000/4633898.stm, accessed December 20, 2006.

Braidotti, Rosi. 2006. *Transpositions: On nomadic ethics.* Cambridge: Polity Press.

Brooks, James F., ed. 2002. *Confounding the color line: The Indian-Black experience in North America.* Lincoln: University of Nebraska Press.

Brysk, Allison. 2000. *From tribal village to global village: Indian rights and international relations in Latin America.* Stanford: Stanford University Press.

Butler, Judith. 1993. *Bodies that matter: On the discursive limits of "sex."* New York: Routledge.

Chakrabarty, Dispesh. 2000. *Provincializing Europe. Postcolonial thought and historical difference.* Princeton: Princeton University Press.

Chung-min, Chen, Chuang Ying-chang, Huang Shu-min, eds. 1994. *Ethnicity in Taiwan: Social, historical and cultural perspectives.* Taipei: Institute of Ethnology, Academia Sinica.

Dagnino, Evelina. 2002. *Sociedade civil e españos públicos no Brasil.* Sáo Paulo: Paz e Terra.

de la Cadena, Marisol. 2000. *Indigenous mestizos: The politics of race and culture in Cuzco, Peru, 1919–1991.* Durham, NC: Duke University Press.

———. 2006. Are mestizos hybrids? The conceptual politics of Andean identities. *Journal of Latin American Studies* 37: 250–284.

De Lepervanche, Marie M. 1984. *Indians in a white Australia: An account of race, class, and Indian immigration to Eastern Australia.* Sydney: Allen and Unwin.

Ehle, John. 1988. *Trail of tears: The rise and fall of the Cherokee Nation*. New York: Doubleday.

Escobar, Arturo. in press. *Places and regions in the global age: Social movements and biodiversity conservation in the Colombian Pacific*. Durham, NC: Duke University Press.

Frazer, James G. 1931 [1888]. *Garnered sheaves*. London: no publisher.

French, Jan. 2004. *Mestizaje* and law making in indigenous identity formation in northeastern Brazil. *American Anthropologist* 106 (4): 663–674.

García, María Elena. 2005. *Making Indigenous citizens: Identities, education, and multicultural development in Peru*. Stanford: Stanford University Press.

García Linera, Alvaro. 2006. El Evismo: Lo nacional-popular en acción. In *Observatorio social de América Latina*, vol. 6, no. 19, July. Buenos Aires: CLACSO.

Guha, Ramachandra. 1989. Radical American environmentalism and wilderness preservation: A Third World critique. *Environmental Ethics* 11 (1): 71–83.

Hale, Charles. 2006. *Más que un Indio: Racial ambivalence and neoliberal multiculturalism in Guatemala*. Santa Fe: School of American Research Press.

Hall, Stuart. 1996. Who needs idenitity? In *Questions of cultural identity*, edited by Stuart Hall and Paul du Gay, 1–17. London: Sage.

Hodgson, Dorothy L. 2001. *Once intrepid warriors: Gender, ethnicity, and the cultural politics of Masai development*. Bloomington: Indiana University Press.

Human Rights and Equal Opportunity Commission. 1997. *Bringing them home: Report of the national inquiry into the separation of aboriginal and Torres Strait Islander children from their families*. Sydney: Human Rights and Equal Opportunity Commission.

Ingold, Tim. 2000. *The perception of the environment*. London: Routledge.

Kirsch, Stuart. 2001. Lost Worlds: Environment Disaster, "Culture Loss" and the Law. *Current Anthropology* 42 (2): 167–198.

Kymlicka, Will. 2001. *Politics in the vernacular: Nationalism, multiculturalism and citizenship*. New York: Oxford University Press.

Latour, Bruno. 1993. *We have never been modern*. Cambridge, MA: Harvard University Press.

——. 2004. Why has critique run out of steam? From matters of fact to matters of concern. *Critical Inquiry* 30 (2): 225–248.

Li, Tania Murray. 2000. Articulating indigenous identity in Indonesia: Resource politics and the tribal slot. *Comparative Studies in Society and History* 42 (1): 149–179.

Mamdani, Mahmood. 2002. *When victims become killers: Colonialism, nativism, and the genocide in Rwanda.* Princeton: Princeton University Press.

———. 2004. Race and Ethnicity as Political Identities in the African Context. In *Keywords: identity,* edited by N. Tazi, 1–24. New York: Other Press.

Moore, Donald. 2004. *Suffering for territory: Race, place, and power in Zimbabwe.* Durham, NC: Duke University Press.

Mouffe, Chantal. 2005. *On the political.* London: Routledge.

Niezen, Ronald. 2000. *The origins of Indigenism: Human rights and the politics of identity.* Berkeley: University of California Press.

Once Were Warriors. 1994. Lee Tamahori, director. 99 min. Fine Line Features.

Office of the High Commissioner for Human Rights. 1989. Convention (No. 169) concerning Indigenous and Tribal Peoples in Independent Countries. Electronic document, http://193.194.138.190/html/menu3/b/62.htm, accessed December 12, 2006.

Oxford English Dictionary. n.d. Electronic document, http://dictionary.oed.com/cgi/entry/50115329?query_type=word&queryword=indigenous&first=1&max_to_show=10&single=1&sort_type=alpha, accessed XXXX.

Piot, Charles. 1999. *Remotely global: Village modernity in West Africa.* Chicago: University of Chicago Press.

Postero, Nancy, and Leon Zamosc. 2004. *The struggle for Indigenous rights in Latin America.* Brighton: Sussex Academic Press.

Quijano, Aníbal. 2006. Keynote address at *Congreso Internacional de Pueblos Indígenas de America Latina,* July 15, Cuzco, Peru.

Ramos, Alcida. 1998. *Indigenism: Ethnic politics in Brazil.* Madison: University of Wisconsin Press.

Reynolds, Henry. 2003. *North of Capricorn: The untold story of Australia's North.* Crow's Nest, New South Wales: Allen and Unwin.

Sheehan, James. 2006. The problem of sovereignty in European history. *American Historical Review* 111 (1): 1–15.

Smith, Linda Tuhiwai. 1999. *Decolonizing methodologies: Research and Indigenous peoples.* London: Zed.

Smith, Paul Chaat. 1994. Home of the Brave. *C Magazine* (Summer): 32–42.

Smith, Paul Chaat, and Robert Allen Warrior. 1996. *Like a hurricane: The Indian movement from Alcatraz to Wounded Knee.* New York: Free Press.

Starn, Orin. 1999. *Nightwatch: The politics of protest in the Andes.* Durham, NC: Duke University Press.

——. 2004. *Ishi's brain: In search of America's last "Wild" Indian*. New York: W. W. Norton.

Stocking, George W. 1995. *After Tylor. British Social Anthropology 1888–1951*. Madison: University of Wisconsin Press.

Stoler, Ann. 2002. *Carnal knowledge and imperial rule: Race and the intimate in colonial rule*. Berkeley: University of California Press.

Stoll, David. 1999. *Rigoberta Menchú and the story of all poor Guatemalans*. Boulder, CO: Westview Press.

Sturm, Circe. 2002. *Blood politics: Race, culture, and identity in the Cherokee nation of Oklahoma*. Berkeley: University of California Press.

Thomson, Sinclair. 2003. *We alone will rule: Native Andean politics in the age of insurgency*. Madison: University of Wisconsin Press.

Thornberry, Patrick. 2003. *Indigenous people and human rights*. Manchester: Manchester University Press.

Toulabor, Comi. 1985. *Le Togo sous Eyeadema*. Dakar: Karthala.

Trouillot, Michel-Rolph. 1991. The Savage Slot: The Poetics and Politics of Otherness. In *Recapturing anthropology: Working in the present*, edited by Richard G. Fox, 17–44. Santa Fe: School of American Research Press.

Tsing, Anna. 2005. *Friction: An ethnography of global connection*. Princeton: Princeton University Press.

Tully, James. 1995. *Strange multiplicity: Constitutionalism in an age of diversity*. Cambridge: Cambridge University Press.

Tylor, E. B. 1903. *Primitive Culture*. 4th edition. 2 Vols. London: John Murray.

Van Cott, Donna. 2000. *The friendly liquidation of the past: The politics of diversity in Latin America*. Pittsburgh: University of Pittsburgh Press.

Wachman, Alan. 1994. *Taiwan: National identity and democratization*. Armonk: M. E. Sharpe.

The Whale Rider. 2003. Niki Caro, dir. 101 min. Newmarket Films.

Williams, Raymond. 1977. *Marxism and literature*. New York: Oxford University Press.

Young, Iris Marion. 2000. Hybrid Democracy: Iroquois Federalism and the Postcolonial Project. In *Political theory and the rights of Indigenous peoples*, edited by Duncan Ivison, Paul Patton, and Will Sanders, 237–258. Cambridge: Cambridge University Press.

Part 1

Indigenous Identities, Old and New

Indigenous Voice

Anna Tsing

The global indigenous movement is alive with promising contradictions. Inverting national development standards, it promises unity
based on plurality: diversity without assimilation. It endorses authenticity
and invention, subsistence *and* wealth, traditional knowledge *and* new
technologies, territory *and* diaspora.[1] The excitement of indigenous rights
claims draws from the creative possibilities of such juxtapositions.

Yet, given this heady brew, it is perhaps not surprising that scholars
have had mixed reactions.[2] Some are excited by the struggle against
discrimination, violence, and resource theft. Others are suspicious of
the support of neoliberal reformers and the movement's inattention
to class. Some note continuities with colonial discourses of race and
cultural essence. Others celebrate cultural revitalization. Meanwhile,
both boosters and critics tend to base their evaluations on one of two
research models: either case studies, with their plethora of distinguishing
particulars, or generalizations about indigeneity at large. Collections
continue to string together cases with the assumption of commonality;
analysis searches for fundamental principles without attention to the
histories that make such principles more or less relevant. Both models
reduce indigeneity to a singular set of logics and dilemmas. Whether
they base their commentary on single cases or on generalizations about
all indigeneity, most scholarly reports have shown little curiosity about
the diversity of indigenous problems, rhetorics, and causes. Those of
us who enter the field to understand how the obscure ethnographic
situation we know best fits into global mobilizations are offered few
clues about divergent histories and conflicting claims. In response, this
chapter begins the task of laying out a historically concrete history of
divergent indigeneities.

My method abandons neither place-based particularity nor the links across places. Instead of imagining links only as a route to homogenization, however, I highlight the friction that creates both grip and gaps, both misunderstandings and common ground. In this spirit, I begin my story with the dynamics of indigeneity in one place, Indonesia, and use the questions raised from that situation to guide my wider inquiry.[3]

Indigeneity is not a self-evident category in Indonesia. Almost everyone is "indigenous" in the sense of deriving from original stocks; Indonesia is not a white settler state. Yet activists and community leaders fighting for the rights of marginal rural communities have increasingly used the rhetoric of indigeneity to draw attention to their causes. In both cities and villages this rhetoric engenders debate; it is difficult to consider "indigenous rights" without running into disagreements about terms. This situation stimulates me to begin with *talk* about indigeneity, rather than jumping immediately to indigenous experience. It also presses me to consider how the national political scene—with its cultural forms and its potential alliances—structures indigenous claims. As I turn from Indonesia to trace indigenous rhetorics more widely, I thus attend to how nations, and the dialogues between nations, shape indigenous voices. In these transnational dialogues, powerful traveling axes of indigenous concern are formed.

I begin, then, with Indonesia, before turning to my general thesis.

Translation Questions

In Indonesia, the phrase used as an equivalent for "indigenous peoples" is *masyarakat adat*. However, the effective translation of the transnational indigenous movement goes beyond the problem of words. Many Indonesians oppose activist attempts to single out certain rural communities as deserving of special rights. Nationalism in Indonesia runs strong, and the directive to blend cultural communities into a common nation—"from the many, one"[4]—is still among the more progressive programs of Indonesian nationalism. In contrast, the division of the nation into ethnic communities is seen as a heritage of colonial "divide and rule" policies.

It is hard to deny that the separation of cultural minorities and majorities throughout Asia and Africa was, and continues to be, a colonial habit. The use of Southeast Asian mountain people by U.S. imperial forces in Indochina serves as an important reminder of the colonial history of nurturing loyal tribes. International identification of "indigenous peoples" in Asia and Africa continues to follow colonial lines of separation, singling out minorities for international protection because they are willing to oppose Muslims, Chinese, and other imagined enemies of the West. In Indonesia, the phrase masyarakat adat, "traditional societies," derives its punch from colonial precedent. Dutch scholars elevated *adat,* perhaps best translated as "custom," to the status of customary law. The notion of adat as law allowed the colonial argument that Islam was a foreign religion that should not be allowed to define native life. At the same time, it also informed those Dutchmen who opposed colonial programs that threatened to plow over all native social forms. Dutch colonial authorities set up adat law courts in only a few places; in terms of power and policy, adat was effective mainly as an *idea* about native difference and, at least potentially, native rights. In the early independence period, nationalists developed contrasting attitudes toward the idea of adat: Some rejected it as archaic; others embraced it as the spirit of the nation. During the New Order regime (1969–98), adat was known through government programs to depoliticize rural citizens through token recognition of harmless cultural forms. When Indonesian environmental and human rights activists of the 1980s and 1990s decided to revive the concept of adat as a tool for the empowerment of rural communities, they had to carry—and transform—this complex and contradictory history.[5]

In 1999, the first archipelago-wide assembly of masyarakat adat was held in Jakarta. The alliance formed from this meeting, Aliansi Masyarakat Adat Nusantara (AMAN), endorses regional campaigns and works to see Indonesia included in international indigenous organizing. Yet the emergence of AMAN has sharpened Indonesian debates about whether indigenous organizing is a good idea.[6] Most government officials argue that the international indigenous movement is irrelevant because there are no "indigenous peoples" in Indonesia. They find common cause with urban professionals who worry about dividing the nation and imagine modernization as the key force for nation-building. Some, including mainstream conservationists, describe adat as "invented tradition" without stability or legitimacy. Many foreign scholars and international donor agencies oppose the idea of working for communal rights, which they see as dangerously exclusive. Supporters of liberal individualism join them, as do those concerned with ethnic violence. In recent years, Indonesia has been torn by ethnic and religious conflicts, many sponsored surreptitiously by the army. In Kalimantan, for example, "indigenous" Dayaks clashed with migrant Madurese in 1997, 2000, and 2001. It was hard to deny that the mobilization of

Dayak identity had been supported by internationally connected NGOs. Few blamed international indigenous politics directly for the violence, but new questions have been raised. For example, there is cause to worry about the role of transnational Christian charities in promoting violence together with indigenous rights. Wherever Christians support minority cultures, missionization and human rights become hopelessly intertwined; anti-Muslim violence is an expectable outcome. Religious rage need not be confused with revolutionary armed struggle. But it is worth noting that where Indonesian communities have turned to revolutionary tactics, they have questioned or refused the indigenous slot. In Aceh and West Papua, activists want *independence* not dependent sovereignty; they find better routes to make their claims than indigenous politics.[7]

All of this points to the impossibility of an Indonesian indigenous politics that can promote social justice, and, yet, those who jump to this conclusion omit the major reason for Indonesian indigenous organizing. Those communities that have placed their hopes in the international indigenous label do so because their land and resources are threatened by corporate and state expansion. Indeed, the destruction of the countryside, with its once vast rainforests, bountiful fishing waters, and richly endowed legacies of culture and community, is the major problem confronting Indonesia today. The policies of the New Order regime, which opened the countryside as a "free" space of exploitation, allowed complementary orders of illegal and legal resource theft to pile atop each other. In Kalimantan, the destructive force of illegal and legal logging and mining tears the countryside apart; few bureaucrats or community leaders can think of much to do except clamor for a share of the spoils. The claim that rural communities might have *rights* based in their traditional cultures is one of the few interruptions of a deadly business as usual. Even if this claim is ultimately unsuccessful in remaking national and international policy, it is worth our attention.

Affiliation with international indigenous politics for this claim follows from a layered history. Colonial administration divided the archipelago into "inner" and "outer" zones with densely populated Java at the center of concerns about the governance of native people. The "outer" islands of Sumatra, Kalimantan, Sulawesi, and Eastern Indonesia were interesting to colonial authorities mainly for entrepreneurial development; the native people were relevant only as exotica. Colonially subjugated Java became the center of the nationalist struggle, and the story of alliance between Javanese peasants and nationalist elites made the nation seem possible. In the early years of independence, non-Javanese elites became increasingly important to nation-building, and a few outer island groups gained prominence. Most rural communities in the outer islands, however, were nationally invisible. Only during the New Order regime were the outer islands targeted—in policies of increasingly massive resource exploitation. The policy of ignoring non-Javanese rural communities facilitated such resource theft. But this meant that rural protest from the outer islands found no channels in national politics. Only the formation of a social justice–oriented environmental movement in the late 1970s and 1980s brought outer-island rural complaints to national attention.

During much of the New Order regime, social protest was censored, and the environmental movement was one of the few sites for public discussion of justice. In the late 1980s and early 1990s, the national environmental movement carried the weight of many progressive hopes. For the movement to endorse the rights of non-Javanese rural communities was an extraordinary political innovation; it brought people who had been historically excluded into the national political process for the first time. Ironically, after the much-anticipated fall of the New Order regime in 1998, the national environmental movement lost visibility, and international conservationists, with their law-and-order nature protection, gained prominence. In this context international affiliations have seemed more crucial than ever to Indonesian activists. To say that masyarakat adat are "indigenous peoples" launches hopes that international legitimacy will give some force to their complaints about land and resource theft. One influential Jakarta activist explained to me that her *definition* of masyarakat adat, the indigenous peoples of Indonesia, was rural communities fighting resource corporations.

Both the force and the idiosyncrasy of this definition raises questions about the transnational field in which "indigenous peoples" has emerged. Can Indonesian activists effectively ally with transnational indigenous peoples? After all, some indigenous peoples—such as those caught up in the U.S. Alaska Native Claims Act—*are* resource corporations. Others, such as those who control Greenland Home Rule, mimic nation-states in their resource management plans. With what strength—and what hesitations—is global indigeneity linked to social justice environmentalism?

Finding myself in the midst of debates about Indonesian indigenous politics, I have turned to comparative readings in indigeneity to find more about the field. Yet comparative exercises are dangerous; they tempt us to assume an imperial perspective: the view from global management.

I have presented this long prologue to suggest another reason for global mapping: to consider how a given set of emergent tactics might thrive or fail in transnational encounters. If we are involved in the politics of particular places, we need some sense of how the plans we advocate articulate with others.

Global indigenous politics is exciting *and* challenging because of its diversity. Its strength is its refusal of pregiven political categories—and its refusal to back down to demands for strict definitions. Almost every international project has adhered to the idea that indigenous peoples will not be predefined. As a Cree spokesperson for the International Working Group for Indigenous Affairs put it, "To assume a right to define indigenous peoples is to further deny our right of self-determination" (Thornberry 2002: 60). Most conventionally, international indigenous spokespeople point to the necessity for self-identification. But self-identification sometimes leads to more layers of contradiction. Consider Central America. Quetzil Castaneda has proposed "We are *not* indigenous!" as a rallying cry for Maya peasants of the Yucatan, who refuse identity politics (2004). In El Salvador, Brandt Peterson has argued that ethnic self-identity exists in a violent gap within speakability; historically only enemies have used the term *indio,* and activists are frustrated by the low levels of interest communities have shown for explicitly "indigenous" programs (Peterson 2005).

Contradictory attitudes about being labeled indigenous lead to two quite different analytic issues. First, all categories arouse varied reactions for the people called to those categories. People whom others label woman, black, or liberal are equally divided and ambivalent. Such issues deserve an analysis of the complex histories of making and claiming identities. This is important work, but it is not my concern in this chapter. Instead, I track variations in the public articulation of indigeneity in different places. I follow not the ambivalence of ordinary people but the claims of those who set the terms of discussion—for example, activists, community leaders, and public intellectuals. Their claims become influential discursive frames to the extent they can gain both a following and an audience. These frames inform what one might call "indigenous voice." By *voice,* I am referring to the genre conventions with which public affirmations of identity are articulated. Because it is the genre convention, not the speaker him or herself, that has power, totally unknown people can speak with this kind of voice; but they must speak in a way an audience can hear. A tree that falls in an empty forest has no voice in this sense; my random complaints similarly have no voice. Only when I find a way to speak that articulates my complaints in a publicly recognizable genre can I gain voice. What can be heard changes. No voices claim all audiences. Yet it seems analytically useful to separate diversity in the public voice of indigeneity from other kinds of indigenous diversity. The rest of this chapter investigates the historical conditions in which a transnational indigenous voice has gained momentum.

Thesis: Cross-National Links Inform Transnational Fora

The meaning of the phrase "indigenous peoples," in its local translations, varies nationally as well as regionally. The contrasts are striking; some versions are contradictory; not all become globally influential. For a particular version of indigeneity to become a transnational model requires linking across national contexts. This linking can amplify indigenous claims in both the places being linked and, thus amplified, make its way into the world. In other cases, the link exists only from the perspective of one nation; in the other nation, no one is even aware that a link was made. Yet, despite this asymmetry, such linking may allow the formation of a powerful traveling model. Traveling models of indigeneity have spread conventions of international indigenous politics. Because they are not readily adapted to every national and regional context, they have also formed nodes of dissension. The inapplicability of powerful frames for the indigenous opens spaces of refusal—and of potential breaks and alliances.

National variation in the meaning of "indigenous" is structured by the exigencies of policy and politics. Nation-state policies have every-where created the conditions for indigenous lives. If the nation-state moves people into reservations, then the fight must continue from the reservation. If the nation-state requires assimilation, then debates will emerge from within the apparatus of assimilation. The form of indigeneity in a particular place cannot be divorced from these histories of national classification and management. Furthermore, indigenous protests must speak to a national audience. Despite the importance of global connections, the nation continues to be the locus of political negotiation in most places. To make a political difference, indigenous leaders must address the nation-state. They must use cultural and political frames that are comprehensible within the nation. Indonesians recognize *adat* whether they agree or disagree with its revival; New Zealanders know the Treaty of Waitangi whether or not they support current interpretations. Recognizable features of the national political and cultural landscape are woven into all indigenous demands. Finally, international fora for indigenous politics reinforce national differences by managing representation by national units. The UN model in which every nation has its spokespeople is replicated in many indigenous working groups. In these, indigenous representatives learn to imagine their transnational status in relation to their national status.

Regional variations in the meaning of indigenous are tied to contingent histories of segregation, alliance, suppression, mobilization, leadership, and political culture. It is important not to lose track of the diversity of subnational regions. Regional contrasts—eastern versus western Guatemala, inner versus outer Indonesia—make all the difference for allegiance to a politics of indigeneity. In this chapter, however, I privilege national variation because it best helps me explore transnationally traveling models.

Powerful transnational models for indigenous organizing are formed in cross-national links. One prominent example is the link between indigenous groups in Canada and New Zealand that formed in the 1970s: From this link, I suggest, the rhetoric of sovereignty came to be a key facet of the international indigenous movement. The link developed from traveling state missions as well as comparative discussion of treaties and governance. The ideas about indigenous sovereignty that developed from the link informed indigenous mobilization in other British settler states, shaping policy debates particularly in Australia and the United States. From this cluster, sovereignty entered the international indigenous agenda, where it has continued to inform almost every document on indigenous rights—despite the fact this rhetoric just does not work in most other places.

Where the Canada—New Zealand link provokes attention to petitions and treaties, a different American connection invokes militant struggle for pluriethnic autonomy. The dialogue linking North and South America around "the Indian question" has been a long one, but one important entry is certainly the inversion of *indigenismo* in the late 1960s, as Mexican activists were stimulated by the U.S. Red Power movement. Instead of imagining a national politics of acculturation, they organized around indigenous cultural rights, beginning the discussion of a multicultural and pluriethnic nation. Red Power activists in the United States did not join Mexican discussion; but the cross-national link still offered it legitimacy and force. Mexican voices have joined other Latin American struggles to transform *mestizaje* and modernization into political autonomy and cultural self-determination. Such narratives invoke inclusion and transformation rather than separation from the nation. As such, they draw directly on earlier peasant organizing, with its nation-making history. They offer transnationally powerful models of militancy—and cooptation—to transnational indigenous concerns.

Sometimes nonindigenous activists make the connections. The Brazilian experience of environmentalist indigenous politics traveled to Malaysia and Indonesia with northern activists who moved from the campaign to save the Amazon to Southeast Asian rainforest campaigns in the 1980s. The alliances between environmentalists and indigenous leaders only worked out well in Brazil at particular historical moments: for example, when the Workers Party helped to domesticate the struggle. But for the environmentalists involved, the idea of alliance with rainforest people was good to travel. National environmentalists in Southeast Asia picked up on the theme—and a global rainforest campaign emerged. From this campaign, indigenous peoples around the world became eligible for the role of environmental steward. But, of course, not all indigenous peoples have wanted this role, and some have actively fought environmentalism.

Rhetorics of sovereignty; narratives of pluriethnic autonomy; environmental stewardship: These are not the only definitional frames for indigenous struggle, but they are among the most powerful. My argument about cross-national connections suggests that they form semiautonomous axes of indigenous voice; they do not always complement each other. I am sure you can already see why the search for a consistent definitional or philosophical basis for indigenous organizing would not help me explain this configuration. Yet definitional and philosophical consistency are demanded not only by skeptical politicians but also by scholars. Is indigenous organizing the dawn of a new cultural era, or, alternatively, the predictable outcome of neoliberal reform on a global scale? Neither approach allows us to consider the making and unmaking of indigenous links. Scholars tend to recognize the importance of an argument only to the extent that it offers a consistent genealogy within an identifiable philosophical tradition. If we have trouble appreciating contingent articulations—even after invoking Antonio Gramsci—it is because we think we have something down only when it repeats political truisms. Yet global connections are not just about repetition. The friction at the heart of global interchange allows new forms and practices to come into being, for better or worse. To recognize the travels of indigenous voice does not mean that indigenous mobilizations are good for everyone. Even if we limit ourselves—as I do here—to the proclamations of eager organizers, their political successes are sporadic and frail. Their frameworks may not excite sympathetic response, and when they do, these may or may not be helpful to anyone. By highlighting the connections, and therefore, too, the disconnections, I hope to show the irregular and contingent development of the indigenous framework.

Voices That Travel

How have indigenous concerns gathered transnational force? Here I elaborate and explain the three axes of connection I introduced briefly in the previous section. Only afterward do I turn to the work that these axes of indigeneity cannot do.

The rhetoric of sovereignty: Two-row wampum at the Tribunal of Waitangi

In the late 1960s, Canada was absorbed by the drama of Quebecois nationalism and the struggle of French Canadians for civil rights. Liberals wanted the federal government to confirm the equality of all Canadian citizens under a single standard. It was in this context that Prime Minister Pierre Trudeau issued a White Paper in 1969 recommending that Indian status be abolished, making Indians Canadian citizens without entitlements. He was unprepared for the uproar that followed. Indians demanded that the government respect their treaty rights and the obligations of their special status. "Red Papers" were issued in reaction, reminding everyone that "equality" in government policy always privileged whiteness. The onslaught of critical reaction forced the government to renounce the White Paper. The ensuing gap in government policy reopened a broad range of questions about the status of Canada's indigenous peoples.[8]

Trudeau returned from a trip to New Zealand in 1970 to address Indian protesters; there he first brought up the New Zealand practice of reserving four parliamentary seats for indigenous Maori (Sanders 1977: 9). New Zealand, like Australia, formed an easy model of proper governance for Canadians. In 1971 and 1972 official missions from Canada were sent to New Zealand and Australia seeking consultation on indigenous governance. Included on the first mission was George Manuel, the president of the influential National Indian Brotherhood—as well as other Canadian Indian leaders. From these contacts, an intertwined story about "indigenous peoples" began to arise.[9] International petition for self-determination and redress was at the heart of it. Indigenous leaders in Canada and New Zealand recalled parallel histories of international petition: Maori delegations traveled to England to meet with the King or Queen in 1882, 1884, 1914, and 1924; chiefs from British Columbia went on similar trips in 1906 and 1909. Representatives of the Iroquois Confederacy traveled to Geneva with grievances for the League of Nations in the 1920s; so did the Maori.[10] This history of petition informed subsequent efforts to form an international organization for indigenous rights. In 1975, the National Indian Brotherhood hosted the formative meeting of the World Council of Indigenous Peoples in Port Alberni, British Columbia. This formative moment has continued to influence subsequent indigenous mobilization.

Indigenous leaders in Canada received particular support from New Zealand Maori for their concerns with treaty rights, which were emerging as the cornerstone of indigenous organizing in New Zealand. In 1840, the British Crown and some five hundred Maori chiefs signed the historic Treaty of Waitangi, which allowed the British to make international claims over New Zealand. Although the treaty did not inform subsequent British policy, "the romantic myth of the treaty as a symbol of the unity and amity of two races" persisted (Howard 2003: 184–185). An annual celebration of the treaty was largely a Pakeha (white) event— at least in 1971, when an emergent Maori protest movement honed in on Waitangi as a site of contest. In 1972, a Pakeha writer brought public attention to the fact that Maori chiefs and British representatives signed different treaties—in Maori and English, respectively. Where the English version supported the idea that Maori had ceded "sovereignty" to the Crown, the Maori version ceded only "governorship" *(kawanatanga),* retaining "cheiftainship" *(rangatiratanga)* over land and property. Both versions gave Maori full rights of British citizenship, but the Maori version makes a Maori–British partnership in sovereignty the goal.[11] This issue of translation set the treaty center stage in Maori struggles for land rights, political autonomy, and culturally appropriate forms of governance. In 1975, a sympathetic Labour government formed the Tribunal of Waitangi to assess government compliance to the treaty. Much of the subsequent success of Maori land-rights and political-autonomy claims depends on this tribunal and its reports. The treaty, then, remains key to Maori assertions—and to Maori influence in Canada and beyond.

In Canada, campaigns to use treaty rights and government settlements to obtain political purchase also heated up in the 1970s as indigenous peoples transformed themselves into First Nations. The Cree and Inuit of northern Quebec won a major settlement in 1975; in the same year, the Dene asserted nationhood. In 1976, the Inuit-controlled territory of Nunuvut was proposed; by 1982, the National Indian Brotherhood had become the Assembly of First Nations. The rhetoric of indigenous sovereignty was further developed in fights to put indigenous rights into the Canadian constitution. Canadian Indians appealed for help to international supporters, especially in London, thus furthering their leadership in promoting indigenous sovereignty on an international level, with a British Empire scope (Sanders 1985). At home, one of the most outspoken indigenous groups was the Iroquois Confederacy. Those Iroquois who allied with the British during the American Revolution were given territories in what became Canada and treated as a sovereign power. The alliance was materialized in the Gus-Wen-Qah or Two-Row Wampum Belt, in which two rows of purple shells, divided by the white sign of peace, signify the Iroquois and English each with their own sovereign path. Two-row wampum became an icon for the struggle for self-determination in Canada (Johnston 2003 [1986]). Like the Treaty of Waitangi, two-row wampum spoke to the possibility of defining sovereignty in culturally appropriate terms. Together, they offer an influential frame for thinking about international indigenous mobilizing.

Almost from the first, indigenous people from the United States, Australia, and northern Europe responded to this axis of mobilization. By 1974, the U.S. American Indian Movement had sponsored the International Treaty Council to seek for UN recognition of tribal treaties (Sanders 2003: 68). As in Canada and New Zealand, Native Americans used the history of treaties as symbolic politics: For example, the Trail of Broken Treaties protest march of 1972 dramatized Indian predicaments. The U.S. government had refused to deal with Native Americans through treaties since 1871. The rhetoric of sovereignty attempted to reverse this history.[12] Meanwhile, Australian aborigines had no treaties to fall back on. Yet their ties to other British settler states—Canada and New Zealand—allowed them to act rather as if they did. The 1976 Aboriginal Land Rights (Northern Territory) Act offered an internationally influential model of building cultural values into entitlements: Aboriginal sacred sites became the basis of land claims (Maddock 1991). The internationalism of all this was further boosted by the involvement of the northern European Sami, who connected the emergent indigenous movement to Scandanavian-based international organizations, such as the International Working Group on Indigenous Affairs (IWGIA), and from there to the United Nations.[13] Many observers of the global indigeneity movement begin here, with the rhetoric of sovereignty. It is the basis of protests to keep the letter "s" in indigenous *peoples* and to remain firm on the language of the UN draft declaration. But it is not the only framing axis of indigenous politics.

Pluriethnic autonomy: An Inter-American dialogue.   The slogan of the 1996 National Indigenous Council of Mexico—"Never again without us"— carries us into another indigenous politics: Latin American struggles for pluriethnic autonomy.[14] "Autonomy is not secession," declared the 1994 National Indigenous Convention; "autonomy is the first opportunity that our indigenous *pueblos* would have to become true Mexicans for the first time."[15] The term *autonomy* is used in indigenous politics around the world. However, only in Latin America is it a term of struggle.[16]

Mexican indigenous mobilization is best known through the 1994 uprising of the Ejercito Zapatista de Liberacion Nacional (EZLN). The EZLN and its political successors have appealed not for sovereignty but, rather, for the remaking of a Mexican nationalism that could work for, rather than against, Indians and the poor. The EZLN carried the Mexican national flag during peace negotiations; indigenous negotiators confirmed without prompting that they were "100 percent Mexican" (Brysk 2000: 81). By remaking the nation in a pluralistic frame for the cause of social justice and cultural rights, the Zapatistas offered a charismatic rendering of an Inter-American story about popular democracy. Drawing from southern "peasant" legacies and from northern multiculturalism, Zapatistas respoke indigeneity, reenergizing earlier Latin American mobilizations, and indeed indigenous campaigns around the world.

One relevant genealogy of this indigenous voice begins with *indigenismo* and the politics of assimilation. In Mexico, indigenismo is associated with the making of the national polity through mestizaje, the European-sponsored cultural uplift and racial mixing of Indians through which civilization was thought to advance.[17] Contemporary indigenous politics in Mexico is a thorough *rejection* of indigenismo. Instead of assimilation, indigenous Mexicans demand self-determination and cultural respect. But indigenismo remains salient: It brought Indians ideologically into national development, even as it attempted to erase them. The power of contemporary indigenous claims to enter national debates on democracy depends on this spectral presence. (North American Indians' claims, in contrast, have trouble being heard in nation-state politics.) In Mexico, indigenismo also ushered in a still-relevant cast of players, including mobilized peasant communities and applied anthropologists.

As an ideology of conquest, indigenismo has depended on travel and dialogue; to track its varied forms across Latin America would be an exciting project—but not one for this chapter. Instead, I concentrate on a little-noticed chapter of its development: dialogue with U.S. Indian politics. In 1940, indigenismo—with all its faults—was revitalized by the first Inter-American Indigenist Congress, held in Pátzcuaro, Mexico. Important Mexican scholars and political figures attended; so too did John Collier of the U.S. Bureau of Indian Affairs.[18] Collier brought funds from the Rockefeller Foundation for the enterprise, which aimed to spread Bureaus of Indian Affairs across Latin America.[19] Collier also came with a new kind of applied anthropology intended to uphold the integrity of native cultures while offering Indians tools to integrate into national society.[20] Hector Díaz Polanco explains how, within the Inter-American discussion, what seemed at first to be a gesture of respect for Indians became yet another charge for assimilation (1997: 68–70). "Integrationism" was the new amalgam of cultural relativism and development formed in this dialogue. This model shaped the International Labour Organization's Convention (ILO) 107 of 1957, which calls for the "progressive integration [of indigenous people] into the life of their respective countries."[21] Marisol de la Cadena adds that "acculturation" as a scholarly concept swept north as well as south from this site and its related discussions (2005b). Meanwhile, indigenous integration blossomed as national policy in Mexico by conflating agendas for state expansion through peasant development and nation making through Indian acculturation.

In the late 1960s, a group of radical Mexican intellectuals launched a fierce critique of indigenismo as a colonial discourse.[22] Their critique was domestic but also transnational: It continued the Inter-American dialogue. One element was their appreciation of the northerners' Red Power movement.

U.S. Native American organizing in the late 1960s and early 1970s was widely influential. As in the Zapatista rebellion, a spectacular symbolic politics was deployed: the occupation of Alcatraz Island; the takeover of the Bureau of Indian Affairs (Smith and Warrior 1996). Furthermore, the Red Power movement caught attention at home and abroad as a transformation of the Black Power and the U.S. civil rights movements. Black Americans were a symbol of struggle not only among minorities all over the world but also among postcolonial nations, who saw anti-colonial energies extended in black movements, and communists, who saw the dirty outcome of advanced capitalism revealed for all in black oppression. The Red Power movement was the first successful exercise in connecting this broad social justice bloc to indigenous mobilization. Demands for civil rights, cultural rights, class struggle, and political freedom were bundled together in the international reception of Red Power. In contrast to many more recent indigenous mobilizations, third world nationalists were not pitted against indigenous activists; here they stood in common ranks against injustice.

Red Power demands were advanced particularly by urban educated Indians, who crossed tribal lines to speak to a U.S. national audience. The later turn to government-to-government negotiations in Native American politics has obscured the importance of pantribal civil-rights-style mobilizations. The inclusive reach of such mobilizations made them appealing in areas without tribal treaty rights and where the rhetoric of sovereignty seemed basically irrelevant.[23] Indigenous organizing in many places was first stimulated by demands for cultural rights, an end to discrimination, and political inclusion. Certainly, this was the case in Mexico.

In the late 1960s, a small group of activist Mexican anthropologists used Red Power to contest Mexican indigenismo and turn indigenous politics into a critique of cultural oppression.[24] In the current climate of Mexican self-examination, their critique was influential; the critical anthropologists were asked to join the National Indigenous Institute (INI) and to reform indigenous policy.[25] According to Courtney Jung, the official result of this reform depoliticized rural communities through its focus on cultural pride and bilingual education; however, the reform had unofficial results in stimulating indigenous self-identification (in press). First, it empowered class-based peasant organizing, if sometimes under an underinterpreted indigenous label. The 1974 Indigenous Congress in San Cristobal, Chiapas, for example, inaugurated an era of Marxist class-based mobilization—just because it brought activists together. Second, indigenous rhetoric familiarized activists with internationally powerful genres that became useful in the early 1990s with the loss of potency of peasant idioms. When Mexico accepted structural adjustment and, most drastically, rewrote the constitution to exclude commitments to peasants, the rhetoric of peasant struggle became ineffective. Peasant activists became indigenous activists to utilize the international cachet of indigenous politics. The conflation of indigenous and peasant demands allowed the indigenous struggle to build directly on the peasant struggle without having to use discredited keywords. EZLN militancy won wide support because it brought together familiar peasant social justice demands and the language of indigenous rights.

Mexican struggles for indigenous autonomy are distinctive; and yet they also partake in a wider Latin American conversation about the possibility of democratic reform through indigenous autonomy. Indigenous organizing for pluralist inclusion is extremely varied, even in neighboring countries. Political scientist Donna Lee Van Cott (2001) contrasts "ethnic autonomy regimes" in nine Latin American countries: Some were put into place in negotiating peace agreements, after armed struggle, whereas others accompanied constitutional reform; some had the support of powerful foreign or domestic allies, whereas others did not; and some were more successful than others in instituting indigenous rights. What they have in common, however, is the struggle to expand the possibilities of the nation, not withdraw from it.

Environmental stewardship: From the Amazon basin to the Malay archipelago

What of forest dwellers who have neither the purchase of national inclusion nor the precedence of treaty rights? Another indigenous axis has brought an alternative set of alliances: the environmental movement. This axis is perhaps the most difficult to present because non-native activists play a central role in it. Northern activists' stereotypes of natives as "close to nature" open the movement to charges of romanticism and colonial discourse. The dramatization of alliance makes the power imbalance between white environmentalists and native spokesmen particularly apparent. In many cases, despite international attention, few benefits have accrued to indigenous communities.[26] And such mobilizations have only occasionally called forth solidarity with other vulnerable people, such as the nonindigenous rural poor.

Yet these occasional moments of solidarity are important: They allow the indigenous–environmental alliance to come to life. This is because such solidarity is produced by the mediation of national Left and opposition movements, which allow indigenous causes—for just a moment—to speak within national political cultures (Tsing n.d.). For marginal peoples who have been excluded entirely from national participation, this is a significant moment of political articulation. The environmental–indigenous axis thus offers an opportunity for "indigenous voice" for those communities with neither treaties nor legacies of national inclusion. Furthermore, although critics have imagined this alliance emerging fully armed from imaginative European foreheads, in fact, it required a history of making links, as in any other collaboration.[27]

One place to begin is Brazil, where international environmental activism honed in on the destruction of the Amazon forest in the 1970s. Margaret Keck tells the story: Brazil was proud of forest destruction (and Indian assimilation) in the 1970s: Brazil was booming—and a leader of the developing world; it was the height of the "economic miracle." At the UN conference on the Human Environment in Stockholm, Brazilian representatives dismissed concern for the rainforest: "Smoke is a sign of progress" (Keck 1995a). In this context, the combination of environmental and indigenous activism seemed downright subversive. Brazilian environmental groups were wary; the generals were alarmed (Hochstetler 1997). The Brazilian Left used Indians to criticize the military government, further excluding them from national influence by identifying them as unpatriotic (Ramos 1998). Both indigenous and environmental organization became known as essentially *foreign*. This only encouraged northerners in their determination to "think globally." The resultant impasse limited action to charges and countercharges.

The impasse broke for just a moment when the environmental–indigenous alliance had an opportunity to become "Brazilian." Perhaps the most important product was not benefits for indigenous communities but, rather, a brief glimpse of solidarity between Indians and the rural poor. The political mobilization of rubber tappers was crucial; tied to Brazil's Workers Party and the tradition of class-based rural organizing, they brought a recognizably Brazilian theme to struggles for rainforest protection (Almeida 2002; Keck 1995b). When the military regime ended in 1985, new kinds of political participation seemed possible; the emergent alliance between indigenous leaders, rural workers, and environmentalists suddenly seemed a *Brazilian* mobilization.[28] The 1988 murder of Chico Mendes moved both progressive Brazilians and foreigners; for a short moment, the national–global alliance seemed potent—and ready to travel. Keck argues that the symbolic potency of environmental–indigenous alliances drew in part from the failure of the developmentalist narrative. By the late 1980s, the Brazilian economy was a mess; the Trans-Amazon highway was impassable. Brazil's rhetoric of development no longer forged cross-national alliances. Instead, global environmental–indigenous alliances could look to Brazil (Keck 1995a, 1995b).[29]

It is undeniable that something "traveled" out from the Brazilian experience, inspiring related mobilizations in other parts of the world. Perhaps the most important thing to travel was the northern environmentalists themselves, who were encouraged by international excitement to form alliances with "forest dwellers" across the globe. Such travels may have used and abused Chico Mendes's commitments.[30] Still, the movement stimulated political eruptions in which spokespeople for marginalized indigenous people became worthy interlocutors.

The political composite melding advocacy for forest dwellers and endangered rainforest ecologies was cemented by the transfer of the transnational rainforest campaign from Brazil to Sarawak, Malaysia (Keck 1995b; Keck and Sikkink 1998). A number of activists worked on both campaigns. Furthermore, new transnational organizations linking environmental protection and indigenous rights sprouted like mushrooms after a rain, and the applicability of their understandings to both Brazil and Sarawak was at the heart of their global appeal.[31] In Sarawak, difficulty in casting the environmental–indigenous struggle as a *Malaysian* struggle caused trouble once again (Brosius 1999).[32] Only when national environmentalists across Southeast Asia took up the struggle as their own did the environmental–indigenous movement come into its strength. In Thailand, Malaysia, the Philippines, and Indonesia, national environmentalists brought social justice struggles into the rainforest in their demands for the land and resource rights of indigenous peoples. Through national mobilizations, indigenous representatives came to speak to both national and international audiences. As in Brazil, the ability of national advocates to make indigenous struggles speak to national political culture gave transnational activism traction.[33] Latin American forest dwellers beyond Brazil have also engaged in related struggles for land and resources, which draw from this same apparatus of transnational support within the context of national mobilization (e.g., Sawyer 2004).

Overlap and convergence

Every group has its own story. But politically effective tales must be crafted to enter emergent channels of public attention, such as those formed in the cross-national axes I have introduced. There is no reason, of course, for speakers to limit themselves to one established axis, and there is plenty of room for maneuver within and across these axes. The story of the Sami of Norway illustrates the simultaneous use of all three axes in creating one indigenous position.

Norwegian Sami have had a formative role in creating international indigenous politics because of their Scandinavian access to international political fora. Henry Minde (2003) notes how Sami—working with other Norwegian representatives—were key players in the 1980s push to revise ILO Convention 107 that led to the drafting of ILO Convention 169.

Sami have had to work against both local and global assessments that they are not indigenous. Not only did Norwegians originally reject Sami claims to indigeneity, citing a long history of assimilation, but New World Indians also questioned their status, for example, at the World Council of Indigenous People's 1974 preparatory meeting in Guyana. Yet Sami claims to membership in the World Council of Indigenous Peoples (WCIP) drew from an earlier, mutually formative history of contact between Canadian Indians and Sami. George Manuel visited Norwegian Sami leaders in 1972 on a trip that helped Manuel imagine the scope and promise of international indigeneity. Calling themselves "White Indians," Sami joined the international indigenism of Canada, New Zealand, and Australia.

Sami were primed for this involvement by a growing sense of Sami cultural pride developed from another axis of connection: The U.S. Red Power movement. In the late 1960s, comparisons between Sami and U.S. Native Americans flourished. A flow of books helped establish the frame: a Swedish edition of Vine Deloria's *Custer Died for your Sins* (1988 [1969]) in 1971; a Norwegian edition of Dee Brown's *Bury My Heart at Wounded Knee* (1971) by 1974. The Red Power movement inspired a radical Sami group, ČSV; a Sami youth culture demanded the revitalization of Sami culture and politics. As in Mexico, Sami pride mixed Marxist militancy and folkloric retrenchment for the wellbeing of the nation. Yet none of this might have made much of a difference except for a dramatic environmental conflict. In 1978, the Norwegian parliament approved plans for the Alta–Kautokeino dam and hydroelectric project in the region of Finnmark. Sami allied with environmental activists in opposition to the dam. In 1979, Sami staged a hunger strike in front of parliament, prompting a rush of media coverage. One particularly effective cartoon depicted Norway as a crocodile with one eye crying for the world's indigenous people ("Poor Indians," the caption says), while its tail sweeps away its own indigenous Sami (Minde 2003: 94–95). Sami involvement in international indigenous politics brought them international support; in turn, Sami used the environmental confrontation to raise their indigenous status. (The Sami representative at a 1981 WCIP meeting explained his stance in an appeal to Brazil: "when you look at everything as a whole, Alta seems like a little branch in the Brazilian jungle" [Minde 2003: 86].) At home, environmentalists brought the conflict inside national debate. When the state mustered police force against Sami protesters in 1981, "Norwegian self-perception as foremost defender of human rights was hanging in the balance" (Minde 2003: 95).

The "Alta affair" changed the climate for Sami politics, opening roads for Sami political claims and enhancing Sami involvement in the international indigenous arena. Sami became spokespeople for indigenous rights at home and abroad. Each of the channels of intelligibility and action I have outlined augmented their ability to imagine themselves within indigenous politics. Indeed, the importance of Scandanavian leadership, funding, and publication in the international indigenous scene has maintained an important presence for Sami there. Not every indigenous leadership, however, has managed to adapt so easily into international conventions.

Nodes of Dissension

Powerful frames for indigeneity are also spaces for disagreement. Not everyone can fit into these frames. Because the frames offer different enmities and alliances, contradictions surface. Considering these irritations and tensions pulls us from past feats toward emergent alliances and divisions.

Too little, and too much, recognition

The rhetoric of sovereignty has many advantages, not least among them its appeal to UN frameworks of self-determination. This appeal is also its main international drawback. Because they need this language for their own sovereignty claims, most nation-state representatives refuse to start a discussion on these terms. The UN draft declaration thus remains a draft.

Within a few countries, the rhetoric of sovereignty has been effective, but this in itself can be cause for alarm. U.S. government-to-government relations with Native tribes offers a ceremonial cover to disempowerment. It also structures conflicts pitting recognized tribal governments against other Native Americans. With limited entitlements available, recognized tribes become allies of the federal government in blocking the aspirations of the nonrecognized.[34] Urban Indians and Indians of mixed tribal origin are similarly disenfranchised.

Sovereignty itself is not uniformly empowering. Often the sovereign nation is defined through male control over women; even oppositional nationalism appeals through patriarchy. (Consider the origin of Gandhi's famous satyagraha: Indian men in South Africa demanded the right to defend their marriages from British colonial law [Mongia 2004].) Courts structure male control into Native sovereignty. Native scholar Renya Ramirez (in press) has analyzed *Santa Clara Pueblo v.*

Martinez, a keystone of Native American sovereignty claims. The 1978 Supreme Court decision established the right of tribes to determine their membership—and, in particular, to ignore federal sex discrimination legislation by excluding women who marry men from another tribe, as well as their children. The irony of the case is that Santa Clara Pueblo was once matrilineal, determining office by connections through women; only federal manipulation established the male line. This is the case to which tribes appeal for authority as nations.

Native American claims are rarely matters of national security in the United States. But where security discourse targets indigenous people, the rhetoric of sovereignty gets very dangerous. Itty Abraham notes that the Brazilian military came to imagine national security through "an east-west axis, penetrating into the depths of the unknown, untamed interior" (Abraham n.d.: 21). Developing the Amazon became a military priority, and the "internationalization of the Amazon" came to seem the nation's worst threat. Wherever indigeneity becomes entangled with national security, the rhetoric of sovereignty does little good.[35] And if fantasy production can be so dangerous, imagine too where U.S. military adventures—as in Nicaragua and Indochina—have armed indigenous people to undermine uncompliant states. Indigenous nationalism rarely stands apart from geopolitics.

In most of Asia and Africa, the rhetoric of indigenous sovereignty is useful at best as performance art. From the perspective of the nation-state, national sovereignty is too recent and precious to be handing it around to small groups—and at the command of northern imperialists. Groups that imagine a real chance at independence—for example, Tibetans—do not need indigenous rhetoric to advance their cause. For most others who claim indigeneity, the rhetoric of sovereignty is only useful at particularly open moments, and then mainly for dramatic effect. Thus, the Indonesian indigenous alliance AMAN took advantage of post–New Order regime freedom to coin the slogan "If the state does not recognize us, we will not recognize the state" (AMAN 1999: 9). The slogan appealed to international indigenous organizations, but it was not clear what forms of nonrecognition indigenous groups could offer. The rhetoric of sovereignty does not travel far here. At the same time, however, asking for inclusion in the nation-state is not so easy either.

Who's in and who's out?

Groups who have organized under the indigenous banner have done so in part because they have been left out of the benefits of national development. Being left out itself might be cause for solidarity—yet there are different ways of being left out, and these divide indigenous perspectives. For groups without treaty rights with which to protest, much comes down to the play of political categories, as these beckon and repulse potential allies. Chiapas militants may bring the power of peasant politics to indigenous struggles, but Peruvian peasants feel disempowered if they imagine themselves as indigenous. Marisol de la Cadena (2000) explains that in highland Peru an elite tradition of indigenous identity and a shame-driven de-Indianization of the poor have gone hand in hand. The only kind of indigeneity that seems empowering to most nonelites is that of the "indigenous mestizo," an oxymoronic paring that denies narratives of popular assimilation and elite purity alike. In the uphill battle for national inclusion, such differences matter.

Such contrasts also assert themselves within nation-states—and, indeed, within communities. Indonesian advocacy for masyarakat adat reaches for groups neglected by national development's largesse. Yet development discourse draws in many rural people, however cheated and disadvantaged; many rural leaders are happier with dreams of progress than with cultural struggle (Li 2000). The distinctions activists make between cultural minorities and ordinary farmers fall apart on the ground. My friends in the Meratus Mountains of Kalimantan are divided about whether to cast their lot with the environmental–indigenous campaign on their behalf or with the apparatus of national development and corporate publicity (Tsing 2005). If they chose the first they are indigenous peoples; if they chose the second they are just another Indonesian rural community. Put this way, it is clear that the choice is one of alliance rather than intrinsic identity. Yet this returns us to the nation-state: The conditions for collaboration have everything to do with the national contours of the discourse on "indigeneity." This is particularly evident where national elites claim indigeneity.

In Indonesia, as in Malaysia and India, the indigenous can look back to the anticolonial project and the alliance between elites and peasants that created the nation-state.[36] The governments of these countries refuse global indigenous politics in part because they hold to this other use of the term. Arguments for indigenous rights are confused in such contexts by the fact that indigenous can mean very different things.[37]

In Indonesia, the term *pribumi*, "indigenous," refers to the native majority. Its major political use has been to legitimate discrimination against Chinese Indonesians, who cannot be pribumi however many generations their ancestors may have been there. Pribumi evokes an urban

discourse of quotas for businessmen and university students; it reaches
to the countryside only in those areas where peasants were historically
active in forming the nation-state. Outside of Java, rural communities
are rarely drawn into pribumi claims. Because this translation of
indigenous is taken for nationalist uses, the environmental–indigenous
movement looked elsewhere, settling on masyarakat adat because it
offered a separate but still recognizable genealogy.

In India, indigeneity in its several meanings has even greater reach.
Indigeneity is just as available for Hindu nationalism as environmental–
indigenous alliances. Furthermore, the long institutionalization of the
term *adivasi* ("tribe") in India creates another legacy of both exclusion
and potential revitalization. Those considered adivasi negotiate between
the pleasures of tenuous acceptance into Hindu politics and culture, with
its nationalist strengths and dangers, and the possibilities of alliance
with well-meaning but stereotyping environmentalists (Baviskar 2003;
this volume).

Natural resource tug-of-war

Meanwhile, not all indigenous peoples support environmental causes;
some are in active conflict with conservation. Two kinds of conflicts
are prominent. The first pits different kinds of environmentalists
against each other: National development conservationists propose
reserves that displace indigenous people, whereas environmental–
indigenous alliances advocate comanagement.[38] The second pits just
those indigenous people who have been most successful in achieving
self-government against environmental causes that might interfere
with economic enrichment. In both cases, the inability of either the
indigenous rights movement or the environmental movement to
displace the hegemony of private property and capitalist development
is evident. Both environmentalists and indigenous rights activists
make demands for land in the incompletely privatized zones where
governments still give things away. In this increasingly narrow space,
turf wars are easy to instigate. "Success" in both movements involves
forming bureaucracies and corporations, which, in search of wealth and
power, convert nature into "resources" to be coveted and destroyed.

Greenland Home Rule illustrates the perils and possibilities of indigenous battles against environmental activism (Caufield 1997).
Greenland is part of Denmark, but since 1979 local government has been
in the hands of a Home Rule administration imagined as empowering
Greenland natives. One of the first actions of the new government was

to take over management of hunting and fishing. Greenlanders had been set off against environmentalists before Home Rule: A 1970s animal rights campaign culminated in the European Economic Community's 1983 ban on sealskin imports, which devastated Greenland's seal industry. The coming of Home Rule allowed Greenlanders to act on their antagonism. To protest European interest in protecting whales, Greenlanders voted to leave the European Community in 1982. In 1991, Greenland Home Rule precipitated a crisis in the International Whaling Commission (IWC) by joining Norway, Iceland, and Japan to demand the reopening of commercial whaling. When this initiative failed, Home Rule helped form the North Atlantic Marine Mammal Commission, an antienvironmentalist alternative to the IWC. Home Rule has also supported the Inuit Circumpolar Conference, an indigenous initiative that presses for whaling rights. Through its connection to Denmark, Home Rule has continued an involvement with the IWC, where it lobbies for bigger quotas. Richard Caufield (1997: 162) calls this organizational assertiveness a form of "weapons of the weak," but it looks to me more like "weapons of the strong." The similarity between Greenland Home Rule and natural resource bureaucracies in the international nation-state system has allowed Greenland natives much the same strategic room for maneuver as other whaling states.

The history of whaling in Greenland is closely tied to state formation. Between 1928 and 1958, Danish authorities caught whales on a British-built vessel and distributed the meat to Greenland's rural communities. (The commercially valued blubber was, of course, shipped to Denmark.) This colonial relation established the centrality of whale meat to state notions of aboriginal subsistence. Now Greenland receives quotas for whaling from the IWC as a part of its aboriginal subsistence hunting calculations. As a member of the IWC, Greenland Home Rule must accept the organization's quotas, but as a self-governing entity it can decide how to allocate them. Like other governments, Home Rule has been impressed into privatization, transforming government-owned trade services into for-profit companies by the early 1990s. Meanwhile, Home Rule divides the whale quota between fishing vessel–based whaling and collective hunt whaling. Fishing vessels require capital and are exclusive to the wealthiest families; skiff-based collective hunting benefits many more people. In the mid-1990s, collective hunters were offered only 34–36 percent of the whaling quota in West Greenland. Everyone else who wanted whale meat had to purchase it from vessel owners. Although it is clear that whaling is important to Greenlanders, the resource management bureaucracy skews it for capitalist development. It is hard not to lend an ear to the critic who wrote: "We are spectators to the development of our own land. Twenty people here in Greenland plan and decide what will happen to 50,000 people" (Caufield 1997: 47).[39]

Other environmental–indigenous conflicts are even more confusing. Perhaps the most disturbing are conflicts between and within indigenous groups: Should Native American tribes, in defense of sovereignty and wealth, put radioactive wastes on their reservations (Harriman 1996)? Should Kayapo leaders be applauded or deposed for making contracts with loggers and miners (Turner 1999)? When resource corporations set up their own "indigenous rights" organizations—as oil companies have in Ecuador, the dizzying conflation between empowerment and destruction is complete (Sawyer 2004). Meanwhile, in the environmental advocacy world, as in the arena of indigenous rights, "success" continues to be measured by the development of capitalism and state forms. As long as capitalist resource use structures even the most oppositional designs for people and nature in indigenous zones, the environmental–indigenous alliance will play a limited role as the utopian dream of losers.

Speaking Globally

Indigenous peoples gain voice through cross-national connections that empower their approach to national dilemmas. Scholars often look to indigenous politics for an example of the growing irrelevance of nation-states, but my investigation suggests their constitutive role. Indigenous leaders convey community perspectives; yet, if they want extralocal clout, their representations must resonate both nationally and internationally. Differences across cross-national framing axes expand the terrain of representational possibilities; nor are these frames stable. Arguments within, across, and beyond these frames enliven indigenous politics, shaping future trajectories. Recognizing the diversity of indigenous challenges is a collective task; this chapter offers one beginning.

In contrast to Enlightenment universals, international indigenous politics opens a global politics in which inconsistency and contradiction become our greatest assets. Not that any old thing will do: Indigenous politics requires us to judge between the real and the fake, empowerment and co-optation, good and bad allies. The call to immerse ourselves in indigenous experience is one starting point for such judgments. Still, indigenous victories depend on mismatching universal rights and local cultural legacies, expert science and place-based knowledge, social justice, and communal precedence.

This is, of course, a challenge so huge it is hard to begin listing what it is up against. To add insult to injury, scholarly conventions continue to plague even the most sympathetic chroniclers. It is hard to describe the inconsistent globality called for here within ordinary scholarly conventions, which either privilege nations, ethnic groups, or communities as units or, alternatively, jump to a transcendent and homogeneous global space. Instead, I have tried to show the potential of tracing links without subsuming them to universals. Such links offer both the *grip* that makes indigenous politics travel and the *irritations* that limit that travel. Elsewhere, I have used the image of "friction" to bring grip and irritation into the same metaphor and to suggest a method for bringing inconsistent global histories to public attention (Tsing 2005). Here, my historical fragments and global tales use this method to bring out both the carrying power and the limiting specificity of indigenous voice.

Notes

This chapter emerged from discussions with my indigeneity reading group: Mark Anderson, Jeremy Campbell, James Clifford, and S. Eben Kirksey. I am indebted to them for introducing me to the literature and ideas here. Marisol de la Cadena kindly continued my tutoring in Latin American studies, yet my preparation is still far from adequate. Charles Hale and Hugh Raffles each pushed me a little further; I know that I have not succeeded in answering their criticisms. Participants in the conference "Indigenous Experience Today" made useful suggestions. James Clifford's "Indigenous Articulations" (2001) guided my search. The attempt to write about disparate regions of the world is humbling. All gaps and gaffs are of course my own.

1. Ronald Niezen (2005: 534) describes "paradoxes" of the indigenous movement: its newness versus its ancient heritage; dependence on the oral and face-to-face as well as international law and governance; subsistence versus high-tech orientations. Clifford (this volume) discusses the interplay of territoriality and diaspora in constituting indigenous identities.

2. Adam Kuper's "The Return of the Native" (2003) and the discussion it raised introduce debates about the indigenous movement. For more of the issues under discussion, see Hale (2002), Li (2003), and Ramos (2002).

3. This chapter concludes a trilogy of works on the development of indigenous politics in and beyond Indonesia. In the first (2002), I chart the history of the Indonesian term for "custom," *adat*, which has been key to the making of Indonesian indigenous claims. In the second (n.d.), I follow the words *indigeneity* and *adat* in and out of Indonesian and transnational conversations. Here, I use Indonesian developments to inspire a transnational analysis of divergent indigenous claims.

4. The Indonesian is "Bhinneka tunggal ika."

5. For a history of the concept of adat in Indonesia, see Tsing 2002.

6. I discuss the wider context of Indonesian indigenous organizing in Tsing 2005; see also Li 2003.

7. I owe my understanding of this point to S. Eben Kirksey. In West Papua indigenous politics is associated with state cooptation.

8. See Perry 1996: 149–151, Cairns 2000, Fleras and Elliot 1992, and Weaver 1985.

9. Maori activist Linda Tuhiwai Smith (conference communication) points out that individual Maori and Canadian Indians worked with each other's campaigns—including her sister, who joined the National Indian Brotherhood.

10. See Sanders 1977 and Johnston (2003 [1986]: 107).

11. See Howard (2003: 186–194) and Fleras and Spoonley (1999: 5–25).

12. Clinebell and Thompson (2003) explain U.S. treaties. The 1975 Indian Self-Determination and Education Assistance Act repealed termination policy, strengthened self-government, and opened a new era of tribal sovereignty claims (Howard 2003: 63).

13. The IWGIA is based at the University of Copenhagen. I discuss the Sami situation in more depth at the end of this section.

14. Brysk (2000: 85) quotes the slogan. Diaz Polanco (1997) is a key source on Latin American dialogues.

15. This quote can be found in Stephen (2003: 203).

16. Elsewhere, the term describes relationships between states and indigenous groups. (See, e.g., Arthur 2001; Jull 1998.) In Latin American, it stretches to mobilize popular support that combines cultural pride and political self-determination. Mexican activist–anthropologist Gilberto López y Rivas (2005) argues that the concept of autonomy reaches out equally to Marxist legacies of struggle and to international legal regimes of recognition. "Furthermore, contrary to the opinions of the supporters of the Unitarian State, autonomy does not fragment national unity. It is discrimination and racism ... that lead to the State fragmentation and to the rupture of the national unity. ... Through its resistance against neoliberalism, indigenous autonomy is broadening its boundaries and widening them, to even include the building of a new kind of

nation ... taking democracy away from the official rhetoric, and converting it into the practice that reaches and fills each space in society, in the economy, in the government, even in the social movements and opposition parties themselves" (2005).

17. Marisol de la Cadena (2005a) points out that "mestizaje" throughout Latin America involved standards of education, propriety, and culture as well as race.

18. Hector Díaz Polanco describes the Mexican delegation: "Among the members of the Mexican delegation to this congress were the most outstanding scholars on indigenous issues, several of whom were also political figures. ... With them there was also a group of younger people, many of whom would become distinguished indigenist intellectuals" (1997: 78).

19. On the funds, see de la Cadena 2005b; on the bureaus, see Brysk (2000: 125).

20. Douglas Sanders (2003 [1983]: 64) explains: "As John Collier later argued in the United States version of indigenism, a healthy Indian community could adapt better than an unhealthy one. Mexican indigenism and the United States 'Indian new deal' came together in 1940 at the First Inter-American Conference on Indian Life."

21. The quotation is from ILO Convention 107, Article 2.1, and can be seen in Thornberry (2002: 433).

22. The rise and fall of applied anthropology in addressing the indigenous question in Mexico is contextualized in Wright 1988.

23. The Red Power movement also inspired urban indigenous people in Canada and New Zealand. I do not include those stories here because their international leadership became known for advancing a different model.

24. These reformers were also influenced by the 1971 Barbados conference on indigenous rights (Jung in press: ch. 4), which was organized by the World Council of Churches and the Ethnology Department of the University of Bern, Switzerland. Latin Americanists tend to see this conference as the origin point of the contemporary international indigenous movement (e.g., Brysk 2000: 86); in contrast, the Anglophone cluster is more likely to point to the World Council of Indigenous Peoples, mentioned above.

25. Jung (in press: ch. 4) writes that President Luis Echeverria was trying to recapture legitimacy after the 1968 student massacre.

26. The critical literature on these topics comes into focus around particular movement "hot spots." For example, when The Body Shop began to deploy the Amazonian Kayapo in their advertising campaigns, criticism exploded. See, for example, Turner (1995), who summarizes criticisms but tempers them with the Kayapo opinion that the alliance represents an opportunity, if not a perfect one.

27. A minor academic industry has grown up to criticize ideas of indigenous harmony with nature. Such criticisms are right in pointing to a history of Western stereotypes; they fail, however, in tracing the collaborative histories in which indigenous spokespeople and their interlocutors engage and enlarge these stereotypes. For a useful attempt to address this problem, see Ramos 2003.

28. Hugh Raffles (personal communication, September 2006) notes the formation of Brazilian NGOs from this moment of coalition.

29. Many caveats are on order, including these: (1) Indigenous organizing against the military regime was an important precedent for environmental mobilization; (2) the alliance between rubber tappers and Indians lasted only a short time; and (3) the current prominence of NGOs has privatized Indian dilemmas, producing "a numbing of the Indian movement as a political force" (Ramos 2002: 269). Chernela (2005) argues that international organizations have damaged community-based conservation in the Amazon by requiring compliance to internationally imposed standards.

30. The death of Chico Mendes unleashed a storm of controversy about how best to interpret Mendes's politics. Was it appropriate to use his charisma to build environmentalism, or, instead, to focus on social justice for the poor? See, for example, Hecht and Cockburn (1989).

31. The term *forest dweller* was introduced in South American indigenous politics and transferred from there to Southeast Asia—and international indigenous rights discourse.

32. The Mahathir regime called environmental–indigenous activism "eco-imperialism" and invoked the indigenous "right to development" as a reason to destroy the rainforest.

33. I review the Indonesian history in Tsing (2005: ch. 6). See also Keck and Sikkink (1998); Brosius (2003).

34. Miller (2003) writes about this process from the perspective of U.S. "invisible indigenes." The structure of recognition, he argues, keeps recognized tribal leaders on the side of the federal government. On page 16, for example, he describes Tulalip leaders of Washington state who argue against extending fishing rights to unrecognized Indians.

35. Hugh Raffles (personal communication, September 2006) points to a recent resurgence of fears of the internationalization of the Amazon. This time, anxieties about this threat to Brazilian sovereignty come from both the Right and the Left. Conspiracy theories of U.S. invasion and annexation, or UN administrative control, have emerged in this climate.

36. The literature and policy nexus regarding "indigenous knowledge" is the chief *cross-national* product of this otherwise mainly *national* set of discourses. In speaking of indigenous knowledge, South Asian postcolonial theorists join

hands briefly with Latin American critics of development (e.g., Agrawal 1995). Yet this nexus stands in an awkward relationship to the indigenous rights movement more generally.

37. Benedict Kingsbury (2003 [1998]) offers a useful review of definitional dilemmas for indigenous groups in Asia, where most governments deny the relevance of the term.

38. Janice Alcorn's (2005) review of political differences in the World Wildlife Foundation offers a useful introduction to such conflicts.

39. Caufield identifies the critic as the writer of a 1990 letter to the editor of *Sermitsiak'*. All the information in this paragraph is from Caufield (1997).

References

Abraham, Itty. n.d. "Security," In *Words in motion*, edited by Carol Gluck and Anna Tsing.

Agrawal, Arun. 1995. Dismantling the divide between Indigenous and scientific knowledge. *Development and Change* 26: 413–439.

Alcorn, Janice. 2005. Dances around the fire: conservation organizations and community-based resource management. In *Communities and conservation: Politics and histories of community-based natural resource management*, edited by J. Peter Brosius, Anna Tsing, and Charles Zerner, 37–68. Oakland, CA: AltaMira Press.

Aliansi Masyarakat Adat Nusantara (AMAN). 1999. *Catatan Hasil Kongres Masyarakat Adat Nusantara, Jakarta 15–22 Maret 1999*. Jakarta: AMAN.

Almeida, Mauro Balbosa. 2002. The politics of Amazonian conservation: The struggles of rubber tappers. *Journal of Latin American Studies* 7 (1): 170–219.

Arthur, William S. 2001. *Indigenous autonomy in Australia: Some concepts, issues and examples*. Technical report discussion paper 220. Canberra: Centre for Aboriginal Economic Policy Research, The Australian National University.

Baviskar, Amita. 2003. Tribal politics and sustainable development. In *Nature in the global South*, edited by Paul Greenough and Anna Tsing, 289–318. Durham, NC: Duke University Press.

Brosius, J. Peter 1999. Green dots, pink hearts: Displacing politics from the Malaysian rainforest. *American Anthropologist* 101 (1): 36–57.

——. 2003. Voices for the Borneo rainforest: Writing the history of an environmental campaign. In *Nature in the global South*, edited by Paul Greenough and Anna Tsing, 319–346. Durham, NC: Duke University Press.

Brown, Dee Alexander. 1971. *Bury my heart at Wounded Knee: An Indian history of the American West*. New York: Holt, Rinehart, and Winston.

Brysk, Alison. 2000. *From tribal village to global village: Indian rights and international relations in Latin America*. Stanford: Stanford University Press.

Cairns, Alan. 2000. *Citizens plus: Aboriginal peoples and the Canadian state*. Vancouver: UBC Press.

Castaneda, Quetzil. 2004. "We are *not* Indigenous!": An introduction to the Maya identity of Yucatan. *Journal of Latin American Anthropology* 9 (1): 36–61.

Caufield, Richard. 1997. *Greenlanders, whales, and whaling: Sustainability and self-determination in the Artic*. Hanover, NH: University Press of New England.

Chernela, Janet. 2005. The politics of mediation: Local-global interactions in the Central Amazon of Brazil. *American Anthropologist* 107 (4): 620–631.

Clifford, James. 2001. Indigenous articulations. *The Contemporary Pacific* 13 (2): 468–490.

Clinebell, John Howard, and Jim Thompson. 2003 [1987]. Sovereignty and self-determination: The rights of Native Americans under international law. In *International law and Indigenous peoples*, edited by S. James Anaya, 117–162. Burlington, VT: Ashgate.

de la Cadena, Marisol. 2000. *Indigenous mestizos*. Durham, NC: Duke University Press.

——. 2005a. Are *mestizos* hybrids? The conceptual politics of Andean identities. *Journal of Latin American Studies* 37: 259–284.

——. 2005b. The production of other knowledges and its tensions: From Andeanist anthropology to interculturalidad? *Journal of the World Anthropology Network* 1 (1): 201–224.

Deloria, Vine, Jr. 1988 [1969]. *Custer died for your sins: An Indian manifesto*. Norman: University of Oklahoma Press.

Díaz Polanco, Hector. 1997. *Indigenous peoples in Latin America: The quest for self-determination*. Translated by Lucia Rayas. Boulder, CO: Westview Press.

Fleras, Augie, and Jean Leonard Elliot. 1992. *The "nations within": Aboriginal-state relations in Canada, the United States, and New Zealand*. Toronto: Oxford University Press.

Fleras, Augie, and Paul Spoonley. 1999. *Recalling Aotearoa: Indigenous politics and ethnic relations in New Zealand*. Auckland: Oxford University Press.

Hale, Charles. 2002. Does multiculturalism menace? Governance, cultural rights and the politics of identity in Guatemala. *Journal of Latin American Studies* 34: 485–524.

Harriman, Ed, director. 1996. *Radioactive reservations* [video recording]. Goldhawk Productions, distributed by Filmmakers Library.

Hecht, Susanna, and Alexander Cockburn. 1989. Lands, trees, and justice: Defenders of the Amazon. *The Nation* 248 (20): 695–697.

Hochstetler, Kathryn. 1997. The evolution of the Brazilian environmental movement and its political roles. In *The new politics of inequality in Latin America,* edited by Douglas Chalmers, Carlos M. Vilas, Katherine Hite, Scott B. Martin, Kerianne Piester, and Monique Segarra, 192–216. Oxford: Oxford University Press.

Howard, Bradley Reed. 2003. *Indigenous peoples and the state: The struggle for Native rights.* DeKalb: Northern Illinois University Press.

Johnston, Darlene M. 2003 [1986]. The quest of the Six Nations Confederacy for self-determination. In *International law and Indigenous peoples,* edited by S. James Anaya, 85–116. Burlington, VT: Ashgate.

Jull, Peter. 1998. *Indigenous autonomy in Nunavut: Canada's present and Australia's possibilities.* Discussion paper, Centre for Democracy, Department of Government, University of Queensland. Electronic document, http://eprint.uq.edu.au/archive/00001190, accessed January 4, 2007.

Jung, Courtney. in press. *Critical liberalism: What normative political theory has to learn from the Mexican Indigenous rights movement.*

Keck, Margaret. 1995a. *International politics in the Amazon.* Paper presented at Environmental Conflicts and Movements conference, Five College Program on Peace and Security, Amherst, MA.

——. 1995b. Social equity and environmental politics in Brazil: Lessons from the rubber tappers of Acre. *Comparative Politics* 27 (July): 409–424.

Keck, Margaret, and Kathryn Sikkink. 1998. *Activists beyond borders: Advocacy networks in international politics.* Ithaca, NY: Cornell University Press.

Kingsbury, Benedict. 2003 [1998]. "Indigenous peoples" in international law: A constructivist approach to the Asian controversy. In *International law and Indigenous peoples,* edited by S. James Anaya, 211–254. Burlington, VT: Ashgate.

Kuper, Adam. 2003. The Return of the Native. *Current Anthropology* 44 (3): 389–395.

Li, Tania. 2000. Constituting tribal space: Indigenous identity and resource politics in Indonesia. *Comparative Studies in Society and History* 42 (1): 149–179.

——. 2003. Masyarakat Adat, Difference, and the Limits of Recognition in Indonesia's Forest Zone. In *Race, nature, and the politics of difference,* edited by Donald Moore, Jake Kosek, and Anand Pandian, 380–406. Durham, NC: Duke University Press.

López y Rivas, Gilberto. 2005. *Neo-liberal etnocide, democracy and indigenous autonomy in Latin America.* Paper presented at Democracy and Domestic Politics: Perspectives from Africa, Asia and Latin America, Kuala Lumpur-South-South Program. Electronic document, http://www.terrorfileonline.org/en/index.php/Neo-liberal_etnocide,_democracy_and_indigenous_autonomy_in_Latin_America, accessed on January 4, 2007.

Maddock, Kenneth. 1991. Metamorphosing the sacred in Australia. *Australian Journal of Anthropology* 2 (2): 213–232.

Miller, Bruce Granville. 2003. *Invisible indigenes: The politics of nonrecognition.* Lincoln: University of Nebraska Press.

Minde, Henry. 2003. The challenge of Indigenism: The struggle for Sami land rights and self-government in Norway 1960–1990. In *Indigenous peoples: Resource management and global rights,* edited by Svein Jentoft, Henry Minde, and Ragnar Nilsen, 75–104. Delft, the Netherlands: Eburan Academic Publishers.

Mongia, Radhika. 2004. Migration, sex, and state sovereignty: Undoing the methodological tyranny of the national. Paper presented at the Simpson Center for the Humanities Conference on the Cultural Logic of Transnational Families, University of Washington, Seattle, June.

Niezen, Ronald. 2005. Digital identity: The construction of virtual selfhood in the indigenous peoples' movement. *Comparative Studies in Society and History* 47 (3): 532–551.

Perry, Richard J. 1996. *From time immemorial: Indigenous peoples and state systems.* Austin: University of Texas Press.

Peterson, Brandt. 2005. *Unsettled remains: Race, trauma, and the politics of identity in millennial El Salvador.* Ph.D. dissertation, Department of Anthropology, University of Texas, Austin.

Ramirez, Renya. in press. Race, gender, and tribal nation: A Native feminist approach to violence against women of color. *Meridian Journal: Feminism, Race, Transnationalism.*

Ramos, Alcida Rita. 1998. *Indigenism: Ethnic politics in Brazil.* Madison: University of Wisconsin Press.

——. 2002. Cutting through state and class: Sources and strategies of self-representation in Latin America. In *Indigenous movements, self-representation, and the state in Latin America,* edited by Kay B. Warren and Jean E. Jackson, 251–279. Austin: University of Texas Press.

———. 2003. Pulp fictions of indigenism. In *Race, nature and the politics of difference,* edited by Moore, Kosek, and Pandian, 356–379. Durham, NC: Duke University Press.

Sanders, Douglas E. 1977. *The formation of the World Council of Indigenous Peoples.* Copenhagen: IWGIA.

———. 1985. The Indian lobby and the Canadian Constitution, 1978–82. In *Indigenous peoples and the nation-state: "Fourth World" politics in Canada, Australia, and Norway,* edited by Noel Dyck, 151–189. Social and Economic Papers, 14. St. John's: Institute of Social and Economic Research, Memorial University of Newfoundland.

———. 2003 [1983]. The re-emergence of indigenous questions in international law. In *International law and Indigenous peoples,* edited by S. James Anaya, 55–82. Burlington, VT: Ashgate.

Sawyer, Suzana. 2004. *Crude chronicles: Indigenous politics, multinational oil, and neoliberalism in Ecuador.* Durham, NC: Duke University Press

Smith, Paul Chaat, and Robert Allen Warrior. 1996. *Like a hurricane: The Indian movement from Alcatraz to Wounded Knee.* New York: The New Press.

Stephen, Lynn. 2003. Indigenous autonomy in Mexico. In *At the risk of being heard. Identity, indigenous rights, and postcolonial states,* edited by Bartholomew Dean and Jerome Levi, 191–216. Ann Arbor: University of Michigan Press.

Thornberry, Patrick. 2002. *Indigenous people and human rights.* Manchester: Manchester University Press.

Tsing, Anna. 2002. Land as law: Negotiating the meaning of property in Indonesia. In *Land, property, and the environment,* edited by John Richards, 94–137. Oakland, CA: Institute for Contemporary Studies Press.

———. 2005. *Friction: An ethnography of global connection.* Princeton: Princeton University Press.

———. n.d. Indigeneity in motion. In *Words in motion,* edited by Carol Gluck and Anna Tsing.

Turner, Terence. 1995. Neoliberal ecopolitics and indigenous peoples: The Kayapo, the "Rainforest Harvest," and the Body Shop. *Yale Forestry and Environmental Science Bulletin* 98: 113–123.

———. 1999. Indigenous rights, environmental protection, and the struggle over forest resources in the Amazon: The case of the Brazilian Kayapo. In *Earth, air, fire, water,* edited by Jill Ker Conway, Kenneth Keniston, and Leo Marx, 145–169. Amherst: University of Massachusetts Press.

Van Cott, Donna Lee. 2001. Explaining ethnic autonomy regimes in Latin America. *Studies in comparative international development* 35 (4): 30–58.

Weaver, Sally. 1985. Political representivity and indigenous minorities in Canada and Australia. In *Indigenous peoples and the nation-state: "Fourth World" politics in Canada, Australia, and Norway,* edited by Noel Dyck, 113–150. Social and Economic Papers, 14. St. John's: Institute of Social and Economic Research, Memorial University of Newfoundland.

Wright, Robin. 1988. Anthropological presuppositions of indigenous advocacy. *Annual Review of Anthropology* 17: 365–390.

Tibetan Indigeneity: Translations, Resemblances, and Uptake

Emily T. Yeh

Why does it seem natural for Tibetans to be included in a volume about indigenous experience today? The term *indigenous*, after all, is not widely used by Tibetans either within Tibet or in exile. And why, considering the wide-ranging, perhaps even "viral" nature of the concept of indigeneity, has its "uptake" not happened to a significant degree among Tibetans? These questions would have made little sense before the 1980s, when the term *indigenous* was rarely used to describe people anywhere in the world. Today, a transnational social movement has made "indigenous peoples" both a legal term and an identity claimed by many peoples with diverse historical situations. It is widely understood to imply, among other things, firstness, nativeness or original or prior occupancy of a place; attachment to a particular territory or homeland; marginalization within a culturally or ethnically different wider society; and often, a history of colonization. As such, it has been used in international conventions, academic works, and activist organizing around issues of sovereignty, dispossession, human rights, and environmental stewardship. Basic demands of the indigenous rights movement include respect for collective rights to land, recognition of cultural difference, and the right to self-determination. Many indigenous struggles are centered around the reappropriation of land, artifacts, and knowledge, and are predicated on a mutual acknowledgement of a historical debt created by dispossession. At the same time, indigenous identity has also come to be associated with a set of ideals of environmental stewardship, connectedness to nature, spirituality, and egalitarianism—ideals that do not similarly adhere to groups more closely identified as "ethnic minorities" and that present both strategic opportunities and challenges.

Despite the transnational indigenous rights movement's success in creating a set of ideas about what constitutes indigenous status, attempts to provide a single, overarching definition have been controversial. A United Nations report by Special Rappateur Miguel Alfonso Martínez (1999) stated the "obvious fact" that in postcolonial Africa and Asia, "autochthonous groups/minorities/ethnic groups/peoples ... cannot ... claim for themselves, unilaterally and exclusively, the 'indigenous' status in the United Nations context." Not surprisingly, this generated considerable opposition from the many groups in postcolonial Asia and Africa who claim an indigenous identity. The UN Working Group on Indigenous Populations has thus avoided a strict definition, instead allowing groups to identify *themselves* as indigenous. There are limits, however, to the ways the term can be stretched. A claim of indigeneity in itself is not enough; that claim must be recognized and legitimated, if not by the corresponding state, then at least by some other audience to which activists wish to speak.

The term *indigenous* invites Tibetans, as it invites many other groups, to be interpellated by it (cf. Castree 2004: 153), and certainly something about the historical, political, and social situation of Tibetans invites others to call them "indigenous." Yet for the most part, neither ordinary Tibetans nor those who might be expected to speak in a public "indigenous voice"—that is, activists, public intellectuals, and community leaders (Tsing this volume)—have claimed the term or the commonality that it suggests with other indigenous peoples. The English word *indigenous* appears only rarely in the copious English-language material produced by the Tibetan government in exile. Tibetan terms describing nativeness, such as *sa skye rdo skyes* ("born of this soil and rock") or tribalness, such as *tsho wa* and *de wa,* are used in everyday speech in Tibet, but they are not deployed to mobilize claims about sovereignty, human rights, national inclusion, environmental stewardship, or to demand rights that accompany the recognition of cultural difference. *Sa skye rdo rkyes* is typically used to indicate one's belonging to a particular village, neighborhood, or town; for example, an elderly couple in Lhasa complained to me about having to rent a threadbare government apartment by stating: "those people one sees buying houses in Lhasa today [i.e., other Tibetans] aren't *sa skye rdo rkyes* Lhasa people. They're all outsiders." Nativeness, at least in current usage, references a scale that is smaller than collective claims-making about political or cultural rights. When Tibetans do make claims to political and cultural rights or ask for recognition of environmental stewardship, they do so based on their identity as "Tibetan," rather than as being *sa skye rdo skyes*.[1] In this sense, they do not currently participate in what Niezen (2003) calls indigenism—the social movement of those indigenous groups who deliberately built translocal and transnational alliances with other indigenous groups to achieve their own goals.

In this chapter, I explore the lack of uptake of an explicitly "indigenous" identity even in the presence of a set of characteristic self-representations that bear what I call a family resemblance to indigenous formations around the world. More specifically, Tibetan claims and representations about environmental stewardship and ecological wisdom resonate strongly with other indigenous formations. This has long been the case in exile, but these representations and associations have only recently emerged in China. At the same time, the political claims of sovereignty that characterize the transnational indigenous movement present a stumbling block for the articulation of an explicitly indigenous identity. For Tibetans in exile, indigeneity is too weak a political claim. Within Tibet, it is too strong under the current political situation; instead, identity claims in the People's Republic of China (PRC) are only considered legitimate if expressed through the category of *minzu* (nationality), which is framed within the larger discourse of *minzu tuanjie*, a phrase meaning both "amity between the nationalities" and "national unity." Bulag (2002) aptly describes minzu tuanjie as a "hegemonic management device to maneuver in the context of China's diversity." Tibetans in Tibet live with the ideology of multiculturalism *(duoyuan wenhua)* but also, simultaneously, repeated state denunciations of "national splittism" *(minzu fenlie)*. The only acceptable cultural difference is that which upholds national unity, and does not split the nation. In analyzing indigeneity, I suggest we need to pay attention to *both* the specific terminology used and the family resemblance of "indigenous" characteristics; under specific historical and political circumstances, the two may not always converge.

My understanding of indigeneity is based on a theory of articulation (Clifford 2001; Hall 1996; Li 2000), a term that Stuart Hall, following Antonio Gramsci, uses in its double sense of both speaking and of a connection or linkage that can be forged under some conditions, but is "not necessary, determined, absolute, and essential for all time" (Hall 1996: 141). A theory of articulation: "is both a way of understanding how ideological elements come, under certain conditions, to cohere together within a certain discourse, and a way of asking how they do or do not become articulated, at specific conjunctures, to certain political subjects" (Hall 1996: 141).

This shifts attention away from questions of "invention" or authenticity, and toward an understanding of indigeneity as a contingent, structured positioning. Tania Li (2000) uses a theory of articulation in a comparison of two groups of farmers in Central Sulawesi, Indonesia, to explore why one has persuasively articulated a collective tribal or indigenous identity, whereas the other has not. Li's notion of a "tribal slot," as a conceptual frame of indigenous recognition is similar to what Tsing (2003) calls the "tribal allegory." Tsing suggests that two distinct story lines—of tribes and peasants—have shaped administrative policies and academic programs concerned with rural peoples. Peasant allegories are associated with populist concerns of class and economic equity. Tribal allegories, by contrast, are concerned with cultural difference, ecological wisdom, and intimate connections with nature. The collective articulation of an indigenous identity requires a particular conjuncture, context, or encounter to make use of an available tribal slot or allegory.

The "tribal allegory" of Tibetan ecological wisdom and deep connection to nature has been an available narrative for Tibetans in exile since the 1980s, and has more recently emerged in China as well. Tibetans within Tibet are beginning to rearticulate their local environmental knowledge in the language of global environmentalism, and in the past few years, Chinese environmental activists and scholars have begun to actively search for the opportunity to support ecologically friendly Tibetan subjects. In this sense, a Tibetan indigenous formation has existed for several decades in exile, and is now emerging within Tibet. In the next section, I briefly describe how Tibetans have been represented, and represent themselves, as wise in the ways of nature and as stewards of the land. The rest of this chapter turns to the larger political choices and constraints that explain why these "Green Tibetan" articulations do not adopt the explicit language of indigeneity.

Ecofriendly Tibetans

Environmental stewardship is one of the most powerful frames of contemporary indigenous activism; in many places, allying with environmental activists around problems of environmental destruction has given indigenous peoples a powerful voice and platform for mobilization (Tsing this volume). As a result, one of the central images made available by the international indigenous peoples movement is that of the inherently ecological Indian. Assertions of Tibetans' natural ecofriendliness are now an indispensable element of both the Tibetan government in exile and the transnational Tibet Movement's representations of Tibetanness.

According to one Tibetan exile writer, for example, "for centuries Tibet's ecosystem was kept in balance and alive out of a common concern for all of humanity" (Atisha 1991). Similarly, a brochure produced by the Environment and Development Desk of the Central Tibetan Administration in Dharamsala, India states:

> Prior to the Chinese occupation, Tibet was ecologically stable and environmental conservation was an essential component of daily life. Guided by Buddhist beliefs in the interdependence of both living and nonliving elements of the earth, Tibetans lived in harmony with nature.

Huber's (1997, 2001) genealogy of the Green Tibetan in exile shows that representations of Tibetans as naturally ecofriendly only began to be produced after 1985. The conjuncture that led to its emergence was the participation of government-in-exile representatives in a series of transnationally organized meetings and events, such as the World Wildlife Fund ([WWF] World Wide Fund for Nature outside of North America)–sponsored Buddhist Perception of nature project, World Environment Day, and the Assai Interfaith Ceremony on World Religions and the Environment. Tibetan assertions of intrinsic ecofriendliness thus appeared relatively late, after the idea of inherent environmental stewardship and knowledge had already been firmly attached to other groups including Native Americans and Kayapo. The congealing of the characteristic of ecological wisdom around a Tibetan identity in exile joined many other cases of indigenous environmental struggles and stewardship in the 1980s and 1990s, and in this sense, was an indigenous formation.

Within China, the emergence of the Green Tibetan as an indigenous formation has been even more recent still. The state's official position on the Tibetan environment attributes all positive environmental stewardship to Chinese science and modernization, not Tibetan tradition; for example, "it was after the peaceful liberation of Tibet that ecological improvement and environmental protection started there, and began to progress along with the modernization of Tibet."[2] Tibetan self-representations of environmental stewardship have become possible only in the space created by China's small but growing environmental movement, and in particular by Chinese staff of transnational conservation NGOs, as well as Chinese social scientists who have become interested in indigenous environmental knowledge (see also Litzinger 2004). Their interest in the relationship between Tibetan culture and nature is itself the result of a contingent convergence of a set of forces, including their own work with international foundations and development agencies, and more broadly, the promotion of the tourism industry as a major strategy for economic development in Tibet, the rise of youth backpacker culture, and a rising interest in Tibetan Buddhism, particularly among residents of wealthy coastal cities. The presence of environmentalists looking actively for evidence of Tibetan indigenous environmental knowledge and stewardship has in turn motivated Tibetans to rearticulate and translate their claims into the language and form understood by the environmentalists.

One important actor is Conservation International (CI), which launched its first program in China in 2000. A major component was the designation of the Mountains of Southwest China as a "biodiversity hotspot." More than 80 percent of this hotspot coincides with places where Tibetans currently and historically have lived. With many years of experience working with Western environmentalists and scientists in these Tibetan areas, the in-country director has implemented a major Sacred Lands program, the premise of which is that Tibetans already have a long history of environmental stewardship which stems from their religious and cultural traditions. Thus, CI is proposing to employ already-existing environmental wisdom toward the new goal of biodiversity preservation:

> The Mountains of Southwest China is rich in culture as it is in bio-diversity. The majority of inhabitants are Tibetans with strong cultural ties to their natural environment. Reflecting the Buddhist reverence for all lives, Tibetan villages and monasteries have for centuries designated mountains, lakes, forests and rivers as holy sites, and have designed local resource management systems to guard the land for exploitation.[3]

The search by this and other similar projects for evidence of local environmental stewardship and reverence for nature has come together with particular local histories, life trajectories, and the agency of Tibetans who have acted as cultural translators to allow a growing number of local villagers, religious teachers, and grassroots organizations to articulate a Green Tibetan identity.

In one case, a cluster of villages in Chamdo, in the eastern Tibet Autonomous Region (TAR), organized a community group for environmental protection after a visit by a new Tibetan environmental NGO, which in turn was being supported by CI. The informal leader of the local environmental protection efforts, who had previously written several essays about the need to rehabilitate and protect the sacred mountain for religious reasons, wrote several documents for the newly formed community group in 2003, including the following text:

> Our forefathers ... always took care of nature and found ways to create a balance in nature. We should pay attention to these rich traditions. ... They have much in common with modern science. They are something that we can be proud of. ... If promoted, these traditions might be helpful for researchers in their search for understanding nature. [Our forefathers] protected mountains, rivers, trees, boulders, and forests. [translation from original in Tibetan][4]

Although his earlier writing was concerned with specific types of illnesses and disasters that result from the disturbance of local beings and spirits, the more recent documents, which reflect an engagement with environmentalists, is couched in the narrative of environmental stewardship made available and pervasive by transnational indigenous movements. In particular, the appeal to the potential that local environmental knowledge has for informing science is a familiar theme in indigenous experience in many settings (see Cruikshank this volume).

There are a number of differences between the articulations of the Green Tibetan in exile and more recently in China, which I do not have space to discuss. What is important here is that in both cases, these self-representations emerged and were given voice through an engagement with a larger set of narratives of traditional environmental stewardship made available by the global discourse of indigeneity. This narrative, positing a distinct and positive relationship between a group of hitherto marginalized people's culture and natural resource management—a relationship from which the industrialized world could learn from and benefit—positions those who identify with it into a "green tribal slot" that is almost always understood as an "indigenous slot." In this sense, the image of the Green Tibetan, among other characteristics of Tibetan communities such as a history of marginalization and representations of exotic spirituality, is a type of indigenous formation. Nevertheless, the term *indigenous* itself is not typically used as part of the self-representation. This is more than just a matter of semantics. The political stakes are high. The rest of this chapter turns to these political stakes that structure the absence of the explicit language of "indigeneity" in Tibetan identification and claims making.

Indigeneity or Independence? Tibetans in Exile

People are not indigenous naturally, but rather by convention and recognition by others; although mutable, the conventions of indigeneity at any particular given time matter a great deal. For Tibetans in exile, the most important convention is the active disavowal by many indigenous groups of secessionist claims.

That one of the central claims of indigenous groups is sovereignty and self-determination has caused a great deal of concern among states that indigenous peoples' demands are threats to their territorial integrity. To allay these fears while convincing reluctant states to accede to their demands, many indigenous leaders have proclaimed that their intention is not to "divide states." Analyzing the draft declaration of the UN Working Group on Indigenous Rights, David Maybury-Lewis finds that it "makes it clear once and for all that secession and separatism are not on the mainstream agenda of indigenous peoples. What they want is a recognition of their rights within existing states" (1997: 56). Similarly, Ronald Niezen suggests,

> Indigenous peoples ... do not as a rule aspire to independent statehood, even though this is a concern mistakenly (or strategically) invoked in response to their claims to self-determination. ... Indigenism can thus be distinguished from ethno-nationalism by the consistent reluctance of indigenous peoples, at least up to the present, to invoke secession and independent statehood as desired political goals. [2003: 203–204]

There are several interrelated reasons for this. First, complete independence would absolve former hosts of treaty obligations. Also, the international nature of the indigenous peoples movement, in which disparate groups are invited to see themselves as part of a global community, means that they "do not need statehood to possess international status" (2003: 203–204). Furthermore, most groups that claim indigenous status are too small and have too few resources to be able to establish economically, politically, and militarily viable states. And finally, independent statehood "would in most cases be antithetical to indigenous peoples' traditional political values," not because they are inherently averse to the use of bureaucracies, but rather because their goals have been geared toward securing "traditional" political identity rather than statehood (Niezen 2000: 142).

Indeed, the fact that indigenous groups generally demand sovereignty without secession is one of the reasons indigeneity has been celebrated as a radical challenge to modern political organization. The argument for nations within nations, and rights to self-determination nested within state citizenship rights, is considered one of the great innovations of indigenism (Dirlik and Prazniak 2001; Niezen 2003). However, this convention of separating sovereignty from secession is precisely why Tibetan exiles have been reluctant to explicitly identify their struggle as an indigenous one. Official exile history describes Tibet (anachronistically) as an independent country whose history stretches back through an unbroken period of thousands of years, up to the Chinese invasion (or, according to the PRC, "peaceful liberation") of 1951. Emphasis is placed not only on a long history of sovereignty and the presence of all of the trappings of statehood but also on Tibet's immense geographical size (the Tibetan cultural region is about the size of Western Europe) and its population of roughly 6 million.[5] In other words, the government in exile and transnational Tibet Movement emphasize several characteristics that are quite different from those of most indigenous peoples. In its transnational scope, the Tibet Movement resembles transnational indigenous organizing, but rather than linking its issues to those of other similarly positioned peoples, it focuses on human rights violations and independence specifically for Tibet.

This brings up the thorny political question of whether complete independence is indeed what is currently being demanded. The PRC has consistently and adamantly opposed independence, viewing it as a deal breaker in all negotiations. Thus, in 1987 the Dalai Lama proposed the "Middle Path," an option of autonomy without independence. This would retain the territorial integrity of the PRC and put China in charge of Tibet's foreign policy while giving the government of Tibet "the right to decide on all affairs relating to Tibet and Tibetans." In the mid-1990s, the government in exile held a Referendum asking Tibetans in exile to choose from among four options: complete independence, the Middle Path, satyagraha (passive resistance), or self-determination; the result was majority support for the Dalai Lama's Middle Path. However, the Referendum was marked by much confusion and controversy. Some Tibetan argued that without the input of Tibetans inside Tibet, the referendum could not be legally binding. Others charged that the resulting vote was not truly indicative of a lack of desire for independence, but rather that Tibetans voted that way only to say "whatever the Dalai Lama says is fine with me."

More recently, Western legal experts working with the Tibet Movement have pointed out that the Referendum was deeply flawed, because self-determination should be considered a universal right of all "peoples," a category for which Tibetans have been determined in other international fora to qualify, rather than one among several options for political status (Herzer 2002). As a result, there has been a shift in rhetoric among some elements of the Tibet Movement toward a focus on self-determination, saving debates about specific political form for later. According to one former government-in-exile minister in 2004, "independence under the present circumstances is something the Tibetans only demand. Self-determination on the other hand, is a right, a principle that the modern world accepts … it is evident that self-determination may be a very important idea, one that can unify our many voices and also find global and legal resonance."[6]

These appeals to self-determination as a globally and legally recognized right come very close to the narratives of sovereignty and self-determination made available by the indigenous peoples movement. The Dalai Lama has also further softened his position, declaring that he is now "completely committed to renouncing independence." Since the late 1990s, he has dropped several conditions that were difficult for China to accept. His calls for genuine regional autonomy have also shifted in focus to cultural heritage, again in language that is strikingly reminiscent of global indigenous voice: "Tibet's religious and cultural heritage is extremely rich. Thus to protect the heritage, Tibet needs some rights of self-government" (Sautman 2002).[7]

However, to date the Chinese government has adamantly rejected these pronouncements, instead denouncing the Dalai Lama as a hypocrite and reactionary "splittist," someone whose true and malicious intent is to "split" the Chinese nation. According to the Chinese government, the Dalai Lama's "Middle Way" is merely a ruse. Indeed, the association of the Dalai Lama with "splittism" is so strong that display of his photographs was once again banned in Central Tibet in the mid-1990s, and as part of "patriotic education" campaigns, monks and nuns have been required to personally denounce him and to "draw a clear line" between themselves and the "Dalai clique" (Tibet Information Network [TIN] 1996). Celebrations of the Dalai Lama's birthday have also been banned, and public denunciation has continued into the present, in cycles of lesser and greater severity. The opening of the Qinghai–Tibet Railway in 2006 drew promises from Beijing of a "fight to the death struggle" against him and his supporters.

Though the Dalai Lama now appeals for real political autonomy rather than independence, the government in exile continues to adhere to the definition and demand for "greater Tibet," which includes not just the TAR alone—the area currently accepted as "Tibet" by the Chinese government— but rather the entire "three provinces of Tibet" (Amdo,

Kham, and U-Tsang), including parts of five provincial-level units in China, with roughly twice the total land area and twice the Tibetan population as lives in the TAR. The insistence on political autonomy not just for the TAR but for greater Tibet has been one of the largest obstacles in attempted negotiations between the government in exile and the Chinese government, with the latter completely rejecting this possibility.

The lack of a solution and apparently deteriorating situation in Tibet has further angered exile activists who openly disagree with the call for autonomy. There is even dissent against the Dalai Lama's message of nonviolence, with some youth leaders claiming that "about 60 percent of Tibetan youth want to take up arms against China" and that "the future will be bloody" if the situation is not resolved during the lifetime of the current Dalai Lama (Chanda 2002). The Tibetan Youth Congress (TYC), counting 20,000 members and calling itself "the largest Tibetan NGO," demands of its members that they "serve one's country ... under the guidance of His Holiness the Dalai Lama" but, simultaneously, that they "struggle for the total independence of Tibet even at the cost of one's life." Among TYC's recent campaigns have been a hunger strike in Geneva in 2004 to protest "UN negligence" on the issue of Tibet, and a call to boycott all Chinese-made goods.

Although groups such as TYC agree that Tibetans are indigenous in the sense of native, prior occupants of a place, they refuse the idea that this place can be properly called China. Yet the current trend in the transnational indigenous movement is precisely for indigenous peoples to speak to and even represent the larger nation-state of which they are a part. The refusal to speak in registers that link smoothly with the narratives of other indigenous rights groups around the world—for example, calls for sovereignty without separate statehood or national inclusion in a multicultural nation—helps explain why Tibetans in exile have not made much use of indigenous status as a claim-making political tool. Even though the official government-in-exile position now emphasizes the familiar indigenous themes of self-determination and sovereignty, there is considerable resistance to these themes from certain fragments of the exile population, as well as suspicion from the audience it was meant to appease—the Chinese government.

Nationalist Protests of the 1980s and the Circulation of Discourses

China's political isolation severely curtailed contact between Tibetans inside Tibet and the refugee community for more than two decades after 1959. Only in the early 1980s were Tibetans allowed to go on pilgrimage and visit relatives in South Asia. During this time, parents began to send their children to schools run by the exile government. After the proindependence demonstrations in the late 1980s, however, travel to India was restricted once more, and families with children there were pressured to bring them back to Tibet. Despite increasing difficulties crossing the border in the 1990s and after, many Tibetan children continue to escape to India to study in Tibetan government-in-exile schools. Of these, a significant number eventually return to Tibet either because their parents are pressured to bring them home, or in some cases because they returned to visit their families and found themselves unable to leave again.

As a result, discourses and ideas (as well as material goods and people) circulate in complex networks between Tibetans in exile and in Tibet, as well as being shaped by notions of Tibetanness produced by Western and Chinese representations. Elliot Sperling's analysis of the rhetoric of dissent in political pamphlets produced in Lhasa around the time of Tibetan nationalist demonstrations in 1987–89 shows "clear evidence of familiarity with information and materials originating with exile Tibetans within dissident circles in Tibet" (1994: 269), but also picking and choosing from among these ideas. In particular, the pamphlets drew heavily on exile materials dealing with the question of human rights, while disregarding other exile discourses, such as the Dalai Lama's statements renouncing independence in favor of the Middle Path. In addition the Tibetan pamphleteers also used vocabulary specific to Chinese Marxism as well as vocabulary shared by many anticolonial movements around the world. Again, the global discourse of indigeneity was not invoked.

The 1987–89 protests resulted in nearly a hundred deaths (including children) from police gunfire, some three thousand arrests followed by imprisonment and usually accompanied by torture, and finally, the imposition of martial law in Lhasa for more than a year (Barnett 1998). The state responded with a two-pronged strategy: a tightening of political control, including increased surveillance to facilitate a shift from "passive" to "active" policing (targeting potential protestors before demonstrations), and a rapid program of marketization that has created new Tibetan class divisions. Given the severity with which "attempts to split the nation" are punished, Tibetans within Tibet must maneuver very carefully when making cultural or political claims. In contrast to the demands of many exiles, as well as the rhetoric of the Lhasa pamphleteers in the late 1980s, many if not most Tibetans living in

Tibet today believe that complete independence is an impossible dream. Do Tibetan leaders, intellectuals, and others who accept (or are resigned to) their status as citizens of the PRC invoke a discourse of indigeneity? How does indigeneity translate into the Chinese context and is it useful for Tibetans? The rest of the essay turns to these questions.

Translating Indigeneity in China

Like the governments of Indonesia (Li 2000), India (Karlsson 2003), and other postcolonial Asian countries, the PRC government has long insisted that the category of "indigenous peoples" is irrelevant because all of the nation's citizens are equally indigenous. China's official position has been that, "as in the majority of Asian countries, the various nationalities in China have all lived for eons on Chinese territory. Although there is no indigenous peoples' question in China, the Chinese Government and people have every sympathy with indigenous peoples' historical woes" (Kingsbury 1998: 417–418). Although China has sent representatives to UN working groups on Indigenous populations, its own ethnic minorities have not been allowed to participate as ethnic representatives, again because China does not consider them indigenous (Gladney 1997).

Despite this official position, the English-language term *indigenous* is in fact being used by a few scholar-activist circles in China. Of these one of the most visible is the Center for Biodiversity and Indigenous Knowledge (CBIK), in Yunnan, which has had long-standing ties with U.S.-based scholars as well as support from international organizations such as the Ford Foundation. Executive director of CBIK Xu Jianchu has published numerous papers about indigenous knowledge and its cultural and environmental importance, with members of various minority minzu in China, and with Western social scientists.

The question of translation, both literal and figurative, is thus of great interest here. If "indigenous knowledge" is used when speaking to an international audience, what concept is used when speaking to a national one? CBIK's Chinese name is "Center for Research on Bio-diversity and Traditional Knowledge." *Indigenous* becomes *tradition,* a general term that can be used in reference to both the Han and non-Han. In fact, however, CBIK's research focuses exclusively on non-Han groups, a fact that is explained on its website in this way (in Chinese): "CBIK's Traditional Knowledge Program is concerned with the impact of socioeconomic changes upon the future of China's Southwest minority minzu." While using *traditional* in its name as a gloss for *indigenous,* the center is also building an understanding of *minority minzu* as being equivalent to *indigenous* as used in global contexts. This appears on the surface not so different from the way adivasi is "indigenous" in India or the way masyarakat adat is used as the translation for indigenous in Indonesia. However, I argue that the specific histories and forms of national classification projects make a difference, and that, at least for now, the category of minzu cannot do the work of indigeneity for Tibetans in the PRC.

Minzu and Autonomy

The genealogy of minzu cannot be separated from the history of nationalism and the transition between the Manchu Qing empire and what is now the PRC. The Qing covered a huge territory that included not just Han dominated areas, but also vast parts of inner Asia. Unlike the Miao, Yi, and other groups of distinct peoples who were not large or widespread enough to compete with the Qing, five constituencies— the Manchu, Mongol, Chinese, Tibetan, and Muslims—were seen as representing particularly powerful and distinct cultural traditions. Tibetans and Mongols were given special treatment by the Qing vis-à-vis groups such as the Miao, a historical difference that continues to have effects today (Tuttle 2005).

After the Qing empire fell in 1911, it took an educational campaign by Chinese nationalists to develop concern for Tibetan territory among the Chinese. In other words, it was not inevitable for modern China's boundaries to be the same as those of the Qing empire; rather, considerable work had to be done, some of which included the promotion of discourses of racial, national, and religious unity (Tuttle 2005). Sun Yat-sen, leader of the Republican movement that toppled the Qing, developed a theory, rife with contradictions, of *minzu zhuyi*, or "nationalism"; it expressed a racial nationalism embodying ideas of both race as lineage and race as nation (Dikötter 1992). On the one hand, the notion of a Han minzu was developed to mobilize the vast majority of people against the Manchu Qing, with the idea that each minzu should decide its own destiny and not be ruled by others (Gladney 1994). On the other hand, Sun also claimed that a larger "Chinese race" (*Zhonghua minzu*) was distinct from all other "races" in the world, and was itself composed of the five major "races" of the Han, Manchu, Mongol, Tibetan, and Muslim. Later, Guomingdang leader Chiang Kai-shek (1947: 40, in Smith 1996: 329), further stated, "that there are five peoples designated in China is not due to difference in race or blood, but to religion and geographic environment."

The transition between the Qing empire and the modern nation-state led to the emergence of two distinct nationalisms, which Louisa Schein calls Han nationalism—"concerned with the boundaries between peoples within the shifting territory of the Chinese polity, specifically between Han and those they designated as 'barbarians'"—and Chinese nationalism, which "rose in response to incidences of foreign imperialist aggression that prompted a unifying within the physical boundary of China against the outside" (2000: 108). Against the foreign imperialists, all of China's minzu, including Tibetans, were said to be united, and part of the same larger "Chinese race."

However useful this discourse was for the Han, its utility was limited for Tibetans. As Uradyn Bulag points out, in the official names of both the Republic of China (Zhonghua Minguo) and the People's Republic of China (Zhonghua Renmin Gongheguo), the Middle (Zhong) Kingdom (guo) is always hyphenated with *Hua,* a term that is used only to denote the Han: "It is this inseparability of Han or Hua from 'China' that makes minority identification with China so ambivalent or difficult. In English we can write Han Chinese, but it is impossible to hyphenate other nationalities with Chinese. Mongol Chinese or Tibetan Chinese are impossibilities" (2002: 18). In the 1930s, a number of Tibetans, particularly from the eastern area of Batang, tried to shape Sun Yat-sen's work to fit their own interests. Applying the logic of "national autonomy" to their own situation lead to a short-lived and unsuccessful movement of "Khampa rule for Kham," in which the Khampas demanded autonomy from both China and Central Tibet (Tuttle 2005: 149; Goldstein, Sherap, and Siebenschuh 2004).

Minzu was also used by the Chinese Communist Party (CCP), which early on adopted Lenin's approach of allowing self-determination for every minzu. This was codified in Article 14 of the 1931 CCP constitution, which recognized the right to self-determination, including complete separation and the formation of an independent state, for each minority minzu (Smith 1996). Indeed, Baba Phuntsog Wangyal (from Batang) founded a secret Tibetan Communist Party in the 1930s, with the idea of an independent Tibet after a communist revolution (Goldstein, Sherap, and Siebenschuh 2004: 47). Later, when political circumstances made their party untenable, he and several others created a Tibetan branch of the CCP, which he believed "would lead to the restructuring of Kham and possibly the whole Tibetan area ... as an autonomous republic that would function in a way similar to the autonomous socialist republics in the Soviet Union (2004: 125).

When the CCP came to power, however, it repudiated its promise of self-determination with the declaration that the "concrete conditions" of China dictated that there would be no option of either secession or a federated system. Instead "autonomous" units, which were to have some measure of cultural and political autonomy, were established at the provincial, prefectural, and county levels, in places where minorities were concentrated. As one of the most populous groups, Tibetans were given the (provincial-level) TAR, roughly consistent with the area directly under the control of the government in Lhasa in the early 20th century, and covering about half of the PRC's total Tibetan population. However, there is in fact little autonomy; the TAR has consistently had much more direct central government involvement in its political, cultural, and economic affairs than other provinces (Yeh 2003). Nevertheless, the TAR is one of the few "autonomous regions" where minorities outnumber the Han; official statistics claim that over 96 percent of the TAR population is Tibetan. However, official documents about the TAR also always describe it as a "multiethnic region," inhabited not only by Tibetans and Han, but also Hui (Chinese Muslims) and smaller groups such as the Lhopa and Menpa. Thus, whereas indigenous cultures are often framed spatially, incarcerated in place or at least tied to specific pieces of land or nature (Baviskar this volume), the PRC's discourse of minzu and autonomy suggest that it is just as "natural" for the Han as the Tibetans to live in the TAR, and for Tibetans to live outside of the TAR.

The Limits of Difference

Soon after the founding of the PRC, minorities were asked to step forward for recognition. More than 400 groups applied, leading to intensive field investigations by research teams of historians, linguists, ethnologists, and economists, who were sent to determine whether the groups that applied were actually distinct minzu, or subgroups of the Han or other minority minzu. The teams made decisions about recognition based on Stalin's definition of a nation, according to which a nation is a group that has a stable community of people, was historically constituted, and is formed on the basis of common language, territory, economic life, and "psychological make-up manifested in a common culture" (Litzinger 2000; Mackerras 1994). By 1979, the team had narrowed the official number down to 55 minority groups, plus the Han, who account for about 92 percent of China's population.

The PRC's official position has always been that it is a multinational state. However, after the Anti-Rightist Campaign of 1957 and throughout the Cultural Revolution, there was a nationwide movement to suppress difference and achieve cultural homogenization; this period emphasized the ideology that minzu would ultimately disappear, and that the faster the "nationality problem" was solved—by assimilating minorities into the Chinese Nation—the better. Indeed, despite his very early revolutionary credentials, Baba Phuntsog Wangyal was arrested in 1958 and held in solitary confinement for 18 years, for fusing Tibetan nationalism to Communist ideals.

Since the cultural and economic liberalization of the 1980s, difference has again become acceptable and, especially since the mid-1990s, encouraged with the commodification of the "exotic" ethnic other (see Schein 2000). The more lenient political atmosphere and critique of "big Han chauvinism" after the end of the Cultural Revolution encouraged a significant number of Han-identified people to reclassify themselves as belonging to other minzu. Gladney (1997) suggests that since the 1990s it has become "popular to be 'ethnic' in today's China." In some cases those who are marked as minority minzu have indeed been able to take advantage of permission to have more children, pay fewer taxes, and other privileges. This shift has been accompanied by a tendency increasingly to translate minzu into English as "ethnic" rather than "nationality." In the past few years, it has also facilitated the emergence of Tibet chic and mass domestic tourism to Tibet. In trendy neighborhoods of major Chinese cities, one can now find boutiques selling Tibetan trinkets (mostly imported from Nepal and India), similar to ones hawked in boutiques and street fairs in the United States. Tibet sells, as evidenced by Shangri-la wine, Tibet grass brand ginseng-berry juice, Tibetan Fragrant spring sorghum liquor, and the growing popularity of Tibetan medicine—everything from pain-relief plaster to "Tibetan secret" potions for curing impotence. The New Age flavor of this commodification of an exoticized Tibetan culture bears a strong resemblance to the marketing of indigenousness (but not ethnic nationalism) around the world.

Although the commodification of Tibetan culture is now encouraged, the deep entanglement of Tibetan culture with religion makes the space permitted by the state's new neoliberal multicultural recognition precarious at best. Monasteries and temples are key tourist destinations, and advertisements for everything from incense to herbal candy to cell phones feature Tibetan monks with the relevant product. At the same time however, since the mid-1990s, all government officials (not just CCP members), their relatives, and students of all ages have been banned from participating in religious practice in Lhasa. More recently, monks and nuns have been banned from setting foot on the campus of Tibet University because of their alleged "splittist" tendencies (see Barnett 2006 for more details). Religion can be sold to tourists, but its practice by locals is increasingly restricted.

The burgeoning popularity of Tibetan religion among the Han is also of particular state concern. Indeed, officials found the large number of Han Chinese followers of Khenpo Jigme Phuntsok in Larung Gar, Serthar, Sichuan particularly threatening. His status among the Han contributed to their decision to impose strict controls on his institute, evict a thousand of his Han disciples, and demolish several thousand of his followers' homes in 2001. This concern with the growing number of Han disciples of Tibetan lamas reflects not only a general concern with any challenges to state authority (as also with Falun Gong) but also a specific concern about Tibetan religious leaders, especially after Agya Rinpoche, abbot of Kumbum Monastery, and the seventeenth Karmapa left China in 1998 and 1999 for the United States and India, respectively. Both were high-ranking lamas favored by the state, and believed to be loyal to China; their unexpected departure has led to further restrictions on contact between Tibetan religious leaders living abroad and Tibetan Buddhists in China (Kapstein 2004).

The recent "ethnicization" of Tibetan representations in China has thus not erased the importance of minzu tuanjie as a hegemonic device to manage a coercive "unity." Neoliberal economic policies have allowed a valorization of Tibetan culture that contrasts with older representations of Tibetans as barbaric and backward, but these new expressions and claims of cultural difference, and any corresponding rights, can only be made within the bounds of minzu tuanjie. Bulag's analysis of the problem for Mongolians in today's China applies equally well to Tibetans; both groups occupy strategic borders and have international ties about which China is concerned:

> If, from the national minority point of view, their demand for greater autonomy is understood as a plea for acceptance of a more diverse China, one that grants equality to minorities, guaranteeing their cultural dignity and difference, the counterargument from the majoritarian state is that such demands threaten minzu tuanjie and are in effect minzu fenlie. The subtext is that the demand for greater autonomy and rights is either the demand of a handful of reactionaries of a minzu, or is instigated by imperialists in order to undermine China's sovereignty. (Bulag 2002: 13–14)

In each unique context, "indigenous" leaders can hope to make a difference in state policy—whether in demanding greater respect for collective rights, recognition of cultural difference, or reappropriation of physical, cultural, or other resources—only by speaking in a register that can be heard by, and makes sense to a national audience (Tsing this volume). Within the PRC, minzu is currently the only available frame for talking about cultural difference. This is why CBIK's (English) "indigenous knowledge" program translates into a program (in Chinese) concerned with the traditional knowledge of minority minzu. But note that CBIK's goal is not to reappropriate cultural knowledge for indigenous groups (see Castree 2004) but, rather, only to understand and document it. This allows it to fit well into minzu discourse, according to which (as one very large sign in Lhasa's Jokhang Square proclaims) "What belongs to minzu, also belongs to the world."

To be a successful user of minzu discourse, one cannot make demands altogether outside the purview of state discourse. Herein lies one of the main difficulties in translating "indigenous" concerns into minzu. Whereas many indigenous struggles work around the mutually ack- nowledged notion of a historical debt or deficit after conquest, the PRC insists that Tibetans were liberated (from local "feudal" overlords), not oppressed, by the PRC. It is no wonder, then, that the notion of indigenousness is rejected by the Chinese state, according to which Tibetans are grateful for liberation, not suffering from the effects of colonization.

The refusal to compare or link the situation of Tibetans with those of other marginalized peoples around the world is a powerful reason why the state has not accepted indigeneity as a palatable alternative to a more explicitly nationalist discourse. Also at issue is the way in which indigenous groups build transnational linkages and alliances with other similarly identified groups to achieve their goals. The Chinese state denies that Tibetans need to struggle for anything that the state does not already provide,[8] and frequently accuses international advocacy groups as well as foreign governments of "meddling" into domestic Chinese affairs whenever the issue of Tibet is raised. Both the severe restrictions on Tibetan cross-border connections, especially those link- ing to Tibetans on the outside (especially the Dalai Lama), and current state policies toward Tibetan religion, are rather incompatible with global practices of autonomy for indigenous groups. At the same time, the state adamantly maintains that Tibetans already have autonomy, in the TAR and autonomous prefectures in other provinces; this further discourages articulations of an indigenous identity based on special cultural rights. The official position is an insistence that whatever is now in place is already providing all the special rights and affirmative action (such as lower standards for college entrance examinations) that

Tibetans need and should rightfully ask for. To demand more is to attempt to split the nation.

Tibetan Minzu in Practice

Tibetan imaginations of minzu are shaped in multiple ways, including through regulation of the language of difference and belonging. One example was an attempt in villages around Lhasa, in 2000–01, by local officials to replace use of the term *rgya mi* with *rgya rigs* in everyday conversation. Both terms refer to Han Chinese. However the term *rigs* means type, kind, or lineage, whereas *mi* simply means "person." *Mi rigs*, a specific type of person, is now the standard Tibetan translation of the Chinese minzu; and *bod rigs* is used in addition to the older term *bod pa* (in which "pa" is a nominalizer) to mean "Tibetan." *Rgya nag* is the term historically used to refer to China, as distinct from Tibet. Thus, the term *rgya* refers somewhat ambiguously to both "Han" and "Chinese," as these were historically conflated and there was no need to distinguish between the two. In the contemporary context, *rgya nag* refers not to the entire territory of the PRC, but rather only to the primarily Han areas of the east; in Chinese, its equivalent is *neidi*, "inner land." Tibet is not considered part of *rgya nag*, but it is part of *Zhongguo*, or "China." The attempt to replace *rgya mi* with *rgya rigs* is an attempt to diffuse the sense of Otherness of *rgya*, and foster instead a sense of being part of the same "family," of belonging to a larger China that encompasses many different minzu, or *mi rigs*. *Rgya*, like *bod*, are merely particular kinds of nationalities (rigs) rather than separate "peoples." *Rgya rig* can only refer to Han ethnicity, whereas *rgya mi* runs the risk of being understood as "Chinese person." The latter may carry residual implications of significant difference, and of not belonging in Tibet, whereas the former does not.

How do Tibetans understand minzu in practice? Consider the case of Drolma, a well-educated young Tibetan woman who grew up in the urban center of Xining, in Qinghai province:

> When I was young I didn't think there was any difference between Tibetan and Han. I didn't think it was a big deal being Tibetan, since we were just another minzu. But other people wanted to make me different. When I go out with my friends in the city and dress like a city girl, no one believes I am Tibetan. Even when I tell them, they always ask me "which one of your parents is Han, your father or your mother?" ... They congratulate me for not being like a Tibetan. ... Whenever a rural

Tibetan gets on a city bus, people hold their noses and walk away and
make very rude comments. ... I started to feel: okay, I am Tibetan. I'm
not at all like you Han people. ... Now I'm proud of being Tibetan. ... I
think it's very important for us to keep our Tibetan culture.

For Drolma, coming to identify with her Tibetanness was a process of
being subject, on the one hand, to negative stereotypes of Tibetans as
backward, lazy, dirty, or barbaric, and, on the other hand, a process
of being misrecognized as Han. Her increasingly strong feelings of
separation and cultural difference from the Han Chinese mean coming
to think of Tibetans as something *other than* "just another minzu." The
difference she now understands there to be between the Tibetan and
the Chinese cannot be contained within the category of minzu. For
some Tibetans, then, the concept of minzu is an inadequate container
of cultural difference; it does not have the power to do the political and
cultural work that "indigeneous" does in other settings.

At the same time that minzu is seen by some as an inadequate marker
for difference, others worry about the political dangers of even using
minzu discourse at all. Consider, for example, the problem of caterpillar fungus *(Cordyceps sinensis)*. Used in Chinese medicine and found
extensively in Tibetan pastures above 13,000 feet, caterpillar fungus
has become one of the most important sources of household income
throughout the Tibetan plateau in the past decade. With prices in Lhasa
now at 10,000–30,000 RMB ($1,200–$3,600) per kilogram, increasing
numbers of conflicts are occurring over rights to harvest. Although all
of the use rights to the high pastures on which cordyceps are found
have been legally allocated to local (Tibetan) households and villages,
many cases have been reported of government officials "selling" the
mountains to private entrepreneurs; of government officials selling
harvesting permits to outsiders without local consent and without
sharing the profits; and of outsiders, including Han and Hui, harvesting
without permission or compensation to local residents. In many ways,
this would appear to be a classic problem of indigenous control over
land and natural resources. And if minzu is the way in which indigeneity
is best translated for a national audience, then Tibetan struggles over
their right to control local land ought to be framed by minzu. Yet, it
is not. A Tibetan social scientist and Party member who has studied
the problem of caterpillar fungus, and who is well-positioned enough
to have the ear of some government officials, explained this to me as
follows: "The most important thing is to have some new laws preventing
outsiders from harvesting caterpillar fungus without permits. Actually,

these are basically Han and Hui. What we need to do is to keep the land for the Tibetans. But we can't say that. We can't say the 'Han,' 'Hui,' 'Tibetan' and so forth. We can't talk about different minzu. We have to find another way to address the problem without mentioning minzu." For him, to even frame conflicts as a minzu question would be to risk being accused of minzu fenlie.

Minzu can only be minzu tuanjie, an always already–existing unity. The case of Woeser, a Tibetan author writing in Chinese, illustrates the hard boundaries of minzu tuanjie and what is considered acceptable difference within the PRC today. The daughter of Party members, college educated with a degree in Chinese literature, and an author who writes only in Chinese, Woeser is, like many others of her generation, a model of national inclusion. Until recently, she held a government position as editor of the official journal of the Literature Association of the TAR. Her most recent anthology, *Notes on Tibet,* is a collection of essays about ordinary people and the absurdities of everyday life in Tibet. The book carefully avoids any outright demand for political and cultural rights; there is no mention of Tibetan nationalism or independence. For the most part, it stays away from explicit attention to minority issues, but in a few cases, descriptions of everyday life lead her to discuss minzu. For example, in one essay about two Chinese tourists taking unwelcome photographs in the Jokhang temple, she writes

> Phurbu was even more angry and said to him, "No photos…"
> Then the other man was furious. "Why can't we take photos of you? What right have you got to stop us from taking photos?" he said loudly, with his face red…
> … These two men seem to think they have the right. … Surely, traveling in the land of one of the [55] minorities you have the right to do what you want. Who can stop you? (TIN 2004: 252)

Another essay describes an incident in which a Tibetan policeman joins a Chinese policeman in beating two Tibetan men on the street:

> "Why do you beat people?" … someone shouted from the crowd…
> "'What? Say that again,' the policeman said in Tibetan, wearing an evil look on his face … [one of the men] was beaten beyond recognition. … They pushed the crying Tibetan man into their car. … Together … [the Tibetan and Chinese policemen] watched as the car drove away. At that moment, I was reminded of the favorite rhetoric of the Party Secretary Ragdi, "Chinese nationalit[y] and Tibetan nationalit[y] are inseparable."

The face of the Han policeman was full of triumphant pride. (TIN 2004: 249)

Soon after it was published in Guangdong in 2003, the book attracted the attention of censors and was banned, first in the TAR and then throughout China. Because the book praised the Dalai Lama as "the person who is loved, revered, and missed by all Tibetans," Woeser was accused of "exaggerating and beautifying the positive function of religion in social life," and of "indulging in nostalgia for the old Tibet." Further, the contents were said to reveal "a rigid thinking on nationalism and opinions that are harmful to the unification and solidarity of our nation"; the book was "divorced from correct political principles" (Wang 2004). Woeser and her family were subsequently the subject to "thought work" (*sixiang gongzuo*), aimed at having her "make herself a new person" (*chongxin zuoren*). Refusing to denounce the Dalai Lama, however, Woeser instead lost her job and went "in exile" to Beijing, where she currently lives without income, social security, job, or option to apply for a passport to leave the country. As Wang (2004) points out, there are far fewer options for economic survival in Tibet compared to other parts of China:

> For people living in free societies or in today's inland China, the sign-
> ificance of this kind of punishment to Tibetans might not be clearly
> understood ... Tibet and its society has been structured to completely
> rely financially on Beijing ... only when inducted as a part of the system
> can one have a chance to become a professional working in the fields of
> culture; otherwise, there is even no guarantee of basic survival.

With this example, I do not mean to suggest that an oppositional voice is the only "authentically" Tibetan one. Many Tibetans in the PRC participate in structures of power; well-educated cadres (as Woeser was until recently) and CCP members are among the most successful. Not all are critical of minzu discourse or policy; not all stand in the same relationship to Tibetan and Chinese nationalisms. My concern here has been to show that, for those who would even gently question "national unity," or ask for greater cultural rights (such as the right to openly praise the Dalai Lama), respect for cultural difference, or demand any sort of self-determination—that is, for those who use minzu discourse to do the work of "indigeneity"—there is at present, very limited space in which to maneuver.

Conclusion

In this chapter, I have agreed that indigeneity, as a concept that is "out there" transnationally, has not been taken up to a significant degree by Tibetans either in exile or in Tibet, for different reasons. The notion of nativeness and belonging within a larger existing state does not help exile Tibetans do their political work of demanding a separate, independent country. Within the boundaries of the PRC, terms referring to nativeness do not signify a scale of identification needed to make collective claims about political or cultural rights, and are not recognized by a national audience. Instead, the history of national classification within China makes minzu the relevant category for making claims about difference. And indeed, scholars within China now who use English terms such as *indigenous knowledge* explain their work in Chinese with the term minzu.

However, minzu does not quite do the work of "indigeneity" for Tibetans. On the one hand, in some contexts and for some Tibetans, minzu is too confined, too narrow to contain and express their felt cultural difference and their desire for greater cultural rights and respect. Being a minority minzu means standing in a hegemonically defined relationship of harmoniousness and unity to the majority minzu, the Han; it also means standing in a certain relationship to the other 54 state-defined minority minzu. But thus far, the most important social scale of identification and solidarity for Tibetans is with the category of "Tibetans" (itself an aggregate of many smaller, disparate socioterritorial identifications). Identification does not extend to any significant extent to a scale encompassing the other 54 minority minzu, nor to other indigenous groups around the world. There is no equivalent in the PRC, in other words, to organizations such as the archipelago-wide indigenous advocacy network formed in Indonesia in 1999 (the Aliansi Masyarakat Adat Nusantrara). The only significant networks that link Tibetans with other minority minzu in China are defined by the state, as part of minzu tuanjie. On the other hand, in other contexts and for other Tibetans, phrasing demands for greater rights or defense of local control of natural resources in terms of minzu is too politically risky. Demanding more autonomy or more cultural rights where one is already supposed to have as much autonomy or rights as is needed, invites accusations of national splittism. Thus, it is not an effective tool.

It is in these senses and for these reasons, then, that Tibetans have not been interpellated as indigenous subjects. Nevertheless, I do not suggest that this is a permanent or unchangeable state of affairs, nor that a more explicit Tibetan indigeneity may not come into being in the future. The articulation of indigenous identity is contingent and without guarantees. Political conditions and national imaginations can change. Indeed, despite the lack of uptake of an explicitly indigenous identity, the growing strength of claims and representations about Tibetan environmental stewardship and ecological wisdom resonate strongly with indigenous formations around the world.

The current tenor of exile discourse, which rejects the assumptions of indigeneity in favor for demands of complete independence, seem unlikely to change in the short term. However, as the Dalai Lama himself stressed during his 2006 Kalachakra teachings in Amravati, India, the future of Tibet depends on the initiative and lies in the hands of those living in Tibet. For Tibetans living in the PRC, the question is not so much an explicit rejection of indigeneity as the very limited space currently allowed for any claims of cultural and historical difference, and for rights based on those claims. Although the Tibet Movement and government in exile play important political roles in the international arena, the ongoing attacks on the Dalai Lama and foreign "interference" as "splittism" and unwanted meddling into Chinese domestic affairs suggests that the best hope for more autonomy and cultural rights for Tibetans may very well lie with Han Chinese citizens, working toward these goals within China itself.

Growing interest among mainstream Chinese in Tibetan culture, religion, and nature is opening up a new space for Tibetans to make claims on local resources and cultural practices. Thus far, these openings are being made without the discourse of indigeneity, but if a political space for it were to become available, indigeneity could open up some strategic possibilities (as well as pitfalls). For example, current efforts by Chinese environmentalists working with international NGOs to codify Tibetan sacred lands as an officially recognized, legal form of community environmental protection in the National Protected Areas Law, fits very well into broader demands for collective rights to land in the global discourse of indigeneity. Another new phenomenon in Tibetan areas, the sale of (use rights to) collective land by government officials to the highest bidder (almost always Han businessmen), against the desires and legal rights of the local Tibetans, raises a new specter of land dispossession, another issue common to many indigenous groups.

As in other parts of the world, then, collaboration between environmental activists and marginalized peoples around questions of environmental protection and land rights could eventually be a catalyst for successful activism, as well as a new conjuncture in which Tibetan struggles and representations are rearticulated with the explicit language of indigeneity. Indigeneity would be, for cosmopolitan Han activists, both safer and more appealing than the more nationalist Tibetan alternative, while also allowing for a much broader range of possibilities of strategy and action than the current discourse of minzu tuanjie allows. This could facilitate the Tibetan uptake of an indigenous identity. Though by no means a guaranteed or even very likely outcome, such an alliance between Tibetans and well-positioned and (relatively) politically protected Chinese activists, based on the premises of Tibetan indigeneity, may also have the potential to lead to greater Tibetan autonomy.

Notes

Acknowledgements. Thanks to all of the participants of the conference on which this volume is based, and particularly to Marisol de la Cadena and Orin Starn, for their stimulating conversation and very helpful suggestions.

1. In exile, the term *bod pa* is used for all Tibetans, but within Tibet, it is still common for most people to use bod pa in reference only to people from central Tibet, in particular the Lhasa and Lhoka areas. Other Tibetans, though recognized as being part of a larger collective group (which is often left unnamed, or sometimes referred to as *bod rigs*) are referred to by their regional names, for example, Amdowa, Khampa, Tsangpa, Dopa.

2. This is from a White Paper on ecological improvement and environmental protection in Tibet. State Council, March 2003, accessed at http://www.china-embassy.org/eng/zt/zfbps/t36547.htm, December 23, 2006.

3. This is from a CI–China brochure, 2000.

4. "Rules and specific places for the voluntary association of Gonjo Zedingsengdzong to protect the environment."

5. This a contested figure. Although the Tibetan government in exile has consistently claimed a population of 6 million, the PRC reported a Tibetan population within its borders of 4.6 million in 1990, and 5.4 million in 2006; another 150,000 live in exile.

6. Tenzin Namgyal Tethong, "Shaping the future of Tibet—Tibetan Self-Determination and Individual Activism" conference, accessed at http://www.tibetanyouth.org/futureoftibet/interview_tnt.htm, December 23, 2006.

7. "Dalai Lama comments on Tibet issue" Chung-Kuo Shih-pao, Taiwan; March 7, 1999, in BBC/SWB, March 11, 1999; quoted from Saumtan 2002.

8. A German NGO dedicated to fixing and preserving historic houses in Lhasa was expelled reportedly after TAR leaders were angered by a television show in which local residents who were interviewed about their work expressed immense gratitude to the organization. According to one government official, "they wanted to know why the locals were praising the Germans instead of China for all China has done."

References

Atisha, Tenzin P. 1991. The Tibetan approach to ecology. Electronic document, http://www.tibet.com/Eco/eco7.html, accessed December 23, 2006.

Barnett, Robert. 1998. Untitled essay. In *The Tibetans: A struggle to survive*, edited by Steve Lehman, 178–196. New York: Umbrage Editions.

——. 2006. Modernity, religion and urban space in contemporary Lhasa. Paper presented at the Association of Asian Studies annual meeting, April 2006.

Bulag, Uradyn E. 2002. *The Mongols at China's edge: History and the politics of national unity*. Boulder, CO: Rowman and Littlefield.

Castree, Noel. 2004. Differential geographies: Place, indigenous rights and "local" resources. *Political Geography* 23: 133–167.

Chanda, Abhik Kumar. 2002. Tibetan youth increasingly frustrated with credo of non-violence. Electronic document, http://www.tibet.ca/en/wtnarchive/2000/2/21_1.html, accessed December 23, 2006.

Chiang Kai-shek. 1947. *China's destiny*. New York: Roy Publishers.

Clifford, James. 2001. Indigenous articulations. *Contemporary Pacific* 13 (2): 468–490.

Dikötter, Frank. 1992. *The discourse of race in modern China*. Stanford: Stanford University Press.

Dirlik, Arif, and Roxanne Prazniak. 2001. Introduction: Cultural identity and the politics of place. *Places and politics in an age of globalization*, edited by R. Prazniak and A. Drilik, 3–14. Boulder, CO: Rowman and Littlefield.

Gladney, Dru. 1994. Representing nationality in China: Refiguring majority/minority identities. *The Journal of Asian Studies* 53 (1): 92–123.

——. 1997. The question of minority identity and indigeneity in post-colonial China. *Cultural Survival Quarterly* 21 (3): 50–54.

Goldstein, Melvyn, Dawei Sherap, and William R. Siebenschuh. 2004. *A Tibetan revolutionary: The political life and times of Bapa Phuntso Wangye.* Berkeley: University of California Press.

Hall, Stuart. 1996. On postmodernism and articulation: An interview with Stuart Hall. In *Stuart Hall: Critical dialogues in cultural studies,* edited by D. Morley and K. Chen, 131–150. London: Routledge.

Herzer, Eva. 2002. *Options for Tibet's future political status: Self-governance through an autonomous arrangement.* New Delhi: Tibetan Parliamentary and Policy Research.

Huber, Toni. 1997. Green Tibetans: A brief social history. In *Tibetan culture in the diaspora,* edited by F. Korum, 103–119. Vienna: Verlag der Östereichischen Akademie der Wissenchaften.

———. 2001. Shangri-la in exile: Representations of Tibetan identity and transnational culture. In *Imagining Tibet,* edited by T. Dodin and H. Rather, 357–372. Boston: Wisdom Publications.

Kapstein, Matthew. 2004. A thorn in the dragon's side: Tibetan Buddhist culture in China. In *Governing China's multiethnic frontiers,* edited by M. Rossabi, 230–269. Seattle: University of Washington Press.

Karlsson, Bengt G. 2003. Anthropology and the "indigenous slot": Claims to and debates about indigenous peoples' status in India. *Critique of anthropology* 23 (4): 403–423.

Kingsbury, Benedict. 1998. "Indigenous Peoples" in international law: A constructivist approach to the Asian controversy. *American Journal of International Law* 92 (3): 414–457.

Li, Tania Murray. 2000. Articulating indigenous identity in Indonesia: Resource politics and the tribal slot. *Comparative Studies in Society and History* 42 (1): 149–179.

Litzinger, Ralph. 2000. *Other Chinas: The Yao and the politics of national belonging.* Durham, NC: Duke University Press.

———. 2004. The mobilization of nature: Perspectives from northwest Yunnan. *China Quarterly* 178: 488–504.

Mackerras, Colin. 1994. *China's minorities: Integration and modernization in the twentieth century.* Hong Kong: Oxford University Press.

Martínez, Miguel Alfonso. 1999. *Human rights of indigenous peoples.* Final Report, United Nations Economic and Social Council, Commission on Human Rights. Electronic document, http://www.unhchr.ch/Huridocda/ Huridoca.nsf/0/696c51cf6f20b8bc802567c4003793ecOpendocument, accessed August 8, 2006.

Maybury-Lewis, David. 1997. *Indigenous peoples, ethnic groups, and the state.* Boston: Allyn and Bacon.

Niezen, Ronald. 2000. Recognizing indigenism: Canadian unity and the international movement of indigenous peoples. *Comparative Studies in Society and History* 42 (1): 119–148.

——. 2003. *The origins of indigenism: Human rights and the politics of identity.* Berkeley: University of California Press.

Sautman, Barry. 2002. Resolving the Tibet Question: Problems and prospects. *Journal of Contemporary China* 11 (30): 77–107.

Schein, Louisa. 2000. *Minority rules: The Miao and the feminine in China's cultural politics.* Durham, NC: Duke University Press.

Smith, Warren. 1996. *Tibetan nation: A history of Tibetan nationalism and Sino-Tibetan relations.* Boulder, CO: Westview Press.

Sperling, Elliot. 1994. The rhetoric of dissent: Tibetan pamphleteers. In *Resistance and reform in Tibet,* edited by R. Barnett, 267–284. Bloomington: Indiana University Press.

Tibet Information Network (TIN). 1996. *Cutting off the serpent's head: Tightening control in Tibet, 1994–1995.* New York: Human Rights Watch–Asia.

——. 2004. Tibetan stories: Extracts from "Notes on Tibet." May 4, 2004. ISSN: 3313–3315. Electronic document, http://www.tibetinfo.net, accessed August 1, 2005.

Tsing, Anna. 2003. Agrarian allegory and global futures. In *Nature in the global South: Environmental projects in South and Southeast Asia,* edited by P. Greenough and A. Tsing, 124–169. Durham, NC: Duke University Press.

Tuttle, Gray. 2005. *Tibetan Buddhists in the making of modern China.* New York: Columbia University Press.

Wang, Lixong. 2004. *Tibet facing imperialism of two kinds: An analysis of the Woeser incident.* Translated from Chinese edition, available on *World Tibet News* archives. Electronic document, http://www.asiademo.org, accessed December 21, 2004.

Yeh, Emily T. 2003. *Taming the Tibetan landscape: Chinese development and the transformation of agriculture.* Ph.D. dissertation, Energy and Resources Group, University of California, Berkeley.

"Our Struggle Has Just Begun": Experiences of Belonging and Mapuche Formations of Self

Claudia Briones

The vehicles that brought the people from Esquel, in the province of Chubut, and from Bariloche, in the province of Río Negro, arrived together late at night in the small town situated in the middle of the Patagonian steppe. As the travelers descended, warm greetings foretold of the joy they would experience when reuniting with other Mapuche brothers and sisters they had met at previous *fvta xawvn*, or parliaments, as well as getting to know other Mapuches for the first time. The affection displayed in every *chalitun* (greeting ritual) drew attention just as much as the different dresses of those who met to "shake hands" or to give a kiss à la Mapuche, on each cheek.

It mattered very little that some dressed in their best *bombacha,* hat, and handkerchief as a sign of rural origin, and that others showed off jean jackets and hoods that left only a small part of a face piercing exposed, anarchist-punk mottos, and Mapuche resistance slogans. Some women wore traditional skirts despite the cold that bit at their legs, while others wore pants and jackets so commonly used by those who live in "los pueblos." However, what mattered most was to perform and enjoy the greeting etiquette on arrival. Later, they would meet up in the school cafeteria respecting everyone's turn to some hot food. There they would continue conversing about the latest news, their expectations of the meeting that would last two full work days, and each person's responsibilities at this encounter. At last they would prepare to wake up early for the first public prayer before formally initiating the parliament that, for the fourth time, was bringing together Mapuche-Tehuelche communities and organizations of Chubut, the hosting province, as well as Mapuches from neighboring provinces. A similar gathering of people had attended previous parliaments in Vuelta del Río (April 2003), in Buenos Aires Chico (October 2003), and in the Prane community (April 2004), all located in the northwest of Chubut. Much like previous parliaments, the last afternoon of the meeting would be open to *wigka* or non-Mapuche (nonindigenous) contributors and organizations that wanted to show "their solidarity for the Mapuche struggle" or to propose some collaborative project. Also, a public announcement would be made to discuss the encroachment of mining companies on Mapuche lands and the legal proceedings that Mapuches were taking to combat this invasion. Perhaps the most novel aspect of this fourth meeting was its location in the Chubutean plateau. The location facilitated the access of people from Mapuche communities and villages placed nearby the zone where Valentín Sayweke, the cacique whose surrender in 1885 signaled the end of the so called Conquest of the Desert, had been "reserved."

In these types of gatherings, Mapuche identity crisis, its loss or strengthening in light of historic stigmatization by *wigka* or non-Mapuche society, is one of the reoccurring topics of debate. But in this chapter I am interested in showing that the concept of identity, including its politicization, is no more than the tip of the iceberg for understanding much more complicated processes of individuation (Grossberg 1996) and communalization (Brow 1990) that diversify, and at the same time assemble, what is understood and felt as "being Mapuche today."

In an earlier work (Briones 2006), I argued that distinct national formations of alterity promote differences in indigenous cultural productions and organizational processes. I explored how the diversification of Mapuche demands in Argentina is influenced by the provincial formations of alterity that are specific to each of the provincial states where the Mapuches are located and have high levels of visibility today: mainly, Chubut, Neuquén and Río Negro.[1] In this chapter, I explore other factors that also influence the diverse proposals and responses that arise in Mapuche cultural politics. I examine what I observed and heard at the IV Parliament, and in other Mapuche meetings, to present examples of diversity within the Mapuche community, such as gender, age, schooling, political participation, and so forth, and to identify activities and arguments that arose despite of and because of this diversity. Because of questions of space, I will focus on *pu wece*, or young people's, reflections and positionalities. For this analysis, I use some specific concepts to help understand what is it that makes a people that claim to be in resistance for over five centuries, and from this experience proclaim that "they are not going to subject our will," to also recognize that "our struggle as just begun."

I refer to the concept of Mapuche formations of self as an alternative to individuation in terms of subjectivity, identity, and agency. These formations of self emerge from specific national and provincial formations of alterity that are based on regional geographies of inclusion and exclusion. These regional geographies delineate a series of structured mobilities for Mapuches that foster to different degrees—or may even preclude—the opportunity and desire to come together despite of differences.

The point here not only is that Mapuche people construct different maps of meaning to interpret regional geographies and make sense of their structured mobilities. These contested maps also promote different strategic installations and affective investments of belonging. Likewise, I use the idea of the political economy of the production of cultural diversity to analyze the hegemonic constructions of aboriginality that are both challenged or reinscribed by Mapuche self-perceptions and the performances through which culture and politics are brought together in enactments that demand a more dignified spaces in the country where they live. A focus on Mapuche formations of self will allow me to explore emerging identities such as the punk Mapuches and the heavy metal Mapuches. I approach these identifications less as political identities spread by globalizing processes (Segato 2002), than as indicators and contemporary manifestations of some of the historical trajectories available to Mapuches since colonization.

I. Personal Experiences of Mapucheness

Once they were ready to begin the parliamentary session in a large circle on the school's covered patio, one of the organizer's requested that everyone prepared brief individual presentations. This round of presentations lasted much longer than anticipated because Don Ruperto, who was participating in this type of parliament for the first time, felt obligated to play host. Being the *logko,* or cacique, of the community closest to where the meeting was being held, he assumed that he needed to proceed with Mapuche etiquette and welcome the participants from other regions and provinces. Don Ruperto had arrived with a small group of representatives that included not only his wife and other elders, but also two adolescent women that held the position of *kallfv zomo,* or "holy girls," in the collective prayers of their Mapuche community. Because they lived closest to the meeting, Don Ruperto also assumed that he should provide the necessary infrastructure, especially ritual instruments, flags, containers to prepare el *mushay* to sprinkle while they engaged in prayer,[2] for the *gijipun* that initiated each day of the parliament.[3] On this occasion, the elders, who usually accompany the organizing committee in carrying out the group's rituals, shared the responsibility with Don Ruperto. During collective debates, this group of elders positioned themselves as "traditional authorities." They shared their thoughts with everyone present, identified community problems, and taught the Mapuche way to resolve certain issues. They also mediated disagreements and gave advice, urging people to preserve the unity of "the Mapuche that we are" and to respect traditional practices and customs. A central concern for the elders is the use and recuperation, according to the situation, of *mapuzugun,* or the traditional Mapuche language. By sharing *pu gvxam,* or truth stories, about suffering in the face of military campaigns and the dispossession of collective land, the elders historicized situations that many participants politicized.

The histories and experiences that the participants shared introduced diverse perspectives and were narrated from different subject positions. Participants who were active in the hosting organization reminded the group that this and previous parliaments were not the property of any one organization, but of all those present. They also emphasized that no topic of discussion was more important than any other because they all affected the Mapuche people. And, thus, the conversations started. A group of people attending the parliament for the first time, showed interest in meeting other Mapuches in order to learn how to organize an urban community in the neighboring localities where they lived. Other attendees—who had been selected as communal representatives of the provincial administration thus becoming functionaries of the non-Mapuche state apparatus—explained that they came together to learn about the problems of the Mapuche that they were supposed to be representing. Some attended to report that their lands where an object of mining prospecting and to solicit help in stopping the miners by force if necessary. Others asked for the parliament to intervene in land litigations that had resulted from disagreements with neighbors and family members. Several participants attended to solicit advice about how to defend their lands from local landowners and property holders. Some representatives spoke about their community's experience resisting eviction and how they had recuperated land through their own initiatives. Although a number of women participated in all the activities, but never spoke in public, other women lively shared how they began to get involved in the Mapuche struggle. For some, it was because they had always been rebels and needed to channel their rebelliousness, and for others, it was because of personal or family injustices that had made them realize the importance of defending their origins. Middle age men also presented contrasted views. One explained that to commit himself to his people he had to disobey advice given to him by the elders who encouraged him to be patient and not to rebel against injustices. Other said that he arrived at this commitment once he was able to understand the many "signs" since birth that had indicated he had received the *newen,* or special force, that marks those who should dedicate themselves to defending their people. Until then, he had been unable to read these signs amidst a life plagued by jails, alcoholism, family abandonment, and conversion to Evangelical cults. It was not until he experienced a more truthful and militant conversion that he was able to confront injustices, discrimination, and inequality.

However, it was the young people that arrived from Bariloche, (a city in the neighboring province of Río Negro well known for its tourist attractions) who consistently solicited the opinions of the elders. Self-defined as "Independent and Autonomous," many of these adolescents were participating in the parliament for the first time. The two young men responsible for supervising them had attended previous gatherings and were recognized as forming part of "the movement" *mapunky* (punk Mapuches) and *mapuheavy* (heavy metal Mapuches). Members of these movements claim that they give them a language through which to discuss rebellion, including the constant use of the letter "k" in place of "c" in names, poems, and messages. For example, Fakundo and Oskar say that to be a young urban indigenous person includes a fusion of experiences and realities that the joint words *mapu-heavy* and *mapunky* help to express. At eighteen, it does not matter to Fakundo that many people say what they declare comes from foreign trends or can be attributed to the fact that "they are at a rebellious age." He explains that:

> Obviously, we are rebels, we are rebels against a system, we are rebels against a form of life that our parents were forced to live … we feel this reflected in the punk attitude. In the city what other option do you have? … the issue is that today Mapuches are in the neighborhoods, today we are the *piqueteros,* the delinquents … the mayor's office is full of Mapuche. And this makes you mad because when it suits them they agree that we exist and when it suits them we are the worst trash

... anarkopunk helped me to think through some things such as how society is run, and from there to get to know about anarchism. ... Over anything else I am Mapuche, but in the city I take these tools ... that is what helps you when you are in the city. (Scandizzo 2004c)

In his early twenties, Oskar runs a program at a community radio in Bariloche that he defines as "underground, intercultural and emancipatory." He agrees with Fakundo that "getting to know punk and heavy helped me a lot to channel my rebellion." However, he recognizes that:

Many Mapuches reject us, they discriminate against us or they leave us out because of the way that we are, because we think this way, because we dress this way ... but today we are another form of expression of our people. ... Mapuche did not freeze in time and if everyone realizes this, many other people in the neighborhoods would also recognize it as a Mapuche way of being. (Cañuqueo 2003)

Mapunkies and mapuheavies take up metaphors from the poet David Añiñir, a self-defined as mapurbe (urban Mapuche), to make sense of their belonging as fusion. I would however contend that the notion of friction is more effective to help us understand how their processes of self-identification both question spaces of identity from the outside and destabilize the spaces that they provisionally occupy within the Mapuche community (cf. Tsing 2005).

Currently, their positionalities create friction with what they call "the system," a set of hegemonic values, practices of social control and effects of the political economy that place them in marginalized neighborhoods and in the margins of society, too close to political repression and too far away from the upper class young people with jobs, dignified housing, schooling and predictable futures. But they also create friction with other youth like themselves who have assumed the stigma of their poverty and given themselves up to distinct addictions, such as gang crime, premature fatherhood, or domestic violence. They view these youth as failing to recognize their Mapuche origins in the city. Furthermore, they create friction with the Mapucheness of their parents from whom they distance themselves because of the passivity that they have seemed to demonstrate in the face of injustices. These youth criticize earlier generations for accepting their invisibility as Mapuches when they arrived in towns to seek work after being dispossessed of their lands by private capital and the state itself. Finally, they place themselves in friction with the idea that Mapucheness is centrally linked to the countryside and rural life, and with cultural activists that vindicate themselves as "strugglers," while they let themselves be seduced by *wigka or nonindigenous* politics, the "old politics" as they call it, and end up concentrating their demands on services from the state, accepting multilateral financing for their projects, or traveling around the world as "grassroots representatives" of communities from which they are evermore distant. Mapunkies and mapuheavies do not only position themselves against power. Their bodily aesthetic also creates friction with dominant Mapuche discourses, resonating from both adults and other young people, who claim that the mapunkies and mapuheavies do not represent indigenous identity.

Some of the youth that were born and continue to live in rural communities, but have been obligated or desired to leave them in search of wage labor, do not necessarily vocalize their sense of belonging centrally in terms of being Mapuche. Despite the fact that some of these young people do accompany adults in community activities, the elderly tend to view them as emblematic of the next disappearance of cultural ancestry. The elders fear their abandonment of the use of traditional language, the gradual transformation of practices, and the decrease in respect owed to "los mayores." It is interesting that these same elders, who remember that when they were young and left the community to find work, they "behaved kind of wildly,"[4] do no make the association that today's youth are passing through a similar experience of momentary distancing from community that could be reversed in the future much like what occurred in their case.

However, for young people that live in rural settings and involve themselves in community problems, the defense of what it means to be Mapuche primarily rests on struggling against the dispossession of land that began with the consolidation of large landholding estates. As Marcelo explained:

> We are indigenous Mapuche communities and we have to make them respect us. ... And if we don't make them respect us, they walk all over us. ... The only solution that we have is that we have to struggle as Mapuches. And if we have to give our blood for our territory, we are going to do so. I am twenty years old and I was born in this community (Vuelta del Río), and if they want to take me away they are going to have to take me dead. Because we are all willing in this community. So I am very much in agreement with what they said, that we as an indigenous people have to make them respect us, we are going to get recognized and

in this way we are going to win the fight for our territories. The little that is left after the landowners took it away from our great-grandfathers. In 1940, the elders, the people had 700 sheep. Today the most that people have is 100 animals. That's what's left. Now we have to stand up and fight to win our territory. (Equipo Mapurbe 2003)

The importance that Marcelo and many communities place on struggling to maintain or to recuperate their land is also upheld by groups of urban young people, or *pu warriache*. However, the difference between these groups revolves around two issues: First, if urban youth will begin to appropriate these agendas so that their activism is exclusively demarcated by its support for the struggles of distinct communities, as has recently been the case with youth in the Centro Mapuche Bariloche, or if they will seek to complement this support with other activities that are more centered on urban problems. Secondly, if the notion of "Mapuche culture" will be restricted to traditional practices that would have to be relearned, or if it will be expanded to incorporate the diverse life trajectories that have occurred as Mapuches relocated to cities. This last idea is one that *mapurbes* explore. *Mapurbes* situate themselves close to the *mapunkies* and *mapuheavies* by questioning discourses that claim that "the face of *kultrún*" (Mapuche drum ritual) or ruralness defines Mapuche belonging, and that being born or living in towns transforms Mapuche into *Wigka*. However, *mapurbes* also distance themselves from *mapunkies and mapuheavies* by recognizing more diverse influences on their identity constructions than anarco-punk and heavy movements. They propose less of a fused identity and more of a notion of the "mapuchization" of places, technologies, and artistic expressions. Lorena, a student of communication science and a member of the Mapuche Communication Working Group that edits the fanzine *Mapurbe*, admits that one of the most frequent errors of urban Mapuche youth is an attempt "to return to their roots" without questioning stereotypes and without it being Mapuches themselves who discuss "seriously what is it that we want to do." When discussing claims about the impossibility of being both urban and Mapuche, Lorena explains:

Even though you are living in the neighborhood Villa Obrera of Fiske Menuko (General Roca) city, you are Mapuche, you have your identity and an immediate origin in that place. You have your roots there. This brings forth a lot of issues, your parents did not come here because they are people who simply cross their arms and do nothing, because they have never done anything to fight. ... What happens with the majority of young people is that they renounce their families, their origins, their roots, they break with their history. ... What we intend to do is to use some basic codes, a way to understand ourselves as young people, being in the city and having a ton of other characteristics in every neighborhood, in every Mapuche ... those of us that are proposing these things from the cities didn't know each other ... in what would have been natural Mapuche settings: not in organizations, not in *kamarikun* (collective rituals) not from anything like this; we met up on the corners, game rooms or in concerts. ... The majority take it: "You can not be Mapuche and walk around with a punk hairdo and hiking boots," "You can't be Mapuche and walk around with your jacket full of shiny things, patches." It's as if something doesn't make sense, but we return to the theme of what is purely Mapuche. This is Mapuche, and this is not. I know that it can be difficult for many of our people, especially the older ones, it can even produce shock. But I also understand that one can not propose a serious reconstruction as a people if they do not take a moment to minimally reflect on how we ended up after the mess that resulted from the invasions by the Chilean and Argentine states. ... I'm not saying that it's going to be massive, but something that little by little will seep into these places, in the different groups in the city that form spaces of resistance. And one begins to fill these spaces with the Mapuche identities even though they were originally created or were made by other types of identity ... like a *lamuen* (sister) says, you can *mapuchizar* these spaces (make them Mapuche) and not always live *awinkándote* (moving forward to being non-Mapuche, whitening you)." (Scandizzo 2004a)

And yet other youth activists, such as the organizers of the Coordinating Organization of the Neuquén Mapuches (COM), question the *mapunky* and *mapuheavy* ideas of "fusion" and the *mapurbes* ideas of "mapuchization." Speaking at length about the objectives of the newspaper they publish, *Tayiñ Rakizuam* (our thoughts), Amankay Ñancucheo, a 19-year-old woman who is one of its editors, explained:

Besides informing and explaining political issues, we also want to reveal our culture, our philosophy. We seek to present what is the essence of our people, their origins, their traditions, because there are many brothers and sisters in the city and in the countryside, many kids like us, who don't know each other, that don't have this type of information, about their *tuwun* (place of spiritual origin), their *kupalme* (principal affiliation with their ancestry). (Pedro Cayuqueo 2004)

Umawtufe, director of the newspaper, explains how these other young people identify themselves as the *pu kona* of the COM:

> We believe that in the twenty-first century, the young people must reassume this role and we do this through the press, the radio, photography, which are non-Mapuche tools, western, but they help us to denounce what is happening in our communities and also, of course, to strengthen our philosophical and cultural ideas. I think that we can not speak about politics without recognizing the Mapuche philosophy, our cosmic vision, which for us goes hand in hand. This is our objective. (Pedro Cayuqueo 2004)

As children of the founders and present leaders of the COM, an organization created in the 1990s to claim for the recognition of Mapuche territory and self-determination (Briones 1999), these adolescents have been brought up in cities, but in a militant Mapuche environment. They share perspectives with their parents, but these perspectives may be different from those of other young people. For example, for some youth, the cultural battle against the dispossession of land implies, above all else, a respect for Mapuche ways that avoids (con)fusions. Pagi, a 20 year old, states: "We have an identity, we listen to heavy and punk every day, but this does not make us mapuche punk. I think that a Mapuche does not have to be known as punk or heavy because you are losing your values, your principals, your identity. You are not recognizing your identity" (Scandizzo 2004b).

Amancay agrees with Pagi in that, "You can not be two things at the same time. You can not be an ambiguous thing. You have to be one thing at a time, and beyond that, if you consider yourself Mapuche, you have a whole culture, a language." In regards to what traditional Mapuche culture offers, Pagi emphasizes that it even offers: "Your own music. .... Instruments. You have everything, it is not necessary to seek out another culture to supposedly fulfill what you are missing out on" (Scandizzo 2004b).

At this point in the interview, Pagi's mothers, a known leader of the COM, intervenes:

> Just as Pagi says, you are Argentine or you are Mapuche; you are punk or you are Mapuche. We do not want a mix of cultures, we want to be

only one. Now, Mapuches can opt to be punk and Mapuche at the same time, Argentine and everything else, but they have an infinite number of identities and neither of these things identify them firmly. It's a little of each thing, and we do not want a little of each thing, we want to be what we are. We do not need a little bit of punk to make us feel better. We would break with our identity, with our characteristics as Mapuche, by being punk. (Scandizzo 2004b)

The examples that I have discussed above do not even exhaust all the positionalities assumed by young Mapuches. For example, at the parliament, a proposal was made in favor of a law that would standardize the teaching of *mapuzugun* in all the provincial schools. They asked: Why do public schools teach English and refuse to teach the languages of the original peoples? In urban contexts, demands usually center around politics to rescue lost or denied cultural elements. However, this proposal brought generational tensions.

Until this moment, the youth of Bariloche and the young adult organizers of the meeting had been in agreement about all the motions proposed. They agreed on condemning the repression of youth protests in Bariloche and to continue requesting the removal of the Julio Argentino Roca monument from the Civic Center of the city. They agreed on supporting the recovery of land and of opposing mining projects. However, when debate touched on making changes to public education, sides divided. The organizers of previous parliaments argued against it. They could not entrust important Mapuche matters to the public school system without first making substantial transformations to the educational system. Without this first, it would be impossible to avoid the continued promotion of a *wigka* education that would at most end up incorporating random Mapuche words into the program of study rather than any substantial Mapuche thought. Although the young people agreed with this, they repeatedly asked the elders to take a clear position on the issue. At this point the coordinator of the discussion tried to ease the tension insisting that the elders needed more time to respond to such complicated matters. At this point, when the issue was the extent to which Mapuche traditional knowledge could provide answers for everything or whether there were questions that could be solved from other cultural perspectives, an elder asked for the floor and negotiated between the two generations:

I am going to speak a little. As the *peñi* (brother) says, we do not understand the complications of the laws. But I tell the brothers and sisters to take their children to the prayer sessions of their elders so that they learn and motivate themselves. The school is not enough because the white *compañeros* laugh at them and this hinders everything (all that had been advanced in strengthening self-esteem) at school.

This example shows that we can not assume the automatic existence of coincidences among Mapuche even if they share generation, gender, place of reference, political commitment, or schooling. Surprising and despite the fact that the mapunky and mapuheavy aesthetic appears to be the most at odds with the rural communities (upheld as the epitome of Mapucheness) elders often demonstrate public affection toward mapunkies and mapuheavies and encourage them showing them affection through gestures and words in more intimate conversations.

II. Making Sense of Diversity

My examples do not exhaust the lived experiences of mapucheness or the political positionalities of Mapuche communities and their organizations.[5] However, these contexts illustrate a series of fragmented experiences that common sense might identify as a weakness for the empowerment of the "Mapuche People-Nation." Elsewhere, I argue that today the force of the Mapuche movement in Argentina resides precisely in the disagreements that have been generated after 20 years of sustained struggle. The more these disagreements stimulate diverse positions, the more dynamic the movement becomes. Thus, it opens a diversity of options for Mapuche subjectivities (Briones et. al 2004). Differences among Mapuches are not anecdotal or obstacles to the production of collective politics. I analyze them as differential formations of self made possible by the dominant national and provincial formations of alterity. These formations produced an image of a white Argentinian society that, on the one hand, excluded Indians, blacks and peasants from national participation, and, on the other hand, produced classificatory categories to discriminate and stigmatize them as "internal others" subject to biopolicies that regulated their differentiated existence (Briones 2002b).

Not an exclusive product of the state, these formations of alterity have predominantly depended on shifting historical geographies of inclusion and exclusion (Briones 2005). To make sense of these geographies, I use Lawrence Grossberg's conceptualization of "identity" as a consequence of the action of a series of stratifying, differentiating and territorializing machines (1992, 1993, 1996) that spatialize differences and, thus, define individual's positions in the socioeconomic structure of the country. I will use my reflections on *mapunkies, mapuheavies,* and *mapurbes* to illustrate some aspects of how these machines operate.[6]

As Grossberg indicates, the stratifying machines provide access to certain types of experiences, and knowledge about the world and about oneself. They thus make subjectivity an unequally distributed universal value. Experiences of the world are produced from particular positions that, although temporary, determine access to knowledge and bring about attachments to places that individuals call "home" and from which they speak. In the case that I analyze, these machines have created positions of subalternity and alterity that, as Fakundo explains, force Mapuches to live in poor neighborhoods in Patagonian cities, suffering hunger and cold. As Mapuches themselves recognize, economic and cultural stigmatizations have led and continue to lead many Mapuches to silence aspects of their identity, and avoid comments against their "*kultrun* face," their illiteracy or poverty. Yet the same circumstances have also led other Mapuches to rebel against these stereotypes. Some such as the *pu kona* of COM, tend to channel this rebellion in the form of political confrontation by reaffirming traditional Mapuche values and practices. For those that did not meet though practical organizations the path was more arduous, as Lorena explains:

> Okay pal, but at the end of the day we are in this, we are feeling this desperation, with this doubt because … is it our heritage? What's going on? And little by little … you came to realize that it was all a process, you are someone that had emerged out of a ton of things that happened to your family. You begin to realize that your parents aren't shitheads: "If it happened to someone here and to someone in that neighborhood also. … What's happening here?" You start to question a bunch of things and you say: "It didn't just begin now since we started to get together here, it began a long time ago." Then you vindicate those stories of resistance that they continuously hide from us (our own families as well as official history). (Scandizzo 2004a)

According to Grossberg, the second group of machines are differentiating machines. These are linked to truth regimes responsible for the production of differentiated identity systems that condition the potential alliances among different people. In Argentina, ethnicized and racialized collectives, ("indigenous," "African," "immigrants," "creoles" and "blackheads") are hierarchically ordered and segregated within a national biomoral system (Briones 2004). This system rests on a political economy of production of cultural diversity that reproduces internal inequalities by rendering invisible certain differences while also insidiously ordering others. Within this political economy, the aboriginality (Beckett 1988; Briones 1998) of some individuals not only impedes their citizenship, but also blemishes the self-proclaimed "Eurocentered" profile of the nation. In the particular case of the Mapuches, stigmatized constructions of aboriginality were not meant to lead to the extreme tropes of savagery and primitivism that befell other original peoples in the country. However, it sought to disqualify Mapuches from citizenship using accusations that they were "belligerent invasive foreigners," eternally Chilean and responsible for the extinction of the *tehuelche* people, the alleged original "Argentines" from Patagonia. Also, narrow constructions of aboriginality produce a fixed Mapuche identity linked to the countryside and a lifestyle dedicated to breeding goats and sheep. These beliefs which confine Mapuches to the past delegitimize their present sense of belonging and their current struggle for their rights as citizens and Mapuches. Additionally, as Fakundo points out, being Mapuche becomes folklore and the "embarrassment of touristic Bariloche," and as Lorena adds, naturalizes an idea of the "Indian" as someone who permanently bows their head, is lazy, a failure or a drunk, neighbors and strangers being convinced that social mobility or urbanization is unusual for Mapuches and therefore dilutes their aboriginality.

Lastly, territorializing machines are the fruit of unequal structures of access and distribution to cultural and economic capital (Grossberg 1992: 106 ff.). They condition structured mobilities that determine what types of places each person can occupy, how they occupy them, how much space they have to move around, and how they can move through these places. These mobilities also provoke differential access to resources affecting an individual's capacity to articulate pleasures and desires and their ability to fight for political, cultural and economic redistribution and spatial reorganization. When Lorena speaks about the places where young Mapuches encounter each other and the strategies that emerge to fight for a dignified identity she discloses:

First you disguise yourself even in those places that are supposedly your places, where you can talk sincerely. You are the *Mecha*, the *Gula*, names that disguise your belonging. "But what's your last name?"— I'm Ñancucheo.—I'm Cañuqueo. You begin to engage in a whole chain narrating your life. "What happened is that my old man came here...—Why did your old man come here?—"Because the military ran him off"; or "There was a need to build a rural school in the province and they threw him out"; or "The Turkish trader arrived and stole the land." And by the end you realize a whole bunch of coincidences and ... your identity, that was initially a punk, enlarges quite a bit. (Scandizzo 2004a)

Mapuche geographies have shifted considerably since early in the 19th century because of birth of private expropriations of land and to official state actions, such as the military occupation of Patagonia (geared to symbolically incorporate the southern portion of the country into the nation). Forced labor migrations have also contributed to the geographic mobility of Mapuches. These migrations resulted in diverse land tenure regimes from the adjudication of land in reservations, or in communal agricultural and pastoral properties (Briones y Delrio 2002). At the end of any these processes Mapuche families were landless rural dwellers, forced to migrate to other rural areas of to the cities in search of a livelihood (Olivera and Briones 1987). Thus, despite hegemonic constructions of aboriginality that proclaim the inevitable deindianization of Mapuches in urban environments, the last national census (2001) showed that today the majority of the self-proclaimed Mapuche in Argentina live in different cities, precisely where their sense of belonging is more systematically questioned and denied.

Given this general situation, suspicions are particularly intense about the authenticity of mapunkies and mapuheavies, as well as indigenous intellectuals whose schooling and political capacity distances them from the image of the "true indígena" (rural, passive, incompetent, submissive, and easily satisfied by basic aid policies). While remaining in communities or rural areas has been a historical obstacle for Mapuche schooling and social mobility, migration to urban centers has made these things possible in a limited way. Thus, a significant professional development of indigenous citizens is still far off. Moreover, when this professionalization does occur, the social pressures in urban areas are so strong that many people render their origins invisible. Although, this process has begun to reverse itself (and Lorena is just one example of young activists from humble families that have struggled to study at the university level), it is exactly in these situations that greater questions and more stringent requirements arise regarding indigenous authenticity, legitimacy and representation.

In sum, the basic panorama that I have laid out should help us understand (1) why Lorena attributes distinct Mapuche urban trajectories to the historic effects of land dispossession; (2) why Mapuches are currently located in the most precarious neighborhoods in Argentine towns and cities and; (3) why Mapuche parliaments reflect such varied demands; and (4) why the recognition of urban aboriginality is so vividly asserted and demanded by some Mapuches.

III. Convergences through Difference, Differentiations through Convergences

The Mapuche struggle has gained considerable force and political visibility in the last 20 years. To explain this achievement in a country that has tried to make invisible and mute its diversity in such a consistent way, we have to pay attention to how the proposals of the "pueblo nación Mapuche" defy stigmatizations and make possible convergences despite of and through differences. In earlier works, I have analyzed the ways in which Mapuches have brought together culture and politics to stage their unity before non-Mapuche society (Briones 1999 and 2003). Here it interests me to point out some of the practices that Mapuches engage in to recreate this sense of unity despite differences from and for Mapuches themselves.

In encounters such as the parliaments, Mapuches mobilize cognitive and affective patterns of communalization. They recreate a sense of belonging together (Brow 1990) in and through practices that are seen as recurring and broadly shared by Mapuches from diverse time periods and places of origin, no matter how innovative these practices are. The greeting, welcoming and farewell rituals, sharing food and housing, or the reaffirmation that takes place in public prayer, stimulate nowadays, as they did before, a sustained and affective investment in displaying a public feeling of being Mapuche. However, not everybody needs to do or know everything. At the parliament while some of the most active participants in the discussions did not engage in the public prayer, others, particularly some local people, arrived early to join others in the orations, but left as soon as debates began.

From the beginning of the parliament, it became clear that different experiences not only produce distinct needs and interests, but they also produce distinct styles of confrontation and consensus building. Convergences thus emerge not necessarily from shared problems, but rather from the performative potential that speaking about "the struggle," *(la lucha)* and projecting a common present and future can provide. This also nourishes a shared sense of becoming through identification with a history of injustice and stories of dispossession and suffering. Moreover, giving testimony to the distinct circumstances that obligate each and every person to defend themselves from some form of subjugation, not only creates a basis for a common conversation, but also articulates strategic installations that help to transform "common people" with disparate life trajectories and structured mobilities into "strugglers." After the Third Parliament, Rosa Rúa Nahuelquir, who along with her husband, Atilio Curiñanco, became famous having been taken to public trial by the Italian corporation, Benetton (Briones and Ramos 2005), explains:

> In the beginning they (the representatives of Benetton) told us to sign and give up the place. We said no because this place belonged to us. We are children of the land, and we want to be here to try to get ahead, progress, and sustain ourselves. So we said no. The struggle is not going to be so easy. When our ancestors lived, they ran them off when they wanted, but today we are going to stand up and fight. I think that Atilio also feels this way, he is not going to give up. ... I feel stronger (after this Parliament). At no time did I feel weak to keep up with the struggle even though I had not done it before. ... I know that some of my brothers and sisters are going to accompany me to see if the courts recognize our rights once and for all. ... I never thought that I would be involved in this. With everything that has happened to us, I (realized that) have to defend my identity. (Moyano 2004)

Now then, if speaking about the struggle and the "more than five centuries of resistance" creates nowadays a common ground, it is paradoxical that it also reinforces the idea that "our struggle has just begun." As a result, middle aged people like Rosa and Atilio feel that much is yet to come. As Rosa explains, this is so because "they ran our ancestors off whenever they wanted." And Atilio laments the faintheartedness of the ancestors that permitted them to do so. He remembers: "my deceased father said, 'Let it be, son. Don't make problems,' and things kept happening."

Young people also explain that the initial channeling of their uncontrollable rebellion against the system and older generations of Mapuches led them to begin to engage in diverse battles, not of them anchored in a Mapuche identification. In time many of them realized that, despite appearances, these battles were a response, although a mediated one, to urban trajectories that have led a large number of Mapuches to live in the poor neighborhoods of distinct towns and cities. They are also a result of the structural conditions that make it hard for them to find work, get schooling, and escape addictions and political persecution.

As shown by the reflective testimonies we shared, these conditions can be more easily grasped or denounced than changed or overcome. Vying to make them visible, mapunkies and mapuheavies articulate their struggles by exploring identifications (age, gender, class, ethnic background, and region) in fusion–friction with distinct places of attachment that render apparent the injustices and inequalities that each of these places are associated with. The mapurbes primarily intend to "Mapuchecize" the distinct contexts in which they live to counteract notions of uprootedness, and avoid renouncing to current Mapuche diversity that they see as a result of *Wigka* supremacy. Curiously, younger groups are affectionate with the generation of elders that Rosa and Atilio hold responsible for their own identity crisis and their late disobedience. Yet young Mapuches not only disapprove of their submissive parents, but also criticize branches of Mapuche cultural activism that, since the 1980s, have fought against the hegemonic invisibilization of indigenous peoples. While perhaps not giving sufficient credit to these activists, today in their forties, for the achievements that resulted from their tenacious crusade in defense of the pueblo, autonomy and territory, mapunkies, mapuheavies, and mapurbes understand that the Mapuche identity that most organizations promote is so one-sided that has become an iron cage. They also claim that much of the organizations' cultural politics amounts to, or favors Wigka realpolitik rather than expressing Mapuche views on the political. Therefore, this Mapuche youth also seems to feel that their struggle has just begun.

It is not easy to explain this convergent, but selective assumption of responsibility that leads both mature and young Mapuche alike to feel disappointed by their parents' generation. It is also curious that the performative potential of speaking about "the struggle" does not suffice to neutralize such an assumption either, even more so when one realizes that any parents' generation forms part of the commonly accepted belief in "more than five centuries of resistance." Perhaps at this point we should think critically about the unintended consequences and side-effects of the affective investments that allow the conversion of categories of oppression into categories of emancipation.

The more these investments are based on self demanding standards of achievement, the more they seem to foster expectations that "the struggle" should effect definitive results. Emancipatory struggles (always open-ended, especially when thought of in the plural form) that are overall conceived as part of a "war of position"—to be conducted across many different and varying fronts of struggle (Hall 1986: 17)—start being judged and felt as part of a "war of manoeuvre," condensed into one front and one moment of struggle to obtain a strategic victory. The impact of moves that challenged cultural hegemonies and forced them to become more refined tends to be overlooked, thus creating a sense of failure or insufficiency. In addition, the more strength needed to challenge the structured mobilities that seem available to us, the more discredited the efforts of those from whom we inherited the struggles seem to appear, thus leading us to feel that "our struggle has just begun." This in turn seems to provoke further attachment to a distant past, the past of the grandparents and the *kujfikece* or ancestors, who can be idealized as bursting with more certainties and direction than the parent generation, and as an untainted incarnation of the "more of five centuries of resistance." In any event, what tends to go unnoticed is that the emergence of (one's own) more expansive conceptions of "autonomy" or "politics" that recreates differences among generations, and even within each generation, feeds on both inherited wisdoms and inherited disappointments.

Notes

1. This is the investigative line of Grupo de Estudios en Aboriginalidad, Provincias y Nación (GEAPRONA) and has also been explored by other members of the team (Cañuqueo et al. 2005; Falaschi et al. 2005; GEAPRONA 2001; Mombello 2005, Ramos and Delrio 2005).

2. *Mushay* is chicha.

3. *Gijipun* is collective prayer.

4. In the sense that they did not understand or forgot the advice of their grandparents.

5. Solely within the field of organizations with Mapuche philosophy and leadership, the use of key concepts such as the right to a territory, to self-determination and to the management of natural resources is widespread. However, different styles of confrontation and strategic installations are tried nowadays. As a result, differences become apparent around the ways in which they address the non indigenous civil society, the extent to which they accept or reject to get involved with state agencies, and agree to multilateral funding for their undertakings. Most of the testimonies that I discuss here belong to

cultural activists that refuse to participate in state-sponsored programs, even more so when multilateral funding is involved. For a broader perspective on the various positionalities of Mapuche communities and organizations in Argentina, please consult Briones 1999, 2002a; Hernández 2003; Kropff 2005; Ramos 2004; Valverde 2004.

6. For a more detailed illustration of state policies that have affected the Mapuche people in Argentina, see for instance Briones 1999; Delrio 2003; Lenton 2005.

References

Beckett, Jeremy. 1988. *Past and present: The construction of aboriginality.* Canberra: Aboriginal Studies Press.

Briones Claudia. 1998. *La alteridad del cuarto mundo. Una deconstrucción antropológica de la diferencia.* Buenos Aires: Ediciones del Sol.

———. 1999. *Weaving "the Mapuche People": The cultural politics of organizations with indigenous philosophy and leadership.* UMI # 9959459: 495. Ann Arbor, Michigan: University Microfilms International.

———. 2002a. "We are neither an ethnic group nor a minority but a Pueblo-Nación Originario. The cultural politics of organizations with Mapuche philosophy and leadership." In *Contemporary perspectives on the Native peoples of Pampa, Patagonia, and Tierra del Fuego: Living on the edge,* edited by C. Briones and J. L. Lanata, 101–120. Bergin and Garvey Series in Anthropology. Westport, CT: Greenwood Publishing.

———. 2002b. Mestizaje y Blanqueamiento como Coordenadas de Aboriginalidad y Nación en Argentina. *RUNA, Universidad de Buenos Aires* 23: 61–88.

———. 2003. Re-membering the dis-membered: A drama about Mapuche and anthropological cultural production in three scenes (4th edition). Special Issue, "Indigenous Struggles and Contested Identities in Argentina," edited by S. Hirsch and G. Gordillo. *Journal of Latin American Anthropology* 8 (3): 31–58.

———. 2004. Construcciones de Aboriginalidad en Argentina. *Bulletin de la Société Suisse des Américanistes* 68: 73–90.

———. 2005. Formaciones de alteridad: Contextos globales, procesos nacionales y provinciales. In *Cartografías Argentinas: Políticas indigenistas y formaciones provinciales de Alteridad,* edited by C. Briones, 11–43. Buenos Aires: Editorial Antropofagia.

———. 2006. Questioning state geographies of inclusion in Argentina: The cultural politics of organizations with Mapuche leadership and philosophy. In *Cultural agency in the Americas,* edited by Doris Sommer, 248–278. Durham, NC: Duke University Press.

Briones, Claudia, Lorena Cañuqueo, Laura Kropff, and Miguel Leuman. 2004. Escenas del multiculturalismo neoliberal. Una proyección desde el sur. Ponencia presentada en la *Segunda Reunión del Grupo de Trabajo CLACSO "Cultura y Poder"* coordinado por Alejandro Grimson. Porto Alegre, 15 al 17 de septiembre. *LACES,* vol. 1. San Diego.

Briones, Claudia, and Walter Delrio. 2002. Patria sí, Colonias también. Estrategias diferenciales de radicación de indígenas en Pampa y Patagonia (1885–1900). In *Fronteras, ciudades y estados, Tomo I,* edited by A. Teruel, M. Lacarrieu, and O. Jerez, 45–78. Córdoba: Alción Editora.

Briones, Claudia, and Ana Ramos. 2005. Audiencias y Contextos: La historia de "Benetton contra los Mapuche." *E-misférica,* Hemispheric Institute of Performance and Politics, New York University 2 (1), spring. Electronic document, http://hemisphericinstitute.org/journal/2_1/briones.html, accessed December, 22, 2006.

Brow, James. 1990. Notes on community, hegemony, and the uses of the past. *Anthropological Quarterly* 63 (1): 1–6.

Cañuqueo, Lorena. 2003. Inche Mapuche Ngen. *Azkintuwe.* Periódico Mapuche, 1, October. Electronic document, http://www.nodo50.org/azkintuwe/furilofche.htm, accessed December, 22, 2006.

Cañuqueo, Lorena, Laura Kropff, Mariela Rodríguez, and Ana Vivaldi. 2005. Tierras, indios y zonas en la provincia de Río Negro. In *Cartografías Argentinas: Políticas indigenistas y formaciones provinciales de alteridad,* edited by C. Briones, 119–149. Buenos Aires: Antropofagia.

Cayuqueo, Pedro. 2004. Los konas de Neuquén. *Azkintuwe.* Periódico Mapuche, 11, pp.: 16–17, December. Electronic document, http://argentina.indymedia.org/news/2004/12/249140.php, accessed December, 22, 2006.

Delrio, Walter. 2003. *Etnogénesis, hegemonía y nación. Construcción de identidades en norpatagonia, 1880–1930.* Tesis de Doctorado, Facultad de Filosofía y Letras, Universidad de Buenos Aires.

Equipo Mapurbe. 2003. II Parlamento Mapuche del Chubut: Taiñ rakizuam. *Azkintuwe.* Periódico Mapuche, 2, December. Electronic document, http://www.mapuche.info/azkin/azkintuwe_02.pdf, accessed December 22, 2006.

Falaschi, Carlos, Fernando Sánchez, and Andrea Szulc. 2005. Políticas indigenistas en Neuquén: pasado y presente. In *Cartografías Argentinas: Políticas indigenistas y formaciones provinciales de alteridad,* edited by C. Briones, 179–221. Buenos Aires: Antropofagia.

Grupo de Estudios en Aboriginalidad, Provincias y Nación ([GEAPRONA]: C. Briones, M. Carrasco, W. Delrío, D. Escolar, L. Kropff, P. Lanusse, D. Lenton, M. Lorenzetti, L. Mombello, M. Rodríguez, F. Sanchez, A. Szulc, and A. Vivaldi). 2001. Lo provincial y lo nacional: Explorando tendencias actuales en los reclamos indígenas en Argentina. Ponencia en el *4° Congreso Chileno de Antropología*. Colegio de Antropólogos de Chile y Universidad de Chile. Noviembre. Electronic document, http://rehue.csociales.uchile.cl/antropologia/congreso/s1612.html, accessed July, 22, 2005.

Grossberg, Lawrence. 1992. *We gotta get out of this place. popular conservatism and postmodern culture*. New York: Routledge.

———. 1993. Cultural Studies/New Worlds. In *Race, identity, and representation in education*, edited by C. McCarthy and W. Crichlow, 89–105. New York: Routledge.

———. 1996. Identity and cultural studies: Is that all there is? In *Questions of cultural identity*, edited by S. Hall and P. Du Gay, 87–107. London: Sage Publications.

Hall, Stuart. 1986. Gramsci's relevance for the study of race and ethnicity. *Journal of Communication Inquiry* 10 (2): 5–27.

Hernández, Isabel. 2003. *Autonomía o ciudadanía incompleta. El Pueblo Mapuche en Chile y Argentina*. Chile: CEPAL y Pehuén Editores.

Kropff, Laura. 2005. Activismo mapuche en Argentina: Trayectoria histórica y nuevas tendencias. In *Pueblos indígenas, estado y democracia*, edited by Pablo Dávalos, 103–132. Buenos Aires: CLACSO.

Lenton, Diana. 2005. Centauros y Alcaloides. *Discurso parlamentario sobre la política indígena en Argentina: 1880–1970*. Tesis de Doctorado, Facultad de Filosofía y Letras, Universidad de Buenos Aires.

Mombello, Laura. 2005. La "mística neuquina." Marcas y disputas de provinciana y alteridad en una provincia joven. In *Cartografías Argentinas: Políticas indigenistas y formaciones provinciales de alteridad*, edited by C. Briones, 151–178. Buenos Aires: Antropofagia.

Moyano, Adrián. 2004. Las voces del Trawün. *Azkintuwe*. Periódico Mapuche, 6, May. Electronic document, http://www.mapuche.info/azkin/azkintuwe_06.pdf, accessed December 22, 2006.

Olivera, Miguel, and Claudia Briones. 1987. Proceso y estructura: Transformaciones asociadas al régimen de "reserva de tierras" en una Agrupación mapuche. *Cuadernos de Historia Regional*. Buenos Aires, UNLU-EUDEBA, 4(10): 29–73.

Ramos, Ana. 2004. *Modos de Hablar y lugares sociales. El liderazgo mapuche en Colonia Cushamen (1995–2002)*. Tesis de Maestría en Análisis del Discurso, Facultad de Filosofía y Letras, Universidad de Buenos Aires.

Ramos, Ana, and Walter Delrio. 2005. Trayectorias de oposición. Los mapuches y tehuelches frente a la hegemonía en Chubut. In *Cartografías Argentinas: Políticas indigenistas y formaciones provinciales de alteridad,* edited by C. Briones, 79–117. Buenos Aires: Antropofagia.

Scandizzo, Hernán. 2004a. Entrevista a Lorena Caniuqueo: El despertar warriache. *Azkintuwe.* Periódico Mapuche, 4, March. Electronic document, http://www.mapuche.info/azkin/azkintuwe_04.pdf, accessed December 22, 2006.

——. 2004b. Inche ta mapunky. Jóvenes en el Puelmapu. *Azkintuwe.* Periódico Mapuche, 10, October. Electronic document, http://www.nodo50.org/azkintuwe/mari_10.htm, accessed July 22, 2005.

——. 2004c. *Tratamos de volver a nuestra raíz desde el cemento.* Entrevista a Fakundo Huala. Electronic document, http://www.mapuexpress.net/publicaciones/mapunky-scandizzo.htm, accessed July 22, 2005.

Segato, Rita. 2002. Identidades Políticas y Alteridades Históricas. Una crítica a las certezas del pluralismo Global. *Nueva Sociedad* 178: 104–125.

Tsing, Anna Lowenhaupt. 2005. *Friction. An Ethnography of Global Connection.* Princeton: Princeton University Press.

Valverde, Sebastián. 2004. *Los movimientos indígenas en la Argentina: Las estrategias políticas de las organizaciones mapuches.* Lanús: Ediciones Cooperativas de la UNLa.

Part 2

Territory and Questions of Sovereignty

Indigeneity as Relational Identity: The Construction of Australian Land Rights

Francesca Merlan

In Australia, positively valued contrasts of indigeneity with non-indigeneity—of "indigenous people" with the nonindigenous or "settler" population—have posited the consubstantiality of Aboriginal being and culture with the "land," in contrast with the externality to it of nonindigenous being. Although "indigeneity" invariably involves the notion of connectedness to territory, the extent of this emphasis in Australia has been extraordinary.

Though the phrase "indigenous people(s)" has become much commoner in recent years, the concept of indigeneity is by no means new. It is relevant, in Australia as elsewhere, at two main levels of relational contrast. First, "indigenous" (native, autochthonous and the like), contrasts with non-native, dis- or re-placed. In this sense, it has long been possible to refer to, for example, "indigenous trees" in contrast to introduced trees, even to "indigenous people" in given places in contrast with nonindigenous ones, although such usage may not previously have been as common as it has become. Second, through a logic of shared difference, many current uses of the term *indigenous* also presuppose commonality among those who are "native" and contrastive, in their specific locales, with the non-native. Thus, indigenous peoples may be envisioned as forming a world collectivity in contrast to their various "others." At this second level of relational identity, the notion of commonality among indigenous people has become much more explicit over several recent decades, in close relation to the growth of international organizations that have made indigenous issues their specific concern (Niezen 2000). Recent times, in short, have witnessed a new collective ethnogenesis, the rise of a category of "indigenous peoples."[1]

But each "indigenous people" as identified in this global intersection comes to it with its distinctive background and set of debates as these have been pursued, mainly (but not only) within particular national spaces, making them different from other "indigeneities." Distinctive indigeneities will intersect in different ways with objectifications and historical structures shaped at the global level. A number of recent critical discussions of indigeneity (Castree 2004; Hirtz 2003; Niezen 2000) have made the points that it is an emergent, relative, "interpellative" term, with relationships to place (Escobar 2001) central to the practical and symbolic contestations involved. Thinking of indigeneity in terms of the two levels of contrast outlined above allows a better understanding of how the history of relationships at the first level has resulted in emphases that intersect in particular ways with dimensions of global indigenism.

Although the strength and widespread diffusion of the notion of Aboriginal consubstantiality with the land might make one think it is of long standing, this emphasis has became common acceptation only within the past 30 years or so. In this chapter, I explore the quality and the conditions of possibility of this identification, as well as current indications of change in it.

The relative recency of these views of Aboriginal relationship to land suggests that their promulgation must be seen as partly, perhaps even largely, independent of Aborigines' practice and thinking. The view of Aboriginal consubstantiality with the land is best seen in constructionist terms, as produced in indigenous–nonindigenous interaction under particular conditions (asymmetrical as between these two categories of actor), rather than naturalistically, as a self-evident aspect of indigenous lifeways that has only lately achieved some wider national acceptance.

Some might think it perverse, and even subversive of indigenous interests, to examine such a prevalent understanding in these terms. By constructionism, Hacking (1998: 54) suggests we mean "various sociological, historical and philosophical projects that aim at displaying or analysing actual, historically situated, social interactions or causal routes that led to or were involved in the construction of an entity." To posit that an entity such as "indigenous landedness" has been constructed does not deny the reality of its constituent elements. But recency and change in these constructs suggests that we may best understand them as time-bound and changing products in which practical and symbolic implications of indigenous–nonindigenous relationship are cast and contested.

Native—Aborigine—Indigene: Terminological Issues and Beyond

Consideration of terminological usage brings to light issues of periodization, generalization, and evolving ethical connotations in the relationship of Australia's indigenous people to the changing nation-state. The continuously contested, unsettled character of designation may help explain the reflux and recent extension of the qualifier "indigenous," given new currency by internationalist usages, to cover some usages previously managed by use of the "A-terms," "Aboriginal" and "Aborigine."

As many have observed (e.g., Attwood 1988; Beckett 1988), there were no "Aborigines" prior to European occupation. The term *Aborigine* was fairly standard national usage by the 1980s, but over the past two decades has begun to be supplanted in some contexts by *indigenous* and, especially, the phrase "indigenous people."

Official and vernacular usages that highlighted "colour," "degree of blood," and the like were common into mid–20th century. The qualifying and referring term *native* remained in use as recently as 1960 (and, indeed, the governmental unit "Native Affairs Branch" was the precursor to "Department of Aboriginal Affairs"), before the Bulletin (an influential national Australian periodical) began setting it off in quotation marks in 1963 (Rowse 1998: 9).

Generalization and nationalization of usage after WWII centered on variants of the terms *aborigine* and *aboriginal,* but instabilities in these terms point to a variety of issues. "Aborigine" had the sense of "originary," but its connotations were not necessarily positive. In vernacular usage this term was often reduced to "abo" and was distinctly pejorative. Only recently have the word *Aborigine* and the phrase "Aboriginal people" come to have more generally positive connotations.

Until the late 1970s, national usage of *aborigine* was not capitalized, and its sense remained linked to the generic referent, aborigine of any colony of settlement. Indigenous historian James Miller conveyed some sense of its feeling–tone: "the word Aboriginal is a Latin-derived English word, which was originally used to refer to any native people of any part of the world ... [it] did not give my people a separate identity" (in Rowse 1998: 10). Replacement of lower- by uppercase "A" signaled national sensitivity to the question of moving from a more generic to a more nationally specific kind of designation, one that could connote special status and belonging. Miller himself preferred "Koori" (his book is entitled *Koori: A Will to Win,* 1985), a native-language-derived term for (indigenous) *person* (a regional term but now of quite extensive distribution, in New South Wales, Victoria, and Tasmania).[2]

Rather than such regional designations, the move to some form of uppercase "A" filled most official usages. But there was trouble not only over the beginning of the word, also the end. For a time, government style manuals preferred *Aboriginal* as the adjective and singular, but accepted both *Aboriginals* and *Aborigines* as the plural. Later style recommendations retained *Aboriginal* as the singular but opted against *Aboriginals* as plural. I have heard a joke made a number of times by educated Aboriginal people that they have trouble knowing whether they are nouns or adjectives—a wry expression of frustration at feeling designated, categorized, "talked about." There has been a tendency for the "-al" forms to be put aside as nouns, and for the adjectival form "Aboriginal" to be coupled with nouns that underline personhood and "peoplehood" (as in "Aboriginal peoples"; cf. "Jews" vs. "Jewish people").

It is probably no surprise that the specific terms *indigenous* and *indigeneity* are of recently revised and limited usage in Australia, as is the case in many other countries where they are current. The recent diffusion of "indigeneity" has seemingly occurred through the work and writing of key participants in UN processes and working groups, that is, those approaching settler–"indigenous" relations through the perspectives and organizational machinery of multilateral organizations, and universalistic terms and values including "human rights." A signal usage in Australia was that by the Aboriginal and Torres Strait Islander Social Justice Commissioner Michael Dodson in his first report of 1995 entitled "Indigenous Social Justice Strategies and Recommendations," a submission to the Parliament of the Commonwealth of Australia. Dodson, the first Commissioner, had been a participant in the Working Group on Indigenous Populations, created (after a number of preliminary meetings, see Niezen 2000: 126–129) as the principal UN group concerned with indigenous people's rights.

In the northern Australian Aboriginal settlements and town camps I know (Merlan 1998), people do not designate themselves as "indigenous" and have no, or only passive, familiarity with the word. Those who work in what is sometimes acerbically called by critics the "Aboriginal industry"—federal bureaucrats in relevant areas; or employees of such State organizations as the Aboriginal Areas Protection Authority—recall the word *indigenous* having come into usage in the 1980s as greater levels of participation came about on the part of rather small numbers of Aboriginal people in the World Council of Indigenous People (formed in Copenhagen in 1977), and which convened its third general assembly in Canberra in 1985.

The recent or refocused terminology of "indigeneity" overlaps and (to date) only in specific contexts supersedes the terminology of reference that had been in place.

But this term, like forms of the "A-word," does not lend itself gracefully to use as a noun. And in any case, the phrase "indigenous people(s)" tends to be the restricted usage of the more activist and educated indigenous few, hardly the vocabulary of local community members. As with the initial vacillation about the capitalization of "Aborigine," there has been some debate in Australia about whether upper- or lowercase "I" is appropriate to this word, partly a question about specificity versus generality, but also about dignifying its reference.

Modes of designating Australian people(s) or "populations" have, in short, been unsettled and contentious. "Indigenous," too, does not solve usage problems, because it belongs to an educated register and also suggests a universalism that many indigenous people find foreign. To acknowledge that "indigeneity" as a conceptual term, and one now used to refer to kinds of persons and interests, has recently been pressed into wider service is to recognize its "constructed" character.

Let us now return to the wider constructionist emphasis of recent decades with which we began, namely, that of Australian indigeneity (still continentally as likely to be called "Australian Aboriginality") as involving consubstantial relationship to land. The national consciousness of Aborigines as "belonging to" the land has emerged in the post–WWII period, as part of the revindication of Aboriginal "difference." During that time, the relationships constitutive of global indigenous organization have increased many fold, with landedness as one of the many issues circulating within them.

Landedness in Sociopolitical Context: The Growth of Culturalist Emphasis

Ideas about the consubstantiality of Aboriginal being with the land now have a wide distribution, especially among those with any positive orientation toward indigenous matters. The following sketches exemplify its circulation in academic writing, as well as among prominent indigenous bureaucrats and other spokespeople.

Indigenous Australian popular musician Kev Carmody is quoted as saying, "The whole culture is based on the spirituality of the land. It's almost as if the whole land was a cathedral" (Maddock 1991: 227, from *Sydney Morning Herald* July 7, 1989). Carmody grew up on a cattle station on the Darling Downs of southeast Queensland, the son of an "Irish-Murri" (Irish Aboriginal) marriage. Sent away from home to a Christian school at age ten, he later spent some years as a back country laborer. At the age of 33, he went to University. He has released song albums steadily since 1989, and works in a variety of styles: country, reggae, and funk. Many of his songs deal with black deaths in custody, land rights, and Aboriginal dispossession, and he espouses broader, left-leaning political concerns and interests.

Galarrwuy Yunupingu, former director of the Northern Land Council, issued a recent collection of papers with the title, "Our Land Is Our Life" (Yunupingu 1997). Born at Yirrkala in northeast Arnhem Land when it was still a Methodist mission, as a promising young man he served as a translator for his elders when, after some years of preliminary disputation, in 1968 the indigenous people of the area brought a suit against Nabalco (a Swiss mining company), and the Australian Commonwealth (which had excised for the company a mining lease from the Arnhem Reserve, gazetted since 1933), in opposition to the takeover of what they regarded as their land for the development of a bauxite mine. The decision, handed down in 1971 by the Northern Territory Supreme Court, found that there was no doctrine of communal native title in Australian law, rendering superfluous more detailed analysis of certain aspects of the claimants' case. It also found that while these Yolngu people had relations to the land amounting to a complex system of tenure, their claim was not proprietary, since it allowed neither for exclusion nor alienation; and the court was not satisfied that the group relationship to land had persisted unchanged since the declaration of British sovereignty over Australia, which it held to be necessary for a positive finding for the claimants (Williams 1986). This long-running case was a key event in the development of "land rights" as a—at times *the*—central indigenous issue on the national agenda.

A kind of social science portrayal that has emerged in recent ethnography may be illustrated by brief quotation from a recent book, entitled *Land Is Life: From Bush to Town, The Story of the Yanyuwa People*:

I have chosen the title "land is life" to stress how important land is to the Yanyuwa. For the Yanyuwa, the land is alive with meanings. The land tells the stories of creation. The spirits of ancestral beings reside in the land and demand respect. The land also tells the story of contact history. For example, the signs of old camps and old cattle yards are there to be read. Yanyuwa travelling the country will often address the land and their ancestors that are embodied in it. The intimate linking of land and life in Aboriginal ways of perceiving the world is well illustrated by the catch phrase of the modern Aboriginal land rights movement "land is life," which takes the famous American geographer Carl Sauer's expression "land and life" one step further. (Baker 1999: 5)

Baker, a cultural geographer, comments that "the Aboriginal understanding that land has a personality that needs to be understood is something cultural geographers have only recently discovered" (Baker 1999: 6). This understanding undoubtedly has been most fully developed in the recent work of anthropologists, and diffused to other disciplines. It has also blossomed in a variety of forms, but probably the most influential have been those of popular culture: novels, documentaries, and films, such as Roeg's film *Walkabout* (1971), Chatwin's book *Songlines* (1987), Marlo Morgan's *Mutant Message Down Under* (2004), and works of biography, history, and song.

Emphases in the Australianist ethnological and anthropological literature on socioterritoriality can be shown to have changed a great deal over time. The classic late-19th- and early-20th-century ethnographies of Spencer and Gillen (e.g., *The Arunta* 1927) described a landscape crisscrossed with what are now called "dreaming tracks," and dotted with named places associated with events of ancestral movement and creation; there was little elaboration of the bodily and personal connections, subsequently documented by anthropologists, in which we now understand relations of people to places to be cast. Evidence and interpretation of these emerged over several decades in the work of T. G. H. Strehlow (1965, 1970), Stanner (1958, 1965), Munn (1970), and others, partly in the context of anthropological studies of religion and symbolism. Anthropological ethnographies of the last several decades have tended to have the dimension of landedness at their core, in a period marked by shift in government policy from emphasis on assimilation—the policy goal of leveling of differences between Aborigines and others—to greater openness to the persistence of difference, a federal policy rubric of "self-determination," and the creation of an organizational framework of land rights, land funds, and sacred sites protection (Bennett 1989: 29–37; Nettheim, Meyers, and Craig 2002: chs. 11–13).

In the period before WWII, calls for social justice and land rights for Aborigines came from churches, unions, Communists and other relatively marginal but socially critical groups, often in collaboration with activist indigenous representatives (Merlan 2005: 478–480 and references therein). In the late 1960s, there developed an urban-based, more radical indigenous activism strongly influenced by American Black Power models (Curthoys 2002; Foley 2001). A call for "land rights" emerged, largely from urban-based indigenous activists in Sydney and Melbourne. Especially at first, this was a political demand strongly grounded in protest of dispossession without a necessarily or strictly traditionalist cultural content. But the next few decades, from the 1970s to the present, were to see the strengthening of requirements that "land rights" be based on traditionalist criteria, without which passage of statutory measures may have been politically indefensible.[3]

The passage of a federal land rights statute in the Northern Territory (the *Aboriginal [Northern Territory] Land Rights Act 1976*), establishment of reserves and land rights regimes in other states, and, most recently, the Mabo High Court decision of 1992 (amounting to a positive finding concerning communal native title, as opposed to the Yirrkala case) and the passage of a federal *Native Title Act 1993,* have created demand for reports and evidence concerning the situation of particular indigenous groups. This work has involved anthropologists, archaeologists, historians, and nonacademic professionals, notably lawyers. Anthropological under-standings of the specific forms of connectedness of people to land have become a resource in legal processes based on traditionalist terms, and played some role in the shaping of public understanding of the strength, if not the particulars, of connection between Aboriginal people and land. The processes of land rights and native title claims have been subjects of anthropological analysis, a lens through which to observe the dynamics of the interaction of governments with indigenous people and organizations created in their interest (Glaskin 2002; Merlan 1998; Povinelli 2002).

Despite all this, there has been call for, but resistance to, recognition of indigenous relation to land on a national level. The federal Labor government of the early 1980s experimented with extending a land rights program to the entire country, but was forced into disarray by objections from its own party politicians at State level, from corporate Australia, and the broader populace (Rowse 1988). Passage of the Native Title Act (1993) came closest, amounting to recognition that "native title" may have survived, and providing the means for this question to be examined in particular instances. It was however, not, straightforwardly a measure of recognition, but partly preemptive: legal findings of communal native title on an island in the Torres Strait between Papua New Guinea and Australia (the 1992 Mabo case) created an atmosphere that, although greeted by some, was seen by others as creating "uncertainty," and requiring statutory management. There has come about an understanding of Aboriginal consubstantiality with the land, and at the same time, struggle to contain what might be the consequences of general recognition of Aboriginal landedness.

Certain obvious ways of explaining the centrality of struggle over land, although relevant, are in themselves insufficient to understanding it. Some might deprecate the coinage, see the intensity of concern with land rights as a consequence of Australia's having so much of it to negotiate with. But the intensity of struggle has shown that land is not freely given. Others would see the emphasis as a natural consequence of the character and intensity of Aborigines' relationship to land; but it is implausible that the emphasis on attachment and "land rights" can be interpreted simply as indigenous initiative or a direct rendering of indigenous priorities. Over 50 percent of those censused as indigenous in 2001 live in or near major cities (although it is equally important that indigenous people account for nearly half of those residents in remote Australia).[4] No single kind of relationship to country can be presumed among the indigenous population. Nor would indigenous people by themselves be likely to project a single kind of representation, though many no doubt profess strong attachment to country. In any event, I take the view of Jones and Hill-Burnett (1982: 235) that although "culture is an important part of the process [of ethnogenesis, or the emergence of identity], the role it plays is neither simple nor direct." It is important to distinguish the expressions of attachment of indigenous people and groups to lands from the "transvalued" national emphasis on consubstantiality with "the land" (cf. Tambiah 1996: 192), which cannot be interpreted as unmediated indigenous expression.

Some theorists have tended to suggest that policy orientations concerning place and territoriality have been principally authored by indigenous people themselves. Escobar (2001), for example, designates "defensive localization" the erection of barriers around place on the part of indigenous people. Castree uses the phrase "strong localism" for the notion of an "exclusionary" place project "pursued at the expense of wider nonindigenous groupings within and beyond national borders" (2004: 163). Such versions may be applicable in some contexts. But despite some defensive populist Australian understandings of land rights in such terms (or ones involving manipulation of indigenous people and interests by others), indigenous "defensive localization" is not an appropriate analysis of Australian versions of land rights. One important reason why is lack of resonance with indigenous understandings, over the length of settlement history. Let us consider some examples of the disparity between what seem to be more direct indigenously authored expressions of intention versus others.

In a number of well-documented instances, Aborigines in earlier colonized parts of Australia demanded land as a matter of right joined to their aim to pursue agrarian livelihood from early colonial settlement (see, e.g., Barwick 1998; Goodall 1996). In the landmark Gurindji walk off of the 1960s, Aboriginal workers subject over many years to poor conditions on the large, English-owned Wave Hill cattle property in the northwestern Northern Territory, initially conceived of their emergent struggle as one for better conditions, better wages, and for "citizenship" rights. The extension to Aborigines of "citizenship" or "citizen's rights" was generally seen in the 1960s as the progressive way forward in the management of indigenous issues, but was then expected to facilitate more or less rapid assimilation to a "mainstream" Australian way of life. Although Wave Hill Aborigines probably did not express themselves in those terms, they clearly wished to have means to pursue an independent livelihood. Eventually Wave Hill workers also demanded a portion of land from the Wave Hill leasehold on which they planned to establish their own cattle company.[5] Their original claims for improved conditions were transmuted into a much broader emergent demand for "land rights" that, although it resonated with Gurindji understandings of their relations to country, was in conception and organization partly of outside origin. Wave Hill Aborigines were advised throughout their struggle by union and Australian Communist Party members (Attwood 2003: 187–190, 260–282; Hardy 1968) a fact that partly accounts for the syndicalist emphasis in their early demands. The conception of "land rights" as stemming from and sustaining a distinctively Aboriginal culture is more recent, and tends to be formulated as a matter of principle and morality, distanced from practical considerations.

The examples given above show that Aboriginal people, too, tended to conceptualize restoration of land partly as a matter of entitlement and justice, but also as the basis of livelihood. At various times policy efforts were made to explicitly link everyday livelihood concerns with land rights. As mentioned above, initial formulation of the federal land rights bill in the mid-1970s included provision for land grants on a "needs" basis (Merlan 1994).[6] But this was dropped as too contentious and politically difficult to achieve: if people are simply "needy," how do they differ from the other needy people? What entitlement can they evince? In 1974, an Aboriginal Land Fund Commission was federally funded to buy land for Aboriginal corporate groups. The later Indigenous Land Fund established by the Keating Labor government in the 1990s (at the same time as a broader "social justice package" was formulated) has been intended to provide for purchase of land for those indigenous people who seem unlikely to benefit from land claims, native title, or other measures that require demonstration of continuous, traditionally based relations to land. However, pressures arising from the modes of government planning, funding and accountability have demonstrably skewed some land-based projects toward unrealistically large, commercially oriented ventures where Aborigines themselves may have had something much more modest, locally focused and continuous with their previous experience in mind (see Cowlishaw 1999; Thiele 1982).

The connection between entitlement (as "traditional owner" or "native title holder") and resource and income issues has been among the liveliest and most contentious questions in relation to land claims and grants among local indigenous people. This must be seen in light of the fact that even land granted through the land-rights process remains, in many ways, permeable to external interventions of many kinds. Notionally "inalienable Aboriginal freehold" that results from grant in the Northern Territory Land Rights process is inherently permeable, in that subsurface mineral rights, though subject to royalty negotiation, remain with the British Crown (as is true of all land in Australia). Negotiations, however, may result in benefit streams. The other side of this coin is that many Aboriginal groups are keen for exploration, and sometimes also mining development, to occur (where this does not meet with strong local objections on particular grounds). Negotiation of possible development has on many occasions revealed diversity of opinion about connection to places, allowable conditions of their exploitation, and intense struggle among indigenous people over criteria and levels of entitlement to involvement and to benefit. They see these issues of "culture" and identity as fundamental, but such struggles often draw adverse comment from observers who have internalized an etherealized culturalist view of indigenous relations to land.

All this points to complex production of connection to land as indigenous issue. The question, "What is indigeneity?" is complicated, and not only at the level of counting noses (Castree 2004; Niezen 2000); so has been the question of whether and how connection to land may be formulated *as* an indigenous issue.

Land rights processes have produced notable outcomes—about half of the Northern Territory is Aboriginal inalienable freehold. Native title results have, on the whole, been protracted and less decisive.[7] But success for those who can achieve it can be disenfranchising and disempowering of those who cannot demonstrate the appropriate kind of relationship; and also, of those who, while they might be able to demonstrate such a relationship to land if pressed, do not see an imperative to do so and therefore can also be judged wanting (see examples in Merlan 1995, 1998; Povinelli 2002).

Since the 1970s, land rights has been constituted as an indigenous issue in pressurized and often adversarial circumstances. Cast by some as a question of national legitimacy, restoration of land to Aborigines is seen by others to imperil the sovereignty of the Australian state. The finding of native title has been understood by some to raise the specter that all of Australia may be subject to contest as "Aboriginal land." Despite some of these perspectives, politicians have generally been pragmatic about what the electorate will accept. And despite assertions of some that relationship to land is integral to Aboriginal culture, forms of land rights and native title repeatedly raise questions in the electorate about "special treatment." From the late 1960s, there has been activist assertion, and at least partial national acceptance, of the view that indigenous recuperation without land rights is impossible. But at the same time, a related, but different, idea had had some currency, that the granting of land to Aborigines would *in itself* be restorative, and allow them to live better lives. Especially in the last several years, consistent reporting of dire Aboriginal living conditions has supported skepticism about the practical and restorative values of land rights, and has stimulated renewed expression of views that Aborigines' entitlements to land should be no different from anyone else's (e.g., Howson 2005).

Constitution of "land rights" as key indigenous issue over the last several decades has been achieved by generalizing, etherealizing and essentializing notions of the relationship of Aborigines to land, and restoration of entitlement to land as crucial to indigenous identity, recuperation as well as national legitimacy. The forms of struggle have seen the construction of land rights pushed in a culturalist direction, and distanced from questions of how indigenous people live, and are to live, that they had themselves often posed.

Australia in Context

"Indigenism," Castree (2004: 151) proposes, is about the control of place; contemporary indigenist struggles are over goods that are all place linked, including land itself, material artifacts, and knowledges. There is palpable anxiety about what control might mean in the context of indigenous–nonindigenous relations in Australia.

Characteristic of Australia is the extent to which Aboriginal (or indigenous) issues touch a raw nerve: they are "unfinished business." Sensitivity is shown by the designation as "History Wars" of recent debates concerning historical interpretation. Recent histories that seek to break what anthropologist William Stanner (1968) called the "great Australian silence" by bringing to light the colonial treatment of indigenous people have been dubbed "black armband" history. The phrase was coined by Australian historian Professor Geoffrey Blainey in 1993, and used approvingly a few years later by Australia's current (1996–2006) Prime Minister, John Howard. These "wars" are highly oppositional, the "history" involved clearly not considered past in terms of its symbolic and practical potential. Over the last 35 years since the Yirrkala decision, they have played a role in a shift from views of settlement history as the occupation of underutilized, perhaps unowned territory,[8] to prevalent (if not universal) views of it as having involved colonial appropriation. This change has been stimulated by debate around many legal decisions on related matters in Australia and the Commonwealth (see, e.g., discussion of Australian and Canadian land rights cases in Nettheim, Myers, and Craig 2002: 86–89), and concomitant debate involving government, academicians, courts and others about history, memory, and possibilities of reconciliation.

But just as with the formulation of land rights, this more revealing history cannot be simply generalized as "indigenous" history. That is, it is not history as a great many indigenous people would narrate their past. Many of their own tellings would be more localistic, inclusive of their own cooptation by settlers and outsiders, and though morally grounded, less judgmental and open to the multifaceted and approachable qualities of outsiders that become evident in close interaction, despite known facts of their having acted cruelly and unjustly (Cowlishaw 1999; Hercus and Sutton 1986; Merlan 1978; Rose 1984; Rowse 1987).

Indigenous localism is related to the incompleteness, or fragment-ariness, of national indigenous action. Some of the most penetrating anthropological accounts have treated localism and small scale as an *essential* characteristic of indigenous Australian social formations.

Anthropologist Basil Sansom (1982) argues that, paradoxically, localism is what social orders across the continent have in common: "particularistic manifestations, consociate experience and a conception of a closed set of others who are truly and really one's Countrymen." This small-scale quality of Aboriginal life constitutes the continental "Aboriginal commonality," and "contains the countervailing forces that would need to be overcome if a pan-Aboriginal ethnogenesis were to be achieved" (Sansom 1982: 135). The building of indigenous translocal solidarities would, on this view, necessarily involve considerable social change. This change, paradoxically, is largely achieved in the extent to which indigenous people become exposed to, and internalize, wider social perspectives and relativize their own situation in terms of them.

Jones and Hill-Burnett (1982) called "ethnogenesis" the development through the 1960s and 1970s of a pan-Aboriginal movement. International linkages (e.g., to UN and other world bodies) were more limited than they are now. They emphasize tension between localism and demands for broader unity in the generation of a common Aboriginality and political mobilization. Indigenous positions became more focused at a national level in the late 1960s and early 1970s. Although certain events were undoubtedly influential (e.g., the establishment of an Aboriginal "tent embassy" in front of Parliament House on Australia Day, 1972), these were organized and carried out by a small group of militants (Foley 2001; Jones and Hill-Burnett 1982: 222)—often called "urban activists"—and could not by themselves bring Aboriginal constituencies from around the country together. The different character and time-depth of settler–indigenous relations in different parts of the continent have resulted in persisting, substantial indigenous differentiation. Radicalism, much to the frustration of "urban" activists, is frequently disavowed and avoided by what are often called "tradition-oriented Aborigines." Arguably, the concerting of indigenous positions is most likely in confrontational dialogue with "outside" agents and organizations. For example, government (and often, the general populace), often take unifying views of Aborigines as a "problem" in terms of economic, health, social and political issues, creating circumstances that effectively require and sometimes produce unity of response. To this day it is meaningful to speak of national dimensions of indigenous social mobilization only as in close interrelation with supporting structures of the wider society.

The late 1960s radicalism referred to above contrasts with, but also makes more sense in terms of, the fact that Australian government has tended to take a controlling role in the formation (and dissolution) of political representative groups among Aborigines. Government has consistently sought to treat peak bodies as advisory, rather than concede them executive powers (see Howard 1977; Rowse 2000; Tatz 1977, among many other references to this issue). This was most recently exemplified by the dissolution of the Aboriginal and Torres Strait Islander Commission (ATSIC), the successor to the federal Department of Aboriginal Affairs and peak indigenous body from 1989, in April 2004, and the mainstreaming of its functions within government departments. The government has named a small indigenous advisory group from across the continent to take its place. Over time, this control has reproduced the tendency for any emergent indigenous elite to be part of, or directly dependent on, governmental structures. Jones and Hill-Burnett (1982: 224) suggested a key problem associated with this is "how a population can produce changes in their status while the consciousness is controlled by the institutions of the larger society" (1982: 239). I would not accept that formulation in full. As I have tried to show elsewhere (Merlan 1995, 2005), efforts at such "control" are often blunted against indigenous forms of understanding that are not in the terms generally formulated in the press and public settings of the dominant society. This "otherness"—or lack of attunement—can inhibit Aboriginal people's ability to make their terms intelligible to a wider public, and to achieve results that reflect them.

While it is easy to point to factors that limit the growth of Aboriginal political solidarity, forms of Australian "semisovereignty" with respect to continental space and national identity play a role in shaping projections of indigeneity capable of generalization and mediation to government and nonindigenous Australian society.

Australia famously emerged as a dumping ground for British convicts, some of whom were not so much criminal as the flotsam and jetsam of British modernization and the effects of its imperial free trade and deagrarianization policies. That kind of self-understanding is now subjectively past (if absorbing) history for most Australians. But that Australia has always, in this and other ways, been directly shaped by the play of international forces is more immediately relevant. Australia developed as a particular kind of colony, bound to its mother society in almost immediate, full-blown dependence on the growth of the world wool trade and Britain's phase of "textile industrialism" and the displacement of sheep farming for wool to the southern hemisphere. Australia's second destiny was to serve as a "geographical branch of English agricultural capitalism" (McMichael 1984: 243). Pastoralism and agriculture have been differentially distributed in accordance with geographical possibility, and have constituted two fairly distinct continental accumulative regimes.

Australia's environmental, social, and historical peculiarities are all linked. Australia was settled from its coasts and its (nonindigenous) population largely lives there. Pastoralism, especially in the north and west, has tended to overlap more completely with those "open spaces" in which Aboriginal systems of law and custom were more likely to survive in recognizable form in their necessary adaptations to settler society. For all its size, Australian metropole–hinterland relations have always been massively skewed toward the urban. Just 40 years after settlement, in the Port Philip region, the urban population of Sydney was double the rural one. Coastal urban areas are widely separated; inland infrastructure is sparse. Today, following trends detectible since the early 20th century, most inland nonmetropolitan areas are losing population, and some assert that the inland has lost its population base (Cribb 1994). Growth areas are metropolitan fringe and coastal. The federalist state system is highly centrist.

The continent is seven-tenths arid or semiarid, and of limited arability (resulting in enormous costs of "productivist" land use practices, Gray and Lawrence 2001: 140, 143). Both rural regimes, pastoral and agricultural, have had to deal over the long term with problems of markets, the tyranny of distances, and susceptibility to foreign ownership. Post–WWII prosperity in the agricultural sector, and the rise of Japan as a major agricultural importer, contributed to reinforcement of Australia's free market orientation as well as its market dependence, and the direct impact of world processes on local productive and social relations. Retreat from land-extensive commodity production in parts of the continent, and conversion where possible to the "amenity" regimes of parks and tourism has been marked (Holmes 1996; Merlan 1999). Mining, the extractive industry par excellence, remains Australia's greatest sector of direct foreign investment by far.

In changing ways over time, these specialized and productivist relations to the Australian continent have readily lent themselves to imaginings of originary indigeneity, focused more on remote than settler-proximate areas (although variations exist, such as portrayal of persisting "traditionality" beneath metropolitan Sydney in the film *The Last Wave* [Weir 1977]). These perspectives are permeated by certain imaginings of indigenous personhood (even if it has become politically incorrect to say so). Australians have always fantasized "undomesticated" Aboriginality, and imagined its continuation in remote spaces. To some extent this has deflected public attention from changing, actual, and often deplorable living conditions of remote-area indigenous people (but representations of this have become more insistent and harder to dispel in recent years). There is, thus, susceptibility to notions of indigenous occupation of the continent on "indigenous terms," precluding (in the view of many) the legitimacy of modified lifestyles and technologies (e.g., Toyotas). Notions of continental indigeneity center representationally on the remote-area population, whose phenotypical and cultural distinctiveness make them most clearly identifiable by the general public as "authentically" continuous with the precolonial population. Onto such indigenous people are projected notions of maximal difference compared to the wider society and its occupancy of land. (However, the view of Aborigines as living in terms of conserving, nontransformative relations to country is now also sometimes debunked as anachronistic.)

On these somewhat problematic bases—despair and celebration of the alien and intractable qualities of the continent, and of Aborigines as "out there" and culturally and physically distinctive—"land rights" have been capable of serving as collective cultural symbol for indigenous and nonindigenous people, and (with some greater difficulty) object of practical struggle. Though earliest and most clearly articulated as a political demand by urban-dwelling indigenous activists, "needs"-based demand and political protest have repeatedly been translated into national representations of indigenous attachment to country featuring a rather metaphysical view of the autochthonous indigene. Paradoxically, institutionalized forms of land rights achieved on the basis of these struggles quickly turn out, problematically, to force the exposure (e.g., through claims and the legal and administrative processes of native title) of what appears, according to the public criteria established, to be the "inauthenticity," the insufficiency according to traditionalist criteria, of all but the few (Merlan 1998; Povinelli 1993).

Contrasting with this nativizing view of the continent, the history of governance and settlement in Australia has always been thoroughly inflected by a carefully considered liberal economism (Collins 1985 suggestively characterizes Australia as "Benthamite"—utilitarian, legalist and positivist) that contains its social and cultural capacity to recognize and value such difference as Aborigines represent, whether fantasized or more objectively appreciated. The formulation of indigenous title under the Land Rights Act in the Northern Territory as "inalienable freehold" enshrines a timeless relation to land. (This also prevents its being sold off, and Aborigines' complete displacement from it.) In terms of what many persons and organizations see as the "real" world, this version of ownership is criticized as singular and an alleged barrier to economic activity. Objections to land rights so far enshrined may come to have renewed significance in the near future, as—given current worldwide sense of energy crisis—larger-scale export of uranium comes back on the political horizon, much of the known reserve in parts of the Northern Territory and remote Australia where Aborigines either have freehold title or forms of pursuable interest.

Nonindigenous and indigenous kinds of relations to land are often considered polar opposites, and irreconcilable. In practice, they some-times are (Merlan 1991). Newer emphases on regional and partnership agreements among Aboriginal organizations and government have produced productive and cooperative models in some instances (see ATSIC 2003: 222 ff.). Benthamite or otherwise, they exemplify possibilities of moderate and outcome-focused approaches to negotiation of interests. Future discussion in these (if not more oppositional) terms seems bound to involve questions of the capacity of Aboriginal-held land to be commoditized and, thus, capable of being more directly brought within the productivist terms of Australian colonial settlement. Such questions may be raised in future by indigenous, as well as nonindigenous people.

Implications

In characterizing indigeneity as emergent, relative, and "interpellative," Castree also recognizes that the recent expansion of translocal interconnection and solidarity represents a shift in scale and intensity of activity; and that such extension "establishes commonality among manifest differences" (2004: 153).

The particular Australian construction of land rights as indigenous issue, always contentious and never wholeheartedly accepted by the wider population, has been molded in the interactions between indigenous and nonindigenous persons and agencies. It has depended on representations of Aborigines and their relations to land in traditionalist and essentialist terms. I have sketched some background to the national susceptibility and tendency to such terms, as well as opposition to them.

Land rights (including, for these purposes, also native title) have made possible great practical gains in some ways, brought about real changes in national awareness and recognition of indigenous people, and played a role, with both positive and negative consequences, in the reinforcement and contestation of identity politics among indigenous people themselves. But land rights have also reinforced already strong, limiting ideas within Australian society concerning authentic Aboriginal identity and being as necessarily linked to land, or else of lesser value; and have delayed recognition of the ways in which, now that indigenous people are no longer chiefly dependent on land for their daily subsistence, their relations to it are recontextualized and relativized to other aspects of their lives. It has recently become more possible to say openly that no return of land to indigenous people will, by itself, be restorative to the extent, or precisely in the ways, imagined by many at the outset by land rights supporters. There is anguished call for improvement in indigenous social conditions, which will probably neither be as "traditional" as the rest of Australia might imagine, nor as fully "assimilated" to dominant Australian ways of life as some might wish.

Recently, some indigenous leaders have moderated the emphasis on indigenous distinctiveness as the basis of (cultural) survival, and have focused on notions of responsibility, livelihood, the need for productive social engagement, as well as the nitty-gritty details of banking, parenting, domestic planning, and other quotidian issues (Pearson 2000). Some of those who espouse this reorientation are criticized as sounding like the conservatives who have dominated the federal political environment for a decade now, virtually unopposed. Since around the mid-1990s in Australia, the ruling conservative government has sought to shift the emphasis away from "indigenous rights" and cultural difference, and engage with indigenous people on a basis of what is termed "practical reconciliation" (Grattan 2000). For many, this sounds uncomfortably like the policy rubric of "assimilation" that predominated into the 1960s, before the era of "self-determination" and the associated heightening of concern with difference in which culturalist notions of Aboriginal landedness flourished. Disparities between specific local indigenous priorities, and those priorities of indigenous people more directly shaped by wider national and international perspectives, is a constant matter for negotiation (and sometimes incomprehension) between members of local communities, and indigenous and nonindigenous people advising them from organizational bases that have a foothold in the wider circuitry of indigenism.

The usual postcolonial paradox remains, that indigenous belonging becomes recognizable by governments only after indigenous expropriation. Indigenous and nonindigenous Australians continue to work through the symbolic and practical meanings of relations to land in ways that are shaped by the globalized historical and contemporary situation of Australia, and not simply interpretable as expression of indigenous interests and aims.

Notes

1. Niezen (2003: 160–165) discusses the "Battle of the S," the plural form ("peoples," "populations") that is taken to raise the issue of self-determination, and is therefore avoided in international fora.

2. Like Miller, many (indigenous activists and others) prefer to use colloquial regional designations: besides "Koori," "Murri" (Queensland), "Nyoongah" (southern Western Australia), "Yolngu" (eastern Arnhem Land), and so forth, most of these native-language terms meaning "person, man" (and contrasting with "European, white person"). The designation "Torres Strait Islanders" has come to be appended to many official names and titles (e.g., the "Australian Institute of Aborigines and Torres Strait Islanders"), to include those whose own sense of relationship to continental Aborigines has been, for many purposes, one of willful distanciation (distancing), but who indeed (at least until the renowned High Court Mabo, or native title, judgment of 1992) tended to be given a much lower profile in considerations of Australia's "indigenous peoples."

3. The *Aboriginal Land Rights (Northern Territory) Act 1976,* and the *Native Title Act (1993)* differ in their bases and formulations, but both require a demonstration of relationship in traditionalist terms. The *Land Rights Act* is a piece of special beneficial legislation, enacted following the negative judgment in the 1971 Yirrkala case discussed above. Framed to make claims possible (but only within the Northern Territory), the *Land Rights Act* requires demonstration of "primary spiritual responsibility" and "common spiritual affiliation" to land on the part of a "local descent group" of Aborigines that may "forage as of right" over land and sites on the land. An original version of the bill introduced in 1974 had allowed greater latitude for "needs" claims to land; but after the removal of the Whitlam Labor government under which the original bill was formulated, the revised version passed in 1976 under the new Liberal–National Coalition government was framed in more exclusively religious and traditionalist terms. When in 1992 the Mabo case changed the situation of Australian land rights with the finding, on the basis of case material from the Torres Strait that is culturally more Melanesian than Australian, that native title could be recognized at the common law, the Labor Government in power hastened to formulate federal legislation. Section 23 of the *Native Title*

Act requires that relationship to land be found to be based on "indigenous laws and customs," and demonstration of continuity in the relationship.

4. ATSIC (2003: 48) cites the 2001 Australian Bureau of Statistics figure for the total Australian indigenous population of 458,520, and attributes the following numbers and percentages to "remoteness" classes as follows: major cities 138,494, 30 percent of total indigenous population; inner regional 92,988, 20.3 percent; outer regional 105,875, 23.1 percent; remote 40,161, 8.8 percent; very remote 81,002, 17.7 percent.

5. All Northern Territory pastoral properties are held as leasehold, of variable term and "rolled over" at expiry on demonstration of fulfillment of covenants.

6. Justice Woodward, who presided in the Yirrkala case, when later appointed to head a commission of inquiry to report on how land rights might be delivered to Aboriginal people, observed that there was little use in recognizing claims to land unless Aboriginal people are also provided with funds to make use of that land. Such plain speaking about "practicalities" was not typical of public high-level government pronouncements favoring land rights.

7. See the National Native Title Tribunal website (http://www.nntt.gov.au) for numbers and details of determinations. As of July 24, 2006, 87 determinations of the existence of native title had been made (60 positive, 27 negative), of hundreds (claimant, nonclaimant, and compensation applications) lodged.

8. "Unowned territory," that is, *terra nullius,* is a phrase that has been circulated as characterization of Australian colonial practice but also sometimes rejected in current debate as anachronistic, not the terms of colonial understanding but of today's interpretation of it.

References

Aboriginal and Torres Strait Islander Commission Report 2002–2003 (ATSIC). 2003. Woden: Commonwealth of Australia.

Attwood, B. 1988. *The making of the Aborigines*. Place: Publisher.

——. 2003. *Rights for Aborigines*. Crows Nest, New South Wales: Allen and Unwin.

Baker, R. 1999. *Land is life: From bush to town, the story of the Yanyuwa people*. Sydney: Allen and Unwin.

Barwick, D. 1998. *Rebellion at Coranderrk,* edited by L. Barwick and R. E. Barwick. Canberra: Aboriginal History.

Beckett, J. 1988. The past in the present; the present in the past: Constructing a national Aboriginality. In *Past and present: The construction of Aboriginality,* edited by J. R. Beckett, 191–217. Canberra: Aboriginal Studies Press.

Bennett, S. 1989. *Aborigines and political power.* Sydney: Allen and Unwin.

Castree, N. 2004. Differential geographies: Place, indigenous rights and "local" resources. *Political Geography* 23 (2): 133–167.

Chatwin, B. 1987. *The Songlines.* London: Jonathan Cape.

Collins, H. 1985. Political ideology in Australia: The distinctiveness of a Benthamite society. *Daedalus* 114: 147–169.

Cowlishaw, G. 1999. *Rednecks, eggheads and blackfellas: A study of racial power and intimacy in Australia.* Sydney: Allen and Unwin.

Cribb, 1994. Farewell to the heartland. *Australian Magazine,* February: 11–16.

Curthoys, A. 2002. *Freedom ride: A freedom rider remembers.* Sydney: Allen and Unwin.

Dodson, M. 1995. *Indigenous social justice: A submission to the Parliament of the Commonwealth of Australia on the social justice package.* Sydney: Aboriginal and Torres Strait Islander Social Justice Commission.

Escobar, A. 2001. Culture sits in places. *Political Geography* 20 (2): 139–144.

Foley, G. 2001. Black power in Redfern 1968–1972. *The Koori History Website.* Electronic document, http://www.kooriweb.org/foley/essays/essay_1.html, accessed December 29, 2006.

Glaskin, K. 2002. *Claiming country: A case study of historical legacy and transition in the Native title context.* Ph.D. Thesis, Department of Archaeology and Anthropology, The Australian National University.

Goodall, H. 1996. *Invasion to embassy: Land in Aboriginal politics in New South Wales 1770–1972.* St. Leonards: Allen and Unwin–Black Books.

Grattan, M., ed. 2000. *Reconciliation: Essays on Australian reconciliation.* Melbourne: Bookman Press.

Gray, I., and G. Lawrence 2001. *A future for regional Australia: Escaping global misfortune.* New York: Cambridge University Press.

Hacking, I. 1998. On being more literal about construction. In *The politics of constructionism,* edited by I. Velody and R. Williams, 49–68. London: Sage.

Hardy, F. 1968. *The unlucky Australians.* Melbourne: Thomas Nelson Rigby.

Hercus, L., and P. Sutton, eds. 1986. *This is what happened: Historical narratives by Aborigines.* Canberra: Australian Institute of Aboriginal Studies.

Hirtz, F. 2003. It takes modern means to be traditional: On recognizing indigenous cultural communities in the Philippines. *Development and Change* 34 (5): 887–914.

Holmes, J. 1996. From commodity values towards amenity values in the northern frontier. *Journal of Australian Studies* 49: 97–104.

Howard, M. 1977. Aboriginal political change in an urban setting: The NACC election in Perth. In *Aborigines and change*, edited by R. M. Berndt, 368–83. Atlantic Highlands, NJ: Humanities Press.

Howson, P. 2005. Aboriginal land rights: The next battle ground. *Quadrant Magazine* 49 (6), June. Electronic document, http://www.quadrant.org.au, accessed December 29, 2006.

Jones, D., and J. Hill-Burnett 1982. The political context of ethnogenesis: An Australian example. In *Aboriginal power in Australian Society*, edited by M. Howard, 214–246. St. Lucia: University of Queensland Press.

Maddock, K. 1991. Metamorphosis of the sacred in Australia. *Australian Journal of Anthropology* 2 (2): 213–232.

McMichael, P. 1984. *Settlers and the agrarian question: Foundations of capitalism in colonial Australia.* Cambridge: Cambridge University Press.

Merlan, F. 1978. Making people quiet in the pastoral north: Reminiscences of Elsey Station. *Journal of Aboriginal History* 1 (2): 70–106.

———. 1991. The limits of cultural constructionism: The case of Coronation Hill. *Oceania* 61: 341–352.

———. 1994. Entitlement and need: Concepts underlying and in land rights and native title acts. In *Claims to knowledge, claims to country*, edited by M. Edmunds, 12–26. Canberra: Australian Institute of Aboriginal Studies, Native Title Unit.

———. 1995. The regimentation of customary practice: From Northern Territory land claims to Mabo. *Australian Journal of Anthropology* 6: 64–82.

———. 1998. *Caging the rainbow: Places, politics and Aborigines in a North Australian Town.* Honolulu: University of Hawai`i Press.

———. 1999. Attitudinal and structural change in indigenous and settler relations to land. In *Reconciliation: Voices from the academy.* Occasional Paper Series 2, edited by L. Manderson, 40–48. Canberra: Academy of the Social Sciences in Australia.

———. 2005. Indigenous movements in Australia. *Annual Reviews in Anthropology* 34: 473–494.

Miller, J. 1985. *A will to win: The heroic resistance, survival and triumph of black Australia.* London: Angus and Robertson.

Morgan, M. 2004. *Mutant message down under. 10th anniversary edition.* New York: HarperCollins.

Munn, N. 1970. The transformation of subjects into objects in Walbiri and Pitjantjatjara myth. In *Australian Aboriginal anthropology,* edited by R. M. Berndt, 141–163. Perth: University of Western Australia.

Nettheim, G., G. D. Meyers, and D. Craig. 2002. *Indigenous peoples and governance structures: A comparative analysis of land and resource management rights.* Canberra: Australian Institute of Aboriginal and Torres Strait Islander Studies.

Niezen, R. 2000. Recognizing indigenism: Canadian unity and the international movement of indigenous peoples. *Comparative Studies in Society and History* 42 (1): 119–148.

——. 2003. *The origins of indigenism: Human rights and the politics of identity.* Berkeley: University of California Press.

Pearson, N. 2000. *Our right to take responsibility.* Self-Published. Available at: eve@capeyork.partnerships.com.

Povinelli, E. 1993. *Labor's lot: The power, history, and culture of Aboriginal action.* Chicago: University of Chicago.

——. 2002. *The cunning of recognition: Indigenous alterities and the making of Australian multiculturalism.* Durham, NC: Duke University Press.

Roeg, N., director. 1971. *Walkabout.* 100 min. Produced by Si Litvinoff, distributed by Films Incorporated.

Rose, D. 1984. The saga of Captain Cook: Morality in Aboriginal and European law. *Australian Aboriginal Studies* 2: 24–39.

Rowse, T. 1987. Were you ever savages? Aboriginal insiders and pastoralists' patronage. *Oceania* 58 (2): 81–99.

——. 1988. Middle Australia and the noble savage: A political romance. In *Past and present: The construction of Aboriginality,* edited by J. R. Beckett, 161–178. Canberra: Aboriginal Studies Press.

——. 1998. Aboriginal nomenclature. In *The Oxford Companion to Australian History,* edited by G. Davison, J. Hirst, and S. Macintyre, 9–10. Melbourne: Oxford University Press.

——. 2000. *Obliged to be difficult: Nugget Coombs' legacy in indigenous affairs.* Cambridge: Cambridge University Press.

Sansom, B. 1982. The Aboriginal commonality. In *Aboriginal sites, rights and resource development.* For the Academy of the Social Sciences in Australia, edited by R. M. Berndt, 117–138. Perth: University of Western Australia Press.

Spencer, B., and F. Gillen 1927. *The Arunta: A study of a Stone Age people.* London: Macmillan.

Stanner, W. E. H. 1958. Continuity and change among the Aborigines. *The Australian Journal of Science* 21 (5A): 99–109.

——. 1965. Religion, totemism and symbolism. In *Aboriginal man in Australia: Essays in honours of Emeritus Professor A. P. Elkin,* edited by R. M. Berndt and C. H. Berndt, 207–237. Sydney: Angus and Robertson.

——. 1968. *After the dreaming: Black and white Australians, an anthropologist's view.* Sydney: Australian Broadcasting Commission Boyer Lectures.

Strehlow, T. G. H. 1965. Culture, social structure and environment in Aboriginal central Australia. In *Aboriginal man in Australia,* edited by R. M. Berndt and C. H. Berndt, 121–145. Sydney: Angus and Robertson.

——. 1970. Geography and the totemic landscape in central Australia: A functional study. In *Australian Aboriginal anthropology,* edited by R. M. Berndt, 92–140. Nedlands: University of Western Australia.

Tambiah, S. 1996. *Levelling crowds: Ethnonationalist conflicts and collective violence in South Asia.* Berkeley: University of California Press.

Tatz, C. 1977. Aborigines: Political options and strategies. In *Aborigines and change: Australia in the 70s,* edited by R. M. Berndt, 384–401. Atlantic Highlands, NJ: Humanities Press.

Thiele, S. 1982. *Yugul, an Arnhem Land cattle station.* Darwin: North Australia Research Unit.

Weir, P., director. 1977. *The Last Wave.* 106 min. Produced by McElroy and McElroy Productions, distributed by United Artists.

Williams, N. 1986. *The Yolngu and their land: A system of land tenure and the fight for its recognition.* Canberra: Australian Institute of Aboriginal Studies.

Yunupingu, G., ed. 1997. *Our land is our life.* St. Lucia: University of Queensland Press.

Choctaw Tribal Sovereignty at the Turn of the 21st Century

Valerie Lambert

The demand for self-determination has become a universal political theme, ranging from competing tribal entities in postapartheid South Africa and other nations of that continent, to the Maoris of New Zealand and the aborigines of Australia, and even to the Hawaiian independence movement. In each of these instances there is a proclivity to compare local situations to that of [U.S.] American Indian tribes which have achieved a high degree of economic and political autonomy within a broader constitutional system.

—Kersey 1996

Many indigenous peoples worldwide indeed seek greater control of their own affairs and the dissolution of structures of discrimination and inequality. Many groups, too, want the national governments under which they live to more fully recognize—or in some cases simply to acknowledge—indigenous rights of self-determination. What gives me pause is the last part of Kersey's statement: his positive valuation of the political rights held by American Indian tribes, together with the suggestion that indigenous peoples throughout the world may be looking to the United States as a model of respect for native autonomy and sovereignty. I examine here a particular case of early-21st-century Indian tribal experience in the United States, that of the Choctaws. Toward this end, I analyze three recent conflicts between the Choctaws and non-Indians. The first involves Choctaw tribal experience selling motor fuels; the second involves the tribe's efforts to expand their tribal gaming enterprises; and the last involves a conflict over water in the

151

Choctaws' southeastern Oklahoma homeland. Each of these conflicts also provides insight into aspects of tribal life and history, and reveals a considerably less rosy picture of the extent of Choctaw sovereignty than might be imagined in an age when some observers want to paint all American Indian tribes as rolling in casino money and unrestricted political power.

Before exploring these conflicts, let me present some material that has significantly shaped my perspective on the issues addressed in this chapter, material drawn from my personal experiences growing up as a Choctaw in Oklahoma and my professional experiences as a cultural anthropologist at the Bureau of Indian Affairs (BIA). During my youth in Oklahoma, then the state with largest Indian population in the United States, I would have been puzzled by the assertion that the United States had made a special accommodation of our distinctiveness. Both my peers and the adults around me in Oklahoma City, where I was reared, characterized Oklahoma as an undesirable place to be, and mention was often made of the reason that we were in this part of the United States: because the federal government had forcibly relocated our tribes to what is now Oklahoma so that non-Indians could have our more fertile land in the Southeast. I spent many summers as a child in the Chickasaw Nation, the tribal nation in which my grandfather, who was of Chickasaw as well as Choctaw ancestry, had taken part of his "allotment" of the Choctaw and Chickasaw tribal estate. The reason that my relations had acquired these parcels of Choctaw and Chickasaw land, I was told, was because an early-20th-century federal law had eviscerated the governments of the Five "Civilized" Tribes, which included the Choctaws, and allotted their lands in severalty to tribal members in an effort to dissolve the Five "Civilized" Tribes. During the late 19th century, many other U.S. tribes were subject to similar legislation.

I have fond memories of a day in sunny August when my sister and I watched brown cattle graze the hills of my grandfather's allotment as we leaned against the fence that bordered a quiet country road. However, the cattle that we watched were not my grandfather's or even my father's. They were the property of a white rancher who had acquired our allotment. My sister and I had leaned against the fence not from within the enclosure but from the roadside. In losing our allotments, my family and I were not alone. Thousands of members of the Five "Civilized" Tribes were dispossessed of their allotments by non-Indians as a result of federal laws at the turn of the 20th century. For Choctaw and Chickasaw children, as well as for many other Indian children in Oklahoma, the lesson was clear: the federal relationship had left us dispossessed—on a large scale—not just once but twice. At that time the only evidence I could see of a federal accommodation of our distinctiveness lay in the fact that the U.S. government permitted us a chief to help manage the 10,000 acres still under tribal control. When I was a young child in the late 1960s, we Choctaws were prohibited by law from selecting this chief. At that time and until 1970, the U.S. government appointed the chiefs of the Five "Civilized" Tribes.

About 15 years after I left Oklahoma to attend college and graduate school, I was recruited to work as a cultural anthropologist at the BIA, an agency that in recent years has been staffed almost entirely by Indians. I accepted this position in part because I was fascinated by federal Indian policy and the policymaking process with respect to Indian affairs. A second and related factor was my strong desire to critically examine what lies within the "black box" that is the BIA, an agency that has been and continues to be of tremendous political and symbolic import for Indians. I served in the BIA central office in Washington, D.C., under two Assistant Secretaries of Indian Affairs—Ada Deer, a Menominee Indian social worker and activist who had spearheaded a successful movement to reinstate her tribe after it had been terminated by the federal government, and Kevin Gover, a Pawnee Indian lawyer from Oklahoma who had used his law degree and the U.S. courts to defend tribes against violations of their sovereignty. I watched both of these Indian leaders struggle against Congress, against U.S. state governments and less frequently, against then–U.S. President Bill Clinton to try to fulfill the federal trust obligation toward U.S. tribes and promote the sovereignty and rights to self-determination of the then 561 federally recognized Indian tribes in the United States.

Deer and Gover treated tribal sovereignty as did most tribal leaders of their time—as, among other things, a bundle of inherent rights. They maintained that the United States is obligated by treaties, by the U.S. Constitution, by federal law, and by federal Indian policy to protect federally recognized tribes against encroachments on their sovereignty, protect tribal property, provide technical assistance to tribal governments, provide health and educational benefits to tribal members, and foster conditions that permit tribes to more fully exercise their sovereignty. Related, they defended what they described as the inherent rights of Indian tribes to elect their own leaders, determine their own memberships, maintain tribal police forces, levy taxes, regulate property under tribal jurisdiction, control the conduct of their members by tribal ordinances, regulate the domestic relations of members, and administer justice. Both Deer and Gover made it clear to us, their staff, that under their watch the highest degree of respect would be given to the bundle of inherent rights that compose tribal sovereignty and that staff were expected to thoroughly understand the legal and political basis of the special status of Indian tribes. For BIA staff, the message was clear: the United States had been built on a legal and political foundation of the political accommodation of Indian tribes and tribal sovereignty. Many in the BIA saw this accommodation as significant. Some even said that they saw it as exceeding any that had existed anywhere in the world at any point in time.

The sometimes arbitrary distinction between federally "recognized" and "unrecognized" tribes framed all of BIA work. At the agency, I was one of only about a dozen staff whose primary job responsibility involved individuals and groups who existed outside what the BIA called its "service population." As part of the Branch of Acknowledgment and Research (BAR), now called the Office of Federal Acknowledgment (OFA), I evaluated the petitions of groups seeking federal recognition as Indian tribes through what is termed the federal acknowledgment process. The existence of this process points to the fact that the federal accommodation of tribes is almost entirely limited to groups whom the U.S. government recognizes as Indian tribes, and to individuals whom federally recognized tribes recognize as their members or citizens. Many members of federally recognized tribes find this limitation and boundary unproblematic, despite the fact that it helps legitimize a continued federal role in deciding who is and is not Indian. This support is partly explained by the widespread fetishization, beginning in the late 20th century, of the category, "federally recognized tribe," among members of the tribes that currently occupy this category.

The branch in which I worked was part of the BIA Office of Tribal Government Services. Partly because of this, my obligations included some work to defend the sovereign rights of federally recognized tribes. The following examples of small actions that I took illustrate the practical uses within the BIA of a sovereignty rhetoric that emphasizes the federal accommodation of recognized tribes and argues that the U.S. government strictly upholds policies of self-determination and of respect for tribal sovereignty and rights. One day after a meeting I returned to my office to find a voicemail message from a caller who claimed that she was being unfairly denied membership in a tribe whom I knew to be federally recognized. She said that she lived on the reservation and that she met the tribe's membership requirements as defined in the tribe's constitution. Yet the tribe allegedly had refused to issue her a tribal membership card and told her that she could not vote in the upcoming tribal election. The reasons were "political," she said; she had been campaigning for the chief's opponent. The caller then asked that the BIA remind the chief that the act of prohibiting an eligible member from enrolling in the tribe violated the tribe's constitution, a document that the chief had sworn to uphold. In sum, she asked that the BIA provide a check on the power of what she described as "that despot." In preparing for my return of this phone call, I perused some files. I was somewhat surprised to find a folder thick with letters from dozens of others who had made the same charges about this chief and had also requested BIA intervention. Alongside each of these letters were letters of response from my colleagues. The letters explained that Indian tribes are sovereign and have exclusive jurisdiction over defining their memberships. The BIA, they continued, cannot and will not intervene in the domestic matters of sovereign Indian tribes. To do so would constitute a violation of the sovereignty of tribes and a violation of the longstanding federal commitment to respecting tribal sovereignty and political rights.

Another time, I fielded a phone call from an angry non-Indian who said that he had stopped for a bite to eat on the reservation of a tribe whom I knew to be federally recognized, and for reasons that he did not reveal, the tribal police had forced him to leave the reservation. "This is America!" he exclaimed. "They [the tribal police] can't do that!" He then said that he told the tribe's police that as soon as he returned from his trip, he would report them—"report them," he said loudly, "to the U.S. government itself!" As a mouthpiece for the BIA sovereignty rhetoric, I told the caller that, yes, this was the United States, a country where there existed a respect for tribal sovereignty and self-determination. Tribes are entitled, by virtue of their sovereignty, to remove individuals like him from their reservation for any reason.

In the Oklahoma of my youth, the federal accommodation of tribes appeared to be minimal. We might have likened it to a small watering hole. At the BIA, the political accommodation of tribes was often seen as ample: as resembling, perhaps, an open pasture. During my youth, it was often taken for granted by those around me that the United States did not respect tribal sovereignty. At the BIA, federal respect for tribal sovereignty was often assumed, but was said to have begun in the 1960s with the start of what scholars often describe as the "era of self-determination" of federal Indian policy. As regards this "self-determination era," an era that continues to the present, many at the BIA simply take it for granted that the United States has become a global leader on issues of respect for indigenous rights and sovereignty.

My research in the Choctaw Nation brought to the fore an on-the-ground experience of tribal sovereignty that differs in critical ways from both of these constructions. As I show, there are three things about Choctaw tribal sovereignty that are not very visible from afar and, thus, might be missed by, for example, indigenous groups elsewhere in the world seeking information about structural accommodations of the sovereignty and autonomy of U.S. tribes. The first thing that risks being overlooked is the intensity and frequency with which the Choctaws experience encroachments on their sovereignty. It is unlikely that even the BIA or most Choctaw citizens fully appreciate the amount of action that the Choctaws and doubtless other tribes see on tribal sovereignty battlegrounds, battlegrounds that, as Biolsi (2001) points out, are concentrated at the local level.

Less opaque to the Choctaw citizenry but perhaps not to the BIA is a second feature of Choctaw sovereignty that the following discussion brings into relief: the fact that, in the context of these encroachments and the political maneuverings that follow them, the sovereignty of the Choctaw tribe is less often recognized and respected than it is challenged, grudgingly tolerated, or even dismissed altogether. Non-Choctaws often resist Choctaw definitions of certain actions as part of the tribe's bundle of inherent rights, forcing the tribe to negotiate and affirm these rights. Through a resulting series of moves and countermoves, Choctaws repeatedly instantiate their sovereignty, and an important aspect of tribal sovereignty is revealed—its identity as a process of negotiation (Clara Sue Kidwell, personal communication; Cattelino 2004).

A third feature of Choctaw sovereignty that is patent in the following discussion is the fact that, when struggling to legally defend themselves against encroachments on their sovereignty, the Choctaws have more at their disposal than is implied by the analogy of a small watering hole, but they do not often experience the unbroken expanse nor the sure and level footing that is implied by the analogy of an open pasture. Their experience more closely resembles that of treading across a thawing lake in the far north at the end of winter. The footing is unsure not only because the ice is slippery and, to use Wilkins and Lomawaima's (2001) analogy, the ground is uneven, but also because the ice often gives way, and it does so in unexpected places at unexpected times. The thawing-lake analogy also captures the harshness and sometimes even the brutality of the present-day Choctaw experience of defending their sovereignty.

* * *

The Choctaw tribe, which numbers about 175,000, inhabits a homeland that spans roughly 7.5 million acres in southeastern Oklahoma. Since the implementation of the allotment laws at the turn of the 20th century, most of this land—land that is termed the Choctaw Nation—has been owned by non-Indians, and the vast majority (perhaps as much as 90 percent) of Choctaw Nation residents have been non-Choctaws, two features that make the relationship between land and Indianness in southeastern Oklahoma complex. A chief heads the tribal government's executive branch and its 6,000 tribal employees. The tribal government's legislative branch consists of a 12-member tribal council, and the tribal judiciary, of three tribal judges.

Two of the conflicts with non-Indians that are discussed below involve tribal efforts to maintain or expand tribal businesses, and efforts by the state of Oklahoma to control or limit the tribe's economic development activities. Since the passage of the Indian Self-Determination and Education Assistance Act of 1975 and other legislation promoting the self-determination and self-governance of U.S. tribes, the Choctaws have pursued an aggressive program of tribal economic development. Its goals are threefold, to (1) stem the flood of urban migration by creating more jobs for Choctaws, (2) continue to expand tribal programs and services to help alleviate high levels of poverty in the Choctaw Nation, and (3) reduce the tribe's dependence on federal funding. Choctaw tribal businesses now generate several hundred million dollars a year, up from zero in 1978. These businesses include travel plazas, bingo palaces, a horse racing track, manufacturing plants, tribal shopping centers, and a resort. Profits from tribal businesses now fund as much as 80 percent of the tribe's programs and services. With some exceptions, the state of Oklahoma is precluded from regulating, controlling, or exercising even limited jurisdiction over tribal businesses and other tribal property. In general, the BIA and federal law construe such acts as violations of tribal sovereignty.

* * *

The first conflict, which was brought to a head in 1996, involved tribal sales of motor fuels at more than a half-dozen tribal travel plazas in the Choctaw Nation. Tribal travel plazas, which the Choctaws began building in 1990, are basically large gas stations. Their primary product is motor fuel, but they also often offer small restaurants, convenience stores, designated spaces for "pull-tab" gaming, and smoke shops.

Clerks, managers, drivers, electricians, accountants, and maintenance workers help staff these mega gas stations, each of which has created between 30 and 50 jobs. Despite the fact that these jobs are few and most are relatively low wage, in most cases their local impact has been important. Poverty and joblessness continue to be significant problems in southeastern Oklahoma.

In the mid-1990s, Oklahoma was imposing a $0.14 per gallon tax on diesel fuel and a $0.17 per gallon tax on gasoline. These taxes generated about $370 million for Oklahoma in FY 1995, about ten percent of total state revenues (Johnson and Turner 1998). Motor fuels sold by tribes are not subject to these taxes by virtue of the sovereign right of tribes to manage tribal property free from intervention or interference by state governments. During the late 20th century, the rapid growth of tribal sales of gasoline in Oklahoma prompted the state to challenge this right. Oklahoma claimed that it was "losing" $3.5 million to tribes in uncollected motor-fuel taxes and that non-Indian owners of gas stations (who put pressure on the state) were facing "unfair competition" from tribes (Johnson and Turner 1998). Oklahoma grudgingly acknowledged that tribes may have a right to sell motor fuels free from state taxes to Indians, but it claimed that the state had the right to impose these taxes on sales by tribes to non-Indians. This particular challenge of tribal sovereignty was sufficiently novel that a case that centered on this challenge, *Oklahoma Tax Commission v. Chickasaw Nation* ([94–771], 515 U.S. 450, 1995), made it to the U.S. Supreme Court.

Before the Supreme Court issued its decision, Choctaw citizens in all parts of the Choctaw Nation expressed concern about the consequences of a possible state victory. If the state won the right to impose taxes on tribal sales of gasoline to non-Indians, would the tribe's travel plazas generate sufficient profits for the tribe to maintain these businesses? Most were aware that the tribe's ability to offer low fuel prices had provided the rationale for building travel plazas and that this rationale would be considerably weakened if the state won. It was simply beyond question that the tribe's travel plazas sold most of their gas to non-Indians.

Another issue was how a decision in favor of the state might be enforced. What method might be used to identify specific transactions as immune from the state tax by virtue of a customer's identity as a Choctaw? A method of external identification based on phenotype would clearly fail to identify all the Choctaw customers. Most Choctaws are phenotypically indistinct from whites, a reflection of a history of extensive intermarriage between Choctaws and whites. As much as

80 percent of all Choctaw tribal members are less than one-quarter Choctaw "by blood." It was clear that either travel plaza staff would have to ask customers whether they were Choctaw, or signs would have to be posted at travel plazas asking customers to expose themselves as Choctaw before they paid for gas.

This, however, raised additional questions. Would Choctaw customers be permitted to self-identify as Choctaw? Or, would they be required to show a Choctaw tribal membership card? Self-identification would capture the most customers and would therefore be in the tribe's best interest. However, since the passage of a tribal constitution in 1983 that defined eligibility for tribal membership on the basis of lineal descent from an ancestor listed as "Choctaw by blood" on the 1906 Dawes (allotment) Rolls, the Choctaw tribal government has limited the right to vote, hold tribal office and receive tribal benefits to enrolled Choctaws. They have also refused to recognize anyone as Choctaw who is not enrolled. Self-identification, an occasional basis for distributing Choctaw tribal benefits between allotment in 1906 and the new constitution in 1983, has been strictly discontinued, as has community identification, the primary criterion for recognizing individuals as Choctaw from at least the 1700s through allotment. In the context of the post-1983 tribal-member-only Choctaw policy and law, the Choctaws in some Choctaw Nation communities have developed a second category of Choctaws, the category, "Choctaw-but-not-enrolled." These individuals live in or are in some way affiliated with Choctaw-Nation communities, have Choctaw ancestry, and are often recognized by their communities as Choctaw; but for various reasons none of their lineal ancestors were listed as "Choctaw by blood" on the 1906 Dawes Rolls and, thus, they are not eligible for Choctaw tribal membership. Because the 1995 motor-fuel tax case threatened to create incentives for the tribal government to define the category, "Choctaw," more broadly than it is currently doing, it raised the possibility of re-introducing community identification or self-identification as bases for defining the set of motor-fuel transactions immune from state taxes.

In 1995, the U.S. Supreme Court effectively ended these local ruminations—at least as they involved the motor-fuels controversy—by ruling that Oklahoma could not impose its motor-fuel tax on tribal businesses, even if sales were to non-Indians. Surprisingly, this did not end the conflict. Within only a few months of the ruling, Oklahoma rewrote its motor-fuel tax law, effectively at the suggestion of the Supreme Court. Instead of levying the tax at the retail level (and, thus, on tribal businesses), Oklahoma levied the tax on consumers. By so doing, Oklahoma could legally tax non-Indian customers of tribal businesses, but not Indian customers. Only enrolled tribal members, not simply self- or community-identified Choctaws, were deemed immune from these taxes.

The revisions to the state tax code sent tribes and the state to the negotiating table to figure out how, specifically, to enforce the state's right to collect motor-fuel taxes from non-Indian consumers of tribal motor fuels. In these extensive negotiations, tribes lost the fight to force non-Indian consumers themselves to send the tax to the state. Tribes also lost the fight to forward to the state only tax monies from sales to non-Indians. In the end, tribes consented to the creation of a two-step process. First, tribes would forward to the state the tax revenues from *all* of their tribal motor-fuel transactions, even on purchases made by tribal members. Then, in lieu of a rebate of taxes paid by each tribal-member consumer, tribes would receive a predetermined percentage of the total tax revenues they had forwarded to the state. To receive the predetermined percentage of these revenues, tribes were required to enter into a compact (a signed, written agreement) with the state. If a tribe chose not to compact, the members of these tribes individually could apply to the state for a rebate of the taxes paid.

When the state initiated this challenge to the sovereignty of the Choctaw tribe (and other Oklahoma tribes), the Choctaws perceived themselves to be on a part of the thawing lake that would fully support their weight. As they made their way across this area, they encountered the icy wind of an only partial and grudging recognition on the part of the state of Oklahoma of the Choctaws' sovereign right to manage their tribal property free from state interference or intervention. When the Supreme Court upheld this right, the Choctaws must have felt that they had successfully made it across this slippery patch. Suddenly, however, the ice gave way. Oklahoma found a way to appropriate a portion of revenues generated by some tribal businesses, penetrating a domain that the Choctaws had treated as solely under tribal jurisdiction. Thus, ended a process by which the Choctaws had not simply asserted and defended their sovereignty but also negotiated it in a context defined by multiple and overlapping sovereignties (Biolsi 2005; Wilkins and Lomawaima 2001).

* * *

During the late 20th and 21st centuries, tribal gaming has also been a contentious issue. Casinos were first proposed as a Choctaw economic development option in the mid-1980s by then-Chief Hollis Roberts. The idea was no doubt informed by the actions of some other tribes who had then only recently decided to use their sovereign status and their immunity from state law to capitalize on the non-Indian appetite for gambling by opening casinos. At that point, it was not yet clear that some tribes would be able to generate, as they have beginning in the late 1980s, hundreds of millions of dollars annually from their casinos. In the mid-1980s, most if not all tribes correctly perceived tribal gaming as financially risky, a reputation that, by the late 1990s, the business had largely been able to shake despite the fact that many Indian casinos fail. The perceived financial riskiness of tribal gaming was of considerable concern to the Choctaws, particularly at that historical moment. One of the tribe's few economic development projects at the time, a fiberglass boat factory, had just failed, and the tribe's resort, Arrowhead Lodge, was floundering.

Chief Roberts nevertheless pressed forward. He spoke individually with council members, grassroots leaders and other Choctaw citizens to generate support for a tribal gaming enterprise. Before long, it became clear that Roberts' primary obstacle was not economic; it was religious. The vast majority of Choctaws are Christian, reflecting a 200-year history of Christian churches and missionaries within the Choctaw homeland. The church has long played a significant role in Choctaw life and politics. Before the tribe's relocation to Oklahoma, churches established and promoted schools for the tribe, a goal that was strongly supported by tribal leaders, and both missionaries and churches were among the strongest non-Indian opponents of the tribe's removal to what is now Oklahoma (Kidwell 1995). When the Choctaw tribal government was eviscerated, and its courts, dissolved as a condition of the allotment legislation at the turn of the 20th century, churches stepped in to fill the institutional void. In fact, from 1906 through the 1970s, churches were probably the tribe's most important social and political institutions (Faiman-Silva 1997; Foster 2001).

In the mid-1980s, Choctaw preachers and church members mobilized against Roberts's proposed gaming venture. Gambling was objectionable on moral grounds, they said; gambling was a "sin." Choctaw preachers argued that the Choctaw tribe was a Christian nation, and as such, the tribe should not only refuse to participate in gaming but also work to prevent the growth of gaming on Indian reservations throughout the country. The most visible such activist was the Reverend Bertram Bobb. For years Bobb, a Choctaw himself, has run a bible camp in the Choctaw Nation and written a Christian column for the Choctaw tribal newspaper *Bishinik*. Several times he was elected to the tribal council. Roberts countered Bobb and the growing movement against gaming in the Choctaw Nation by arguing that the tribe was in desperate need of income to help fund and expand tribal programs and services. In 1987, two years after Roberts's reelection to another four-year term as chief, Roberts succeeded in opening a tribal gaming enterprise. It was not a casino but a somewhat less morally objectionable high-stakes bingo palace.

The almost overnight success of this 28,000-square-foot facility considerably weakened the opposition to tribal gaming among the Choctaw citizenry. In only its second year, the bingo palace, built in the midsized city that houses the Choctaw tribal headquarters, made a profit of more than $1 million (Faiman-Silva 1997). In addition, this controversial tribal business provided jobs for 140 people. By decade's end, the tribal government, with the consent of all but a small minority of the Choctaw citizenry, had begun exploring ways to expand Choctaw gaming operations. The Choctaw tribal council made an official trip to Connecticut to the Mashantucket Pequot tribe's Foxwoods Casino, the largest grossing casino in the world, where they toured the facility and met with casino personnel and tribal leaders. The Mashantucket Pequot tribe pledged to help the Choctaws build a casino of their own.

The passage of the Indian Gaming Regulatory Act (IGRA) by the U.S. Congress in 1988 forced the Choctaws to place their hopes of building a casino on an indefinite hold. IGRA limits the type of gaming in which tribes can engage on the basis of the gaming laws of the state(s) in which tribes are located. It also gives states limited regulatory powers over tribal gaming operations. In so doing, IGRA contradicts the general federal policy—which is grounded in federal law, as well—of prohibiting the involvement of U.S. states in tribal property management (see Biolsi 2005). Under IGRA, Indian gaming is divided into three classes, with the highest class being Class III. Class III Indian gaming includes casino gambling. IGRA requires tribes who operate Class III gaming enterprises to obtain a compact with the government of their state. These agreements set procedures for regulating tribal gaming operations and often require tribes to share a percentage of their profits with the state. In general, if a state does not permit a statewide lottery and if the citizens of the state have not specifically approved tribal gaming (through, e.g., a referendum), the highest level of gaming in which a tribe in that state can engage is Class II gaming. Class II gaming includes high-stakes bingo, pull tabs, and a limited number of electronic games.

Faced with these new federal and state limits on their sovereignty, limits that prohibited them from opening a casino, in the 1990s and early 2000s the Choctaws expanded their gaming operations by expanding their bingo operations. The tribe built three other bingo palaces. In addition, they focused on increasing the number of their customers. They provided free roundtrip bus transportation (on tribal buses) from Dallas, Texas. Highlighting the fact that in a single game, a customer could win $1 million, tribal leaders also promoted Choctaw bingo through the advertising media of radio, television, billboards, and newspapers. By the early 2000s, the tribe was following the lead of other tribes in Oklahoma, most notably the Cherokees, by renaming their gaming facilities "casinos." To enhance their credibility as casinos, the businesses formerly known as bingo palaces were stocked with electronic games manufactured to resemble slot machines. As mentioned above, a limited number of electronic games are permitted under Class II Indian gaming.

The state of Oklahoma responded with resistance to the growth and development of tribal gaming in Oklahoma at the turn of the 21st century, challenging the rights of the Choctaws and other Oklahoma tribes to engage in the type of gaming that was going on in these "casinos." In this the state was abetted by the strong fundamentalist Christian presence in Oklahoma, the most potent expression of which is the Oral Roberts headquarters in eastern Oklahoma, the area where the Five "Civilized" Tribes are located. For years the fundamentalist Christian constituency in Oklahoma has kept an eye on actions oriented toward instituting a statewide lottery; at several different points they have led the charge to defeat such initiatives. Well aware that in Oklahoma it is politically popular to challenge not simply the sovereign right but also the moral right of tribes to operate gaming facilities, the state adopted a position of hostility to tribal gaming. In the early 2000s, with help from the federally housed National Indian Gaming Commission (NIGC), Oklahoma began shutting down selected tribal gaming operations. The tribes operating these facilities, the state said, were crossing the line between Class II and Class III gaming, a line that was so ill defined that certain machines soon became popularly known as "grey-area gaming devices."

In November of 2004, Oklahoma tribes delivered a counterpunch. Through an extensive public-relations campaign and widespread political mobilization, they helped secure the passage of a referendum, State Question 712, that permits Oklahoma tribes to offer certain Class III games, including video poker and blackjack. The price, however, is high:

tribes must share a percentage of their gaming revenues with Oklahoma and permit some state oversight of tribal gaming operations.

In their quest to establish and expand their gaming operations, the Choctaws have been treading across a thawing lake that has cracked beneath their feet several times, most notably when IGRA was passed. Since that time, the tribe has experienced unsure footing as a result of the mobilization of antigaming constituencies and events such as the shutdown by the state in the early 2000s of certain tribal gaming establishments. In negotiating their sovereignty during this conflict, the Choctaws and other Oklahoma tribes have experienced some success—reestablishing, for example, their right to operate casinos. The compacts that regulate these operations, however, allow a certain level of state involvement in tribal affairs that tribal leaders tend to treat as an erosion of tribal sovereignty.

* * *

In 2001, a 27-year conflict over water rights ended with a tentative agreement between the Choctaw and Chickasaw tribes, on the one hand, and the state of Oklahoma, on the other hand. For most of the conflict, Chickasaw involvement in this essentially Choctaw–Oklahoma conflict was limited to the fact that the Chickasaws have a one-fourth interest in the Choctaw estate by virtue of a 19th-century intertribal treaty. The following discussion of the act that precipitated the water conflict, which was the building of a reservoir in the Choctaw Nation, and its aftermath, which culminated in the 2001 agreement, help illustrate the fact that non-Indian efforts to dispossess U.S. tribes of their property did not end at the turn of the 20th century, as is often assumed. Tribes in the United States continue to experience significant threats to their ownership and control over natural resources within their borders, as will be seen, and on occasion, such as in the case described below, tribes continue to encounter a federal government that not simply fails to meet its legal obligation to protect tribal property but also abets local non-Indian efforts to appropriate tribal property. The vast majority of tribal water-rights cases in the United States, it should be pointed out, involve tribal rights to water outside of tribal boundaries. In the case described below, the water that was at issue was limited to the water within Choctaw—and as it turned out in the final agreement, also Chickasaw—tribal boundaries.

A primary basis for U.S. recognition of tribal rights to water are the reservation-creating treaties of the 19th century. For the Choctaws, this is specifically the Treaty of Dancing Rabbit Creek, which in 1830 created a new homeland for the tribe in what is now Oklahoma. *Winters v. U.S.* (207 U.S. 564, 1908) affirmed that such treaties imply tribal ownership and control over all the water within the boundaries defined in and by these treaties. In addition, *Winters* and subsequent case law (esp. *Arizona v. California* [373 U.S. 546, 1963]) stated that if the water within a tribe's homeland is insufficient to enable a tribe to develop and maintain a vibrant, growing economy in their homeland—which is not the case for the Choctaws but is often the case for tribes in the U.S. Southwest—tribes also have rights to off-reservation water sufficient to service all "practically irrigable acreage" in the tribe's homeland. Tribal water rights survive statehood, an act that confers on states ownership of all other water within state borders. Tribal water rights also survive the "checkerboarding" of reservations and tribal homelands, a pattern of land ownership in which, as a consequence of allotment, non-Indian-owned land exists alongside Indian or tribal land within tribal boundaries (see O'Brien 1989). In 1970, three of the Five "Civilized" Tribes, including the Choctaws, won a Supreme Court case that is water related and, thus, has a direct bearing on the conflict discussed below. The Supreme Court found that the Choctaw, Chickasaw, and Cherokee tribes, not the state of Oklahoma, owned the beds of a commercially valuable river that runs through their homelands. The state had not gained ownership of this natural resource, as the state claimed, when it achieved statehood in 1907; the tribes owned this resource on the basis of the early-19th-century treaties that created their homelands.

Despite the Supreme Court's affirmation in 1970 of the continued existence of treaty-based Choctaw water rights, in 1974 the state of Oklahoma crossed Choctaw tribal boundaries and dug a large hole in the middle of the Choctaw Nation with which to capture what state officials often described during my field research as the "excess" water in the Choctaws' homeland. Located in an area that receives an average annual precipitation of 56 inches in some parts (an area that sits on the eastern edge of the eastern woodlands region of the United States), the Choctaw Nation is water rich. In fact, 500 billion gallons of water per year flow over a dam at Hugo Lake in the southern part of the Choctaw Nation and into the Red River (the river that marks the Choctaw Nation's southern boundary), where the water becomes contaminated by minerals. Faced with an impending water shortage in the state's capital city of Oklahoma City because of expected population growth, and protracted endemic water shortages in western Oklahoma because of the region's natural aridity and its heavy reliance on intensive wheat-field irrigation, in the early 1970s the state of Oklahoma hatched a plan to pipe Choctaw Nation water to Oklahoma City and western Oklahoma. They called this plan the Water Conveyance Project, and the large hole that they had dug in the Choctaw Nation, Sardis Lake Reservoir.

The Choctaws did not consent to the building of Sardis Lake Reservoir in their homeland. They also did not consent to the seizure of their water, a tribal resource that the state no doubt believed had been sadly underutilized and underdeveloped by the tribe. The federal government did not intervene to protect this Choctaw property from its seizure by the state. Instead, it built the reservoir for the state of Oklahoma and loaned Oklahoma more than $38 million for the project.

Construction of the 13,610-acre reservoir and its 14,138-foot rolled earthfill dam was completed by the U.S. Army Corps of Engineers in 1982. The project flooded the Choctaw Nation town of Sardis, a small farming and ranching community that sported a school, a post office, and a grocery store. This town had been called Bunch Town during the 19th century when its primary institutions included two blacksmith shops, two grist mills, a saloon, and several churches. Also flooded by the building of the reservoir were the graves of at least 20 private cemeteries, including a 1,000-year-old burial ground of the Caddo Indians who had inhabited the area prior to the Choctaws' relocation in the 1830s. Citing the federal right of eminent domain, in the early 1980s the federal government forcibly relocated Sardis area residents, both living and dead.

Less than a decade after the lake was filled, Oklahoma state leaders and legislators decided to scrap the state's plan for the lake and default on the federal loan. State finances did not permit the state to make the annual loan payments, the state said, and state legislators had been unable to reach a consensus on which communities would be the first to receive Choctaw water. The state decided to sell Choctaw water to the highest bidder. Talks with the North Texas Water Agency (NTWA), a consortium of municipal governments in water-starved north Texas, had revealed that the NTWA was prepared to offer the state of Oklahoma $400 million for the rights to 130 million gallons of Choctaw water per day for a period of 100 years. The rights of the Choctaws to this water were ignored.

When the idea of building Sardis Lake Reservoir and creating the Water Conveyance Project was conceived in the early 1970s, the Choctaws were ill prepared to defend their water rights and sovereignty. In 1906, federal allotment legislation had dissolved the legislative and judicial branches of their tribal government and had left the executive branch a shell of an institution. Perhaps most significantly, from 1906 to 1970, as was alluded to earlier, the Choctaw chief was appointed by the U.S. government. Partly because of this, the work of rebuilding the tribe's formal political institutions did not begin in earnest until the late 1970s. By the mid-1990s, extensive rebuilding had taken place, helping better equip the tribe to defend their water rights and resist other encroachments on their sovereignty and property.

In August of 1992, tribal leaders informed the Choctaw citizenry of the tribe's intention to challenge the state's assumption of ownership over Choctaw water. Choctaw Chief Roberts, Assistant Chief Greg Pyle, and Speaker of the Choctaw Tribal Council Randle Durant then began laying the groundwork for the public announcement in late 1997 of the tribe's water-rights claim. They knew the battle would be bloody. After all, "the state [of Oklahoma] has been using tribal water since its creation, without regard for tribal interests," and under the assumption that it owns the water (Helton 1998: 1000). Choctaw leaders therefore consulted with tribal attorneys, participated in informal meetings with state officials, prepared materials for distribution to Oklahoma state legislators, and talked with the NTWA and other bidders about the idea of leasing Choctaw water. They also mobilized support for the tribe's impending claim by educating Choctaws about the tribe's rights, the illegality of the state's actions, and the necessity of taking action to defend Choctaw water rights and sovereignty. Several times I observed Choctaw leaders electrify crowds of Choctaw citizens with their words about the water.

Especially after the public announcement of the tribe's water-rights claim, tribal leaders launched a public relations campaign to mobilize support from non-Choctaws. The tribe began using full-page newspaper ads, door-to-door solicitors and public meetings to promote tribal sovereignty over the water and the leasing of Choctaw water by the tribe to the NTWA. Tribal control of the water, said tribal leaders, would bring "an unprecedented economic boon to the region." The tribe sponsored dinners to which they invited journalists, bankers, and county commissioners. They also hired Tommy Thomas, a former legislator, to promote public acceptance of a water lease that would still leave "plenty of water for Oklahoma's needs" and would permit unprecedented amounts of capital to flow into the Choctaw Nation.

On November 14, 2001, a draft agreement was reached between Oklahoma and the Choctaw and Chickasaw tribes. At virtually the last minute, it was decided that the water within Chickasaw tribal boundaries would also be a part of the agreement. Despite the Choctaws' extensive preparations for this battle with the state, the outcome was disappointing for both tribes. The agreement stated that Oklahoma, on the one hand, and the Choctaw and the Chickasaw tribes, on the other hand, would evenly split the revenues from leasing southeastern Oklahoma water. The Choctaws would get 37.5 percent; the Chickasaws would get 12.5 percent. All of the state's share, however, was to be spent on economic development in southeastern Oklahoma. A board of southeastern Oklahomans, with only limited representation on the part of the state, would decide how, specifically, to spend the state's share. The tribes' failure to gain recognition of their full treaty-based water rights in this draft agreement can be explained by the historic failure of U.S. state and federal governments to honor treaties with American Indian tribes. It can also be explained by the relative weakness of the Choctaw and Chickasaw tribes relative to the state. An important factor in obtaining tribal consent to this agreement was the sense of urgency that the leaders of both of these tribes felt about the need to create new jobs and businesses in their homelands. The tribes agreed to work toward forging an agreement outside of court to more quickly gain access to capital from water leasing, and they agreed to a deal that ensured that all such capital would be spent in their homelands. In one sense, then, the agreement represents a small victory for Choctaw and Chickasaw self-determination. It is, however, a significant loss for Choctaw and Chickasaw tribal sovereignty, as well as for the honoring of treaties by U.S. federal and state governments.

By 2005, however, the tribes and the state still had not reached an agreement with the NTWA for leasing the water. Moreover, the tribes and the state still had not ratified, through a vote of the Oklahoma state legislature, the terms on which they agreed to "comanage" this resource (see Biolsi 2005). In June of 2005, I had a long conversation with my chief, Greg Pyle, about this conflict and other matters. Pyle told me that the principal cause of the impasse was that the NTWA had been unwilling to offer a price that the state and the tribes found acceptable.

Especially in the late 20th and early 21st centuries, the United States has held itself up as a model nation in its respect for the political rights of minority populations within its borders and its promotion of multiculturalism. It claims to provide a safe haven for its indigenous peoples, offering them ample room to exercise their sovereignty, pursue their rights to self-determination, and achieve a high degree of economic and political autonomy. However, this state model of the political accommodation of tribes in the United States, a model that has received a great deal of international attention, cannot itself accommodate the tribal experiences described in this chapter. Choctaws and doubtless other tribes in the United States continue to experience repeated assaults on their sovereignty, the imposition of unreasonable constraints on their pursuit of self-determination, and attempted and actual seizures of their property. Indigenous peoples would best look elsewhere for an ideal for which to strive.

References

Biolsi, Thomas. 2001. *"Deadliest enemies:" Law and the making of race relations on and off Rosebud Reservation.* Berkeley: University of California Press.

——. 2005. Imagined geographies: Sovereignty, indigenous space, and American Indian struggle. *American Ethnologist* 32 (2): 247–259.

Cattelino, Jessica. 2004. *High stakes: Seminole sovereignty in the casino era.* Ph.D. dissertation, Department of Anthropology, New York University.

Faiman-Silva, Sandra. 1997. *Choctaws at the crossroads: The political economy of class and culture in the Oklahoma timber region.* Lincoln: University of Nebraska Press.

Foster, Morris W. 2001. Choctaw social organization. In *Choctaw language and culture: Chata Anumpa,* edited by Marcia Hagg and Henry Willis, 250–254. Norman: University of Oklahoma Press.

Helton, Taiwagi. 1998. Indian reserved water rights in the dual-system state of Oklahoma. *Tulsa Law Journal* 33: 979–1002.

Johnson, Richard R., and Alvin O. Turner. 1998. *Oklahoma at the cross-roads.* Dubuque: Kendall–Hunt Publishing.

Kersey, Harry A. 1996. *An assumption of sovereignty: Social and political transformation among the Florida Seminoles, 1953–1979.* Lincoln: University of Nebraska Press.

Kidwell, Clara Sue. 1995. *Choctaw and missionaries in Mississippi, 1818–1918.* Norman: University of Oklahoma Press.

O'Brien, Sharon. 1989. *American Indian tribal governments.* Norman: University of Oklahoma Press.

Wilkins, David E., and K. Tsianina Lomawaima. 2001. *Uneven ground: American Indian sovereignty and federal law.* Norman: University of Oklahoma Press.

Sovereignty's Betrayals

Michael F. Brown

The worldwide campaign for indigenous rights invokes few words as reverently as it does *sovereignty*. Even when undeclared—and in many contexts it must remain so—sovereignty is the proverbial elephant in the room during global forums on indigeneity. Those who use the term sometimes disagree about its meaning and implications, but its centrality to the political agenda of the contemporary indigenous-rights movement is indisputable.

One might expect that anthropologists, whose occupational reflexes include skepticism toward received categories, would have brought sovereignty under the microscope, but examples of this kind of critical analysis are few. The most likely explanation for such diffidence is the broad support that the indigenous-rights movement enjoys within the profession. It is also the case, as Anna Tsing (this volume) observes, that indigenous leaders often reject suggestions that they should define precisely the movement's central concepts, including sovereignty and indigeneity itself.[1] Nevertheless, in view of the importance of indigenous activism on the world stage and the accelerating diffusion of sovereignty rhetoric to regions where it was previously unknown, we may have arrived at a moment when the notion of the sovereignty of indigenous peoples—of *any* people, for that matter—warrants critical attention.

In this chapter, I review the history and multiple meanings of sovereignty to highlight some unwelcome effects of its application to indigenous-rights debate and the formulation of relevant social policy. The analysis is offered in the spirit of a provocation or thought exercise, undertaken not because I am hostile to indigenous rights but because in the main I support them. Indigenous peoples should be as free as other communities to govern themselves, to promote traditional languages and social practices to the extent that these are compatible with international human-rights norms, and to exercise a high level of control over their lands and natural resources. For me, the question is not whether indigenous peoples merit redress of grievances but whether such redress is most constructively framed in the language of sovereignty. Sources of inspiration for my approach include recent articles by Thomas Biolsi (2005) and Taiaiake Alfred (2001). Biolsi reviews the current state of American Indian citizenship and tribal sovereignty to underscore the startling complexity of everyday political relations between Indians and the U.S. federal government. The variegated pattern of tribal sovereignty and its unusual interweaving with U.S. national sovereignty, Biolsi insists, make it necessary to rethink our ideas about the state. Alfred, in contrast, questions the legitimacy of sovereignty itself. His argument—a bold and iconoclastic one for a Native intellectual—is that sovereignty is so freighted with Western assumptions about power and social control that it offers a deeply flawed roadmap for the reconstitution of vibrant, authentic Native polities.

Sovereignty holds particular interest because of its talismanic status within the indigenous-rights movement. The sanctity of the term, and its utopian connotations, echo other utopian ideologies that shaped human experience in the 20th century and that continue to affect us today. Utopias have not fared well in recent social thought. The historian Robert Conquest (2000) argues that utopian political programs— those advancing simple, comprehensive solutions to complex social problems—inevitably give rise to totalitarianism. Commentators such as David Harvey (2000) identify neoliberal economics as the dominant utopian ideology of the postsocialist era, and its coercive strategies are almost universally deplored by anthropologists. Yet Harvey, in common with many others, hesitates to forsake utopias. Without them, he says, we lose the sense of open-ended possibilities needed to transcend the stunted political imagination of our time. The view of utopian ideologies that informs the following assessment of indigenous sovereignty is most compatible with the tragic sensibility championed by Terry Eagleton (2003: 186), who calls on social theorists to acknowledge the imperfections of social action without abandoning all ideals or hopes. Where sovereignty is concerned, this means that sovereignty's troubling side—its dystopian arrogance, its need to clarify lines of power by separating one people from another—must be faced squarely if we are to draw from it something useful.

Genealogies of Sovereignty

For a term of great political consequence, *sovereignty* has a surprisingly unstable meaning. The obvious etymological link is to the idea of "the sovereign," a leader imbued with both secular and sacred power. With the rise of the secular state, however, sovereignty came to signify the autonomy and independence of the nation-state vis-à-vis other similar polities. Sovereign nations, in other words, were seen to enjoy an unrestricted right to govern their own internal affairs. State sovereignty was long considered absolute, or nearly so, but in the 20th century the emergence of international law and human-rights protocols has undermined the ability of states to claim that external intervention in their internal governance is always improper. According to the legal scholar Hurst Hannum, the issue about which there is the most agreement at the global level is that "sovereignty is an attribute of statehood, and that only states can be sovereign" (Hannum 1996: 15).

The link to statehood explains why the term *sovereignty* appears so rarely in indigenous-rights documents crafted by the United Nations, UNESCO, and related institutions, including the *Draft Declaration on the Rights of Indigenous Peoples* (1994). The UN charter underlines the importance of "national sovereignty," which prevents it from explicitly identifying ethnic communities as sovereign nations (Köchler 2001: 137). Assertion of a "right to ethnic sovereignty" for indigenous peoples or any other community would place the United Nations in violation of its own foundational principles. Hence, the regular use of "self-determination" as a proxy for sovereignty in UN policy statements.[2]

Outside the walls of the United Nations, a desire for sovereignty is voiced freely and often. Robert B. Porter (2002: 101), an American Indian legal scholar, puts the strong version of indigenous sovereignty in the bluntest possible terms: "We maintain the right to do whatever we want in our own territory without limitations."[3] Within indigenous-rights debate, the meaning of sovereignty has steadily broadened from its conventional implications to encompass every aspect of indigenous life, including education, language, religion, and the expressive arts. Sovereignty is reimagined as a condition of autonomy from other cultures and political entities—an autonomy inseparable from a hoped-for return to primal authenticity. As such, it stands as the culmination of a slow, painful process of decolonization under way throughout the indigenous world.

Such expansive views of sovereignty have a long history in political philosophy. Although *state* sovereignty is arguably the dominant expression of the concept, notions of popular and even self-sovereignty can be traced back the foundational works of Locke, Hobbes, and Rousseau (see Hoffman 1998). This current of sovereignty thought is often antistatist in its principal thrust, insisting that the state's coercive powers and monopolistic control of force are fundamentally at odds with the freedom of individuals and communities to chart their own political course.

Making an impassioned case for an expanded notion of sovereignty that transcends the merely political, Wallace Coffey and Rebecca Tsosie (2001: 196) insist that indigenous peoples must fight for *cultural* sovereignty, which serves as a bulwark against the "forces of mass media, the educational system, and a host of court decisions failing to protect the religious or cultural rights of Native peoples." For them, sovereignty is an almost mystical state that arises spontaneously within the social life and traditions of a people. Coffey and Tsosie identify repatriation as a dominant theme for this indigenous version of sovereignty—not just repatriation of religious objects and human remains, but the recovery of languages, religions, and values, as well as a purging of unwanted influences originating in nonindigenous cultural life. Inseparable from the project of repatriation is the assertion of control over all representations of indigenous lifeways. What diffuses out from a native nation, in other words, is as important to sovereignty as what does, or does not, flow in. In a similar vein, but with particular attention to the Maori of New Zealand/Aotearoa, Stephen Turner (2002: 75, 92) insists that sovereignty is expressed in the "palpable silence" of indigenous New Zealanders, whose unique experiences cannot and should not be shared with non-Maori.

The status of sovereignty as an untouchable article of faith is made equally clear by Andrea Smith, who struggles to reconcile her commitments as a Native feminist with the sometimes negative impact that indigenous sovereignty has had on American Indian women. Smith (2005: 123) notes that decisions of the U.S. Supreme Court (notably, *Santa Clara Pueblo v. Martinez* [436 U.S. 49, 69, 1978]) have affirmed the right of federally recognized Indian nations to exclude from membership the children of female members who married outside their tribe while recognizing the children of male members involved in similar extratribal unions. This gender-based discrimination, welcomed by many as a ratification of the sovereign right of Indian nations to determine their own membership, raises troubling questions for Native feminists. Unwilling to jettison faith in sovereignty despite this betrayal of feminist principles, Smith claims that achievement of true sovereignty would lead to liberation for all peoples, not just Native ones. She ultimately rejects the possibility that sovereignty emerged from and is an organizing principle for the oppressive system she so vigorously resists.[4]

The last stop on sovereignty's journey from the political to the metaphysical is the power attributed to it by people involved in libertarian populism and "common law" resistance, an unstable movement in which elements of far right and far left mutate and fuse. I do not wish to imply that the indigenous-rights movement has inspired or promoted contemporary Anglo-American theories of popular sovereignty, some of which (e.g., Aryan Nation militias) are actively hostile to nonwhite peoples. Such theories date to the French Revolution, if not earlier. At the same time, the centrality of a totalizing, mystical notion of sovereignty to both movements is hardly coincidental. Both arise from the same *Zeitgeist*—the fear, for example, that local values and self-governance are under assault by distant powers who stand to benefit from a compliant, culturally uniform populace. Both are also profoundly antimodernist, rejecting modernity's disembedding of social institutions and its marked tendency to universalize time and space (Giddens 1991: 20–21). And both repudiate liberal cosmopolitanism in favor of a sacralization of the local.

Sovereignty Rhetoric in the Global Indigenous-Rights Movement

As far as I have been able to determine, the invocation of sovereignty when discussing indigenous rights first arose in North America, particularly in the United States, because of a century-long history of formal treaty making between the U.S. government and Indian nations, a process that was far rarer in other colonized regions of the New World. Until the practice of negotiating treaties with North American tribes was ended in 1871, the U.S. government officially regarded Indians as autonomous nations to be dealt with at the federal rather than state level, and they were not automatically treated as U.S. citizens until 1924.[5] This acknowledgment of indigenous nationhood is, however, famously conditional. In many treaties, the government promised to defend Indian land, resources, and the general welfare of Indian people, an expression of paternalism known as the "federal trust responsibility." And Congress assiduously protects its "plenary power" to redefine the federal government's legal relationship to Indian nations as it sees fit. Although this power is occasionally invoked by federal authorities (and never forgotten by American Indians), a multitude of legal precedents and institutional practices make it unlikely that Congress would take the extreme step of voiding the many treaties that underpin relations between the United States and Native America.

Practical acknowledgment of tribal sovereignty within American political life was slow in coming. The 20th century was characterized by a seesaw pattern of rising tribal autonomy punctuated by periods of federal resistance and retrenchment. Nevertheless, the last 50 years have seen an impressive strengthening of independent tribal governance and a routinization of the social arrangements that give it life, including tribal management of education, public safety, judicial process, and civil administration.[6]

The particular notion of indigenous sovereignty that has arisen in the United States and Canada (the latter involving a different administrative history) has broad significance because of the pivotal role that Native American activists and intellectuals have played in the indigenous-rights movement worldwide. However difficult the experience of U.S. and Canadian Indians, their overall situation is better than that of their counterparts in most other parts of the world. Growing numbers have been able to pursue higher education and professional training, and advocates for indigenous rights in North America now present their views forcefully in courtrooms and other public arenas.

The global reach of U.S. media has insured that Indians are seen almost everywhere as the archetype of the indigenous. It is hardly surprising, then, that the North American view of Native self-determination has diffused steadily from its historic hearth to other communities that have come to identify themselves as indigenous. The word sovereignty is increasingly deployed in indigenous-rights advocacy in Australia, New Zealand, and, with reference to the Sami population, in Scandinavia. It has been slower to gain a foothold in other parts of the world. Latin America may be most notable, especially considering the extraordinary rise of indigenous political power during the 1990s. In some contexts—Bolivia comes immediately to mind—indigenous peoples represent a numerical majority, making *indigenous* sovereignty, as such, a less salient issue. In other parts of the region, nationalist leaders repress indigenous-rights debate that even hints at sovereignty claims, perhaps because states are threatened by the prospect of losing access to subsurface oil and mineral resources (see Jackson and Warren 2005). In Southeast Asia, Africa, and India, indigeneity itself is a problematic concept that, even if it can be institutionalized in some politically acceptable way, seems unlikely to lead to the widespread creation of autonomous homelands in the foreseeable future (Bowen 2000; Karlsson 2003; Kuper 2003).

Critiques of Indigenous Sovereignty

Political scientists have proven less reluctant than anthropologists to raise questions about sovereignty's moral standing. One critical strain comes from advocates of classic liberalism who worry that sovereignty, as well as other expressions of cultural separatism, could readily shield illiberal practices from external scrutiny, especially in such areas as the treatment of women or religious nonconformists. Although this is a valid concern, the evidence that indigenous communities are more given to illiberal practices than nation-states is unconvincing. A more provocative question has been posed by the legal scholar Jeremy Waldron (2003): What are the moral and political implications of the role played by the doctrine of "firstness" in the indigenous-rights movement, especially claims to land alienated from indigenous peoples during the colonial era? Waldron wonders how we are to identify the (truly) first occupants of specific territories and assess the standing of indigenous groups who acquired their lands through military conquests that may be as morally questionable as those of colonialists, or nearly so. This question bears less on the issue of sovereignty than on indigeneity broadly construed. As we shall see, however, the complex relationship between land (already possessed or sought through a process of reparations) and indigenous identity is deeply implicated in notions of sovereignty.[7]

Other critiques focus on the alleged tactical drawbacks of sovereignty rhetoric. Assertions of sovereignty raise the specter of secession and potentially of civil war, thereby alienating members of the majority society who might otherwise sympathize with indigenous demands when these are framed in the idiom of human rights (see, e.g., Corntassel and Primeau 1995). Although there is little question that local opposition to indigenous sovereignty sometimes evokes "one-nation-for-all" rhetoric (Mackey 2005), in many settings the idea of indigenous self-rule has become so familiar that most nonindigenous citizens accept it, even if grudgingly. The country offering the highest level of indigenous sovereignty, the United States, provides scant evidence that the political autonomy enjoyed by members of federally recognized Indian tribes has lessened their commitment to the defense of the nation-state. Native Americans have amassed an unassailable record of distinguished service to the nation's armed forces, and their public ceremonies emphasize the strength of their dual allegiance to an Indian nation and the United States (Limerick 2005).

Thus far, then, there is little evidence that indigenous sovereignty fuels secessionist tendencies, although how demands for local autonomy might play out in settings of fragile national unity remains unclear. A stronger case can be made that indigenous-rights discourse has the unhappy effect of driving apart politically subordinate groups that otherwise might present a united front against powerful national interests. This is the principal point made by Sangeeta Kamat, who has studied the rise of indigenous-rights politics in Maharashtra, India. Kamat alleges that anthropology's current infatuation with indigenous peoples—"tribals" in the South Asian context—stifles critiques of neoliberal economics by severing the links between indigenous peoples and ordinary peasants, all of whom are trapped by the same system of exploitation. "Such claims to [indigenous] identity and autonomy," Kamat says, "serve to empower individuals on the basis of being different from others and construct a new elitism, but provide little opportunity to build solidarity for a new cultural politics. In this way, they help contain the discontent of the subaltern who can refer to a new romanticized identity of tribal that is placed in a new hierarchy with other subaltern groups" (2001: 44).

Perhaps the most trenchant critique of the notion of indigenous sovereignty is put forward by the Mohawk political scientist Taiaiake Alfred, whose article "From Sovereignty to Freedom" (2001; see also 2005) develops ideas first explored in the work of Vine Deloria Jr., and others. Alfred argues that sovereignty is a profoundly ethnocentric concept predicated on European attitudes toward governance, political hierarchy, and the legitimate uses of power. He finds these values and practices incompatible with an authentically indigenous politics, which rejects, among other things, "absolute authority," "coercive enforcement of decisions," and the separation of political rule from other aspects of everyday life. To subscribe to a doctrine of sovereignty is, in Alfred's opinion, to evade a moral duty to decolonize indigenous life. "Sovereignty itself implies a set of values and objectives that put it in direct opposition to the values and objectives found in most traditional indigenous philosophies," he insists (Alfred 2001: 27, 28).[8]

The alternative that Alfred sketches is evocative but indistinct. A nonsovereignty-based system of traditional governance would repudiate coercion and foster healthy relationships with the land. "Indigenous thought is often based on the notion that people, communities, and the other elements of creation co-exist as equals—human beings as either individuals or collectives do not have special priority in deciding the justice of a situation" (Alfred 2001: 31). Alfred ends his article on a utopian note, observing that prior to the rise of European colonialism, indigenous peoples had "achieved sovereignty-free regimes of conscience and justice" that, if revived, could help to make the world a better place for everyone (2001: 34). Admittedly, Alfred's conviction that Native people are always and everywhere paragons of participatory democracy is hard to square with historically documented cases of indigenous imperialism and social stratification. Given the modest scale of most Native American tribes or bands today, however, they may be amenable to the retraditionalized systems of governance that Alfred advocates, although most would, as he himself acknowledges, have to adapt such practices to the challenge of dealing with a hierarchical and bureaucratic state.[9]

Alfred's hopeful vision of a sovereignty-free world is echoed in the work of other political scientists, notably, James Tully and Iris Marion Young. Young (2000: 253), for instance, makes a case for what she calls "decentered diverse democratic federalism" inspired by precisely the forms of Iroquoian self-rule with which Taiaiake Alfred identifies. Although localities down to the hamlet level would enjoy a broad right of self-determination, they would not possess sovereignty in the sense of being closed to the opinions of outsiders who can reasonably claim to have a stake in local decisions. This pattern of nested autonomy articulating with consultation at higher levels would be extended to the international level. States would cede some of their powers to global governing institutions and some to localities. Like Alfred, Young holds that massive changes along the lines she proposes are a moral imperative for anyone committed to advancing the postcolonial project.

From Theory to Practice

Discussions of indigenous sovereignty need not be conducted at the level of theory alone: the high level of self-determination enjoyed by federally recognized tribes in the United States offers ample evidence of sovereignty's possibilities and perils. A thorough review the economic and political history of Indian nations is beyond the scope of this chapter. That said, there is little question that tribal self-governance has been beneficial to Native Americans over the past two decades. A study released early in 2005 by a Harvard think tank reveals that almost every index of economic development showed dramatic improvement in Indian Country during the 1990s. This growth was substantially greater than that of the U.S. economy as a whole. Indian reservations still lag far behind the rest of the United States in such indexes as per capita income and employment levels, but the disparity is shrinking. The authors of the study attribute this improvement almost entirely to the benefits of tribal self-determination (Taylor and Kalt 2005).

The Harvard study shows that the economic picture for the subset of Indian nations that run casino operations (currently more than 200) is better still, although the advantage is not as marked if one brackets from consideration the experience of a handful of tribes who have reaped enormous profits. With few exceptions, gaming is seen by American Indian leaders and policymakers as having had a positive impact on their nations. It has been a formidable engine of economic growth and raised the profile of Native sovereignty in the public mind.

Yet amid all the favorable talk about Indian gaming there are conspicuous zones of silence. It is difficult, for instance, to find works in the humanities and social sciences that ask hard questions about the morality of the gaming industry, a surprising reticence for disciplines that show little reluctance to assert a moral stance toward other corporate enterprises that prey on human vulnerability.[10] The prevailing attitude in this case is strictly utilitarian. Legalized gambling is going to take place anyway, the argument goes. We should celebrate because the proceeds benefit Native Americans rather than Donald Trump. Gaming tribes have generally done a good job of redistributing profits to their citizens in ways that genuinely improve their individual and communal lives, unlike non-Native gaming corporations, whose activities benefit only affluent owners or shareholders. Still, to hold that gaming has been a good thing for American Indians is a far cry from concluding that, on balance, it benefits the larger society of which Indian nations are a part.

The effects of Native gaming on surrounding non-Native communities are mixed. Non-Native employment in counties with casinos tends to increase, mostly because reservations often lack a labor force sufficiently large to staff a casino operation. According to one recent study (Evans and Topoleski 2002: 48), however, this benefit is realized at the cost of "a ten percent increase in bankruptcies, auto theft and larceny rates, plus violent crime four or more years after a casino opens in a county." In broader terms, legalized gambling, whoever conducts it, is inseparable from the slow-motion demolition of progressive taxation policies and the U.S. social safety net. Gaming revenues are drawn disproportionately from low-income citizens and (as the tired joke goes) those who failed math in high school. One need not be a card-carrying member of the Traditional Values Coalition, in other words, to regard the dramatic expansion of the gaming industry with a degree of moral ambivalence, regardless of whether it is managed by Indian nations, private corporations, or state lottery systems.

Even if one is convinced that legalized gambling is a Faustian bargain worth making, the cash flowing into gaming tribes has given their sovereignty a new robustness that inclines Indian nations to implement policies previously unfamiliar to them. Some of these are admirable—for instance, the impressive donations that wealthy tribes made to the National Museum of the American Indian and their efforts to direct financial support to less fortunate tribes. Others are disquieting:

- As sovereign nations, Indian tribes regard themselves as exempt from federal and state laws that permit labor unions to organize in tribal businesses. After a California tribe blocked a union's effort to organize casino employees, the National Labor Relations Board (NLRB) intervened on the union's behalf. The NLRB decision, which is certain to be challenged in federal court, prompted the newspaper *Indian Country Today* (2004) to insist in an editorial that "this is not a question of tribes being anti-union, or even more pertinently, anti-worker. In principle, it is a question of tribal sovereignty." Given prior federal court decisions, it is likely that tribes will retain the power to close their businesses to union organizers and to dismiss workers who demonstrate pro-union sympathies.[11] The sovereignty doctrine also puts tribal businesses beyond the reach of state or federal worker-compensation laws. In California, gaming tribes have apparently agreed to meet statewide worker-compensation standards, but as sovereign nations the tribes are responsible for policing their own compliance, a significant conflict of interest in view of the financial stakes. The lack of external oversight has given rise to credible accusations that prevailing standards are routinely ignored when workers (especially Mexican immigrants in the tribal workforce) suffer work-related injuries (Millman 2002: A1).
- Many Indian gaming operations have been financed by non-Native investors, who provide backing for the acquisition of land (a process known as "reservation shopping"), help effect its transformation from private property to trust status, and sell lucrative management services that may continue on a consulting basis long after the transition to local control required by the Indian Gaming Regulatory Act. One of these firms, owned by a controversial

South African entrepreneur, also managed similar operations in several tribal homelands in Southern Africa. Because disclosure requirements are routinely ignored, the true scale of consulting contracts with outside (i.e., non-Native) investors and management firms is not a matter of public record (Perry 2006: 125–126; *Time Magazine* 2002).

■ Conversion to trust status of lands acquired for Native American business operations frees these firms from burdensome state and local environmental protection codes. This has led a land development firm to propose donating its property in Anne Arundel County, Maryland, to the Delaware Nation of Oklahoma, the tribe's goal being to secure conversion of the land to trust status and then to receive royalties from the developer's landfill operation on the site (Davenport 2004). (As I write, the issue has still not been resolved.) To my knowledge, the Delawares have made no claim that this transaction would restore to them tribal lands lost long ago. It is strictly a business arrangement in a place located hundreds of miles from their reservation.

■ The doctrine of tribal sovereignty exempts tribes from state campaign-finance laws that limit contributions to political candidates and stipulate public disclosure of such contributions when they occur. It also invites influence peddling of the sort that came to public attention beginning in 2004, when it was revealed that Washington lobbyists with close ties to the Republican party had received payments exceeding $66 million from a half-dozen Indian tribes for lobbying services that in some cases were never actually provided (Committee on Indian Affairs 2006).

It might be argued that these problems tell us less about sovereignty than about morally flawed leadership, which can afflict any community.[12] There is some truth to this, yet it is impossible to ignore the extent to which the implacable logic of sovereignty prompts decisions and policies that favor one's own citizens at the expense of others. Indeed, if I were serving as an elected official of a federally recognized tribe, charged with the responsibility to make decisions that primarily or perhaps even exclusively benefit members of my nation, I might be guilty of malfeasance if I pursued any policy *other* than opposing unionization, denying non-Native workers adequate compensation for injury, and so on. This is sovereignty's power and its tragic flaw.

Sovereignty of the micronational variety is clearly implicated in the rise of minimally regulated political spaces that are immensely useful to global capital. The blandishments of well financed corporations may be irresistible to impoverished Native nations with no other obvious source of income for the provision of basic community needs, a situation illustrated by the courtship of the Goshutes of Utah by a consortium of utility companies interested in finding a permanent resting place for tons of highly radioactive waste from U.S. nuclear power plants (Fahys 2002; Johnson 2005). As is frequently observed, in a globalized economy one underregulated nation's success in manufacturing and resource extraction tends to push others in the same direction as part of a "geo-spatial race to the bottom" (Perry 2006: 126) involving the abandonment of burdensome environmental regulations, accounting rules, and worker benefits. There is no reason to expect that indigenous nations would be worse in this respect than nation-states; neither is there cause to believe that they would be better, especially considering their often stark economic circumstances. Rogue micronations located in settings characterized by a weakly developed civil society and a tradition of political corruption offer the prospect of becoming to commerce and resource extraction what Liberian registry is to the global shipping industry and the Cayman Islands are to international banking. Observers such as Richard Warren Perry contend that even in North America the "irruption of spectral sovereignties" is bringing on "new privatized and market-rationalized spatial regimes of enclosure and exclusion" (2006: 125, 127) that remain disquieting even if we acknowledge the economic benefits they have brought to the indigenous communities participating in them.

Another bundle of problems that have arisen during the past two decades concerns sovereignty's impact on relations *among* indigenous peoples. The rhetoric and practice of sovereignty drive a wedge between landed and landless indigenous peoples. Appeals to the notion of sovereignty make little sense without land, which helps to explain why a link between indigenous peoples and land has emerged, at least in some international venues, as the sine qua non of indigenous identity. But with thousands of indigenous people living in ethnically mixed rural regions and urban centers in Latin America, Africa, and Asia, it is hard to see how the struggle for indigenous rights is advanced by emphasizing a monolithic vision of indigenous territorial sovereignty that is likely to remain unattainable for many.

As noted earlier, advocates for indigenous rights often appeal to the principle of cultural sovereignty when discussing problems occasioned by unwanted flows of information and artistic productions between indigenous societies and the wider world. In this arena, indigenous leaders increasingly speak the same language as nation-states, many of whom back the efforts of UNESCO to promote international conventions that validate the right of states to control importation of alien cultural products, including films, recorded music, and television programming, in the interest of "protecting cultural heritage."

These discussions address legitimate problems created by the growing power of global mass media and the predatory Information Economy (Brown 2005; Watkins 2005). Nevertheless, sovereignty logic leads down a blind alley when directed to matters of intellectual property. Was there ever a time in human history when peoples enjoyed "sovereign" control of their languages, biological knowledge, or forms of artistic expression? I find no evidence to suggest it. The metaphor of sovereignty implies that each culture's heritage is sui generis: unique, bounded, and subject to conscious control, none of which is true. A logic of sovereignty rooted in the 17th-century Treaty of Westphalia simply is not up to the task of dealing with problems arising from the exploitative potential of global information networks. Even the most muscular sovereign of the moment, the United States, struggles with limited success to defend its intellectual property resources from large-scale industrial piracy in China, Pakistan, Indonesia, and elsewhere, suggesting that sovereignty provides little purchase in this situation.

An example inspired by recent events illustrates the problem. When indigenous leaders or indigenous-rights advocacy groups denounce an alleged instance of biopiracy, as they did when the ICBG-Maya project was still under way in Chiapas prior to 2001 (Brown 2003: 114–125), they typically argue that the indigenous groups being studied have sovereign rights of control over traditional ethnobotanical knowledge. But one group or community alone rarely harbors this knowledge. It is likely that neighboring communities, indigenous or otherwise, also possess this information if they have occupied a biogeographic region long enough. If any one of these peoples decides to share the knowledge with outsiders, they violate the "sovereign" rights of their neighbors. Yet declaring an indefinite moratorium on all forms of bioprospecting (and increasingly, any kind of research that even vaguely resembles bioprospecting), as some activists insist, denies indigenous communities badly needed revenues they might have earned had they abandoned sovereignty discourse, with its misguided assumptions of absolute possession and control, in favor of more flexible approaches to the protection of their economic and moral rights in commercially valuable information.

After Sovereignty

The political scientist Anthony Burke has condemned sovereignty as a "complex and malign articulation of law, power, possibility and force," possessed of a "suffocating ontology" (Burke 2002: para. 6). Burke's language may be excessive, but like Taiaiake Alfred he voices the conviction that sovereignty is too burdened with connotations of arbitrary power, unrealizable ambitions, and the relentless policing of boundaries to help us imagine a world in which indigenous communities balance their collective sense of purpose with the legitimate needs and concerns of their neighbors. Admittedly, this leaves American Indians in an awkward position. Their political reality has been defined by the history of treaty making, a quintessential expression of the pragmatics of sovereignty played out in a colonial North America reshaped by European ideologies and expressions of power. For now, this is the logic by which American Indian aspirations are framed. American Indian sovereignty, like all institutions, is not a creation of the gods but of humankind, afflicted by human limitations and reshaped through time by individual choices and the Law of Unintended Consequences.

Less clear is whether those who support indigenous aspirations should encourage the viral spread of the idiom of sovereignty to new settings in which the appropriateness of its application is at best questionable— parts of Latin America, say, where Native people and others of mixed heritage live side by side or regions in Africa where deep histories of migration and ethnogenesis make it difficult to distinguish between "original" inhabitants and more recent arrivals (Nyamnjoh this volume). A rejoinder is that "modular" models of sovereignty (Biolsi 2005: 245) are but one facet of sovereignty's kaleidoscopic significance.[13] As we have seen, the term is also deployed as shorthand for the collective freedom of one group to live unconstrained by the histories, values, and power of others. Complete sovereignty is obviously an unattainable ideal, but a case can be made that it provides a tactically useful goal for indigenous peoples to foreground when communicating their political demands, provided that they can resist the tendency to invest it with transcendent moral significance. Nevertheless, can a concept so burdened by history shed its dark legacy? On a shrinking planet, is any good purpose served by pretending that one people can stand alone from others? There are many reasons to think not.

If not sovereignty, then what? "Self-determination" is the current alternative of choice. It has obvious virtues. It emphasizes a group's desire to manage its own affairs and selectively perpetuate its own traditions.

Yet in common with sovereignty, it implies that any people is capable of "determining" itself independent of others, a dubious assumption in an interconnected world. It slides too easily into the language of cultural purification and forced sorting along ethnic lines.[14] Another plausible candidate, James Clifford's "articulation theory" (2001), offers intriguing suppleness, readily accommodating the contingencies of place and of history. But it may be too demanding and subtle for ready application in the policy world. Others insist that approaches focusing on cultural rights are superior to sovereignty rhetoric because they emphasize the immediate needs of indigenous peoples without directly challenging the territorial integrity of nation-states (Robbins and Stamatopoulou 2004). Still others propose rehabilitating sovereignty by recasting it in reciprocal terms that repudiate the concept's legacy of hierarchical control (Hoffman 1998: 96–107).

Whatever approach emerges as an alternative to sovereignty in indigenous-rights discourse, to be convincing it must advance arguments in support of self-governance, freedom of religion, and the right to benefit directly from the use of local cultural or natural resources. It must also be flexible enough to accommodate certain realities of indigenous life that are widely recognized but rarely articulated: that countless individuals of indigenous descent live far from the lands that their ancestors called home; that their family lines are likely to be intertwined with those of nonindigenous populations; and that, in the context of many developing countries, their legitimate economic and social needs must be weighed against those of thousands of nonindigenous people who may be just as poor and politically marginalized, or nearly so. To lose sight of the wider context is to fall victim to sovereignty's seductions yet again.

Afterword

Most scholars, I expect, experience moments when they fear that their work has sunk to the level of a word game, a worrying of subtle differences that count for little in the turbulence of human affairs. Writing about sovereignty's betrayals has prompted me to wonder whether I have not fallen into this trap. Against the limits of words I weigh the promise of the locally controlled Navajo schools where I taught during the summers of my undergraduate years or the sense of optimism afforded by large land concessions given by the Peruvian government to a few lucky communities of Aguaruna Indians, with whom I lived in the Alto Río Mayo in the 1970s. In both situations there was a palpable sense of hope and pride—complicated, of course, by internal strife and external meddling. Indigenous people were pleased to be in charge of some important aspect of their lives, and they struggled to acquire the skills that would allow them to succeed on their own terms despite a legacy of outside control by paternalistic colonial states. When indigenous people speak of sovereignty, the word's meaning is shaped by context and by the aspirations of particular communities. Centuries of confrontation have given Native leaders an advanced education in the fine art of negotiation, and most recognize that absolute sovereignty of the sort claimed by nation-states (and rarely achieved in practice) is neither imminent nor desirable. Some indigenous people may embrace visions of sovereignty that, as Jessica Cattelino (2006: 723) puts it, are "based on interdependency, in which the multiple governments of reservation, tribal nation, and settler state exist in tension and mutual constitution." Nevertheless, powerful words shape habits of mind. Inextricably tied to notions of sovereignty is a clear boundary between us and them. Sovereignty sets the terms by which this boundary is enacted in everyday life. In some situations a doctrine of sovereignty may clarify relationships in useful ways. Applied to the more ambiguous circumstances of indigenous identity in other settings, however, sovereignty becomes a mandate to exclude, a warrant to indulge the narcissism of small differences, and a license to advance one people's goals at the expense of another's. If the term is used at all, it should be deployed with awareness of the pathologies lying just beneath its glittering surface.

The global movement for indigenous rights today presents anthropology with knotty dilemmas. Must we accept or perhaps even promote the transfer of research records—field notes, audio tapes, photographs—to the indigenous communities that now claim them as cultural property? Should we hold our tongues when advocates for indigenous rights traffic in essentialist ideologies? To what extent, if any, should our political commitments trump intellectual detachment and impartiality? How do we maintain the double vision that allows us to see simultaneously the benefits that certain policies bring to Native communities and the harm these same policies may visit on others?

When perplexed by these difficulties, I find consolation in Max Weber's 1918 meditation on the emotional and moral demands of scholarly life, "Science as a Vocation." Anthropology and sociology may seem less like sciences today than in Weber's time, and his masculinist language has not aged well. But we are no less obliged to communicate "inconvenient facts" (Weber 1958 [1918]: 147) than were the thinkers of Weber's era, no less called to disenchant the world. And in the world of indigenous affairs, few words remain as resolutely enchanted as sovereignty.

Notes

Acknowledgments. This chapter benefited from the comments of other participants in the "Indigenous Experience Today" symposium at the Villa Luppis. I am especially grateful to the organizers, Marisol de la Cadena and Orin Starn, and to the Wenner-Gren Foundation for Anthropological Research, for bringing all of us together around a single table. Earlier versions of the chapter received critical readings by Thomas Biolsi, Molly H. Mullin, and Gary Wheeler, as well as a anonymous reviewer. My thanks in no way imply that these colleagues agree with my analysis, and all errors of fact or interpretation are my own.

1. The Seneca legal scholar Robert B. Porter (2002: 101) illustrates Tsing's point when he "rejects the notion that there is some universal definition of indigenous national sovereignty that applies across indigenous, colonial, and international perspectives."

2. The circulation of a UN subcommittee report entitled *Indigenous Peoples' Permanent Sovereignty over Natural Resources* (Daes 2004) suggests that the reluctance to talk about indigenous rights in terms of sovereignty may be changing even in international organizations.

3. In a recent review article, Les Field (2003: 448) observes that the range of concerns brought together under the rubric of sovereignty is expanding rapidly among indigenous activists. He also notes that indigenous commitment to the idea of sovereignty seems to be intensifying even as nation-state sovereignty has become more precarious.

4. In the context of women's rights, the legal scholar Madhavi Sunder has described culture (and religious elements of culture in particular) as the "New Sovereignty" because of what she sees as a growing inclination to claim that it must be insulated from law and the global discourse of human rights. Indeed, Sunder (2003: 1409) observes an "increasing use of law to protect and preserve cultural stasis and hierarchy against the challenges to cultural and religious authority emerging on the ground."

5. Robert Porter (1999) has labeled the 1924 assignment of American citizenship to American Indians a "genocidal" act because it undermined indigenous

sovereignty, the framework of American Indian social identity. Such language says a great deal about how the concept of sovereignty can colonize the imagination of a Native thinker.

6. For a less optimistic view of the recent trajectory of tribal sovereignty, see McSloy 2003, Wilkins and Richotte 2003, and Lambert, this volume. Those who perceive American Indian sovereignty as imperiled point to recent decisions of the U.S. Supreme Court that limit tribes' power, although it may be too early to say whether this is a durable trend or merely one of the cyclical reversals noted earlier. Without disputing the significance of recent legal decisions, I would argue that the perception that sovereignty is under siege arises because Indian nations now increasingly exercise elements of self-determination rarely tested in the past, thus provoking new conflicts with local governments. To some extent this issue has a glass-half-full–glass-half-empty quality.

7. Waldron briefly discusses the history of New Zealand's Chatham Islands (Rehoku), which were invaded in 1835 by two Maori groups, Ngati Tama and Ngati Mutunga. The islands' native inhabitants, the Moriori, a peaceful people poorly versed in the arts of war, were killed or enslaved by the Maori occupiers, reducing their population from 1600 to 200 in a generation. One of the issues under adjudication by the Waitangi Tribunal was the percentage of Rehoku that should be seen as belonging to surviving Moriori rather than to the more numerous Maori.

8. See also Burke 2002 and Clifford (2001: 482) for reflections on the political risks of the sovereignty doctrine or, in Clifford's words, an "absolutist indigenism" in which "each distinct 'people' strives to occupy an original bit of ground." Speaking specifically of American Indian tribal sovereignty, Fergus Bordewich (1996: 328) questions the "ideology of sovereignty [that] seems to presume that racial separateness is a positive good, as if Indian bloodlines, economies, and histories were not already inextricably enmeshed with those of white, Hispanic, black, and Asian Americans."

9. Critics of Native American sovereignty argue that the small size of many Indian tribes or bands militates against meaningful nationhood because the communities cannot provide public services associated with complete self-determination. See, for example, Flanagan 2000: 95–99.

10. James V. Fenelon (2000), a Native sociologist, offers a nuanced assessment of the social divisions that gaming has exacerbated on several reservations, usually between "traditional" and "progressive" factions, but he has little to say about whether corporate-scale gambling operations are compatible with traditional indigenous values.

11. Native American arguments against unionization of tribal workforces note the dependence of Indian communities on services funded by tribal

enterprises, usually in lieu of taxes. A strike could jeopardize the operation of these businesses—an argument, of course, that can be made by management anywhere, including the nation's municipal governments. From the perspective of tribal governments, says *Indian Country Today* (2004), "the prospect of incorporating such a potentially crippling element as a union (or unions) is most threatening." For a study of the successful unionization of Navajo health workers in the Navajo Nation, see Kamper 2006.

12. An example of abuse attributable largely to moral frailty is the practice of revoking the tribal membership of individuals and families to settle personal grudges and increase per capita distributions to remaining members. For a description of how this process has affected Indian nations in California, see Beiser 2006.

13. Biolsi (2005: 245) observes that "the modular model is very much the vision and goal of tribal advocates" in the North American context.

14. Self-determination may invite solutions as problematic as the circumstances it claims to rectify. A striking example, drawn from the proceedings of an international conference on the right to self-determination held in Geneva in 2000, is the proposal of a group called the Republic of New Afrika that the United States make reparations to the descendants of slaves by, among other things, ceding the states of Louisiana, Mississippi, Alabama, Georgia, and South Carolina to African Americans willing to establish their own nation there (Killingham 2001: 162). The proposal makes no mention of the fate of the region's two dozen federal and nonfederal Indian tribes were this new African American nation to be created.

References

Alfred, Taiaiake. 2001. From sovereignty to freedom: Towards an indigenous political discourse. *Indigenous Affairs* 3: 22–34.

——. 2005. *Wasáse: Indigenous pathways of action and freedom.* Peterborough, ON: Broadview Press.

Beiser, Vince. 2006. A paper trail of tears: How casino-rich tribes are dealing members out. *Harper's Magazine,* August: 74–77.

Biolsi, Thomas. 2005. Imagined geographies: Sovereignty, indigenous space, and American Indian struggle. *American Ethnologist* 32 (2): 239–259.

Bordewich, Fergus W. 1996. *Killing the White Man's Indian: Reinventing Native Americans at the end of the twentieth century.* New York: Doubleday.

Bowen, John R. 2000. Should we have a universal concept of "Indigenous Peoples' rights?" Ethnicity and essentialism in the twenty-first century. *Anthropology Today* 16 (4, August): 12–16.

Brown, Michael F. 2005. Heritage trouble: Recent work on the protection of intangible cultural property. *International Journal of Cultural
Property* 12: 40–61.

——. 2003. *Who owns Native culture?* Cambridge, MA: Harvard University
Press.

Burke, Anthony. 2002. The perverse perseverance of sovereignty. *Borderlands* 1 (2). Electronic document, http://www.borderlandsejournal.
adelaide.edu.au/vol1no2_2002/burke-perverse.html, accessed 20
January 2005.

Cattelino, Jessica. 2006. Florida Seminole housing and the social meanings of sovereignty. *Comparative Studies in Society and History* 48:
699–726.

Clifford, James. 2001. Indigenous articulations. *Contemporary Pacific*
13 (2): 468–490.

Coffey, Wallace, and Rebecca Tsosie. 2001. Rethinking the tribal sovereignty doctrine: Cultural sovereignty and the collective future of
Indian nations. *Stanford Law and Policy Review* 12: 191–221.

Committee on Indian Affairs, U.S. Senate. 2006. *"Gimme five"—
Investigation of tribal lobbying matters.* 109th Congress, Second Session,
22 June 2006. Washington, DC: Government Printing Office.

Conquest, Robert. 2000. *Reflections on a ravaged century.* New York: W.
W. Norton.

Corntassel, Jeff J., and Tomas Hopkins Primeau. 1995. Indigenous
"Sovereignty" and International Law: Revised Strategies for Pursuing
"Self-Determination." *Human Rights Quarterly* 17 (2): 343–365.

Daes, Erica-Irene A., Special Rapporteur. 2004. *Indigenous peoples' permanent sovereignty over natural resources (advance edited version). Prevention
of discrimination and protection of indigenous peoples.* Vol. E/CN.4/
Sub.2/2004/30. 56th Session, 13 July. Geneva: United Nations.

Davenport, Christian. 2004. Surprising ally joins landfill quest: Thwarted
developer would make Indian tribe owner of Arundel Site. *Washington
Post,* November 1: B1.

Draft Declaration on the Rights of Indigenous Peoples. 1994. United Nations
Document E/CN.4/Sub.2/1994/2/Add.1. Geneva: United Nations.

Eagleton, Terry. 2003. *After theory.* New York: Basic Books.

Evans, William N., and Julie H. Topoleski. 2002. *The social and economic
impact of Native American casinos.* National Bureau of Economic
Research Working Paper, W9198. Electronic document, http://papers.
nber.gov/papers/w9198, accessed January 20, 2005.

Fahys, Judy. 2002. Drafts show seamy side of N-waste deal: Private fuel
storage tried to get the Goshutes' land for bargain-basement rate.
Salt Lake Tribune, September 29: A1.

Fenelon, James V. 2000. Traditional and modern perspectives on Indian gaming: The struggle for sovereignty. In *Indian gaming: Who wins?*, edited by Angela Mullis and David Kamper, 108–128. Los Angeles: University of California, Los Angeles, American Indian Studies Center.

Field, Les W. 2003. Dynamic tensions in Indigenous sovereignty and representation: A sampler. *American Ethnologist* 30 (3): 447–453.

Flanagan, Tom. 2000. *First Nations? Second thoughts.* Montreal: McGill-Queen's University Press.

Giddens, Anthony. 1991. *Modernity and self-identity: Self and society in the late modern age.* Stanford: Stanford University Press.

Hannum, Hurst. 1996. *Autonomy, sovereignty, and self-determination: The accommodation of conflicting rights* (Revised Edition). Philadelphia: University of Pennsylvania Press.

Harvey, David. 2000. *Spaces of hope.* Berkeley: University of California Press.

Hoffman, John. 1998. *Sovereignty.* Minneapolis: University of Minnesota Press.

Indian Country Today. 2004. Steadily Come the Unions. Editorial, June 18. Electronic document, http://www.indiancountry.com, accessed January 20, 2005.

Jackson, Jean E., and Kay V. Warren. 2005. Indigenous movements in Latin America, 1992–2004: Controversies, ironies, new directions. *Annual Reviews in Anthropology* 34: 549–573.

Johnson, Kirk. 2005. A tribe, nimble and determined, moves ahead with nuclear storage plan. *New York Times,* February 28: A15.

Kamat, Sangeeta. 2001. Anthropology and global capital: Rediscovering the noble savage. *Cultural Dynamics* 13 (1): 29–51.

Kamper, David. 2006. Organizing in the context of tribal sovereignty: The Navajo Area Indian Health Service campaign for union recognition. *Labor Studies Journal* 30 (4): 17–39.

Karlsson, Bengt G. 2003. Anthropology and the "indigenous slot": Claims to and debates about indigenous peoples' status in India. *Critique of Anthropology* 23 (4): 403–423.

Killingham, Marilyn Preston. 2001. The black nation in North America. In *In pursuit of the right of self-determination: Collected papers and proceedings of the First International Conference on the Right to Self-Determination and the United Nations,* edited by Y. N. Kly and D. Kly, 161–163. Atlanta, GA: Clarity Press.

Köchler, Hans. 2001. Self-determination as a means of democratiza-tion of the UN and the international system. In *In pursuit of the right* of self-determination: Collected papers and proceedings of the First International Conference on the Right to Self-Determination and the United Nations, edited by Y. N. Kly and D. Kly, 133–142. Atlanta, GA: Clarity Press.

Kuper, Adam. 2003. The return of the Native. *Current Anthropology* 44 (3): 389–402.

Limerick, Patricia Nelson. 2005. Live free and soar. *New York Times*, June 29: A23.

Mackey, Eva. 2005. Universal rights in conflict: "Backlash" and "benevolent resistance" to indigenous land rights. *Anthropology Today* 21 (2) April: 14–20.

McSloy, Steven Paul. 2003. The "miner's canary": A bird's eye view of American Indian law and its future. *New England Law Review* 37: 733–741.

Millman, Joel. 2002. House Advantage: Indian Casinos Win by Partly Avoiding Costly Labor Rules. *Wall Street Journal*, May 7: A1.

Perry, Richard Warren. 2006. Native American tribal gaming as crime against nature: Environment, sovereignty, globalization. *Political and Legal Anthropology Review* 29 (1): 110–131.

Porter, Robert B. 1999. The demise of the *Ongwehoweh* and the rise of the Native Americans: Redressing the genocidal act of forcing American citizenship upon indigenous peoples. *Harvard Black Letter Law Journal* 15 (Spring): 107–183.

———. 2002. The meaning of indigenous nation sovereignty. *Arizona State Law Journal* 34 (Spring): 75–112.

Robbins, Bruce, and Elsa Stamatopoulou. 2004. Reflections on culture and cultural rights. *South Atlantic Quarterly* 103 (2–3): 419–434.

Smith, Andrea. 2005. Native American feminism, sovereignty, and social change. *Feminist Studies* 31 (1): 116–132.

Sunder, Madhavi. 2003. Piercing the veil. *Yale Law Journal* 112 (6): 1399–1472.

Taylor, Jonathan B., and Joseph P. Kalt. 2005. *American Indians on reservations: A databook of socioeconomic change between the 1990 and 2000 censuses.* Harvard Project on American Indian Economic Development. Cambridge, MA: Malcolm Wiener Center for Social Policy, Harvard University. 59 pp.

Time Magazine. 2002. Who Gets the Money? December 16: 48–50.

Turner, Stephen. 2002. Sovereignty, or the art of being native. *Cultural Critique* 13 (Spring): 74–100.

Waldron, Jeremy. 2003. *Indigeneity? First Peoples and last occupancy.* New Zealand Journal of Public and International Law 1 (1): 55–82.

Watkins, Joe. 2005. Cultural nationalists, internationalists, and "intra-nationalists": Who's right and whose right? *International Journal of Cultural Property* 12 (1): 78–94.

Weber, Max. 1958 [1918]. Science as a vocation. In *From Max Weber: Essays in sociology,* edited and translated by H. H. Gerth and C. Wright Mills, 129–156. New York: Oxford University Press.

Wilkins, David E., and Keith Richotte. 2003. The Rehnquist Court and indigenous rights: The expedited diminution of native powers of governance. *Publius: The Journal of Federalism* 33 (3): 83–110.

Young, Iris Marion. 2000. Hybrid Democracy: Iroquois Federalism and the Postcolonial Project. In *Political theory and the rights of indigenous peoples,* edited by Duncan Ivison, Paul Patton, and Will Sanders, 237–258. Cambridge: Cambridge University Press.

Part 3

Indigeneity Beyond Borders

Varieties of Indigenous Experience: Diasporas, Homelands, Sovereignties

James Clifford

We shall visit our people who have gone to the lands of diaspora and tell them that we have built something, a new home for all of us. And taking a cue from the ocean's everflowing and encircling nature, we will travel far and wide to connect with oceanic and maritime peoples elsewhere, and swap stories of voyages that we have taken and those yet to be embarked on.

—Epeli Hau'ofa, on the Oceania Centre for Arts and Culture, Suva

Home is where the navel cord was cut.

—A Melanesian saying

"What contradictory people we are!"

—Linda Tuhiwai Smith, at the Wenner-Gren international conference,
"Indigenous Experience Today," March 2005

"Indigenous experience" is difficult to contain: the senses of belonging evoked by the phrase are integral to many, and diverse, localisms, and nationalisms.[1] Sometimes it comes down to a minimal claim, relational and strategic: "we were here before *you*." Feeling indigenous may crystallize around hostility to outsiders, to invaders or immigrants. Many forms of nativism sustain these sorts of borders, reflecting immediate political agendas, self-defense, or aggression (Amita Baviskar and Joseph Niamnjoh this volume, offer cautionary examples). The anteriority claimed can be relatively shallow and fundamentally contested: all sorts of people, these days, claim "indigeneity" vis-à-vis someone else. There are, nonetheless, many social groups with undeniably deep roots in a familiar place, and they are the subjects of this chapter. The peoples in question are called aboriginal, tribal, first nations, native, autochthonous, or a range of more particular, local names. They may or may not (or may only sometimes) claim the identity "indigenous." Whatever names these people take or are given, they are defined by long attachment to a locale and by violent histories of occupation, expropriation, and marginalization. A diverse range of experiences falls within this loose grouping, and its boundaries, despite attempts by the International Labour Organization (ILO) and UN agencies to formally define indigenous peoples, are fuzzy (Brown 2003; Niezen 2003).

This fuzziness suggests a certain open-ended historical dynamism. People are improvising new ways to be native: articulations, performances, and translations of old and new cultures and projects. The increase of indigenous movements at different scales—local, national, regional, and international—has been one of the surprises of the late 20th century. Tribal ("archaic" or "primitive") peoples were, after all, destined to wither in the relentless wind of modernization. This was a historical *fact*, understood by everyone—except the people in question, busy with difficult and inventive survival struggles. This "survival" has been an interactive, dynamic process of shifting scales and affiliations, uprooting and rerooting, the waxing and waning of identities. In the current moment these processes take shape as a complex emergence, a *présence indigène* or a performative indigenous "voice" (Tsing this volume). What experiences of loss and renewal, what shifting past and present attachments, what social, cultural, and political strategies are active in these rearticulations? A growing body of scholarship grapples with these questions: for example the programmatic overview of Sahlins 1999 and the complex Native American histories described by Harmon 1998 and Sturm 2002.

To grasp the active, unfinished, processes at work in various articulated sites of indigeneity it helps to open up, or at least "loosen" (Teaiwa 2001), common understandings of key terms like *native, authochthonous,* and *sovereign.* The definitional closures built into these words, the cultural and political practices they authorize, are both necessary and dangerous. The strong claims they express contribute centrally to indigenous social movements. They also close down possibilities, and are, in practice, supplemented and cross-cut by less absolute experiences and tactics. There are various ways to be "native" in relation to a place;

assumptions of firstness or "autochthony" often obscure important histories of movement; and "sovereign" control is always compromised and relative. More happens under the sign of the indigenous than being born, or belonging, in a bounded land or nation.

This chapter works to make space for contradiction and excess across a broad spectrum of indigenous experiences today by loosening the common opposition of "indigenous" and "diasporic" forms of life. The goal is a richer and more contingent realism, a fuller sense of what has happened, is happening, and may be emerging. The argument does not deny claims for landed, rooted or local identities, asserting that they really are, or ought to be, diasporic. Nor does it assume that cosmopolitan experiences are historically more progressive—even though new scales and dimensions of indigenous life are proliferating in a globally interconnected, locally inflected postmodernity. Questioning an essential opposition does not eliminate the historical differences or tensions expressed by the contrast. Native or tribal peoples claim, often with strong historical justification, to belong in a place, a densely familiar and deeply inhabited landscape. Australian Aborigines, for example, have been living in and with their "country" for an extremely long time—long enough to persuade even skeptics committed to a linear historical ontology, that it makes sense to say they have been there "forever," or "from the beginning." Such quintessentially "mythic" assertions of ancient origins evoke a "historical" continuity. With varying degrees of archaeological support, Inuit, Pacific Islanders, the various native peoples of North and South America; Sami in Norway, Sweden, Finland, and Russia; the Dayaks of West Kilimantan, and others, all make credible claims, if not to autochthony, at least to deep local roots: an indigenous *longue durée*. Such historical experiences begin and end with lives grounded, profoundly, in one place. What could be more distant from diasporic identifications, experiences that originate in, are constituted by, physical displacements, uprootings?

Yet many of the experiences made visible and intelligible by diaspora theorists such as Hall (1990), Gilroy (1993), Mishra (1996a, 1996b), or Brah (1996), the transmigrant circuits revealed by Roger Rouse (1991) and Nina Glick-Schiller (1995), and the historical pressures and structures analyzed by comparative sociologists like Robin Cohen (1997) have their equivalents, or near equivalents, in contemporary indigenous life. In everyday practices of mobility and dwelling, the line separating the diasporic from the indigenous thickens; a complex borderland opens up. Contested lines of indigenous autonomy and sovereignty are drawn across it: the fraught relationship of "off-island" Hawaiians to movements of native nationalism (Kauanui 1999), or tensions between urban-dwelling Aboriginals or Indians with those living close to ancestral lands. Indigenous attachments to place are complexly mediated and do not necessarily entail continuous residence, especially in contexts such as the United States, Canada, Australia, and Aotearoa/New Zealand, where a majority of native people now live in cities. Thus, it makes some sense to speak of "indigenous diasporas."

What kind of sense? Translation is continually at issue. One cannot simply import a concept that is associated with, say, the North Atlantic slave trade's aftermath (Gilroy) or with postcolonial migrations to former imperial centers (Brah) into situations of profound, ongoing connection with land and country, experiences associated with Australian Aborigines, with Pacific Islanders, with Arctic Inuit, or with Mayan Indians. We need to explore the specificity of indigenous diasporas, or perhaps better, diasporic *dimensions* or *conjunctures* in contemporary native lives. To bring the language of diaspora into indigenous contexts is to confront its built-in difficulties. Among recent critiques of diasporic or postcolonial theorizing, native scholars (e.g., Teaiwa 2001) observe that when traveling, displacement and migration are seen as normative, or at least characteristic of the contemporary world, the focus tends to relegate native peoples, yet again, to the past or to the margins. For example, when cultural-studies diaspora theorists reject "nativism" in its racist, little England, Thatcherite forms, they can make all deeply rooted attachments seem illegitimate, bad essentialisms. Genuinely complex indigenous histories, which involve mobility as well as staying put, and that have always been based on transformative, potentially expansive interactions, become invisible. The native is thrown out with the bathwater of nativism (for correctives, see the articles in Diaz and Kauanui 2001).

The result is to obscure specifically indigenous forms of interactive cosmopolitanism: genealogical inclusion of outsiders; trading relations; circular migration; vernacular discourses of "development"; mission, maritime, and military contexts of travel (Chappell 1997; Gegeo 1998; Gidwani and Sivaramakrishnan 2003; Phillips 1998; Sahlins 1989; Swain 1993). Exclusivist nativism is, of course, prominent in political indigenism: for example, the nationalist rhetoric of "Red Power," of Hawaiian sovereignty movements, of Native Fijian attacks on diasporic Indians. However, such claims are not sustainable in all, or even in most, lived circumstances. Across the current range of indigenous experiences, identifications are seldom exclusively local or inward looking but, rather, work at multiple scales of interaction. The language of diaspora can be useful in bringing something of this complexity into view. It cannot transcend the tension between the material interests and normative visions of natives and newcomers, particularly in structurally unequal settler colonial situations (Fujikane and Okamura 2000). But when diasporic displacements, memories, networks, and reidentifications are recognized as integral to tribal, aboriginal, native survival and dynamism, a lived, historical landscape of ruptures and affiliations becomes more visible.

"Diaspora theory" may have enjoyed its 15 minutes of academic fame. Aihwa Ong (1999) and others writing about overseas Chinese have questioned its extension. Some cultural studies writers—like Ien Ang in her recent collection, *On Not Speaking Chinese* (2001)—have backed away from an earlier positive embrace of diasporic self-location, now grappling with the absolutist dimensions of what Benedict Anderson (1988) calls "long-distance nationalisms." In his accounts of Indian diaspora cultures, Vijay Mishra avoids celebration, always keeping the constitutive tension between essentialism and hybridity clearly in view, showing the "interrelated conditions" of what he calls diasporas of "exclusivism" and of "the border," the former focused on return the other on interaction and crossover (Mishra 1996a, 1996b). Celebratory visions of diaspora, whether they take nationalist or antinationalist form, are permanently troubled by their opposites. This dialectical instability can be an analytic strength: the opposed tendencies of diasporic experience, exclusivism and border crossing, are good to think with. Indeed, a contradictory complexity with respect to belonging—both inside and outside national structures in contemporary multisited social worlds—may turn out to be diaspora's most productive "theoretical" contribution. The last section of this chapter argues that indigenous claims to "sovereignty" contain analogous contradictions, and possibilities.

* * *

Colin Calloway, an ethnohistorian of the Abenaki Indians in the U.S. state of Vermont, uses the term *diaspora* to describe the dispersal of local Indian groups in the face of settler encroachments during the 19th century (Calloway 1990). The apparent melting away of the Abenaki, which was interpreted as a disappearance (there were of course the usual military pressures and epidemiological disasters) was, according to Calloway, in part at least a movement to different, safer, places in the neighboring state of Maine, and in Canada (see also Ghere 1993). According to this account, diaspora was a means of survival for the

Abenaki, who did not entirely lose contact with each other and are still around, reconstituting elements of their culture in new circumstances. For relatively mobile native groups, the experience of moving away from homelands under pressure may not be adequately captured by the notion of "exile." "Diaspora" gets somewhat closer to a sociospatial reality of connectedness-in-dispersion.

"Exile" denotes a condition of enforced absence, with the sustained expectation of returning home as soon as the conditions of expulsion can be corrected. The term thus applies to a broad range of displaced native peoples, even to those still living on their ancestral lands in reduced reservations or enclaves without the ability to freely hunt, fish, gather, travel, or conduct ceremonies in appropriate sites. The goal of an actual return remains alive, and it takes concrete political form in land claims and repatriations. At the same time, many people give up the idea of a physical return to traditional communities and land, focusing instead on ceremonial observations, seasonal visits to reservations or "country," and symbolic tokens or performances of tradition. To the extent that later generations, forced or drawn into towns or cities, have no realistic intention of actually living continuously in traditional places, then the connection to lost homelands comes closer to a diasporic relation, with its characteristic forms of longing, long-distance nationalism, and displaced performances of "heritage." Diaspora classically presupposes distance from the place of origin and deferred returns. This distinguishes it from the "circuits of migration" and "borderlands" experiences of many Mexicanos in the United States or Caribbeans in New York City, where coming and going is frequent. Yet modern communications can shrink distances and make many diasporas more like borderlands in the frequency and intimacy of possible contacts (Clifford 1994).

Indigenous populations actively sustain these sorts of diasporic borderlands, as we will see in an Alaskan example discussed in detail below. It will be no surprise to anyone who studies labor migrations that many native populations are spatially far flung. Indians from Michoacan inhabit Mexico City and do farm work in California. There are many thousands of Samoans in Auckland, Tongans in Salt Lake City, and Hawaiians in Los Angeles. Significant Navajo populations can be found in the San Francisco Area (the result of government relocation programs in the 1960s). Examples could be multiplied: the classic portrayal by Mitchell (1960) of Mohawk steel workers, Gossen's early account of Chamulan migration as expansive cosmology (1999 [1983]), the Kabre diaspora and travel circuits integral to Piot's recent ethnography,

Remotely Global (1999), Darnell's (1999) grounded "accordion model of nomadic Native American social organization."

When addressing the lived spectrum of indigenous separations from, and orientations to, homeland, village, or reservation, we need to complicate diasporic assumptions of "loss" and "distance." Likewise, urbanization should not be conceived as a one-way trip from village to city. Gidwani and Sivaramakrishnan (2003) provide a sophisticated critique of both Marxist and liberal modernisms in an ethnographically persuasive account of "circular migration" by "tribals" and "dalits" in India. Embodied practices of work and desire are portrayed in Gramscian terms as entangled counterhegemonic projects opening up "rural cosmopolitan" possibilities for identity and cultural assertion. The same can be said of much contemporary "indigenous" migration—coerced, voluntary, or specific combinations of the two. Avoiding a modernist teleology of urbanization as the simple abandonment of rural life, ethnographic accounts now follow the "routes" of multisited communities (Lambert 2002 provides a rich West African case study). The focus shifts to particular connections and translations, intermediate stopping places and circuits of return. For example, in Merlan's finely detailed ethnography, Australian Aboriginal "mobs" have clustered on the outskirts of towns, and at cattle stations, while orienting these settlements in the direction of traditional "country" and making regular journeys "out bush" in groups to gather traditional foods and to dance and sing at sacred sites (Merlan 1998; also Christen 2004). Relations of kinship with country can, in practice, be sustained, even when the land is legally owned by non-Aboriginals. Of course there are struggles over multiple "uses" and access is not always negotiable (the same goes for hunting, fishing, and gathering rights in North America). But the essential fact of pragmatic, if not legally recognized, sovereignty is that concrete ties to ancestral places have not been severed. "Diasporic" distance is specific and relational.

These partially displaced, sustained relations to "country" need to be compared, along a continuum, with the seasonal, or deferred, "returns" of more distant city dwellers. Recent scholarship in Australia has invoked the language of diaspora when addressing differential attachments to land in the "Native Title Era." (Rigsby 1995; Smith 2000; Weiner 2002; see also Lilley's archaeological interventions 2004, 2006) Without reducing Aboriginal identity to a single nexus of struggle, it is worth dwelling on how key issues of articulated continuity are being debated in the emerging land claims context. Benjamin Richard Smith (drawing on Rigsby) questions a rigid distinction, prevalent in both scholarship and law, between "traditional" and "historical" people. The former live in proximate relationships with ancient lands and customs and express this in "mythic" claims to have "been here forever;" the latter trace their "Aboriginal" heritage through colonial histories of displacement and recovered genealogies. Native Title law has tended to recognize the claims of locally based groups while denying those of Aboriginals whose physical distance from country is viewed as an index of lost authenticity. Smith makes clear that many of the people he calls "diasporic," living in towns and cities, do not fall readily into either historical or traditional categories. He sees negotiable differences not an essential opposition. City dwellers tend to subscribe to a more homogenous "tribal" model of Aboriginality than local people whose sense of belonging and ownership is based on specific clans and responsibilities to sites. This difference of perspective may lead to incomprehension and mutual suspicion. But in the process of making land claims, the two groups can overcome initial suspicions and work together. One group learns to defer, at least some of the time, to the local knowledge of elders; the other, at least pragmatically, comes to embrace a wider "Aboriginal" mobilization and future. Of course there is no guarantee of unity in these contingent alliances. Drawing on what Merlan (1997) observes is an "epistemological openness" in Aboriginal connections to country, and on a common, underlying sociocultural structure, diasporic and local people fashion new coalitions and scales of identification. Rather than embodying the "mythic" past and the "historical" future, local and diasporic groups represent "two trajectories of cultural continuity articulating with changing contexts" (Smith 2000: 8; see also Sutton 1988, for practical fusions of myth and history).

James Weiner (2002) challenges legal and anthropological notions of "continuity" that see specific traits (such as physical proximity to country, language fluency, religious observance, etc.) as make-or-break conditions of identity. He recognizes a more polythetic and dynamic ensemble-through-time (see also Clifford 1988, 2001). The reproduction of social life is always a matter of recurring "loss" and "recovery," of selective transmission and reconstructed history in changing circumstances. Urban Aboriginals who reconnect identities and affiliations are doing nothing fundamentally new. Drawing on Jewish diaspora experiences, Weiner lends support to land rights for displaced Aboriginals: "the *idea* or *image* of a homeland, such as has sustained diasporic populations throughout the world in countless examples through the centuries, would be sufficient to maintain something that the legal profession would have to call proprietary rights to country" (2002: 10) This rather strong culturalist position is kept in tension with a materialist criterion deployed by Australian courts (and more than a few hard-nosed Marxists) that would require native title to be based on continuing use, "a system of economic and adaptational relations to a particular territory" (Weiner 2002: 10). Accepting the tension, and properly rejecting any ideational/ materialist dichotomy, Weiner concludes: "Somewhere between these two poles—as imaginary as they are unrealistic in Australian terms—lie *all* of the native title claims in Australia" (2002: 10). Between these poles, too, lies an uneven continuum of ideational, embodied, structural, and material practices that needs to be understood as both complexly rooted and diasporic.

Confronting the actual diversity of indigenous societies, one works with a series of contexts and scales, new terms of political mobilization and expanded social maps. Collective terms such as *Native American, Native Alaskan, First Peoples* (in Canada), *Kanak* (in New Caledonia), *Mayan* (in Guatemala), *Aboriginal* (in Australia), *Masyarakat Adat* (in Indonesia) represent large-scale *articulated* identities—alliances of particular "tribes," language groups, villages, or clans. They include people sustaining different spatial and social relations with ancestral places, a range of distances from "land." For all who identify as "native," "tribal," or "indigenous, a feeling of connectedness to a homeland and to kin, a feeling of grounded peoplehood, is basic. How this feeling is practiced, in discursive, embodied, emplaced ways, can be quite varied. Urban populations may or may not return to rural places for family gatherings, ceremonial events, dance festivals, subsistence activities, pow wows, and so forth. For some it is a matter of frequent visits; others go once a year, for summer or midwinter social activities; some return rarely or never.

The varieties of indigenous experience proliferate between the poles of autochthony (we are here and have been here forever) and diaspora (we yearn for a homeland: "Next year in the Black Hills!"). Seeing an articulated continuum, a complex range of affiliations, offers a fresh perspective on both ends of the spectrum. If there are diasporic aspects of indigenous life, the reverse is also true. For something like an indigenous desire animates diasporic consciousness: the search for somewhere to belong that is outside the imagined community of the dominant nation-state. In diaspora, the authentic home is found in another imagined place (simultaneously past and future, lost and desired) as well as in concrete social networks of linked places. This whole range of felt attachments is crucially a part of what Avtar Brah has called "a homing desire" (Brah 1996: 180). Diasporic dwelling practices (as distinct from the absolutist ideologies of return that often accompany them) avoid the either–or of exile or assimilation. People make a place here by keeping alive a strong feeling of attachment elsewhere. The all-or-nothing of naturalization, of proper citizenship, is sidestepped, but without condemning oneself to a condition of permanent marginality. This, at least is the project of diasporic belonging: to be black *and* British, Muslim *and* French, Latino *and* U.S. American. In this lived practice, various strong forms of "cultural citizenship" emerge and become battlegrounds, as the hyphen in "nation-state" loosens (Flores and Benmayor 1997; Ramirez in press).

Analogues from indigenous experience are not hard to find: it is common, for example, to be a tribally enrolled American Indian, to love baseball and be proud of one's service in the U.S. Army. Such "double belonging" (a phrase applied to Turks in Germany by Riva Kastoriano 2003) requires a portable sense of the indigenous. It is why claims to ethnic identity or peoplehood can be profound yet not nationalist in a bounded, territorial sense (Hall 1989). In lived practice, then, indigenous and diasporic multiple attachments are not mutually exclusive. And although there are certainly situations of political struggle in which the ideological opposition indigenous–diasporic is activated, there are also a great many relatively invisible intermediate, pragmatic experiences where the two kinds of belonging interpenetrate and coexist. The purpose of opening up the borderland between diasporic and indigenous paradigms is to recognize an uneven terrain of spatial scales, cultural affiliations, and social projects (Tsing 2000 offers a lucid and complex map). A realistic account of "indigenous experience" engages with actual life overflowing the definitions, the political programs, and all the museums of archaism and authenticity—self-created and externally imposed.

* * *

Let us now turn to a particular case, drawn from the work of Ann Fienup-Riordan (1990, 2000), an anthropologist who has worked closely for nearly 30 years with the Nelson Island Yup'ik of western Alaska. Fienup-Riordan and her native collaborators have described Yup'ik society, colonial and postcolonial, in considerable detail. What follows are the broad outlines.

Before the arrival of the Russians in the late 18th century the inhabitants of the Kuskokwim and Yukon deltas lived a life of settled mobility, "nomadic" within discrete territories. Hunting, gathering, and fishing (freshwater and ocean) provided a relatively rich livelihood. Long classified as "Eskimos" (based on linguistic and social similarities to Inupiaq and Inuit), Yup'ik have never lived in igloos or speared seals through the ice. In many ways, they defy common stereotypes (Fienup-Riordan 1990). The colonial impact of the Russians was relatively light, because there were no sea otters to hunt along the Bering Sea coast. The aboriginal inhabitants of western Alaska did not suffer the harsh conquest and forced labor regimes imposed on their neighbors to the south, "Aleuts"—a Russian catch-all term now distinguished as Onangan (Aleutian Islanders) and Alutiiq (former Pacific Eskimos). Later, the absence of gold in Yup'ik territories spared them the heavy disruptions experienced by other native populations in Alaska. Yup'ik did suffer from contact diseases, and their societies underwent disruptive changes.

If Russian influence was more gradual than elsewhere, it did result in widespread conversion to Russian Orthodoxy (albeit with syncretic indigenous components), the presence of creole kinship (Russian colonization encouraged intermarriage), and new trade and commercial relationships. After the Americans took control of Alaska in the 1870s, fresh missionaries arrived, and new indigenized Christianities took hold, particularly Catholic and Moravian. Over these years, native kinship structures, village affiliations, subsistence food consumption, and language use, while undergoing transformations, remained viable. In recent decades, with the renewal of native land claims in Alaska, heritage displays, development activities, and identity politics, Yup'iit have sustained their reputation as a locally rooted people, confident in their sense of identity, still connected with traditional affiliations while pragmatically asserting new ways to be native.

There is no need to paint a romantic picture of sociocultural survival. Many Yup'iit continue to suffer the pernicious effects of colonial disruption, economic marginalization, and blocked futures. As elsewhere in native Alaska, alcoholism and high suicide rates take their toll. Welfare dependency coexists with independent, subsistence hunting and fishing. The sweeping land settlements of 1971 (the Alaska Native Claims Settlement Act [ANCSA]) were a mixed blessing. ANCSA stabilized land holdings in a state where indigenous populations, while dispossessed of much territory, had never been subjected to the forced localization of a reservation system. And although it brought considerable new resources to tribal communities, ANCSA capped indigenous title to land and introduced property boundaries between native communities and native corporations. The settlement subsidized new forms of economic activity and the emergence of corporate elites. It also supported a broad range of heritage projects, the articulation, translation, and performance of what Fienup-Riordan calls "conscious culture" (2000: 167). In Yup'ik country this involved the revival of mask making and dancing, once banned, now encouraged, by Christian authorities—part of a more general context of native resurgence, alliance, and entanglement with state structures (Dombrowski 2002 and Clifford 2004a offer contrasting assessments of these developments). In this ongoing period of Native Alaskan sociocultural realignments, tribal governments and liberal state structures can neither be separated nor melded in a functioning hegemony. Fienup-Riordan documents a generally hopeful story of Yup'ik continuity: a dynamic local tradition is sustained, refocused, and in certain respects strengthened by experiences of mobility and diaspora.

In *Hunting Tradition in a Changing World* (2000) Fienup-Riordan shows that movement out of traditional Yup'ik villages into regional towns and state urban centers has markedly increased. Although the story she tells may have a class bias, focused as it is on Yupiit who have the means to create extended networks, to travel and distribute food in the city (2000: 279, n. 13), the phenomena she traces are far from limited to a narrow elite. Most importantly, this migration does not conform to the one-way "urbanization" of modernization models. There is considerable circulation between traditional Yup'ik country and new centers of native life in Anchorage, Alaska's largest city. Fienup-Riordan portrays these movements as part of an emerging Yup'ik "worldwide web:" multicentered native life at new social and spatial scales. In 1970, 4,800 Alaska natives were living in Anchorage more-or-less permanently ("more-or-less" is an important qualification). By 1990 the number had risen to 14,500, and by 2000 it was approaching 19,000. In Fienup-Riordan's assessment, the trend reflects not so much an emptying of Yup'ik country as its extension.

Yup'ik circulation between village and city adapts and transforms traditional exchanges and seasonal rhythms. Formerly, the summer was a time of mobile hunting and gathering in small family units, the winter a time for coming together in large social groupings, intense ritual life, festivals, and exchanges. For urban-based Yupiit similar social activities are performed in new ways and sometimes at different times. This is the result of many factors, including employment patterns and vacations as well as transportation possibilities. Yup'ik community is stitched together today with snow machines, telephones, and, especially, airplanes, large and small. Yupiit living in Anchorage regularly return to villages around Nelson Island and the Kuskwokwim Delta to engage in fishing, hunting, and gathering of seasonal foods. "Subsistence" activities (widely identified in Alaska with native identity and "tradition") can be combined with commercial projects. In Winter, recently revived dance festivals, Catholic and Moravian holidays, and the Orthodox Christmas and New Year draw return visitors. During an especially intense period in early and mid-January, old midwinter traditions of social gathering and exchanges meld with Christian rituals brought by the Russians two centuries ago (Fienup-Riordan 1990).

Yupiit who dwell in regional villages and towns visit Anchorage for a variety of reasons, including marriages, births, deaths, and shopping, dropping off frozen and recently gathered "native foods." They also travel to the Alaska Native Medical Center (ANMC is something more than a medical establishment; it is specifically designed for Native Alaskan health needs and organized with local cultures in mind. Its gift shop offers an important outlet for arts and crafts). Political and educational gatherings are also a draw, for example the convention of Alaskan bilingual teachers that annually draws more than 1,000 participants from all over the state. Heritage performances and sharing of native foods play a central role in all such encounters.

Patterns of visiting and circulation between village and city are driven by interlocking social, economic, political, and cultural forces. Clearly many of the pressures and opportunities that are familiar from modernization theories, forces that work to "disembed" local societies (Giddens 1990 [1983]), are responsible for the movement out of villages and into cities: an erosion of traditional subsistence, rural poverty, a search for employment, for wider sociocultural horizons, for gender equality, and so forth. But what emerges from Fienup-Riordan's account is a recognizably "indigenous" form of modernity, or at least its entangled possibility. Traditional hunting, fishing, and gathering, while they are threatened and regulated, have not been wiped out by capitalist modes of production and distribution. They take new forms alongside, and in conjunction with, modern economies. Communal (familial, village-level) affiliations and exchanges are extended by movements into and out of cities. Rather than a linear process of disembedding (or deterritorializing), one observes a transformation and extension of culturally distinctive spatial and social practices: reembedding, extending territories, dwelling with airplanes.

Fienup-Riordan sees strategies of survival and "development," individual and communitarian, that are pursued to significant degrees on native terms (cf. work on indigenous conceptions of development in Melanesia by Curtis 2002; Gegeo 1998; Sahlins 1989, 1993 and in Africa by Peel 1978). This agency is not free or unconstrained. Nor is it simply coerced. For example, more young women than young men from Yup'ik country are going to Anchorage—both in search of education and escaping village restrictions. Such "modernizing" strategies are not experienced as a loss of native identity—quite the contrary. In Anchorage, Yupiit enter extended networks of economic exchange, politics, and culture—connections at state, national, and international levels. In these networks they come to feel "Yup'ik," rather than primarily rooted in specific kin groups or villages. This tribal or national ethnonym, which only began to be widely used after the 1960s, now marks distinction in multiethnic neighborhoods, in pan-Alaskan native settings, in Fourth World contacts, in relations with non-natives, in a variety of cultural performances, exhibits, websites, and the like.

Clearly, an increase of traveling and dwelling beyond local villages and regional centers has contributed to an expanded articulation of "Yup'ik" identity. The experience is far from unique. A comparable, though differently compelled, Solomon Island experience is evoked by David Gegeo in which Malitans migrating away from their homeland "will see their movement as *an expansion of place,* and attendant on it will be a strengthening of the sense of indigeneity" (2001: 499). Indeed, many nationalisms have first been articulated by exiles or students in foreign capitals (e.g., Rafael 1989 on José Rizal and the Filipino "ilustrados"). Indigenous "tribal," as opposed to place-based or clan, affiliations, tend to be more characteristic of displaced populations living in urban settings where language, extended kinship, and consumable symbols of objectified "heritage" predominate over specific local ties with land and family. It would be wrong, however, to turn a contrast into an opposition. In practice, identifications are plural and situated: one is from a village, from Nelson Island, from the Kuskokwim region, a Yup'ik, or an Alaska Native, depending on the situation. Local affiliations are not replaced by wider "indigenous" formations in a zero-sum relation. Linda Tuhiwai Smith suggested a similar complexity at the Wenner-Gren conference originating this volume, saying she grew up thinking that being bicultural was being a Maori person (because women's roles were so different in her mother's and father's tribes). Being "indigenous," she observed, has been a way of working through the different layers of her identity: "What contradictory people we are!"

In Alaska, the emergence of larger-scale "tribal" and "Native Alaskan" social formations is bound up with liberal multiculturalism and governmentality: ANCSA, native art markets, heritage venues, tourism,

NGOs, and corporate sponsors. *Présence indigène* comes at a price (Hale 2002, Clifford 2004a). The new scales and performances of identity are "called out," by hegemonic structures of managed multiculturalism. Yet the new identifications also transform and translate deep, if not always continuous, local roots (Friedman 1993). The range of phenomena sometimes lumped together as "identity politics" includes processes of interpellation, performativity, translation, and political strategy. When associating new tribal identifications with displaced populations it is critical to recognize the specificity and flexibility of native landedness, expansive senses of "place" evoked by Gegeo. Large-scale tribal identities can remain in close articulation with other levels of affiliation and with homelands, both geographically and socially defined.

> At a time when men and women go from and come back to their home villages in greater numbers for longer periods of time, the villages themselves take on special importance. Personhood and "placehood" are closely intertwined in contemporary Yup'ik life. Although a person does not need uninterrupted residence on the land for that relationship to continue, the existence of the homeland is at the core of contemporary Yup'ik identity. (Fienup-Riordan 2000: 156)

This perspective is echoed in the final sentences of "Yup'iks in the City," an article by radio journalist John Active that is included in *Hunting Tradition*. Active suggests something of the performativity of native identity in urban settings: "All in all, Anchorage is a fun place to visit, but I wouldn't want to live there. Besides, the pavement is too hard on my ankles, and I always have to prove my Yup'icity to the kass'aqs [white people]" (Active 2000: 182).

As this view of the city and "Yup'icity" suggests, different kinds of performance are required in specific relational sites. For Active, the city is a nice place to visit, but also a place of uncomfortable encounters and coerced performances. For other Yupiit it feels like an extension of home. For others (or at different times) it is an exciting new place to branch out. Fienup-Riordan clearly insists that "the existence of the homeland is at the core of contemporary Yup'ik identity" (2000: 184), but she also rejects any linear progression between rural and urban, old and new, performative sites. Tribal diaspora is not a condition of exile, of obstructed return; it is more multiplex, relational, and productive (cf. Darnell's account of traditional Algonquian "semi-nomadic" social structure, "a process of subsistence-motivated expansion and contraction," sustained and translated in new historical contexts 1999:

91). Fienup-Riordan offers concrete examples of ways that contacts with villages (kin ties) and land (subsistence activities) are sustained by urban Yup'iks from a connected distance that is not that of an émigré or an exile. Research on Indian communities in the San Francisco Bay area by Native American scholars Kurt Peters 1995 and Renya Ramirez in press echoes this complex experience of networking and multiattachment. The language of "diaspora" (in its recent versions overlapping with paradigms of extended borderlands and migrant cycles) renders something of these mobile, multipolar, practices of belonging. "Transmigrants," who create and sustain very particular "transnational communities" might seem a more exact analogue (e.g., Levitt 2001). But although here is considerable overlap, the newly articulated sense of tribal identification at something like a national scale combined with renewed yearnings for a return to tradition and land, are more suggestive of diasporas.

* * *

No single analytic language can exhaust what is at stake in these complexly rooted and routed experiences. Diaspora discourse is good at keeping multisited, multiscaled predicaments in view and resisting teleological narratives of transformation. It acknowledges but does not adequately analyze the political, economic, and social forces at work in contemporary displacements: histories of violent dispossession, the material push–pull of labor mobility, collective strategies of circular migration, individual flights from oppressive social conditions, consumerist desires, the lure of the modern, and "development." Obviously, the sociocultural connections sustained in diaspora networks cannot compensate for, though they may make more livable, the poverty and racial exclusions typically suffered by indigenous people. Moreover, there is an "indigenous" specificity that eludes diaspora's central emphasis on displacement, loss, and deferred desire for the homeland. People who identify as first nations, aboriginal, or tribal share histories of having been invaded and dispossessed within fairly recent memory. Many currently dwell either on reduced parcels of their former territory or nearby. The feeling that one has never left one's deep ancestral home is strong, both as a lived reality and as a redemptive political myth. This affects the ways space and time are experienced, distances and connections lived. Urban-based Yup'it, as understood by Fienup-Riordan, are not so much displaced from a homeland as extensions of it. She points to similar patterns for other Alaska native groups. Thus, it is not a question of the center holding or not, but rather one of open ended social networks sustaining transformed connections to land and kin, The tribal home—its animals, plants, social gatherings, shared foods, ancestors, and spiritual powers—is not imagined from a distance. It is activated, "practiced" (De Certeau 1984), made meaningful in a range of sites by seasonal rituals, social gatherings, visits, and subsistence activities. "Diasporic" natives are more like offshoots than broken branches.

No doubt this is an idealization. Negative experiences of exile, poverty, alienation from family, despair, loss of language and tradition, endlessly deferred returns, nostalgia, and yearning, are certainly part of the varied experiences of native peoples living in settings removed from their homelands. The physical separation and different knowledge bases of "diaspora" and "local" peoples cannot always be bridged by kin ties, exchanges, and political alliances. The politics of culture and identity at new "tribal," regional, and international scales cannot avoid failed, or very partial, translation between sites and generations, social exclusions, tests for racial purity and cultural authenticity. New leaders, culture brokers, and economic elites, new dependencies on governmental, corporate, academic, and philanthropic resources are inextricably part of the processes by which extended indigenous connections are being made. Fienup-Riordan's Yup'ik "worldwide web" is both a description and a hope that cannot be automatically generalized. Yup'iit, who enjoy relatively strong ongoing connections with language, land, and tradition, are able to sustain social ties across an enlarged space. And in this rooted experience of routes, they represent one example from a spectrum of decentered indigenous stories. Yet if the locally grounded "worldwide web" in Fienup-Riordan's account is an idealization, it is not a delusion. For it describes established native practices and aspirations in many parts of the world today. The rather bright Yup'ik picture will always be shadowed by other realities of poverty, racial subjugation, inferior health care, and education. Diasporic consciousness expresses contradictory experiences of loss and hope, despair and messianism (Clifford 1994). Thus, in thinking about indigenous diasporas, one necessarily confronts the disastrous histories of oppression that have created them and simultaneously the sociocultural connections that sustain a sense of peoplehood and, in tangled political–economic situations, project a rooted, expansive future.

Although this chapter has suggested some of the characteristic features of "indigenous diasporas," it has not drawn a sharp contrast with the experiences of other migrants and transnational dwellers. What has emerged is an uneven, overlapping range of experiences, constraints, and possibilities. In practice, for those many self-identified natives who dwell in, and circulate through, urban and semiurban settings, there can be no essential, privative opposition between "indigenous" and "diasporic" experiences. The terms break down in the compromises and inconsistencies of everyday life. We struggle for languages to represent the layered, faceted realities of the "indigenous" today, without imposing reductive, backward-looking criteria of authenticity. What is at stake in this representational struggle is an adequate *realism* in our ways of thinking comparatively about a range of old and emergent histories.

Realism is a term that needs to be used carefully. Here, it is evoked in both its descriptive–historicist and pragmatic–political senses. The main problem with much descriptive realism is that it projects its vision of what is really there and what is really possible from an unacknowledged vantage point in time and space. Sooner or later, "full," "realistic" accounts of historical development, modernity, progress, Westernization, capitalism, and national liberation will be situated (Haraway 1988), or provincialized (Chakrabarty 2000) by the emergence of new historical subjects. Of course, some of these "new" subjects, whose interventions trouble formerly settled projections of the real, are not new (recently invented) but formerly silenced, marginalized peoples who, in specific conditions, attain a widely recognized presence or voice. The continuity (Friedman 1993) and ethnogenesis (Hill 1996) at work in these processes of survival and emergence include political *articulations,* conjunctural *performances,* and partial *translations* (Clifford 2004a). New historical subjects (in the present context, those loosely labeled "indigenous") are seen and heard in translocal circuits, exerting enough political pressure to make them more than marginal actors in a broad historical field of forces.

Historical (historicized and translated) realism does not project one synthetic big story. It works with open ended (because linear historical time is ontologically unfinished) "big enough stories," sites of contact, struggle, and dialog (Clifford 2002). What counts as a big enough story—representing a force, happening, or presence that "matters"—is not something that can be finally decided by scholarly expertise, cultural, or political authority. Every projection of "the real," however diverse, contested or polythetic, presupposes exclusion and forgetting: constitutive outsides, silences, or specters from unburied pasts that can reemerge as "realistic" in conjunctures or emergencies either currently unimaginable or utopian (Benjamin 1969). The current persistence and renaissance of so many different small-scale tribal and native societies rearticulated under the sign of the "indigenous" is just such a critique and expansion of the historically real. *Real* refers here, simultaneously, to something that actually exists and that has a future in a nonteleological postmodernity.

In this perspective, the present chapter questions a conceptual opposition (diaspora vs. indigenous) that has impeded understanding of how native peoples have reckoned with experiences of genocide, material dispossession, forced assimilation, political, cultural, racial, and economic marginality, opportunities for change and reidentification. (De la Cadena 2000, does similar work by opening up of the opposition or *indio* and *mestizo*.) This kind of realism foregrounds complex histories: the syncretic experiences of diverse native Christians; or "travels" with Buffalo Bill, on whaling ships, as coerced and contract laborers; or the work of Aboriginals on cattle stations, Mayans in coffee plantations, Indians on high steel; or the broad range of "urban indigenous" experiences. This perspective struggles for a lucid ambivalence with respect to tribal engagements with tourism, with capitalist development, with museums and art markets. It views these activities as "historical practices" integral to "traditional futures" (Clifford 2004b). This, like any realism, is deployed at a particular moment and from a specific location.

Recognizing one's own standpoint is, of course, difficult. Others can be counted on to help, not always generously. The present chapter may be criticized as overly invested in the interactive, spliced, spatially dispersed aspects of tribal or native lives at the expense of continuities in place, kinship, language, and tradition. And this emphasis may be read as unfriendly to the necessary essentialist claims of nationalist movements for independence and sovereignty. There is warrant for this reading. The chapter does argue that indigenous historical experiences are layered and fundamentally relational, that ethnically or racially absolute assertions foreshorten lived reality and foreclose crucial possibilities. Diaspora has not, however, been proposed as an alternative or cure for strong identity claims. Diasporic *dimensions* are understood as aspects of an uneven, continuum of attachments. Strong alternate claims to autochthony, localism, and cultural or racial essence are equally part of the process. Indeed, groups and individuals migrate between these apparently contradictory positions depending on situation, audience, or pragmatic goals. An adequate realism needs to grasp specific interactions of diasporic–cosmopolitan and autochthonous–nationalist experiences—ongoing historical dialogues and tensions performed under the contested sign of "indigeneity". (For an exemplary study, which keeps these dialogues and tensions in view, see Mallon 2005, "Samoan *tatau* as global practice.")

It is not simply a matter of richer "historicist" description: telling it as it was or like it is. Realism has inescapable political and even prophetic dimensions, for it prefigures what does and does not have a "real" chance of making a difference. The aspirations of indigenous movements today for self-determination and sovereignty reflect an altered balance of forces, a post-1960s shift in what may, in certain circumstances, and without guarantees, be possible. Much is emerging under the sign of indigenous sovereignty, and the term's range of practical meanings is difficult to circumscribe, taking into account specific local and national contexts as well as uneven conditions of "globalization." Exercised and negotiated at different scales, sovereignty's meanings today are different from those projected at the treaty of Westphalia or imposed by Louis XIV and Napoleon. And they exceed the visions of integration and independence associated with either Wilsonian internationalism or anticolonial national liberation. Sturm's (2002) subtle exploration of the Gramscian "contradictory consciousness" that has historically made and remade an irreducibly diverse "Cherokee Nation" is a case in point. Indigenous sovereignty, in its current range of meanings, includes the "domestic dependent nation" status of Native Americans, the semi-independence of Nunavut, the national status of Vanuatu (and its transnational tax shelters), the bicultural polity emerging in Aotearoa/New Zealand, the cross border institutions of the Saami, the federalism of New Caledonia's Matignon and Noumea Accords, the "corporate" institutions of Native Alaskans, the broad range of agreements that govern uses of Aboriginal country in Australia, and intensifying struggles around natural resources and "cultural property."

Roger Maaka and Augie Fleras explore this "proliferation of sovereignty discourses" arguing that they do not reproduce the 19th-century models underlying settler-colonial states. The current discourses express "patterns of belonging that accentuate a sovereignty without secession, involving models of relative yet relational autonomy in non-coercive contexts" (Maaka and Fleras 2000: 93, 108). Indigenous movements take advantage of interstitial possibilities, failures and openings within national–transnational governmental structures of "graduated sovereignty" (Ong 2000). James Tully, drawing on Taiaiake Alfred's trenchant Mohawk vision (see Brown this volume), sees indigenous social movements not as struggles *for* freedom (in the older sense of absolute independence, but as "struggles *of* freedom to modify the system of internal colonization from within" (Tully 2000: 58). Charles Hale (2002), in his Gramscian assessment of Mayan social movements, unevenly articulated with neoliberal multiculturalism, comes to a similar conclusion. Attaining formal independence does not necessarily change the situation, as the predicament of Pacific microstates struggling to reconcile cultural–political autonomy with economic (inter)dependence shows (Bensa and Wittersheim 1998). "Sovereignty," understood as a range of current practices, evokes pragmatic possibilities and structural limits. Thomas Biolsi's (2005) analysis of four distinct sovereignty claims currently made by Native Americans is a pointed reminder of this strategic complexity, as is Andrea Muehlebach's (2001) account of mobile "place-making" in struggles for self-determination and sovereignty at the United Nations.

Within each context, appeals to all-or-nothing ("ideological") sovereignty combine and alternate with negotiated ("pragmatic") sovereignty. A nonreductive assessment of the historically possible, a political and prophetic realism, recognizes this necessary alternation and tactical flexibility. Without radical visions and maximalist claims indigenous movements risk cooptation. Without ad hoc arrangements and coalitions, in which economic and military power remain overwhelmingly unequal, little can be gained in the short term. And the risk of backlash is great. One of the values, perhaps, of bringing diaspora into the complex domain of the indigenous is to import a constitutive ambivalence. Diasporic experience is necessarily both nationalist and antinationalist. Absolutist invocations of blood, land, and return coexist with the arts of conviviality, the need to make homes away from home, among different peoples. Diasporic ruptures and connections—lost homelands, partial returns, relational identities, and world-spanning networks—are fundamental components of indigenous experience today.

Note

1. The present chapter expands and refocuses a paper, "Indigenous Diasporas," forthcoming in *Diasporas: Après quinze années de ferveur*, edited by William Berthomière and Christine Chivallon. Paris: Maison des Sciences de l'Homme. The volume collects papers from a conference, "La Notion de Diaspora," Poitiers, May 15–16, 2003. I thank the organizers and participants for stimulating discussions, in a context of comparative diasporas. I am also grateful to Orin Starn and Marisol de la Cadena, as well as to participants in

the Wenner-Gren Conference, "Indigenous Experience Today," who helped me find my way through a different comparative landscape.

References

Active, John. 2000. Yup'iks in the city. In *Hunting tradition in a changing world*, edited by Anne Fienup-Riordan, 169–182. New Brunswick, NJ: Rutgers University Press.

Anderson, Benedict. 1998. Long Distance Nationalism. In *The spectre of comparisons: Nationalism, Southeast Asia, and the world*, 58–74. London: Verso.

Ang, Ien. 2001. Indonesia on my mind. In *On not speaking Chinese: Living between Asia and the West*, 52–74. London: Routledge.

Benjamin, Walter. 1969. Theses on the philosophy of history. In *Illuminations*, edited by Hannah Arendt, 256–265. New York: Schocken.

Bensa, Alban, and Eric Wittersheim. 1998. Nationalism and Interdependence: The Political Thought of Jean-Marie Tjibaou. *Contemporary Pacific* 10 (2): 369–391.

Biolsi, Thomas. 2005. Imagined geographies: Sovereignty, indigenous space, and American Indian struggles. *American Ethnologist* 32 (2): 239–259.

Brah, Avtar. 1996. *Cartographies of diaspora: Contesting identities*. London: Routledge.

Brown, Michael. 2003. *Who owns native culture?* Cambridge, MA: Harvard University Press.

Calloway, Colin. 1990. *The Western Abenakis of Vermont, 1600–1800: War, migration, and the survival of an Indian people*. Norman: University of Oklahoma Press.

Chakrabarty, Dipesh. 2000. *Provincializing Europe: Postcolonial thought and historical difference*. Princeton: Princeton University Pres.

Chappell, David. 1997. *Double ghosts: Oceanian voyagers on Euroamerican ships*. Armonk NY: M. E. Sharpe.

Christen, Kimberley. 2004. *Properly Warumungu: Indigenous future-making in a remote Australian town*. Ph.D. dissertation, History of Consciousness Department, University of California, Santa Cruz.

Clifford, James. 1988. Identity in Mashpee. In *The predicament of culture*, 277–346. Cambridge, MA: Harvard University Press.

——. 1994. Diasporas. *Cultural Anthropology* 9 (3): 302–338. Reprinted in *Routes* (1997), 244–278. Cambridge, MA: Harvard University Press.

——. 2001. Indigenous Articulations. *Contemporary Pacific* 13 (2): 468–490.

——. 2002. Post-neo colonial situations: Notes on historical realism today. In *Literatura e viagens pós-coloniais (ACT, No. 6)*, edited by Helena Carvalhão Buescu and Manuela Reibeiro Sanches, 9–32. Lisbon: Edições Colibri.

——. 2004a. Looking several ways: Anthropology and native heritage in Alaska. *Current Anthropology* 45 (1): 5–30.

——. 2004b. Traditional Futures. In *Questions of tradition,* edited by Mark Phillips and Gordon Schochet, 152–168. Toronto: University of Toronto Press.

Cohen, Robin. 1997. *Global diasporas: An introduction.* London: University College London Press.

Curtis, Tim. 2002. *Talking about place: Identities, histories and powers among the Na'Hai speakers of Malakula (Vanuatu).* Ph.D. dissertation, Department of Anthropology, The Australian National University.

Darnell, Regna. 1999. Rethinking the concepts of band and tribe, community and nation: An accordion model of nomadic Native American social organization. *Papers of the Twenty-Ninth Algonquian Conference/Actes du congres des Algonquinistes,* 90–105. Winnipeg: University of Manitoba.

De Certeau Michel. 1984. *The practice of everyday life.* Berkeley: University of California Press.

de la Cadena, Marisol. 2000. *Indigenous mestizos: The politics of race and culture in Cuzco, 1919–1991.* Durham, NC: Duke University Press.

Diaz, Vicente, and Kehaulani Kauanui, eds. 2001. Special Issue: "Native Pacific cultural studies at the edge," *Contemporary Pacific* 13 (2).

Dombrowski, Kirk. 2002. The praxis of indigenism and Alaska Native timber politics. *American Anthropologist* 104: 1062–1073.

Fienup-Riordan, Ann. 1990. *Eskimo essays: Yup'ik lives and how we see them.* New Brunswick, NJ: Rutgers University Press.

——. 2000. *Hunting tradition in a changing world.* New Brunswick, NJ: Rutgers University Press.

Flores, William, and Rina Benmayor, eds. 1997. *Latino cultural citizenship: Claiming identity, space, and rights.* Boston: Beacon Press.

Friedman, Jonathan. 1993. Will the real Hawaiian please stand: Anthropologists and natives in the global struggle for identity. *Bijdragen: Journal of the Humanities and Social Sciences of Southeast Asia and Oceania* (Leiden), 49 (4): 737–767.

Fujikane, Candace, and Jonathan Okamura, eds. 2000. Special issue: "Whose vision? Asian settler colonialism in Hawai`i," *Amerasia Journal* 26 (2).

Gegeo, David Welchman. 1998. Indigenous knowledge and empowerment: Rural development examined from within. *Contemporary Pacific* 10 (2): 289–315.

——. 2001. Cultural rupture and Indigeneity: The challenge of (re)-visioning "place" in the Pacific. *Contemporary Pacific* 13 (2): 491–508.

Ghere, David. 1993. The "disappearance" of the Abenaki in western Maine: Political organization and ethnocentric assumptions. *American Indian Quarterly* 17: 193–207.

Giddens, Anthony. 1990 [1983]. *The Consequences of modernity*. Cambridge: Polity Press.

Gidwani, Vinay, and K. Sivaramakrishnan. 2003. Circular migration and the spaces of cultural assertion. *Annals of the Association of American Geographers* 93 (1): 186–213.

Gilroy, Paul. 1993. *The black Atlantic: Double consciousness and modernity*. Cambridge, MA: Harvard University Press.

Gossen, Gary. 1999. Indians inside and outside of the Mexican national idea: A case study of the modern diaspora of San Juan Chamula. In *Telling Maya tales: Tzotzil identities in modern Mexico*, 189–208. London: Routledge. (Originally published in Spanish, 1983)

Glick-Schiller, Nina. 1995. From immigrant to transmigrant: Theorizing transnational migration. *Anthropological Quarterly* 68 (1): 48–63.

Hale, Charles. 2002. Does multiculturalism menace? Governance, cultural rights and the politics of identity in Guatemala. *Journal of Latin American Studies* 34: 485–524.

Hall, Stuart. 1989. New ethnicities. In *Black film, British cinema*, edited by Kobena Mercer, 27–30. London: Institute of Contemporary Art.

——. 1990. Cultural identity and diaspora. In *Identity, community, culture, difference*, edited by Jonathan Rutherford, 222–237. London: Lawrence and Wishart.

Haraway, Donna. 1988. Situated knowledges: The science question in feminism and the privilege of partial perspective. *Feminist Studies* 14 (1): 167–181.

Harmon, Alexandra. 1998. *Indians in the making: Ethnic relations and Indian identities around Puget Sound*. Berkeley: University of California Press.

Hill, Jonathan, ed. 1996. *History, power, and identity: Ethnogenesis in the Americas, 1492–1992*. Iowa City: University of Iowa Press.

Kastoriano, Riva, 2003. Diaspora, transnationalism and the state. Paper presented at the La Notion de Diaspora conference, Maison des Sciences de l'Homme, Poitiers, May 16th.

Kauanui, Kehaulani. 1999. Off-island Hawaiians "making" ourselves at "home": A [gendered] contradiction in terms? *Women's Studies International Forum* 21 (6): 681–693.

Lambert, Michael. 2002. *Longing for exile: Migration and the making of a translocal community in Senegal, West Africa.* Portsmouth, NH: Heinemann.

Levitt, Peggy. 2001. *The transnational villagers.* Berkeley: University of California Press.

Lilley, Ian. 2004. Diaspora and identity in archaeology: Moving beyond the black Atlantic. In *A companion to social archaeology,* edited by L. Meskell and R. Preucel, 287–312. Oxford: Blackwell.

——. 2006. Archaeology, diaspora and decolonization. Journal of Social Archaeology 6 (1): 28–47.

Maaka, Roger, and Augie Fleras. 2000. Engaging with indigeneity: Tino Rangatiratanga in Aotearoa. In *Political theory and the rights of indigenous peoples,* edited by Duncan Ivison, Paul Patton, and Will Sanders, 89–111. Cambridge: Cambridge University Press.

Mallon, Sean. 2005. Samoan *tatau* as global practice. In *Tatoo: Bodies, art and exchange in the Pacific and the West,* edited by Nicolas Thomas, Anna Cole, and Bronwen Douglas, 145–170. London: Reaktion Books.

Merlan, Francesca. 1997. Fighting over country: Four commonplaces. In *Fighting over country: Anthropological perspectives,* CAEPR Research monograph, 12: 4–15. Canberra: Centre for Aboriginal Economic Policy research, The Australian National University.

——. 1998. *Caging the rainbow: Places, politics, and Aborigines in a North Australian town.* Honolulu: University of Hawai`i Press.

Mishra, Vijay. 1996a. The Diasporic imaginary: Theorizing the Indian diaspora. *Textual Practice* 10 (3): 421–447.

——. 1996b. (B)ordering Naipaul: Indenture history and diasporic poetics. *Diaspora* 5 (2): 189–237.

Mitchell, Joseph. 1960. Mohawks in High Steel. In *Apologies to the Iroquois,* edited by Edmund Wilson, 3–38. New York: Vintage. (Originally published in *The New Yorker,* 1959)

Muehlebach, Andrea. 2001. "Making place" at the United Nations: Indigenous cultural politics at the U.N. Working Group on Indigenous Populations. *Cultural Anthropology* 16 (3): 415–448.

Niezen, Ronald. 2003. *The Origins of indigenism: Human rights and the politics of identity.* Berkeley, CA: University of California Press.

Ong, Aihwa. 1999. *Flexible citizenship: The cultural logics of transnationality.* Durham, NC: Duke University Press.

——. 2000. Graduated sovereignty in South-East Asia. *Theory, Culture and Society* 17 (4): 55–75.

Peel, J. D. Y. 1978. Olajú: A Yoruba concept of development. *Journal of Development Studies* 14: 139–165.

Peters, Kurt. 1995. Santa Fe Indian Camp, House 21, Richmond California: Persistence of Identity among Laguna Pueblo Railroad Laborers, 1945–1982. *American Indian Culture and Research Journal* 19 (3): 33–70.

Phillips, Ruth. 1998. *Trading identities: The souvenir in Native North American art from the Northeast, 1700–1900*. Seattle: University of Washington Press.

Piot, Charles. 1999. *Remotely global: Village modernity in West Africa*, Durham, NC: Duke University Press.

Rafael, Vicente. 1898. Imagination and imagery: Filipino nationalism in the 19th century. *Inscriptions* 5: 25–48. (Center for Cultural Studies, University of California, Santa Cruz)

Ramirez, Renya. in press. *Native hubs: Culture, community, and belonging in Silicon Valley and beyond*. Durham, NC: Duke University Press.

Rigsby, Bruce. 1995. Tribes, diaspora people and the vitality of law and custom: Some comments. In *Anthropology in the native title era: Proceeedings of a workshop,* edited by Jim Fingleton and Julie Finlayson, 25–27. Canberra: Australian Institute of Aboriginal and Torres Straits Islander Studies.

Rouse, Roger. 1991. Mexican migration and the social space of post-modernism. *Diaspora* 1 (1): 8–23.

Sahlins, Marshall. 1989. Cosmologies of capitalism: The trans-Pacific sector of "the world system." *Proceedings of the British Academy* 74: 1–51. (Reprinted in *Culture in Practice* [2000]: 415–469. New York: Zone Books.)

——. 1993. Goodbye to *tristes tropes*: Ethnography in the context of modern world economy. *Journal of Modern History* 65: 1–25. (Reprinted in *Culture in Practice* [2000]: 471–500. New York: Zone Books.)

——. 1999. What is anthropological enlightenment? Some lessons of the twentieth century. *Annual Review of Anthropology* 28: i–xxiii. (Reprinted in *Culture in Practice* [2000]: 501–526. New York: Zone Books.)

Smith, Benjamin Richard. 2000. "Local" and "diaspora" connections to country and kin in Central Cape York Peninsula. In *Land, rights, laws: Issues of native title,* vol. 2, issue 6, edited by Jessica Weir, 1–8. Canberra: Australian Institute of Aboriginal and Torres Straits Islander Studies.

Sturm, Circe. 2002. *Blood politics: Pace, culture and identity in the Cherokee Nation of Oklahoma*. Berkeley: University of California Press.

Sutton, Peter. 1988. Myth as history, History as myth. In *Being black: Aboriginal cultures in "settled" Australia*, edited by Ian Keen, 251–268. Canberra: Aboriginal Studies Press.

Swain, Tony. 1993. *A Place for Strangers: Towards a History of Australian Aboriginal Being*. Cambridge: Cambridge University Press.

Teaiwa, Teresia. 2001. *Militarism, tourism and the native: Articulations in Oceania*. Ph.D. dissertation, History of Consciousness Department, University of California, Santa Cruz.

Tsing, Anna. 2000. The Global Situation. *Cultural Anthropology* 15 (3): 327–360.

Tully, James. 2000. The Struggles of indigenous peoples for and of freedom. In *Political theory and the rights of indigenous peoples*, edited by Duncan Ivison, Paul Patton, and Will Sanders, 36–59. Cambridge: Cambridge University Press.

Weiner, James. 2000. Diaspora, materialism, tradition: Anthropological issues in the recent High Court appeal of the Yorta Yorta. In *Land, rights, laws: Issues of native title*, vol. 2, issue 6, edited by Jessica Weir, 1–12. Canberra: Australian Institute of Aboriginal and Torres Straits Islander Studies.

Diasporic Media and Hmong/Miao Formulations of Nativeness and Displacement

Louisa Schein

For Hmong/Miao scattered across the globe, a common identity is typically posited through shared narratives of displacement. A collection of historical moments are threaded together by the theme of loss of lands: Beginning in central China, Hmong/Miao were dislodged southward over centuries by hostile Chinese, eventually migrating into Southeast Asia where those involved on the U.S. side in the Vietnam war were uprooted from Laos to Thailand, and eventually relocated to Western countries. "Hmong have never had a country." "Hmong are seminomadic." "Hmong people are always on the move." "We lost our country." These are the tropes that have been used by themselves and others as characterizations of Hmong/Miao over the centuries. How to think these identity motifs in relation to the theme of indigeneity? While the notion itself has not been taken up in these self-characterizations, the unjust expropriation of native lands is a discourse shared with those who would identify themselves as indigenous peoples. Indeed, as James Clifford holds (this volume), in cases in which indigenous peoples were forced or drawn into cities and towns, "the connection to lost homelands comes closer to a diasporic relation, with its characteristic forms of longing, long distance nationalism and displaced performances of 'heritage.'" Andre Beteille, however, is cautiously skeptical, charging anthropologists with overusing the indigenous category because it arouses their "moral excitation" and asking "How widely can people move and still retain the entitlement of being indigenous for themselves and their descendants?" (1998: 190). Given such discrepant views of distance and mobility, what can be gained by bringing diasporic and indigenous identity motifs into dialogue?

My point of entry for this chapter is the translocal relations between Hmong Americans and their coethnics in Southeast Asia and in China (where they are called Miao).[1] What is striking about the contemporary era—since a cohort of perhaps 200,000 Hmong took up residence in the United States as refugees beginning in 1975—is that the migration trajectory enshrined as unidirectional in the exilic narrative has become multidirectional in practice. In other words, Hmong in the United States, along with those in France and Australia, have been in the position to reverse direction, to travel "back" to their remembered homelands. No longer is Hmong/Miao diaspora the singular process of a people spreading outward from the epicenter that was China. What the most recent moves have enabled is a crisscrossing of the globe, with those Hmong privileged to have accumulated resources and travel documents in some of the world's wealthiest countries journeying with frequency to China, Laos, Thailand, and even Vietnam and Burma.

Hmong/Miao social intercourse now takes place at a global scale, rather than only within localities or national boundaries. And spatial subjectivities have shifted accordingly. Not only do Hmong in *Western* countries think of themselves as linked and—for some—shuttling back and forth to Asian homelands, but those who host them in Asia are also coming to perceive their lives as imbricated with their overseas coethnics. The types of engagement are numerous. Some Hmong émigrés travel back to tour, usually visiting relatives along the way. Some are pursuing transnational business ventures, such as imports or media productions, about which I will have a great deal to say presently. Some are looking for sexual trysts or marriage partners. Indeed, the flow of brides to the West has created a set of durable affinal ties that further solidify the transnational character of Hmong/Miao social life. Finally, in addition to actual traveling bodies, there has also been a constant flow of remittances from relatives in the West to kin in Asia.

In the last two decades, Hmong Americans at the farthest reach of the diaspora, then, have begun to engage in activities of reterritorialization as they recuperate pasts, roots, and homelands through concrete practices of trans-Pacific travel and business. Certain places, even as they are increasingly transected by the flows of persons from abroad, are becoming fixed, even frozen, in memory and in cultural production as icons of pure Hmong origins. These origin places are portrayed as lands legitimately occupied by Hmong/Miao over history, lands from which they were unwillingly wrenched away by war and exile. Yet in the memory practices through which involuntary displacement is elaborated, the notion of indigeneity has not come into play.

In this chapter I offer an analysis of powered "relational" and gendered place making and constructions of nativeness among the Hmong/Miao through the lens of their burgeoning media practices.[2] Since the early 1990s, I have documented the Hmong media scene, collecting nearly 250 videos as well as some audio tapes, interviewing directors and audiences, visiting sites of distribution, and watching and interpreting videos alongside Hmong consumers. Focusing on video, my ethnography encompasses both the production–consumption of forms of grassroots media about Asia by Hmong in the West and the ethnotextual analysis of the contents of certain media texts.

Here, I explore how Hmong media produce, comment on, and process both emerging translocalisms and the remembered places that Hmong in the West hail from. I make the methodological argument that an understanding of Hmong/Miao reterritorialization practices must encompass not only consideration of representations of lost lands, but also investigation of the material processes and relations of media production that give rise to such representations. I show that both are characterized by a gendered regime in which homelands are feminized. And I suggest that the absence of address to external powers in Hmong transnational practice may shed light on their indifference to the category of the indigenous.

Narrating Loss of Land

In comparing Hmong, as they are called in Southeast Asia and the West, with Miao, as they are called in China, one sees a predictable intens-ification of narratives of displacement and exile the further one gets from China. In the eastern part of China's Guizhou province, where I have done extensive fieldwork, Miao peasants have tilled the same fields for several centuries and have a sense of themselves as legitimately occupying their lands. Nonetheless, this is an uneasy legitimacy, always crosscut by Miao histories of conflict with the Chinese imperium. In the present day, the ancient struggle over lands has been replaced with the marginality of minority status. The late Maoist period implemented a household registration system that effectively tied all Chinese citizens to their places of birth and prohibited migration, thus legally encoding Miao entitlement to the lands they occupied. But at the same time the era institutionalized a minority policy that froze identity as either Han or not, with the Han constituting over 90 percent of the population, and the 55 minority nationalities framed as less advanced and less worthy of official positions.

Outside the purview of the so-called Miao pale, a region in Hunan and eastern Guizhou provinces where Miao reside in great density of population and have for centuries, narratives about land shift dramatically. Even within China, in the border regions of Yunnan and Guangxi provinces abutting Vietnam and Laos, Miao portray themselves as latecomers to the land, and as occupying the least arable, most forbidding, steepest, most isolated sectors of whatever region they inhabit. They explain their economic marginality precisely through the account of exilic flight that deposited them in their current dwellings long after the lower and better irrigated land was already occupied. In the mountains of Vietnam, Laos, Thailand, and Burma, such self-portrayals as interlopers, as sojourners on land that was never granted to them, but on which lowlanders tolerated Hmong residence, are ubiquitous. Those Hmong of Laos who had assisted the U.S. Secret War during the Vietnam era and were exiled once again by their political vulnerability after U.S. withdrawal in 1975, recount an even more involuntary flight. That they have been uneasily accommodated in the West, targeted with racist sentiment held over from the war and with more generalized anti-immigrant reaction is in complete accord with their self-perception over the centuries as unwanted late arrivals competing for scarce resources.

The theme of Hmong as interlopers on already occupied lands took a strange and terrible historical twist in the fall of 2004 when a Hmong American man, Chai Soua Vang, shot and killed six hunters in the woods of Wisconsin. The accounts are contradictory, with the white Americans maintaining that the shooting was unprovoked, and Vang maintaining that he was subjected to racial slurs and harassment, then fired at, before he snapped. But what is telling is that there is no disagreement that Vang was on private hunting land. As Orecklin recounts in *Time Magazine*, "white hunters have complained that Hmong do not respect private property. In the North Woods, private and public lands abut each other, and the only way to know the difference is to consult maps issued by the state or look for NO TRESPASSING signs. Landowners routinely find unauthorized hunters on their property. Etiquette calls for asking the interloper to leave or phoning the sheriff or game warden" (2004: 37).

Refracted through the lens of the longue durée of Hmong/Miao migration, it is not difficult to imagine that the construct of "respect" for private property would have been of dubious merit, a luxury in which only the comfortably landed, not the Hmong nomads, could indulge. As longtime latecomers, whose occupation of ill-defined terrains was the only means of livelihood for generations, and whose residence in highland regions was eventually to become legitimate and recognized by Southeast Asian states, it may have made little sense for Hmong hunters to assiduously avoid wandering across the invisible lines demarcating private woods, especially because white hunters apparently did so routinely as well. This is not to imply a cultural essentialist move of designating property sense as "lacking" in Hmong culture, but rather to suggest the possibility of an historically conditioned structure of feeling that would render a clean counterposition of public and private land somewhat nonsensical to Hmong who had long lived in liminal space. After the incident, Hmong activists and hunters mobilized quickly to counter what was foreseen as an onslaught of racial backlash against them, attesting en masse to experiences of racial harassment while hunting (Moua 2004: 7). Opined one man in an editorial in the St. Paul newspaper, the *Hmong Times*, "The example of hunting 'without' regulations and private land in Laos has been used to pin down and drive the issue that Hmong hunters do not understand the concept of the regulations and rules. … Throughout the whole tragic event, hunting has been claimed as an historical Wisconsin tradition passed on from generation to generation. Surely hunting is in the roots of Wisconsin, but what is failed to be acknowledged is that hunting also happens in other states and countries" (Xiong 2004: 2).[3]

The Problem of Indigeneity

For a people so on the move, so multiply displaced, it may seem counter-intuitive to entertain issues of indigeneity. Attachments to territory appear over time as ephemeral for Hmong/Miao, not as definitive of who they are or what claims they can make. Yet the theme of violent and unjust colonization by Chinese settlers, one that over centuries broke the hold Hmong/Miao had on their territories and rendered their cultural practices less than hegemonic, would seem to lend itself to this terminology. Indeed, within the contemporary Chinese purview, one might especially expect activism around indigeneity to have arisen within Tibet, where the tie-ins with transnational activists are so dense, and where the territory has more of a constant association with Tibetans. Yet, as seen in Emily Yeh's contribution to this volume, indigenous terminology is not prevalent in Tibet either. These absences push us to entertain the utter contingency of indigenous discourse. A morphological analysis of social forms and histories (relation to land, to dominant groups, etc.) cannot account for the differential insertion of minoritized peoples into circuits of language and activism that may or may not call out the indigenous term. Chinese and Southeast Asian sites, as seen also in Anna Tsing's chapter (this volume), have taken up the term unevenly, and largely, I would argue, because of external or relational factors such as the specific transnational alliances that particular groups may have formed in recent decades.

Nonetheless, there is much to be learned from thinking the transnational strategies of identity production and political mobilization within and beyond the indigenous label. One of the things Hmong/Miao narratives share with those more typically associated with indigenous peoples is the attribute of chronic statelessness as a result of unjust expropriation of land. This is a fundamental organizing principle of Hmong/Miao identities; their folklore delves in great depth into the origins of this deprivation, usually citing instances of Chinese trickery and deceit in ancient times as the cause (Tapp 1989). We might, then, think of indigenism or nativeness more capaciously. As Clifford (this volume) points out, "there are various ways to be 'native' in relation to a place; assumptions of firstness or 'autochthony' often obscure important histories of movement; and 'sovereign' control is always compromised and relative." The Hmong/Miao, having been perennially on the move, emerge out of these definitional discrepancies as eschewing firstness per se, but still as stateless, minoritized, and socially marginal peoples, in diaspora as well as in Asia. Some of the questions that could be posed include: Why is it that those Hmong furthest from the lands of origin—that is, those in the West—appear to be the ones most mobilized in terms of identity politics? And why is it those most far-flung who most champion territories in Asia as "homelands"? How is it that those in diaspora are the most active in striving to preserve cultural heritage and find ways of conveying it to their youth? How does the lived practice of translocality across the Pacific articulate with the activities of place-making that consolidate certain sites as Hmong or Miao? And why has indigeneity never become a key term in the identity productions of Hmong/Miao anywhere?

It is elucidating here to reread the much-cited definition of indigenous peoples by Jose Martinez Cobo, of the UN Subcommission on the Prevention of Discrimination and Protection of Minorities: "Indigenous communities, peoples and nations are those which have a historical continuity with pre-invasion and pre-colonial societies that developed on their territories, consider themselves distinct from other sectors of societies now prevailing in those territories, or parts of them. They form at present non-dominant sectors of society and are determined to preserve, develop, and transmit to future generations their ancestral territories, and their ethnic identity, as the basis of their continued existence as peoples, in accordance with their own cultural patterns, social institutions and legal systems" (Cobo 1986: 5). What emerges from this formulation is an important conceptual alliance—to be expected—between ties to "ancestral territories" and the status of being "nondominant" sectors in the present day. What I am going to suggest for the Hmong/Miao, however, is that the vicissitudes of diaspora be considered the analytical counterpart of invasion and colonization, as both operate to effect minoritization and to put the inhabitation of ancestral lands at risk. Steeped in the memory of being flung, repeatedly, from those lands, the determination to "preserve, develop and transmit to future generations" their ethnic identity takes on a particular, and particularly acute, cast. Those Hmong in the West recall, and attempt to recuperate through travel, lands that are halfway around the world. Distance notwithstanding, they recall them with immediacy, even a sentimental intimacy. They site the culture that they are in peril of losing as intact and persisting on those lands.

The diasporic project of transmission also references those spatially remote Asian territories where culture is envisioned to be best preserved. But transmission poses a dilemma: the younger generations are not as likely to make return voyages, because parents as well as children are likewise struggling to fashion themselves as members of western societies. Hmong-produced media about the homelands comes to be imbricated in this concern for cultural integrity, comes to be seen as a key technology of transmission that can effect a bridging of space, the space that otherwise keeps diasporic Hmong who do not travel back from their past. My exploration will show that other internecine cultural politics emerge from this bifurcation of space.

Media Production and Resource Politics

Dozens of the primarily male Hmong American travelers to Asia, then, are involved in the production of videos that constitute diverse representations of the lands they call home. This media entrepreneurship has become one of the strategies by which Hmong refugees have made their way in the neoliberal U.S. economy. Arriving in the United States, refugees, typically with limited language, job skills and capital begin as wards of the welfare state. Yet this status is ultimately an unsustainable one because the economic milieu into which they are inserted premises their membership in society, their good citizenship, on swift "autonomization," on taking responsibility for themselves as a demonstration of their "freedom" (Burchell 1996: 27–29). Hence, they immediately become liminal, because their host's agenda, even as it initially extends to them a charitable safety net, is, from the moment they set foot on U.S. soil, to remake them into "self-sufficient" contributors to the U.S. economy. Since 1975, many Hmong have supported their own resettlement process through taking up this latter role. They have taken responsibility for their livelihood not only through language and employment programs that channel Hmong into low-paying jobs in manufacturing and service; neoliberal governmentalities privilege instead the refashioning of refugees into entrepreneurs. Independent ventures have become the ever more inexorable solution to underemployment given the America Hmong inhabit, one that, as Bourdieu and Wacquant have put it, is characterized by "the generalization of precarious wage labor and social insecurity, turned into the privileged engine of economic activity" (2001: 3). Canny as they are about the contraction of the welfare state, and deeply savvy about the betrayals that the United States is capable of ever since the latter's precipitous withdrawal from Laos in 1975, many Hmong immigrants have not waited for their social welfare safety net to be pulled out from under them or for the tenuous security of their menial jobs to be shattered by more offshore relocations. They have adopted instead what has been portrayed as the hallmark of neoliberalism: "enterprise culture" (Heelas and Morris 1992), specifically, that which generates income *within their own communities*. Their ventures include small businesses such as restaurants, groceries, video shops, auto shops, and laundromats. But of interest here is the production of media, which is quite distinct as a Hmong livelihood strategy.

To my knowledge, no other immigrant group to the United States has undertaken to produce their own commercial entertainment videos to the extent that Hmong have done so. It is noteworthy that Hmong/Miao status as stateless minorities everywhere means that, unlike, say, their Vietnamese or Indian counterparts, there is no national cinema in their own language to import. Entrepreneurs have spotted a market, particularly among those diasporics of older generations, who remember life in the old country and, isolated in their American lives as new immigrants alienated by language, long to consume simulacra of their pasts. What the trans-Pacific traveling Hmong entrepreneurs have offered them is an array of videotapes. These tapes, shot, edited, and marketed all by Hmong, take their place in the context of a huge Hmong media scene in which hundreds of newspapers, magazines, audio cassettes, CDs, music videos, and videotapes are produced and sold, all within the Hmong market. Videos are made by a range of amateur and semiprofessional producers, many of whom have established companies with names such as Hmong World Productions, Asia Video Productions, Vang's International Video Productions, and S. T. Universal Video. The tapes are in Hmong language and targeted exclusively for intraethnic consumption. Shrink-wrapped and usually copyrighted, they sell for $10–$30 apiece. They are marketed at Hmong festivals, through Asian groceries and video shops, and by mail order.

Among this large volume of videos are dramas, martial arts thrillers, documentaries of important events, performance or "music" videos of singing and dancing, historical reconstructions, and Asian feature films dubbed into Hmong. A moderate proportion concern Asian home-land sites. There are tapes that portray Laos, birthplace of almost all Hmong Americans and scene of the Secret War orchestrated by the CIA in which Hmong fought as guerillas during Vietnam. There are those set in Thailand, where Hmong sojourned in refugee camps before being granted permission to migrate to the West. And there are those that document a mythologized land of origins in the mountains of southwest China. As an aggregate, these products can be distinguished by what Leuthold (1998: 1–3) refers to as "indigenous aesthetics": they demonstrate place attachment and through their contents and styles their creators express their belonging and accountability within their communities.

It bears emphasizing that although much Hmong media production spans continents, bringing Asia and the West together in both production relations and in content, it is Hmong Americans who are owners of the means of production and who profit from the ventures. How are Hmong/Miao abroad incorporated into video projects? On the basis of my interviews with producers and directors in the United States, those who go abroad typically develop bases of operations in Thailand, sometimes in Laos. They find close relatives, clan members, or coethnics, who facilitate productions by organizing casts and space for shooting. Local actors can be paid almost nothing and they have that aura of authenticity that actors who had sojourned in the states would have been hard pressed to effect. Locals have also been trained to do camera and crew work, making the costs of production unimaginably low.

Hmong Americans can arrive with one or more video cameras, and a feature-length video can be shot in a week or two.

Another model for involving Asian Hmong in U.S.-owned ventures has been sponsorship—especially in the music business. A producer will locate a talented and aspiring singer, dancer, or other performer and put up money for them to train and record music in their home country, whether Laos or Thailand. Music and lyrics might be written in Asia, by the performer or others, or might be provided by the U.S. producer. For music videos, great care is taken with settings and costumes, offering the Hmong American consumer aural and visual indulgences in motifs from remembered village life, or eye candy in the form of lavish costumes—traditional Hmong or other Southeast Asian styles all being popular among the nostalgic audiences in the West.

There are several aspects that contribute to the politics of value for these performers. Much like the resources of lands deemed indigenous, they are struggled over with great exertion. Sponsors strive assiduously to make exclusive arrangements with talents they feel have promise. A great deal of backbiting goes on between producers about who has control over hot stars in Asia and, once someone shows signs of potential success, producers frequently poach on each other's terrain. Likewise, the rising stars are often willing to play the field, making agreements with various producers for different projects. However, some are also careful to maintain one patron, who will be loyal to promoting them over other competitors on the market.

The more relevant aspect of value for this discussion pertains to the homeland cache of these artists. The homeland artists' appeal is often largely based on their traditional aura. Indeed, there is yet another genre of music video, that of the singers of time-honored Hmong *kwv txhiaj*—improvised antiphonal songs—who are located in villages as keepers of traditional lore and recorded or shot in their localities without the technologies of recording studios. Although popular, there is a limited market, mostly among the elder generations, for these old folk melodies. Those singers who dress in Hmong or Southeast Asian attire, sing in Hmong language, but sing the soft pop style that was fashioned toward the end of the war and in the refugee camps, have a wider marketability. There is a premium placed on Asian locations, and the desire for consuming the East is a crucial element of fans' subjectivities.

For Hmong American entrepreneurs, then, the homeland serves as resource in at least two mutually reinforcing ways. It provides profitable conditions for production—with abundant labor and costs at rock bottom prices—and it provides invaluable material for cultural imaginaries. There is no substitute for the effects garnered from narrative, music and documentary videos shot before the craggy backdrops of the Southeast Asian or Chinese highlands, or in the gritty mise-en-scène of dusty village roads, makeshift homes and rice cooked over wood fires that evokes refugee camps and peasant agriculture. Notably, although it is specific lands—and the traditions fixed to these sites from which value can be derived, it is those with access to transnational circuits of mobility, commerce, and representation who are positioned to reap rewards. It is, in other words, the articulation (Clifford 2001) of carefully rendered place-based authenticity with the ready mobility of transnational Hmong entrepreneurs that makes for lucrative ventures.

Place Making, Translocally

As I have suggested, while narratives of displacement and landless-ness have over history characterized almost all Hmong and Miao, even those within China, what the meaning production of Hmong American video reveals are myriad efforts to stabilize Asian sites as loci of cultural continuity, places not of transience, but of fixed significance for roots-seeking Hmong. We might call the practice of consuming music and video produced in Asia one of place making, a kind of virtual or remote place making from afar that is born out of translocal activity and imagination. As commentators on indigenism have pointed out, the place making on which indigenous claims are made is also routinely premised on translocal alliances. As Castree puts it: "People laying claim to the title 'indigenous' have ... created a 'resistance identity' that is avowedly international in compass. It is at once territorially rooted ... and yet a prime instance of translocal solidarity" (2004: 136). But what Castree describes is a circumstance in which locals concerned with *their own* locale, tap into the force of translocal organizations and discourses as a way of pursuing their ends. The Hmong/Miao version of place making differs in that it is specific translocals, what Glick-Schiller, Basch, and Blanc-Szanton (1994) call "transmigrants," who engage in fashioning, even bounding, the local and impose this meaning of place on those who inhabit Asian sites. Those represented are rendered relatively inactive through the action of translocals on them. Although we could say, then, that localism and translocalism are mutually constitutive here, as they are with indigenous movements, we can identify a distinct mode of interaction that may be more typical of the activities of diasporics canonizing the lands they call home.

It might be argued that transnational activists for indigenous peoples take their place in a long line of Orientalists, exoticist tourists, heritage preservationists, government conservationists and the like who also traffic in imposing the "tribal slot" *on others* (Li 2000: 153). Hmong Americans, with their apparatuses of representation could be seen to be not so different from these historical agents who affirm their own modernity by freezing others in alteric traditions. It is crucial, then, that we explore the specifics of that "slot" into which homeland Hmong/Miao are placed through the discursive and productive activities of media. As Tania Li suggests: "Agency is involved in the selection and combination of elements that form a recognizably indigenous identity, and also in the process of making connections" (2000: 157). In Hmong/Miao translocal media, where does that agency lie, and, if not indigenous, what identity is fashioned?

What is notable about Hmong/Miao practices of homeland recuperation is that they are about *internal* connections and *internal* differences. Perhaps the *indigenous* term does not come into relevance precisely because these practices are not concerned with articulating nativeness or making claims to dominant states or institutions. Rather, they are about internally complex identity formation. Both social and media practices are premised on and reinforce a disparity, both economic and gendered, between homelands and the West. Lands of origin, as we shall see, are constructed as impoverished, dependent, feminine. Those actors, mostly men, who traverse transnational space are masculinized by their economic power and in turn by their sexual access. Such internecine cultural politics, while thickly imbricated with a nostalgia for lost homelands, do not particularly interface with indigeneity politics that are much more about minoritization vis-à-vis ethnic others.

Reading Homeland Videos

As I have said, Hmong American video concerning the homeland comprises several distinct genres. The most salient distinction is that between videos that portray Asia intact and those that portray Hmong sites transected by returnee travel. Let me first discuss portrayals of Asia as they work to evoke the Hmong past. In these texts, the diasporic Hmong subject is centered as the cinematic eye gazing on former times; indeed, for migrant subjects, there is a way in which Asia is literally the past of their earlier lives, for many the site of their coming of age. Youth as an object of nostalgic memory is much of what fuels the desire for videos that travel backward in time. But there is also a geopolitical mapping implicit in these evocations, one that is reinforced through gendered imagery and positions Hmong in the West as those most advanced within global Hmong society. Below are some of the typical genres.

Homeland Documentaries

Videos in documentary style have been made concerning every country of Hmong residence—China, Vietnam, Laos, Thailand, and Burma. They usually feature the director as guide, narrating the images with heavy interpretation designed to allow viewers to reflect on where they have come from. Shot from airplanes or speeding busses, features of the land—the arc of mountains, the lush of gardens and fields, gurgling streams, peasants with draft animals—are stock images, as are festivals or cultural events that feature singing and dancing. Typically, there is a dwelling on the rudiments of living, emphasizing—tacitly or explicitly—what has become the stark difference between rugged village lives in Asia and such urban comforts as running water and vehicular transportation. Sometimes, the relevant Asian towns and cities, say Vientiane or Kunming, will also be sketched. Although the viewer knows that these images come from the present time, narration often adopts a tone of "this is where we came from." Ponderous songs, in the traditional *kwv txhiaj* style or the nostalgic light pop of Asia enhance the emotional impact of the visuals.

Among the documentarians of Asia, Su Thao, one of the very earliest to make commercial Hmong videos, is perhaps the best known. His videos cover all of the countries listed above, and he was the first among Hmong émigrés to document Vietnam and Burma. Each video case offers a lavish collage of costumed Hmong, often with Thao nestled somewhere among them. The contents then deliver this promised dream world of travel back to the cultural womb. We see all through Thao's panoptical eye, and we encounter villagers all along the way through Thao's pat interviews asking the interviewees to identify themselves, their clan, their village, the event, if relevant. A characteristic feature of Thao's work is the heavily gendered dimension of the encounter: a male gaze falls on the feminized beauty of Asia (often through zooms of unwitting young women's faces), and then concretizes the fantasy in the form of flirty interviews with women as to their marital status and clan affiliations. As I have argued elsewhere (Schein 1999, 2004), media are intrinsic to the cultivation and actualization of desire for homeland women as mistresses or wives, a desire that also in turn propels Hmong transnationality. Such documentaries are the most explicit example of this.

Another form of documenting the past is in returning to the specific sites of Hmong refugee history, specifically, Long Tieng, the CIA airbase in the Lao mountains where so many Hmong refugees worked or spent their childhoods, or Ban Vinai, the main Hmong refugee camp. These sites are nothing but overgrown rubble now, but the returnee camera wanders lovingly over every detail, looking past the decay to reevoke pasts lived in these locales.

Certain more specialized genres have also developed in the documentary vein. Tapes of actual *kwv txhiaj* singing have always been popular, and feature costumed singers, either staged for the camera or in the context of Asian festivals. A typical editing technique is to enrich the contents of the songs with visual cutaways to scenes of the land—mountains, fields, village life. More recently, documentaries of bullfights, a favorite festival pastime for Hmong/Miao in China and Southeast Asia, have appeared on the market. Even more recent is the new genre of hunting videos that take the viewer on actual hunting trips deep into the jungles of Laos or Thailand to stalk the birds or small animals that audiences remember as their special quarry in times gone by.

Historical Accounts

Other documentarians have undertaken to represent less timeless images of the Hmong past in favor of concrete accounts of the specific Hmong histories of migration, war and displacement. These tapes often rely on archival footage that has been passed down since the war, or that is obtained through Freedom of Information Act requests. Yuepheng Xiong, who studied history at the graduate level and now runs the only Hmong bookstore in the United States, is perhaps best known for this genre. In *Royal Lao Armed Forces* (1998), for instance, we see an 85-minute black-and-white film, narrated in Lao, showing soldiers in training and in uniform, learning maneuvers, marching in formation, catapulting themselves over walls, climbing ropes, parachuting into fields, training with multifarious weaponry, loading cannons, being reviewed by decorated officers, participating in any number of formal ceremonies.

Xiong's best seller, however, is a roots-seeking journey to China (*Taug Txoj Lw Ntshav: Keeb Kwm Hmoob Suav Teb,* "Following the Trail of Blood: Hmong History in China," 2000), which traces the putative migration trajectory of the Miao southward across China to their current locations in the southwest. Now in *Part Three,* it does not use archival footage, but rather was shot by Xiong himself with the help of a Miao crew in China. One of the reasons for the tape's popularity is that it bestows a deeper genealogy on the Southeast Asian Hmong, a genealogy that suggests a time before the waves of displacement began. Xiong's inspirational narration peppers most of the footage, beginning with the opening lines: "Hello. I am Yuepheng Xiong. There have been times when I wondered who I really was. I am Hmong, but what are Hmong? And who are Hmong? Do we have a history like other people?" In addition to visiting several key sites of Miao migration in China, Xiong takes the viewer to Zhuolu, 75 miles northwest of Beijing and much canonized as the origin place of the Miao people, where a statue of Chiyou, claimed to be the original Hmong progenitor, is regularly worshipped on Hmong returnee pilgrimages. He describes the conflict between the original inhabitants of this region—Chiyou, the putative Miao ancestor, and Huangdi, the Chinese Yellow Emperor. He describes the superior defenses of the Miao people, how they were victorious nine times before defeat. "Because of these wars," he laments, "Hmong were forced to go live in the mountains. They left behind their prosperous lives and had to resign themselves to backwardness." Here the video carries on the perennial account of Hmong loss of land and kingdom, mobilizing it to explain backwardness in the present day. In the process, it renders the acute losses of the Vietnam era continuous with millennia of like tragedies.

Folk Stories and Other Timeless Tales

Rising in popularity in recent years are dramatic recreations of ancient Hmong/Miao folk stories, complete with special effects. Children and elderly are especially fond of this genre, which features ghosts, spirits, and animals in abundance. The folk tale genre traffics in timelessness, clothing its actors in traditional Hmong dress and dwelling affectionately on the imponderabilia of village life anywhere. Stock characters—an orphan boy, a good-hearted stepdaughter, an evil second wife—people the scripts, which often stay quite faithful to specific tales that have been passed down for generations.

Related to the actual folk tales are dramas set in the village life of old, especially romances and yarns about gender and kinship struggles. A "second wife" genre has become popular as Hmong Americans reflect on a tradition of polygyny that was technically terminated on arrival in the

United States, but that de facto persists when married Hmong Americans pursue transnational liaisons. Both tragic and comic figures abound in these tales of family intrigue that often build on the time-honored tropes of older lore—tropes such as the would-be lovers divided by wealth and poverty, the enduring first wife persecuted by a headstrong second wife, the child separated from parents by a cruel remarriage.

The other form of nostalgia drama that has overwhelming popularity is martial arts thrillers. While some producers have made good money by buying the rights to Chinese, Hong Kong and other martial arts features and dubbing them in Hmong language, a few have tried their hand with original dramas played by Hmong actors who are martial arts enthusiasts themselves. These tapes usually mimic the themes of the classical Chinese genre, with bits of Hmong accent added in for good measure.

All these genres of drama tapes are usually quite didactic, and moralize about good kinship, honor, and personal conduct. But my work with audiences indicates that it is not the messages about the vagaries of social life per se that bind their viewers so loyally to the screens. Rather, it is the erasure of temporality and change that makes them a salve to the wounds of perennial displacement. Even if it means dressing present-day Asian Hmong in old-fashioned attire—pleated batiked skirts, for instance, instead of the sarongs that have been adopted by most Hmong in Thailand—having them till the fields in full festival costume, or insuring that they speak in the "old Hmong" language specified in the scripts, directors strain to offer these "collective wish images" (Watts 1999) to their voracious viewers. As Hmong anthropologist Gary Y. Lee puts it, "to the Hmong in diaspora, these video images may be more real than the reality of their dreary surroundings that are often devoid of familiar cultural practices and self-presentations" (2004: 16). Here we see clearly the agentive constructedness of a past that becomes a currency in the business of Hmong video. Comparable to the international NGOs that must construct enticing evocations of indigenous peoples' traditional lives to draw donor funds, Hmong directors strive to authenticate their images for maximum salability in the entertainment market.

Lis Txais and the Inspirational Genre

Akin to the plethora of new age media that glut the mainstream market with motifs and recreations of indigenous peoples' lore, a series of videos featuring the cult figure Lis Txais bring messages of unity and traditional values to dislocated Hmong struggling to find meaning in alienating urban American lives. Lis Txais has been a self-appointed guru since the days of Ban Vinai refugee camp when he constructed a temple and preached a new Hmong religion. After the camp era came to a close, Lis took up residence in a Hmong area in a remote corner of the Thai mountains. From there he has recorded audio tapes that have been widely distributed across the oceans instructing émigrés about how to stay Hmong in a threatening world. A few years ago, a relative in Wisconsin got the idea of preserving his teachings through video. The result is a series of tapes that feature Lis dressed in various kinds of ethnic or Western garb engaged in such activities as strolling through the mountains, picking berries, playing a flute, playing the *qeej* (bamboo reed pipe), blowing leaves, or singing, in a range of styles, about what it means to be Hmong and the importance of loving one another around the world. In one of the most striking sequences, he appears in a field of variegated poppies, introduces their varieties, then takes the viewer through an extended how-to lecture about cultivating the flower and harvesting opium. Lis's videos operate like sermons, drawing together fragments of tradition to fashion teachings for the future. "Never forget" is the overarching message.

Trials of Transnationality

Videos that deal with the new tribulations of acutely asymmetrical relations in diaspora also have wide viewership. Hmong American audiences desire not only the frozen images that evoke memory, but also a vehicle for working through the traumas that geopolitical separation have precipitated. These stories dwell noticeably on gender struggles, highlighting the harsh actuality that gender asymmetry also structures much of the transnational interchange between Hmong in the West and those in Asia. They also function didactically, warning philandering Hmong Americans of the perils of overseas excess.

In *Mob Niam Yau* (Sick for a Second Wife [2000]), a scheming middle-aged womanizer plays sick to get his wife to agree to consult a shaman whom he's secretly paid off to diagnose that he needs a second wife. He goes off to Thailand to woo a beautiful young girl, who seduces him into living with her parents and working in the fields for the household. In cahoots with her local boyfriend, she sets up a kidnapping in which the boyfriend and his gang take the hapless Hmong American captive at gunpoint, humiliate him, and call his U.S. wife to bail him out. She does so, dutifully, and he returns, chastened, to the United States.

One might summarize the moral message as: If you tamper with the homeland, it will tamper with you.

Commodified Places and Translocal Longing

At first blush, the Hmong diaspora appears quite divergent from those social movements that are organized around the notion of indigenous ties and rights to land. In some ways, their centuries of geographic dispersal mitigate toward viewing the Hmong and other diasporics as contrapuntal to those collectivities whose identity claims are based on rootedness. What a reading of Hmong media brings into focus, however, is that the *discourses* both of diasporic longing and those championing preservation of indigenous lifeways are not so far apart. As Clifford has suggested, "We are left with a spectrum of attachments to land and place—articulated, old and new traditions of indigenous dwelling and traveling" (2001: 477).

Together indigenous and diasporic discourses may be part and parcel of a worldwide malaise that prompts those with means of representation to offer recuperations of the traditional, the untouched, and the timeless alongside cautionary tales about too much intercourse with the outside. These discourses, of course, have measurable material dimensions. In the case of diasporic media, they comprise media commodities that sell in the West; in the case of indigenous movements, they are in large part what generates the flow of donor funds. As such, we might view both the retrograde discourses and the material practices they imply as indexical of an overarching commodity logic that compels indigeneity and tradition toward the market, or even *accounts* for the visibility of indigeneity/tradition through the work of market forces. Watts reminds us that: "Markers of identity may become themselves commodities in a way that the histories of interrelated peoples become spatialized into bounded territories" (1999: 88). In thinking the contingency of the emergence of indigenous identification, we might pose questions such as "Who profits?" And "In what ways and under what circumstances do neoliberal economic formations call out certain strategies of indigeneity?" Again, one of the ways that Hmong/Miao homeland activity diverges from that of indigenous struggles is that, although it is called out in large part by neoliberal economic formations, its economics are internal. Profits are extracted from the production of goods and their sale *within* Hmong/Miao community, accounting perhaps for why "indigenous" rhetoric would not apply.

This raises the question of minority status and its concomitant derogations. However indigenous and diasporic peoples carve out their identities, it is consistently as outside or marginal to dominant states and ethnicities. But as de la Cadena (2000) stresses in her discussion of "indigenous mestizos," these exclusions are always partial, dialogic, contested. Hmong Americans experience what she calls a "fractal hybridity" (2000: 318–319) similar to that of the Indians she described in Peru who are both of the dominant society and yet its other, similar in some ways, yet ever alteric. Hmong membership in Americanness is in part achieved by wielding means of media representation and orientalizing their counterparts in Asia; it is, in turn, this practice that internally fractures "the Hmong/Miao" into geopolitical sectors. And yet the longing that propels these acts is at the same time one of identification, born in part of the racism and discrimination that brings Hmong/Miao together in common experience over time and space. It is here that we can better perceive the interdependence of translocality and place making, for the highly marked places of Hmong/Miao authenticity reveal themselves to be artifacts of transnational processes just as the inception of indigenous identities is "grounded in international networks" (Niezen 2000: 120). These transnationalities are inflected differently however, for while mobilizations of the indigenous deploy the term to speak legitimacy to dominant others, Hmong/Miao media producers ignore those others, deploying their voices instead to engage in naming their less powered, feminized coethnics on ancient lands as part of their own diasporic process.

Notes

1. The term *Miao* has a long history of various usages to denote non-Han peoples in China. In the Maoist era, the term was stabilized to refer officially to a large umbrella category, the fifth largest minority in China, within which researchers included several subgroups, including the people that call themselves "Hmong." For the purposes of this article, the Miao term appears when I refer to Hmong coethnics in China. Although readily adopted by many in China, the term remains highly contested outside the mainland. For more detailed discussion of the politics of ethnonyms, see Schein (2000: xi–xiv, 35–67).

2. See Castree (2004) and Massey (1999) for discussions of relationality in regard to space and place.

3. For an extended exploration of these issues around the property and the hunter incident see Schein and Thoj (n.d.).

References

Beteille, Andre. 1998. The idea of indigenous people. *Current Anthropology* 39 (2): 187–191.

Bourdieu, Pierre, and Loic Wacquant. 2001. New liberal speak: Notes on the new planetary vulgate. *Radical Philosophy* 105 (January–February): 2–5.

Burchell, Graham. 1996. Liberal government and the techniques of the self. In *Foucault and political reason: Liberalism, neo-liberalism and rationalities of government,* edited by Andrew Barry, Thomas Osborne, and Nikolas Rose, 19–36. Chicago: University of Chicago Press.

Castree, Noel. 2004. Differential geographies: Place, indigenous rights and "local" resources. *Political Geography* 23: 133–167.

Clifford, James. 2001. Indigenous articulations. *Contemporary Pacific* 13 (2): 468–490.

Cobo, Jose Martinez. 1986. The study of the problem of discrimination against indigenous populations, vols. 1–5, United Nations Document E/CN.4/Sub.2/1986/7/Add. 4. Geneva: United Nations.

de la Cadena, Marisol. 2000. *Indigenous mestizos: The politics of race and culture in Cuzco, Peru, 1919–1991.* Durham, NC: Duke University Press.

Glick-Schiller, Nina, Linda Basch, and Cristina Blanc-Szanton. 1994. Transnational projects: A new perspective. In *Nations unbound: Transnational projects, postcolonial predicaments and deterritorialized nation-states,* edited by Nina Glick-Schiller, Linda Basch, and Cristina Blanc-Szanton, 1–19. Langhorn, PA: Gordon and Breach Science Publishers.

Heelas, Paul, and Paul Morris. 1992. *The values of the enterprise culture: The moral debate.* London: Routledge.

Lee, Gary Y. 2004. *Dreaming across the Oceans: Globalisation and Cultural Reinvention in the Hmong Diaspora.* Paper presented at a workshop at The Australian National University, Nov. 20–21.

Leuthold, Steven. 1998. *Indigenous aesthetics: Native art, media and identity.* Austin: University of Texas Press.

Li, Tania Murray. 2000. Articulating indigenous identity in Indonesia: Resource politics and the tribal slot. *Comparative Studies in Society and History* 42 (1): 149–179.

Massey, Doreen. 1999. Spaces of politics. In *Human geography today,* edited by Doreen Massey, John Allen, and Philip Sarre, 279–294. Cambridge: Polity Press.

Moua, Wameng. 2004. Hunters Speak Out to DNR Directors: "Stop the Racism!" *Hmong Today* 1 (26): 7.

Niezen, Ronald. 2000. Recognizing indigenism: Canadian unity and the international movement of indigenous peoples. *Comparative Studies in Society and History* 42 (1): 119–148.

Orecklin, Michelle. 2004. Massacre in the woods; Why did a man open fire on a group of hunters? He says it was about race, but a survivor disagrees. *Time Magazine,* December 6: 37.

Schein, Louisa. 1999. Diaspora politics, homeland erotics and the materializing of memory. *Positions: East Asia Cultures Critique* 7 (3): 697–729.

——. 2000. Minority rules: The Miao and the feminine in China's cultural politics. Durham, NC: Duke University Press.

——. 2004. Homeland beauty: Transnational longing and Hmong American video. *Journal of Asian Studies* 63 (2): 433–463.

Schein, Louisa, and Va-Megn Thoj. n.d. *Occult racism: Masking race in the Hmong hunter-incident a dialogue between anthropologist Louisa Schein and filmmaker-activist Va-Megn Thoj.* Unpublished MS.

Tapp, Nicholas. 1989. Sovereignty and rebellion: The white Hmong of Northern Thailand. Singapore: Oxford University Press.

Watts, Michael John. 1999. Collective wish images: Geographical imaginaries and the crisis of national development. In *Human geography today,* edited by Doreen Massey, John Allen, and Philip Sarre, 85–107. Cambridge: Polity Press.

Xiong, Gaoib. 2004. Hunting tragedy opens up questions of: Race, class, sanity, competence and tradition. *Hmong Times* 7 (23): 1–2.

Videography

Mob Niam Yau (Sick for a second wife). 2000. VHS. Directed by Su Thao. Fresno, CA: S. T. Universal Video.

Royal Lao Armed Forces. 1998. VHS. Produced by Yuepheng Xiong. ST. Paul, MN: Hmong ABC Publications.

Taug Txoj Lw Ntshav: Keeb Kwm Hmoob Nyob Suav Teb (Following the Trail of Blood: Hmong history in China). 2000. VHS. Directed by Yuepheng Xiong. St. Paul, MN: Hmong ABC Publications.

Bolivian Indigeneity in Japan: Folklorized Music Performance

Michelle Bigenho

From the 1960s through the early 1990s, what was called "folklore" (*fōkuroa*) in Japan—"Andean music" in other global contexts—experienced a worldwide boom especially in Europe and Japan. Musicians at the center of this boom now talk of saturated audiences and lament that their music is too cheaply heard in the subways of any major city; Andean music has become, as one musician who plays Irish music in Tokyo expressed it "the Chinese food of ethnic music." But the Andean music boom in Japan took on particular characteristics, as Japanese fans of this music moved beyond the position of passive listeners and began to learn to play the instruments that attracted them to this music in the first place. The *charango* (small plucked-stringed instrument), *quena* (notched flute), and *zampoñas* (panpipes) evoke for the Japanese images of a distant indigenous world, a world of non-Western Others with whom the Japanese imagine a shared non-Western Otherness. In this chapter I analyze Bolivian folklore performances in Japan, and I draw on performers' perspectives—those of both Japanese and Bolivian musicians—to examine the contemporary imaginings of "Andean music" in Japan and the place of indigeneity in these intercultural articulations.

Although this chapter springs from the world of music, its insights speak to broader issues of how representations of indigenous culture have entered global circulation, and more specifically, how these representations have entered the markets of a non-Western world. Positive ideas about indigenous peoples circulate through multiple realms (United Nations, NGOs, tourists, etc.) and back to local indigenous groups (Clifford 2001: 472), often creating the impossible "hyperreal Indian" as the perfect Noble Savage subject and the alter ego to all negative characteristics of the modern Western subject (Ramos 1998). Even as indigenous peoples' use of such representations should not be viewed in purely instrumental terms (Graham 2005), indigenous peoples adopt and manipulate Western representations of indigeneity to articulate with tourist markets (see Zorn 2005), and to make demands on local, regional, and state entities (see Turner 1991). As a way to move beyond the conundrum of indigenous essentialism or indigenous constructivism, and to grapple with both the rootedness associated with indigeneity and the uprootedness of diaspora experience, James Clifford addresses these circulations as "indigenous articulations" (2001; this volume). But what about those networks that sustain so many good feelings about indigenous peoples and indigenous things? Focusing on representations of indigeneity, this chapter addresses how Bolivian musicians renegotiate Japanese expectations of indigenous performance, and how Japanese musicians who become involved in these traditions may move far beyond the stereotypes in their knowledge of Bolivian music while still pinning on indigeneity a nostalgia for what they perceive as lost in Japanese modernity.

In addressing this circulation of ideas, I find useful Anna Tsing's concept of "indigenous voice"—"the genre conventions with which public affirmations of identity are articulated" and through which genres, rather than the speakers, hold persuasive power (this volume). The difference here is that for the most part I am not writing about musicians who affirm their own indigenous identity in relation to the worldwide "powerful definitional frames of indigenous struggle": sovereignty, national inclusion, and environmental stewardship (Tsing this volume). Rather, this chapter reflects on representations of indigenous voice that become marketed to a global audience. If this volume takes as a starting point the idea that indigenousness, like any identity, is relational, articulated, and "without guarantees" (de la Cadena and Starn in the Introduction), indigenous identities depend in part on the circulation of images and sounds of indigeneity, often as created, modified, and sustained by nonindigenous Others. In this sense, labels of indigeneity circulate as commodities that are sometimes taken up by or forced on those who self-identify as indigenous. In a world of music and dance, these representations often take folklorized forms. By *folklorization*, I refer to the multilayered process whereby groups consciously choreograph, compose, and perform for themselves and others, what they want to represent as distinct about their identity (local, regional, national), and how this performance is also filtered through a set of audience expectations about the Other. The debated middle ground in folklorization of indigeneity is between performers' desires, audiences' expectations, and the different meanings that folklore performances acquire as they move between international, national, and local contexts.

Through folklorization, Bolivian musical representations of indigenous voice have come to represent the national within a country where powerful frames of indigenous struggle continue in a parallel fashion. Bolivian 1992 census statistics on indigenous languages reflect an indigenous majority, with Quechua and Aymara spoken in the highlands and 30 different indigenous languages spoken by over 33 different ethnic groups in Bolivia's eastern lowlands (Albó 1999). In relation to 2001 census data, in which 63 percent of the population declared an indigenous identity and only 49.4 percent claimed to speak an indigenous language, Andrew Canessa suggests that language is an inadequate marker of indigenous identity in Bolivia (2006). In any case, it would be a mistake to treat this statistical majority as a single unified block, and in some cases the differences between highland and lowland indigeneity have been manipulated by Bolivian state policies (Gustafson 2002). Nevertheless, recent social movements, all depicted to varying degrees as "indigenous," have converged to produce significant effects around issues like control over gas resources and the production of coca.

The historicization of indigenous voice in Bolivia should take into account the Spanish colonial administration that maintained "Spanish" and "Indians" as separate republics, and the popular memory of 18th-century uprisings against this colonial rule. In 1781 an indigenous Aymara man, Tupac Katari, led an uprising that fenced off the city of La Paz for three months. Tupac Katari's rebellion, along with others of the period, proposed alternative projects that featured a return to indigenous rule (see Thomson 2002). Tupac Katari was publicly executed by troops sent from Buenos Aires, but he has lived on the in collective memory of Bolivian Aymaras.

In the 1970s, a radical indigenous politics emerged around the experience of Aymara intellectuals in the city of La Paz, and through a peasant union that interpreted Bolivian history through "the theory of two eyes": exploitation as a class and exploitation as distinct ethnic or racial groups (Rivera Cusicanqui 2003b; Sanjinés 2002). These movements took their name from the 1781 hero, and one Katarista, Felipe Quispe (El Mallku) constitutes a prominent figure within these contemporary indigenous articulations. Quispe makes statements that hark to Aymara firstness and recall the 1780s uprisings: "*Q'aras* (whites) who think with foreign heads must be Indianized"; Indians need to "unthink" mestizo ways (after Sanjinés 2002: 52–53); and "If you quartered Tupaj Katari with four horses, you can quarter me with four tanks or four airplanes" (after Patzi Palco 2003: 221). Quispe's political momentum, shaped around issues of land, water, and coca eradication policies, coalesced as a political party called the Indigenous Movement Pachakuti (*Movimiento Indígena Pachakuti* [MIP]).

Indigenous voice in Bolivia is also connected to a defense of the coca leaf because this plant has been used in the Andes for centuries, within traditional ritual and working contexts. The current coca growers' movement has been profoundly shaped against the backdrop of (1) the neoliberal economic policies that in the 1980s led to the closure of mines and the relocation of miners to coca-growing regions, and (2) the U.S. pressures for eradication of coca production, even in zones that had been labeled for "traditional" production and consumption (see Léons and Sanabria 1997; Rivera Cusicanqui 2003a; Spedding 1997). Coca growers *(cocaleros)* emerged as a significant social movement that struggled to defend the small-scale, peasant producer from the criminalizing politics of the state and international sphere. Evo Morales emerged as the leader of this movement that took electoral form in 2002 as Movement to Socialism (*Movimiento al Socialismo* [MAS]).

The "October agenda" of 2003—dramatically expressed through the popular ousting of President Gonzalo Sánchez de Lozada—brought into high profile Bolivia's management of hydrocarbon resources, the cry for a constituent assembly to reconstitute the Bolivian nation-state, and the 2005 special electoral process through which Evo Morales won the presidency with a record percentage of the vote. Morales's indigenous roots—something that has already come under critique as a more recently elaborated narrative—have been central to framing the moment in which it is felt that an indigenous majority is finally represented in the highest office of the land. Although Morales's politics have been interpreted as merging multiple interests including those based on class, indigenous ethnicity, and antiglobalization discourses (Canessa 2006; Postero 2005), the national and international coverage of his victory and inauguration have overwhelmingly emphasized his indigenous identity. Morales's international presence as an indigenous president may mark a shift in how Bolivia's local indigenous articulations travel.

In my course on indigenous politics of Latin America, my students usually arrive with general knowledge of the Mexican Zapatistas and this movement's great cultural translator, Subcomandante Marcos. Marcos's sharp-edged writings (1995) have done much to connect tourist worlds with this Mexican social movement that carries a distinctly indigenous face. Tourists may enjoy the indigenous connections of this movement and appropriate its image for a representation of the exotic (Martin 2004: 119), but even the greatest skeptics (see Gómez-Peña 2000) have come to see positive outcomes in Zapatista-inspired tourism. However, before Morales's 2005 electoral victory, my students usually arrived with no knowledge of Morales or Quispe as international representatives of Bolivian indigeneity, and tourism to Bolivia has not included solidarity moves with the Kataristas or cocaleros. Nevertheless, most of my students have heard a poncho-clad Andean band playing on the streets or in a subway of some cosmopolitan urban context. This chapter explores this other circulation of indigeneity, one that seems rather disconnected from the pressing indigenous politics of the contemporary Bolivian context and one that is too often dismissed as mere commodification of the exotic.

Within the Japanese context, indigeneity becomes a point of identification between Bolivian musicians, who do not usually identify as indigenous, and Japanese enthusiasts of these "Andean" traditions. Rather than dismiss these representational practices as merely indigenous ventriloquism, I want to consider them as folklorization— as a genre of indigenous voice that shapes global impressions of Bolivian indigeneity and that may have worked, until recently, to foreclose the international circulation of other Bolivian genres of indigenous voice. First, I address the folklorization of indigenous expressions as a national project and detail how Bolivian music arrived in Japan through new valorizations of imagined indigenous and "Andean" expressions. Second, I address how representations of Bolivian indigeneity have changed in Bolivia and the extent to which these transformations have made it to Japanese stages. Finally, I consider the symbolic work of Japanese identifications with this folklorized indigeneity that remains so disjointed from the pressing demands of indigenous social movements in contemporary Bolivia.

National Folklorization through World Tours

While Japanese folklore musicians today will talk about the central place of Bolivian music within Andean traditions, they very frequently mention that their own interests in this music were first ignited by hearing Paul Simon and Art Garfunkel's rendition of "El condor pasa." Just as the Argentine *tango* had to go through US and European metropoles on its way to a Japanese market (Savigliano 1995), Bolivian music that became folklore in Japan, had to pass through metropoles that were quite distant from the imagined sources of this music. These "schizophonic" shifts (Feld 1994, 1996) were not just about getting the music out there and finally heard by a wide global audience. It was about an increased value attributed to indigenous cultural references that came, in part, through a circuitous route of foreign associations.

"El condor pasa" is a composition by the Peruvian Daniel Alomía Robles (1871–1942). Alomía Robles traveled extensively in Peru, collected folklore of his country, studied classical music, and lived for many years in the United States. One could view Alomía Robles's composition within the *indigenista* expressions of the period, as music that was inspired by indigenous expressions, crafted within certain principles of Western musical forms, and then presented as part of regional or national identities.[1]

Folklorization of indigenous expressions has often been interpreted as a uniform attempt to paper over a hierarchical divide between whites and Indians that has marked Latin American societies since colonization. Without disagreeing with this general interpretation, I want to complicate this overall story. The folklorization tale draws on international artistic interactions that crafted Bolivian "national music" and "Andean music" out of indigenous inspirations. From the late 1930s, several mestizo–creole (glossed as nonindigenous or white) women vocalists began to put aside the popular "foreign" genres of the time (i.e., *vals*, tango, and *bolero*) and to take on the self-ascribed roles of folklore pioneers, transforming sounds that were previously disliked by their own social classes into Bolivian national music, making expressions of marginalized Indian music the root of a mestizo–creole patriotic core (see Bigenho 2005). Following the Chaco War of the 1930s, the 1952 Revolution not only moved marginalized Indian expressions to the center of a nationalist cultural project, but also brought universal suffrage, universal education, the abolition of the hacienda system (Agrarian Reform of 1953), the nationalization of mines, the unionization of peasants, and a nationalist discourse of *mestizaje* (glossed as a discourse of racial and cultural mixing). Within relatively recently formed political parties, the marginalized flesh and blood "Indians" came under the new label of "peasants" ([*campesinos*]; Albó 1987: 381), and the symbolic world of indianness moved into the service of symbolically representing the nation.

National folklorization of indigenous expressions was evident in popular staged musical reviews like *Fantasía Boliviana* (*Bolivian Fantasy*)— a 1955 production that was organized through the government-backed Bolivian Motion Picture Institute. The production featured different music and dance traditions of Bolivia, and toured Bolivian cities as well as Asunción (Paraguay), Montevideo (Uruguay), and Buenos Aires (Argentina) (Cerruto Moravek 1996). Although the ideas of Bolivian Fantasy fit the mestizo Revolutionary project like a glove, its 60 participants came from varied backgrounds—mestizo–creoles as well as indigenous Aymaras, and several key protagonists in this production had cultural and artistic ties with Buenos Aires (Bigenho 2006a).

In the 1960s, Simon and Garfunkel shared a stage in Paris with the group "Los Incas" and it was here that the singers first heard "El condor pasa." (see Meisch 2002: 138). The duo rearranged the piece, added their own lyrics ("I'd rather be a sparrow than a snail."), and released the song to an enthusiastic world audience. On Simon and Garfunkel's album, Alomía Robles is credited as one of three composers of the tune (along with Paul Simon and Jorge Milchberg; 1972). In Paul Simon's concert recording *Live Rhymin'* (1974) Simon is joined in several tunes by his Paris connection, then using the name "Urubamba," and Simon presents them by mentioning that this ensemble introduced him to "South American music" in 1965, and that their group's name is that of a river that "runs past the last Inca city, Machu Picchu in Peru." A great deal of ambiguity surrounds these schizophonic practices that are both critiqued as "cultural imperialism" and "cultural appropriation," and praised as "transcultural inspiration" or "borrowing" (Feld 1996: 14; Meisch 2002: 182). From the release of Simon and Garfunkel's song to the present day, "El condor pasa," in a variety of interpretations, has become the piece that most foreigners request to hear from Andean musicians. It is also the piece that Bolivians often dislike playing—for nationalist reasons ("It isn't even Bolivian!"), and for reasons of burnout. In Japan, "El condor pasa" is almost always on the program of a Bolivian music performance, and the piece is often required implicitly as part of the contract for touring Japan.

At about the same time Simon and Garfunkel made their hit, a Swiss man, Gilbert Favre (also known as "El Gringo Favre"), was making quite a sensation in Bolivia with his interpretation of the quena. It would be wrong to give the impression that the new value given to indigenous expressions came *only* through foreign associations. If I single out Favre in my discussion of how Andean music made it to the global market,

I do so because Bolivian musicians on many occasions have done so when they speak about the international boom in Andean music. As a Bolivian living in Japan told me: "When El Gringo [Favre] stepped out … it was something revolutionary. … The quena was dressed in gala clothes! A gringo played it! So the people said, 'Listen, if a gringo plays it we can play it.' That's how it was at that time." With this comment, the musician referred to the ongoing racism in Bolivia that continued to discredit "Indian things" until foreigners gave these instruments and expressions new cachet. "El Gringo" Favre played quena with "Los Jairas," a Bolivian ensemble founded in the mid-1960s. When Los Jairas appeared on the Bolivian music scene, they built on the ongoing process of folklorizing indigenous musical expressions, developing virtuosity on the iconic "Andean" instruments of quena, zampoña, and charango, and specifically shaping a small ensemble that fit the logistics of international travel and performance. Los Jairas in particular would form the model of the "pan-Andean bands" that would become ubiquitous in a global market (Céspedes 1984). The musicians in Los Jairas included Ernesto Cavour on charango, Gilbert Favre on quena, Edgar "Yayo" Joffré on vocals, and Julio Godoy on guitar.[2] Los Jairas went to Geneva in 1969 and several members settled in Europe as the Andean music boom took off in this region.[3] Cavour was the first person to leave the ensemble and return to Bolivia, and he would eventually play a key role in popularizing Andean music in Japan.

As Bolivian folklore was taking off in Europe, Bolivians at home were living through several military regimes that often clashed with popular mining sectors. The Military–Peasant Pact, initiated by the government of René Barrientos Ortuño in the mid-1960s and lasting into the early 1980s, was designed to co-opt and control the agricultural sector and to pit peasants against popular urban sectors and miners. With the exception of the above-mentioned Kataristas, indigenous politics of this period seemed rather hidden within the political scene, as politics proceeded through Cold War structures of class organizing and anticommunism. With this political backdrop, the contacts between Bolivians and Japanese emerged in Argentina, from an intricate circuit of musicians, their different sonorous productions, and particular imaginings about exotic instruments believed to be connected to an indigenous Andean world. Japanese and Bolivian musicians talk about the initial presence in Japan of Uña Ramos, an Argentine quena player. He was followed by "Los Laikas" and then Cavour—Bolivian musicians who all received their first invitations to Japan based on the merits of their playing within the context of the Argentine folklore boom. By the

1980s, Bolivian musicians were traveling directly from their country to Japan and Japanese folklore musicians came to see Bolivia as the heart of what is called "Andean music."

Representing Bolivian Indigeneity in Japan

Few of the Bolivian musicians who travel to Japan self-identify as indigenous and for those who do, their work in the musical world has pulled them into the ambiguities of a mestizo world. This said, Bolivian musicians would often describe passionately a point of self-identification with representations of indigenous music; often these narratives were about discovering the national cultural self as one began to musically perform "Bolivia" within a foreign context (e.g., Brazil, Argentina, the United States, France, Japan). Just as the Hmong/Miao, away from home and with the view from afar, structured their nativeness in their media practices (Schein, this volume), several Bolivian musicians discovered the indigenous side of their Bolivianness by playing music outside of their national territory. On the one hand, from the 1960s to the 1980s, indigeneity was referenced internationally through the instruments used in the pan-Andean bands. On the other hand, beginning in the mid-1970s and moving into the 1990s, Bolivian musicians' imperative *at home* was to conduct research in the countryside, to study the precise ways that different indigenous instruments were played, and to replicate that performance practice in an urban setting.

At home in Bolivia, the troupe-style performance of highland indigenous wind instruments became one of these new markers of "authentic" indigenous music performance. Twelve to 20 musicians perform a single kind of instrument, the players varying only in the size and register of the instruments they play. The Bolivian rock band "Wara" greatly boosted this trend when, in 1975, they recorded interludes of indigenous troupe-style performance within their own rock compositions (1975). The musical representation of indigeneity in Bolivia has become marked by this troupe-style playing, and these practices provide ways that young people in La Paz, sons and daughters of Aymara migrants, come to express their urban indigenous identity (Archondo 2000; Bigenho 2002: 109–113). These transformations in musical representations of indigeneity are not as quick to enter the Japanese performance context. When Bolivian musicians tour Japan today, their performances still resemble the solo-driven pan-Andean model, even if Japanese musicians within these musical traditions have become experts in distinguishing the complexity of different Bolivian music performance styles. In this section, I discuss transformations of indigeneity that occur as Bolivian bands move from their local performance context to the stages of Japan. I draw from the interviews I conducted with Bolivian musicians who have toured Japan, and I will focus on the performances of "Música de Maestros" or "Music of the Masters"—the ensemble with which I toured and performed in 2002.

In the case of Music of the Masters, the invitation to tour Japan arrived directly to the ensemble's founder and director, Zacarías Encinas. The Japanese company originally wanted to contract Encinas as a quena soloist with his accompanying musicians. Encinas chose instead to foreground what for him has been his favorite musical project, the ensemble Music of the Masters. In Bolivia, Music of the Masters usually includes more than 24 musicians: guitars, mandolins, concertina, cello, viola, violins, charango, quenas, and zampoñas. This ensemble formed in the 1980s with the agenda of recording the works of Bolivian master composers. Their name consciously references the Western classical concept of "great composers," but the ensemble also extends the idea of composership from inspired individuals to indigenous groups within Bolivia. Their initial recordings emphasized musical compositions of the 1930s, a period considered to mark a golden age for music composed within genres that carry more mestizo–creole associations than indigenous ones. But the ensemble also considers music of indigenous association and their recordings have emphasized a geographic spread that attempts to represent musically both highland and lowland indigeneity (see Bigenho 2002: 121–135).

Only five Bolivian musicians of the ensemble travel to Japan, a significant reduction in the group's size that stirs jealousy at home and also significantly limits their ability to perform pieces in the troupe style. Music of the Masters also has toured France, Germany, Switzerland, and China. Although many of these other tours were more about "showing one's music," tours built around festivals that work more through discourses of "sharing one's culture" than about a well-remunerated contract (Bigenho 2002: 84–95), music work in Japan is overall one of the best remunerated gigs for Bolivian musicians. Musicians who go to Japan with this group are already in rather flexible and unstable labor relations at home: playing gigs in nightclubs with multiple ensembles, teaching music, making recordings, and preparing new repertoire. Earnings from work in Japan can significantly shift musicians' home economic situation out of perpetual precariousness (see Bigenho 2006b).

As a reduced ensemble, Music of the Masters tours Japan for three-month periods, under the sponsorship of a small Japanese company. The company organizes different cultural activities for school presentations and for concerts in regular theaters. In three months, Music of the Masters might give 70–90 performances, most of them in schools. The company pays the Bolivians' airfares, arranges for their visas, provides all transportation and hotel accommodations, and pays both a daily item for food and, at the close of the tour, a fixed sum for the work during the three months.

My participation on this tour was ten years in the making. I first became involved with Music of the Masters in 1993 when I lived for two years in Bolivia conducting my doctoral dissertation research. Since that time, I have been performing and recording with Music of the Masters on annual return trips to Bolivia. When I was approaching a semester sabbatical at Hampshire College that coincided with one of these tours, I asked the director if I could join them, paying my own way and donating my performances to the tour. In other words, I would not be taking the place of a paid Bolivian musician. The director was thrilled at the possibility, but my presence on the tour had to be vetted by the Japanese company. The initial contact with the company had come through a Japanese musician, Koji Hishimoto, who had lived for seven years in Bolivia, worked as a key performer on quena and zampoñas, and created many of the musical arrangements for Music of the Masters. When Hishimoto returned to Japan, he obtained employment as a guide and translator with this Japanese cultural performance company. While the company also sponsored Japanese cultural presentations, both within Japan and internationally, a good part of their work focused on contracting foreign cultural performances for Japanese school settings. Musical and theatrical groups were invited from China, Korea, Mexico, Russia, Norway, Kenya, and Australia. According to Hishimoto and another employee of the company, the government recommends that schools sponsor at least one of these international cultural performances each year.

When Hishimoto first began to work for the company, he wanted to perform with the Bolivian bands on tour. Within Bolivia he had already gained notoriety as one of the best interpreters of quena and zampoña, but it took a few years of work before the Japanese company would allow him to move beyond the role of cultural translator, and actually join the Bolivians on the music performance stage. In a similar way, my participation with the band stirred some controversy before my arrival in 2002. Perceptions of cultural purity haunted this dispute as the Japanese company worried that the Bolivian band's authenticity would be compromised by my presence in the group. Like the insistence on cultural purity within other niche music markets of Japan (see Hosokawa 2002: 298–303), the cultural otherness of Bolivian music was supposed to be uncluttered by anything or anyone who was not essentially Bolivian. I do not know how they came to the decision to accept my presence on the tour, but they did, and I met up with the Bolivian musicians in Tokyo on a hot summer evening.

Our performances on this tour always began with the highland indigenous references that Japanese have come to associate with Andean music. "El condor pasa" was the first piece we performed and Hishimoto introduced our interpretation with explanatory discourse about the South American region, the existence of the Andes mountains, and the location of Bolivia in the region. During the entire first half of our performances, we wore costumes that were associated with highland indigeneity—not specific costumes from distinct villages but rather generic wide gathered skirts or white pants, and colorfully woven belts, hats, and bags. In Bolivia, members of Music of the Masters did not wear this attire, but rather donned a more mestizo–creole look of black pants, white shirts, black vests, and fedora hats. The ensemble had to cite the world of highland indigeneity the Japanese have come to associate, not necessarily with Bolivia, but with "the Andes." World performances of Bolivian music work under this "reiterative power of discourse" that constrains the performers' acts (Butler 1993: 2).

If citing highland Andean indigeneity through "El condor pasa" got them through the door to these Japanese performance contracts, Music of the Masters hardly stopped there. During the second half of the show, the ensemble featured music of African Bolivian, mestizo–creole, lowland indigenous, and Chaqueña associations, and for this part of the show, we would change into our "regular" mestizo–creole look, what we always wore when performing in Bolivia. I moved from a woman's dress during the first half of the program, to a man's clothes in the second half of the program. The only other woman on the tour would change into the costume of African Bolivians, then into a costume of a *cholita paceña*,[4] and then finally into a long flowing skirt for the performance of music from the Chaco region. These kinds of costume changes were particular to the performances in Japan and have not been part of our performance practices in Bolivia. Costume changes in Japan were, on the one hand, about showmanship and spectacle. But on the other hand, they were also about Encinas's consistent desire to show world audiences that Bolivian music went far beyond the ubiquitous pan-Andean bands whose fringed ponchos have become iconic in the international representation of this country's music. His perspective represented an alternative pursuit of authenticity, an attempt to perform his concept of a multicultural Bolivia and evidence that these performances are constrained but never fully determined in advance (Butler 1993: 95). Music of the Masters rarely made costume changes in Bolivia, but on national as well as international stages, the multicultural music performance was the ongoing project of the ensemble.

Even within the presentation of this musical variety, the focus remained on the exotic instruments. During the first half of the show, we performed a segment that was introduced as "the Aymara fiesta" and that featured our playing of distinct instruments that are usually performed in the troupe style (*tarka, pinquillo,* and zampoña). At one point two musicians would leave the stage and return in *kusillo* costumes (a jesting figure that appears within some Aymara regions), playing the pinquillo instrument, and literally acting out the part of the kusillo. Although this dramatization of highland indigeneity gave many more details than one might encounter in a watered-down version of Andean folklore, it is difficult for a group of seven musicians to achieve the sonorous effect of a full troupe-style performance. Throughout this research, I have only heard of one complete troupe that made a brief tour of Japan. Because of the daily costs of maintaining musicians on the road, companies rarely seem to move beyond the sponsorship of five or six musicians.

During two parts of Music of the Masters' performance, the ensemble would leave the stage and Hishimoto would explain some of the instruments that were unknown to the Japanese audiences, having the individual musicians demonstrate their use, and asking the students if they could guess certain materials that were used to construct the instruments. Performing indigenous Bolivian music in Japan was about performing an exotic Other, but for Bolivians and Japanese there was something intimate about the cultural distances being represented. Throughout the wider interpretation of this work with Bolivians and Japanese, I find useful the concept of "intimate distance" by which I refer to a broad set of issues, including folklorization, through which Bolivians and Japanese, at the meeting place of Bolivian music performance, simultaneously find points of intimacy and great difference between their ways of being in the world. In organizing our show, Hishimoto attempted to draw a common thread between a Japanese sonorous environment and a Bolivian one. During the demonstration of the quena or notched flute, Hishimoto would show the *shakuhachi,* a Japanese notched flute. Throughout my fieldwork, Japanese and Bolivians consistently drew lines of similarity between this "traditional"

Japanese instrument and the Andean notched flute. After comparing the quena and shakuhachi, Hishimoto and Encinas would interpret on quenas the song that runs through the credits of Hayao Miyazaki's popular Japanese animated film—*Spirited Away.* The initial phrase of the tune always provoked a reaction of gleeful surprise, as the students heard a known tune on an instrument that was unknown yet somehow familiar.

Other parts of the show were designed to connect unknown instruments to known sonorous environments. When Victor Hugo Gironda demonstrated the panpipes, he played a tune often heard in Japanese supermarkets as an advertising jingle for selling fish. Backstage, Gironda would refer to this part of the show as "going to sell fish," and his intervention was guaranteed to provoke laughter from the younger audiences. If from back stage we heard no response to the playing of this ditty on the panpipes, we knew we had a difficult audience to please.

The aesthetic strategies at work in meeting the expectations of Japanese audiences included making this Bolivian music seem less Other, foregrounding pieces with straightforward rhythmic patterns, and designing a program that aimed to produce audience identification and participation. The strange and exotic was made approachable by featuring Bolivian instruments that were "like traditional Japanese ones," and by referencing familiar sonorous landscapes of supermarkets, Japanese animated films, and popular Japanese songs. Bolivian cultural work for Japanese school audiences entailed a transformation of a nationalist music project and its substitution by an imagined indigenous voice of the Andes. Bolivian musicians had to cite the expected, but their overall presentation went beyond these limits.

Japanese Identification with Folklorized Indigeneity

The Japanese have gained a reputation for getting deeply involved in many different musical traditions of Others—jazz, salsa, blue grass, tango, hip hop, and so forth (see Atkins 2001; Condry 2001; Hosokawa 2002; Mitsui 1993; Savigliano 1995). Japanese interest in Bolivian music began in the 1960s trajectory I described earlier. Under very different conditions from those in which Bolivian musicians toured, Japanese traveled to Bolivia as tourists and volunteers for the Japanese government. They traveled in search of something that inspired them in these musical sounds. While some of them went home after a short trip and perhaps started a hobby group of Andean music back in Tokyo, others remained in Bolivia for extended periods of time, forming a noticeable presence within the community of Bolivian musicians. Next to the myriad of encounters with others' music, Bolivian music in Japan is hardly significant statistically, but the presence of Japanese musicians in the Bolivian music context and the Bolivian musicians' tours of Japan are of considerable significance, and are particularly revealing examples of how this intercultural nexus transformed a Bolivian political economy of music. One Bolivian musician from Catavi, Potosí referred to Japanese presence in Bolivian music as "a friendly invasion." Bolivian ensembles like "Wara," "Luz del Ande," "Los Kharkas," as well as Music of the Masters have all experienced a significant presence of Japanese as performing musicians and even as directors. All of these ensembles, and a few others ("Ernesto Cavour y su Conjunto," "Los Caballeros del Folklore," "Kallawaya," "Grupo Aymara," and "Taypi K'ala") have benefited from the remuneration of music tours in Japan.

The most serious Japanese folklore musicians, like the best of the anthropological tribe, make their claims to having "been there," in Bolivia: they discuss their musical training; they list the years they have resided in Bolivia, they name their master teachers; and they name the groups with which they have played and recorded. I would suggest that for the more serious Japanese folklore musicians (those who have played in the ensembles I mentioned and who have lived in Bolivia for extended periods), a major point of identification is at the assumed universal level of "musician." These Japanese musicians compose in Bolivian genres, express desires to contribute artistically to the tradition, innovate within these "traditions," and, along with other Bolivian musicians, worry about the decline of Andean music in world markets. But Japanese folklore musicians will also describe formative moments when they were participating in Bolivian ritual contexts, and will comment on the inspirational indigenous connections of these moments. Through ritual connections and associations, Japanese folklore musicians and enthusiasts will identify with a represented indigeneity, but they locate their point of intersection in a past. By denying coevalness (Fabian 1983) to Bolivian indigeneity as represented in folklore, Japanese can identify with this native world of difference without contradicting the Japanese narrative of national homogeneity and without engaging with the other genres of indigenous voice as expressed through the pressing demands of Evo Morales and Felipe Quispe.

The Japanese uptake of folklorized Bolivian indigeneity hangs heavily on ritual worlds, imagined ones for those who have not been in Bolivia, and experienced ones for those who "have been there." One Japanese charango player told me his story: he had studied sociology in graduate school and was teaching at a university in Japan when he gave up his job to live several years in Bolivia and study the charango. He has acquired a distinctive style on charango, even composing his own pieces in Bolivian genres. Although he was careful to mention that much of the "folklore" music played in Japan had more Spanish than indigenous roots, he conceded that "The native music they play by the Lake [Titicaca] is somewhat like the music they play in Japanese rituals." The charango player's expressions were far from a simple romanticized view of the Andean music world, but his classifications followed an obsession with "real" native origins, and he drew connections between that imagined pure native (often rural) space and his perceptions of Japanese ritual worlds.

Japanese imaginings of Bolivian indigenous ritual seem to emerge through feelings of a crisis of authenticity at home. In La Paz, I met a young Japanese man who went by the nickname "Apache," a moniker that calls forth another imagined indigenous connection. In our conversation, he drew connections between the Andean indigenous ritual world and a Japanese ritual world that he perceived to be disappearing in post–WWII Japan. In Japan he had studied politics and economics at the university. Then he worked as a plumber for six years before hitting the road with his savings. During his general world tour, he had settled in Bolivia for a few years, learning Bolivian wind instruments and teaching Japanese drum playing. In his discussion of Bolivian music he pointed to perceived similarities between indigenous languages of Aymara and Quechua and his own native Japanese. When he finishes traveling the world, he told me, he plans to return to Japan and teach young people about their roots, "the elements of spirit that have been lost with economic development." Bolivian indigeneity is narrativized within a Japanese past—a past that is perceived to contain something of Japaneseness, something that is thought to be slipping away through Japan's modernity.

The ritual worlds of represented indigeneity also get taken up in the form of "new age" associations, ones that seemed to float through Apache's narrative, and that become a marketing strategy in Japan. In Tokyo, I met another Japanese musician who, at the age of 37, was making quite a successful career as a star of Andean panpipe music in Japan: performing concerts, selling his signature quenas, and signing his albums that had titles like *Songs of the Wind* (2000), *Nieve* ([Snow] 1996), *Luna* ([Moon] 1997), *Forest Rain* (1998), *Silencio* ([Silence] 1999), and just plain *Andes* (2001). Although he is not fond of the label, he said his music has been marketed under "what in the U.S. is called 'New Age' and what in Japan they call 'Healing Music.'" His album titles bring in references to the natural world and the compositions on these recordings place Bolivian instruments of indigenous association in relation to this world of naturalized indigeneity and Japanese longing for nature.

To put in perspective how Japanese audiences and musicians respond to represented Bolivian indigeneity it is useful to examine Japanese encounters with alterity, and the structuring of the Ainu as the aboriginal people of Japan. The Ainu of northern Japan are often narrativized as the geographically marginal internal other, the native, against which Japaneseness became articulated (see Howell 2005). The Ainu have lived by hunting, fishing, and gathering, and in this way they go against the grain of Japanese agrarian myths that place Japanese identity in relation to the agricultural production of rice (Ohnuki-Tierney 1998). Since the 19th century, the Japanese government has implemented assimilationist policies like the Hokkaido Former Aborigine Protection Act (in effect 1899–1997) that provided agricultural land to the Ainu, and encouraged them to become agriculturalists (Howell 2005: 172). Today, the Ainu still represent Japan's internal exotic other (Ohnuki-Tierney 1998: 44), but within overarching ideologies of Japanese homogeneity. The Japanese state upholds an ideology of a homogeneous national community in which hyphenated categories are avoided and cultural differences are classified through the dubious Japanese–foreigner dichotomy (Kelly 1991: 413; Masden 1997: 56). The myth of Japanese homogeneity, based on the metaphorical associations of "Japanese blood," has come under increasing strain within the contexts of Japanese returnees and foreign workers in Japan (Roth 2002; Yoshino 1997). As pluralization of Japanese society challenges the long-standing myth of homogeneity (Murphy-Shigematsu 2000: 215), many of the official policies of the Japanese Ministry of Education continue to uphold this myth (Masden 1997: 29). Next to and in association with this strong national ideology of homogeneity, Japanese producers and consumers express strong desires to internationalize (Yoshino 1998: 15). In finding a connection to an imagined Bolivian indigeneity, some Japanese are finding an international connection that appears as an alternative to those with the United States or with the West.

Japanese uptake of folklorized Bolivian indigeneity seems to be about the paradox of wanting what the Japanese perceive themselves to be losing in the modern world. The attitude of the Japanese musicians echoes that marked by Louisa Schein in her work on Hmong/Miao diasporic longing (this volume). Schein locates this longing as part of a "worldwide malaise" that motivates those with the power of representation to engage in projects of cultural recuperation, while putting up shields against too much contact with outsiders (this volume). The imagined native subject of the past creates a great nostalgic package and a longing that can never be totally satisfied. Identification with imagined Bolivian indigeneity hardly contradicts Japan's ideologies of homogeneity, as ties with folklorized indigeneity are located in foreign lands and in mythical pasts.

Conclusions: Folklorized Indigeneity and Longing

In this chapter, I have presented the musical constructions of the Andean native as represented on Japanese stages, and the nexus that Bolivian and Japanese musicians discursively construct between their worlds. I have underscored two ironies in this particular uptake of indigeneity: (1) the absence of indigenous subjects in the performance space where folklorized indigeneity becomes a shared point of contact for Bolivian and Japanese musicians, and (2) the chasm between this genre of indigenous voice and the other genres that frame contemporary indigenous social movements in Bolivia. There is a third irony to consider. Nostalgia for the native is usually articulated through Western–non-Western discursive practices (see Hall 2002). Whether it is the discussion of authenticity "made possible by the metanarrative of progress" (Errington 1998: 5), the identification with the other that replaces the departed love object (Fuss 1995), or the concern with "endangered authenticities (Clifford 1988: 5), all of these ways of framing Western identity and loss in postcolonial modernity depend on the production of the native as the "symptom of the white man" (Chow 1994: 127).

But what is to be made of a Japanese nostalgia for the native, a supposedly non-Western subject's longing for the ways of another so-called non-Western subject? I would suggest that insights into this inquiry require a second look at modernity and particularly at how the different histories of colonialism and nationalism have shaped distinct perceptions of indigeneity. Spanish colonial organizations left a hierarchical divide between Indians and whites, one of the most debilitating legacies of the Conquest (Hale 1994), and a legacy that persists in contemporary nation-states of the Andean region (see Canessa 2005; Weismantel 2001). Since the early 20th century, Bolivian nationalism has included the symbolic work of representing folklorized indigeneity and part of this folklorization process was articulated through international contacts and associations. The Bolivian pageant that celebrates folklorized indigeneity is not completely outside of assimilationist politics. In fact, Bolivian folklorization processes of the 1950s developed parallel to the nationalist ideology of mestizaje that claimed national inclusiveness through an erasure of cultural differences. With the neoliberal reforms of the 1980s and the 1990s, "mestizaje" was replaced by "multiculturalism," but such politics have been viewed suspiciously by indigenous groups (Rivera Cusicanqui 2003b; Gustafson 2002). With the baggage of its colonial heritage, Bolivian nationalism continues to swing back and forth simultaneously, or vibrate, between the poles of multiculturalism and assimilation, even as in practice not all of this country's citizens receive equal invitations to the national banquet. The Bolivian "imagined community" (Anderson 1991), like that of other Latin American nations, sustains dependent and subordinate relations as a central part of its nationalist project (see Lomnitz 2000).

Japanese nationalism emerges in a different way, through a narrative of cultural–racial homogeneity in which local natives (the Ainu) are expected to become Japanese by transforming themselves into agriculturalists. Japanese historiography has underscored the ambivalent position of Japan's national identity within discourses of East and West (see Tanaka 1993), and Koichi Iwabuchi has suggested that "Japan's modern national identity has ... always been imagined in an asymmetrical totalizing triad between 'Asia,' 'the West,' and 'Japan,'" in which "the West" stood for the modern other and "Asia" for Japan's past (2002: 7). Framed within these arguments that decenter any straightforward East–West dichotomy, Japanese identifications with folklorized Bolivian indigeneity seem to resemble the Western-to-non-Western pattern without falling completely within it.

If identification is "the detour through the other that defines the self" (Fuss 1995: 2), both Bolivian and Japanese musicians made this detour in identifying Bolivian and Japanese selves. Bolivian national music emerged through global contacts that created limits and expectations of indigenous performance, but Bolivians' performances were not completely determined by this existing external discourse. Japanese musicians and enthusiasts of Andean music first entered the world of Bolivian music through three instruments that globally came to stand for Andean indigeneity: quena, panpipes, and charango. Although the experts moved beyond this simple trio, the trio stuck in the imaginaries of the wider population, and also proved malleable to a process of global commodification and international performance tours. In the intercultural nexus between Bolivian and Japanese musicians, both groups seemed to commune with an imagined indigenous world as located in a past, and as disconnected from contemporary indigenous politics in Bolivia. Although the Japanese identification with Bolivian folklorized indigeneity expresses a nostalgia for things perceived to be disappearing in Japan's trajectory through modernity, the Bolivian identification with folklorized indigeneity has been a central part of symbolic nation-making—also a part of modernity—even as this project has excluded socioeconomically the majority of those who might self-identify as indigenous. As the world registers Evo Morales as representative of an indigenous voice out of Bolivia, one wonders how this genre will differ from that of Andean music, and how both genres of indigenous voice ultimately depend on the global circulation of multiple and interconnected forms of indigeneity.

Notes

Acknowledgments. For their insights and stimulating discussion I would like to thank the participants of the conference "Indigenous Experience Today." I am grateful to Marisol de la Cadena and Orin Starn, the conference organizers who first gave me the opportunity to participate in this intellectual exchange and whose feedback helped me in my revisions. I have also benefited tremendously from comments and suggestions from Andrew Canessa, Julie Hemment, Beth Notar, Joshua Roth, Barbara Yngvesson, and an anonymous reviewer for Berg. I am also indebted to Rolando Encinas whose continued willingness to welcome me into his ensemble has made possible several unique fieldwork experiences, including my work as a "Bolivian" musician in Japan. Of course, I am ultimately responsible for any shortcomings in this analysis. Initial research in Bolivia was funded by Fulbright (1993) and Fulbright-Hays (1994) grants. Research in Japan was made possible by a Whiting Foundation Grant (2003) and a semester sabbatical leave from Hampshire College (2002). Summer research trips to Bolivia have been possible with Hampshire College faculty development grants in summers 1999–2002 and 2004.

1. Indigenismo, as a politics of culture, took different paths within different national contexts. For details from the Peruvian context, see Marisol de la Cadena (2000) Zoila Mendoza (2004) and Deborah Poole (1997). For details

from the Bolivian context, see Josefa Salmón (1997), Javier Sanjinés (2004), and Michelle Bigenho (2006a).

2. Alfredo Dominguez would join the group as an invited guest guitarist.

3. Gilbert Favre died in 1998 but a group in France called "Los Gringos" holds an annual celebration in his honor, bringing together many musicians who had contact with El Gringo (personal communication, Zacarías Encinas, 2004).

4. The term *chola*, as a loaded racial category between Indian and white, has its own accompanying set of pejorative uses, fantasies, and fears (see Weismantel 2001).

References Cited

Albó, Xavier. 1987. From MNRistas to Kataristas to Katari. In *Resistance, rebellion, and consciousness in the Andean peasant world: 18th to 20th centuries,* edited by Steve J. Stern, 379–419. Madison: University of Wisconsin Press.

——. 1999. *Iguales aunque diferentes: Hacia unas políticas interculturales y lingüísticas para Bolivia.* La Paz: Ministerio de Educación, UNICEF, CIPCA, Cuadernos de Investigación 52.

Anderson, Benedict. 1991. *Imagined communities: Reflections on the origin and spread of nationalism.* Revised edition. London: Verso.

Archondo, Rafael. 2000. Existencias fronterizas: ser "chango" en El Alto: entre el rock y los sikuris. *T'inkazos* 3 (6): 67–78.

Atkins, E. Taylor. 2001. *Blue Nippon: Authenticating jazz in Japan.* Durham, NC: Duke University Press.

Bigenho, Michelle. 2002. *Sounding indigenous: Authenticity in Bolivian music performance.* New York: Palgrave Macmillan.

——. 2005. Making music safe for the nation: Folklore pioneers in Bolivian indigenism. In *Natives making nation: Gender, indigeneity, and the state in the Andes,* edited by Andrew Canessa, 60–80. Tucson: University of Arizona Press.

——. 2006a. Embodied matters: *Bolivian Fantasy* and indigenismo. *Journal of Latin American Anthropology* 11 (2): 267–293.

——. 2006b. Laboring in the transnational culture mines: The work of Bolivian music in Japan. In *Culture and development in a globalising world: Geographies, actors, and paradigms,* edited by Sarah Radcliffe, 107–125. New York: Routledge.

Butler, Judith. 1993. *Bodies that matter: On the discursive limits of "sex."* New York: Routledge.

Canessa, Andrew. 2005. Introduction: Making the nation on the margins. In *Natives making nation: Gender, indigeneity, and the state in the Andes,* edited by Andrew Canessa, 3–31. Tucson: University of Arizona Press.

——. 2006. "Todos somos indígenas": Towards a new language of national political identity. *Bulletin of Latin American Research* 25 (2): 241–263.

Cerruto Moravek, Karina. 1996. *Crónicas históricas documentadas.* La Paz: Librería Editorial "Juventud."

Céspedes, Gilka Wara. 1984. New currents in música folklórica in La Paz, Bolivia. *Latin American Music Review* 5: 217–242.

Chow, Rey. 1994. Where have all the natives gone? In *Displacements: Cultural identities in question,* edited by Angelika Bammer, 125–151. Bloomington: Indiana University Press.

Clifford, James. 1988. *The predicament of culture: Twentieth-century ethnography, literature, and art.* Cambridge, MA: Harvard University Press.

——. 2001. Indigenous articulations. *Contemporary Pacific* 13 (2): 468–490.

Condry, Ian. 2001. Japanese hip-hop and the globalization of popular culture. In *Urban life: Readings in the anthropology of the city,* edited by George Gmelch and Walter Zenner, 357–387. Prospect Heights, IL: Waveland Press.

de la Cadena, Marisol. 2000. *Indigenous mestizos: The politics of race and culture in Cuzco, Peru, 1919–1991.* Durham, NC: Duke University Press.

Errington, Shelly. 1998. *The death of authentic primitive art and other tales of progress.* Berkeley: University of California Press.

Fabian, Johannes. 1983. *Time and the Other: How anthropology makes its object.* New York: Columbia University Press.

Feld, Steven. 1994. From schizophonia to schismogenesis: On the discourses and commodification practices of "world music" and "world beat." In *Music grooves,* by Charles Keil and Steven Feld, 257–289. Chicago: University of Chicago Press.

——. 1996. Pygmy pop: A genealogy of schizophonic mimesis. *Yearbook for Traditional Music* 28: 1–35.

Fuss, Diana. 1995. *Identification papers.* New York: Routledge.

Gómez-Peña, Guillermo. 2000. *Dangerous border crossers: The artist talks back.* London: Routledge.

Graham, Laura R. 2005. Image and instrumentality in a Xavante politics of existential recognition: The public outreach work of EtÉnhiritipa Pimentel Barbosa. *American Ethnologist* 32 (4): 622–641.

Gustafson, Bret. 2002. Paradoxes of liberal indigenism: Indigenous movements, state processes, and intercultural reform in Bolivia. In *The politics of ethnicity: Indigenous peoples in Latin American States,* edited by David Maybury-Lewis, 267–306. Cambridge, MA: Harvard University Press.

Hale, Charles. 1994. Between Che Guevara and the Pachamama: Mestizos, Indians, and identity politics in the anti-quincentenary campaign. *Critique of Anthropology* 14 (1): 9–39.

Hall, Stuart. 2002. The West and the rest: Discourse and power. In *Development: A cultural studies reader,* edited by Susanne Schech and Jane Haggis, 56–64. Oxford: Blackwell.

Hosokawa, Shuhei. 2002. Salsa no tiene fronteras: Orquesta de la Luz and the globalization of popular music. In *Situating salsa: Global markets and local meanings in Latin popular music,* edited by Lise Waxer, 289–311. New York: Routledge.

Howell, David L. 2005. *Geographies of identity in nineteenth-century Japan.* Berkeley: University of California Press.

Iwabuchi, Koichi. 2002. *Recentering globalization: Popular culture and Japanese transnationalism.* Durham, NC: Duke University Press.

Kelly, William W. 1991. Directions in the anthropology of contemporary Japan. *Annual Review of Anthropology* 20: 395–431.

Léons, Madeline Barbara, and Harry Sanabria. 1997. Coca and cocaine in Bolivia: Reality and policy illusion. In *Coca, cocaine, and the Bolivian reality,* edited by Madeline Barbara Léons and Harry Sanabria, 1–46. Albany: State University of New York Press.

Lomnitz, Claudio. 2001. *Deep Mexico, silent Mexico: An anthropology of nationalism.* Minneapolis: University of Minnesota Press.

Marcos, Subcomandante. 1995. *Shadows of tender fury: The letters and communiqués of Subcomandante Marcos and the Zapatista Army of National Liberation,* translated by Frank Bardacke, Leslie López, and The Watsonville Human Rights Committee. New York: Monthly Review Press.

Martin, Desirée A. 2004. "Excuse the inconvenience, but this is a revolution": Zapatista paradox and the rhetoric of tourism. *South Central Review* 21 (3): 107–128.

Masden, Kirk. 1997. The impact of ministry of education policy on pluralism in Japanese education: An examination of recent issues. In *Emerging pluralism in Asia and the Pacific,* edited by David Y. H. Wu, Humphrey McQueen, and Yamamoto Yasushi, 29–63. Hong Kong: Hong Kong Institute of Asia-Pacific Studies–The Chinese University of Hong Kong.

Meisch, Lynn A. 2002. *Andean entrepreneurs: Otavalo merchants and musicians in the global arena*. Austin: University of Texas Press.

Mendoza, Zoila. 2004. Crear y sentir lo nuestro: La Misión Peruana de Arte Incaico y el impulso de la producción artístico-folklórica en Cusco. *Latin American Music Review* 25 (1): 57–77.

Mitsui, Toru. 1993. The reception of the music of American southern whites in Japan. In *Transforming tradition: Folk music revivals examined*, edited by Neil V. Rosenberg, 275–293. Chicago: University of Illinois Press.

Murphy-Shigematsu, Stephen. 2000. Identities of multiethnic people in Japan, In *Japan and global migration: Foreign workers and the advent of a multicultural society*, edited by Mike Douglass and Glenda S. Roberts, 196–216. London: Routledge.

Ohnuki-Tierney, Emiko. 1998. A conceptual model for the historical relationship between the self and the internal and external others: The agrarian Japanese, the Ainu, and the special-status people. In *Making majorities: Constituting the nation in Japan, Korea, China, Malaysia, Fiji, Turkey, and the United States*, edited by Dru C. Gladney, 31–51. Stanford: Stanford University Press.

Patzi Paco, Felix. 2003. Rebelión indígena contra la colonialidad y la transnacionalización de la economía: Triunfos y vicisitudes del movimiento indígena desde 2000 a 2003. In *Ya es otro tiempo el presente: Cuatro momentos de insurgencia indígena*, edited by Forrest Hylton, Felix Patzi, Sergio Serulnikov, and Sinclair Thomson, 199–279. La Paz: Muela del Diablo Editores.

Poole, Deborah. 1997. *Vision, race, and modernity: A visual economy of the Andean image world*. Princeton: Princeton University Press.

Postero, Nancy. 2005. Indigenous responses to neoliberalism: A look at the Bolivian uprising of 2003. *Political and Legal Anthropology Review* 28 (1): 73–92.

Ramos, Alcida Rita. 1998. *Indigenism: Ethnic politics in Brazil*. Madison: University of Wisconsin Press.

Rivera Cusicanqui, Silvia. 2003a. *Las fronteras de la coca: Epistemologías coloniales y circuitos alternativos de la hoja de coca. El caso de la frontera Boliviana-Argentina*. La Paz: IDIS-UMSA y Ediciones Aruwiyiri.

——. 2003b [1984]. *Oprimidos pero no vencidos: Luchas del campesinado aymara y qhechwa de Bolivia, 1900–1980*, Con nuevo prefacio de la autora. La Paz: Aruwiyiri–Yachaywasi.

Roth, Joshua Hotaka. 2002. *Brokered homeland: Japanese Brazilian migrants in Japan*. Ithaca, NY: Cornell University Press.

Salmón, Josefa. 1997. *El espejo indígena: El discurso indigenista en Bolivia 1900–1956*. La Paz: Plural Editores-UMSA.

Sanjinés, Javier. 2002. Mestizaje upside down: Subaltern knowledges and the known. *Nepantla: Views from the South* 3 (1): 39–60.

——. 2004. *Mestizaje upside-down: Aesthetic politics in modern Bolivia*. Pittsburgh: University of Pittsburgh Press.

Savigliano, Marta E. 1995. *Tango and the political economy of passion*. Boulder, CO: Westview Press.

Segi, Takamasa. 1996. *Nieve*. Tokyo: Polystar.

——. 1997. *Luna*. Tokyo: Polystar.

——. 1998. *Forest Rain*. Sapporo, Japan: Polystar.

——. 1999. *Silencio*. Sapporo, Japan: Polystar.

——. 2000. *Songs of the Wind*. Tokyo: Polystar.

——. 2001. *Segi/Andes*. Cochabamba, Bolivia: Polystar.

Simon, Paul. 1974. *Live rhymin': Paul Simon in concert, with Urubamba and the Jessy Dixon Singers*. New York: Warner Brothers.

Simon, Paul, and Art Garfunkel. 1972. *Simon and Garfunkel's greatest hits*. New York: Columbia CBS.

Spedding, Alison L. 1997. Cocataki, taki-coca: Trade, traffic, and organized peasant resistance in the Yungas of La Paz. In *Coca, cocaine and the Bolivian reality*, edited by Madeline Barbara Léons and Harry Sanabria, 117–137. Albany: State University of New York Press.

Tanaka, Stefan. 1993. *Japan's orient: Rendering pasts into history*. Berkeley: University of California Press.

Thomson, Sinclair. 2002. *We alone will rule: Native Andean politics in the age of insurgency*. Madison: University of Wisconsin Press.

Turner, Terence. 1991. The social dynamics of video media in an indigenous society: The cultural meaning and the personal politics of video making in Kayapó communities. *Visual Anthropology Review* 7 (2): 68–76.

Wara. 1975. *Maya/Paya*. La Paz: Discolandia.

Weismantel, Mary. 2001. *Cholas and pishtacos: Stories of race and sex in the Andes*, forward by Catherine R. Stimpson. Chicago: University of Chicago Press.

Yoshino, Kosaku. 1997. Discourse on blood and racial identity in contemporary Japan. In *The construction of racial identities in China and Japan: Historical and contemporary perspectives*, edited by Frank Dikötter, 199–211. Honolulu: University of Hawai`i Press.

——. 1998. Culturalism, racialism, and internationalism in the discourse on Japanese identity. In *Making majorities: Constituting the nation in*

Japan, Korea, China, Malaysia, Fiji, Turkey, and the United States, edited by Dru C. Gladney, 13–30. Stanford, CA: Stanford University Press.

Zorn, Elayne. 2005. From political prison to tourist village: Tourism, gender, indigeneity, and the state on Taquile Island, Peru. In *Natives making nation: Gender, indigeneity, and the state in the Andes,* edited by Andrew Canessa, 156–180. Tucson: University of Arizona Press.

Part 4

The Boundary Politics of Indigeneity

Indian Indigeneities: Adivasi Engagements with Hindu Nationalism in India

Amita Baviskar

In the late 1990s, sections among Bhilala adivasis, members of a "Scheduled Tribe" in western India, joined the battle for Hindu supremacy, attacking Christian adivasis and, later, Muslims. At issue was indigeneity, the politics of place and belonging in the Indian nation. The affiliation with Hindu nationalism marked a radical departure from the previous decade's politics when adivasis had asserted a separate tribal identity and sought to reclaim rights to resources. These claims, articulated with great eloquence during the course of a campaign against dam-induced displacement, were shaped and strengthened by globally circulating discourses of indigeneity and indigenous peoples. How did these discourses, and the distinctive meanings of adivasi indigeneity to which they lent themselves, come to be superseded? Instead of signifying a subaltern experience of adivasi dispossession and resistance, how are discourses of indigeneity deployed to support the claims of the politically dominant Hindu Right, disenfranchizing religious minorities and legitimizing a politics of hate? How do Bhilala adivasis participate in this transformation in the valences of indigeneity? In this chapter, I trace adivasi mobilization across three sites: rights to place and natural resources, religious reform, and electoral representation, to examine how discourses of indigeneity are differently constructed and contested across the terrain of class, caste, and citizenship.

Footsoldiers for Lord Ram

In March 2002, I was walking along the dirt track from Kakrana to Kulvat, to catch the early morning bus that would take me to Alirajpur, the subdistrict headquarters of district Jhabua. Kakrana is a sprawling village on the bank of the Narmada river in central India in the state of Madhya Pradesh (MP); the local geography of hills that march along the river's flow make it a staging post on the long hike to and from other villagers along the river banks. Outsiders consider these villages "remote," inaccessible except on foot, nestled in the fastnesses of forested hills. The Bhilala and Bhil *adivasis* who live here have long been viewed by the rest of the world as "backward."[1] The valences of that term extend beyond the material poverty of most adivasis here who eke out a living from farming tiny plots of land and collecting forest produce, forms of livelihood that barely see them through the year. "Backwardness" is more general attribute—the failure to conform to the "civilized" standards set by nonadivasis in matters of dress and deportment, and lifestyle and aspirations.[2] The difference is also marked in terms of adivasi religious beliefs and practices that are centered on the worship of ancestral spirits and gods personifying nature. I was returning from one such religious ceremony—*indal,* celebrating the union of the earth and rain that brings forth grain. Indal is a complex of rites performed by a family, elaborated over a day and night, in which the singing of the Bhilala myth of creation induces spirit possession. Goats and chickens are sacrificed to the gods and everyone feasts and gets drunk.[3] What nonadivasis notice the most about indal is its excess—the wildness of possession, sacrifice, dancing and drunkenness, qualities that contrast with the more austere spirit of upper-caste Hindu rituals and festivities. There have been strenuous attempts to "reform" adivasis by inculcating in them more upper-caste modes of religious virtue, but the villages along the river had been largely untouched by such campaigns.

Or so I thought. I was walking alone, savoring the bright morning and the sounds and smells of the Bhilala countryside, feeling a pleasant lassitude after a convivial night with friends. As I paused at the top of a small rise where the ridge marked the boundary between two villages, a spot where a small cement platform encircled a *boor* (*Zizyphus jujuba*) tree under which offerings of shredded tobacco marked past journeys and passages, I saw four figures in the distance, their rapid strides swallowing up the gap between us. I lingered to let them catch up with me, looking for some company on the rest of the way to Kulvat. But as they drew nearer, and I saw what they were wearing, a great unease overtook me. They were young men, in their late teens or early twenties, and adivasi, judging by their features and the tattoos at the corner of their eyes. They were dressed in white shirts and khaki shorts, generic boy scouts or school uniforms, except that they wore black caps on their heads. The attire signified that they were members of the Rashtriya Swayamsevak Sangh ([RSS] National Volunteer Union),[4] the Hindu nationalist organization known for its hate-based politics, admired and/or feared for its vast network of disciplined cadres committed to the cause of Hindu supremacy. The confident presence of these RSS youth in this place, in uniform and marching in step, was an assertion of the strides that Hindu fundamentalism had made in the adivasi heartland.

Just 50 kilometers away lay the adjacent state of Gujarat where, at that very moment, shops and houses owned by Muslims still smoldered. They had been looted and burnt by mobs out to avenge an alleged attack on a train carrying Hindutva activists through the state. The Bharatiya Janata Party ([BJP] Indian People's Party) government in the state ensured that the civil administration and police remained passive spectators of the violence; in places even overtly encouraging it (Varadarajan 2003). Over the month of March, about 2,000 Muslims had been killed in Gujarat, women raped and mutilated; several thousands more were driven out and displaced by the destruction of their homes and workplaces. There were two novel features that made these communal riots a departure from previous incidents: one, violence was not confined to urban areas but also occurred in the countryside; and two, adivasis participated in the attacks against Muslims. Muslim traders, whose families had been settled for generations in the villages and small towns across the region, had to run for their lives when adivasis wielding swords and sickles, shouting Hindu slogans, stormed into their houses. Reflecting with satisfaction on their success, an adivasi man remarked, "*Ame shakti batavi*" ("we showed our strength") (Lobo 2002: 4845). Adivasis had converted to the Hindutva cause with deadly effect.

The violence in Gujarat had been contained at the state border. MP state was ruled by a Congress Party government that took strong measures to defuse communal tensions instigated by the Sangh Parivar. The police was deployed on an unprecedented scale in border towns like Alirajpur. District officials held meetings with community leaders. "Bad characters" were taken into preventive custody. Large gatherings were prohibited. But for this mobilization, Muslims in MP would have suffered the same fate as members of their religious community in Gujarat. In this context, the sight of adivasi men flaunting their RSS affiliation as they walked along a village path was an ominous reminder that a communal conflagration had just barely been averted in MP. In this moment, adivasi engagements with Hinduism, centuries of complex and contentious collective negotiations, seemed to have been reduced to the chillingly familiar binaries of hate politics—adivasis conscripted into a monolithic Hinduism confronting the Muslim Other.

Adivasis

The use of the term *adivasi* (lit., "original dwellers") or "indigenous people" for the groups classified under the Indian Constitution as "Scheduled Tribes" in India has now become commonplace. Despite its passage into everyday usage, scholars have voiced their misgivings about the applicability of terms such as "tribe" and "indigenous people" in the Indian context (Beteille 1986, 1998). Andre Beteille points to the theoretical and practical difficulties of distinguishing adivasis from the castes around them, given their long histories of cultural exchange. Nandini Sundar (1997) and Ajay Skaria (1999) have elaborated this theme in their ethnographies and histories. Other scholars such as G. S. Ghurye have pointed to the colonial provenance of the term and its origins in the imperatives of imperialist politics (Ghurye 1963). Sumit Guha (1999) traces the connections between anthropological understandings of "tribes" and the structures of colonial power. Guha also shows how racial anthropometry, a "science" pursued by colonial administrators like H. H. Risley and enthusiastically seized by upper-caste Indians, fused ideas of race with caste and tribe. The notion of shared Indo-Aryan origins were used by Indian elites to assert parity with Europeans while also emphasizing their distance from lower caste and tribal "aborigines," beneath them in the social hierarchy.[5] Sundar (1997: esp. ch. 6) also presents a nuanced account of the multiple ideologies and interests at work in colonial and postcolonial practices regarding "tribes." The sum of this scholarly writing is to deconstruct the notion of "tribe" and "indigenous people" in the Indian context.

And, yet, the term *adivasi* (or *tribe*, or *indigenous people*, or *aborigines*) is not easily dismissed. Although scholars have contested its sociological validity and disputed its precise meanings and characteristic attributes, and nationalists exposed its dubious genealogy, the accretions of political and administrative usage over time have rendered the term a social fact. Various conventions of the International Labour Organization from 1957 onward and the Working Group on Indigenous Populations set up by the United Nations have sought to protect the interests of "indigenous and other tribal and semi-tribal populations" (Xaxa 1999: 3590). As a signatory, the Indian government is bound by several of these conventions. The rights of adivasis are protected under the Fifth and Sixth Schedules of the Indian Constitution that designate adivasi-populated parts of the country as subject to special laws and procedures.[6] These rights have recently been added to under the Panchayati Raj Act for Scheduled Areas (PESA) and may be further augmented by the proposed Scheduled Tribes and Forest Dwellers (Recognition of Forest Rights) Act.[7] Even more important, various social groups—Bhil, Bhilala, Gond, Santhal, Munda, and hundreds of others whose presence is depicted by clusters of ink spots dotted across the demographic map of India—use the term *adivasi* to define themselves as a collectivity and to stake claim to material and symbolic resources. The combined weight of international and national law, administrative practice, similar histories, and political internalization by the people thus designated, has imparted to the term a legitimacy that is hard to ignore. Once created, the concept of "adivasi" has taken on a life of its own, animated by the complex social practices that have accrued around it. It has become a part of received wisdom, internalized and acted on. To respect the political weight of the concept is not to subscribe to the implicit notion of essential difference that it invokes, but to recognize the power of this regime of representation.

Are those groups who are designated as adivasis, and who identify themselves as adivasis, characterized by any "objective" markers of subordinate status and social deprivation? In terms of economic and political indicators, it is easy to make the general case that adivasis in peninsular India lag behind the average Indian with respect to basic human development indicators such as income, literacy, life expectancy, infant mortality, and the like.[8] The poverty of adivasis is generally linked to a lack of access to productive resources, whether land based or industrial–urban. Poverty is combined with political powerlessness that constrains their ability to bargain for secure and remunerative livelihoods. More and more adivasis today make up the gangs of seasonal laborers migrating in search of wage employment to urban centers and areas of intensive agriculture. The failure of the welfare state to substantially improve the lives of adivasis is evident in their impoverished everyday lives. Deprivation is not a natural state for adivasis; it is produced and reproduced by the policies and practices that characterize India's postcolonial development. The landscape that adivasis inhabit has been the internal frontier for an expanding Indian economy—a source of minerals and timber, a site for mines, dams and heavy industries, and they have experienced the resultant erosion of their agriculture and forest-based economy.

Economic and political subordination is buttressed by the ideology of caste pollution and purity. Unconverted adivasis face the social stigma of being considered "savage" and "backward" by dominant groups such as caste Hindus as well as by Muslims and Christians. This stigma facilitates the brutal, often sadistic, treatment meted out to adivasis by dominant groups (Baviskar 2001). To cite one ubiquitous instance: poor adivasis in western India are actively discouraged from sitting in the front of the bus if there are caste Hindus traveling. Adivasi women are typified as "promiscuous," making them fair game for sexual harassment. To be an adivasi in western India is to be at the bottom of the social hierarchy.

However, the stark social differences in public dealings between adivasis and *bazaarias* (townspeople, upper-caste Hindus and Muslims) are now less well-defined for a section of adivasis. Educated in government schools, fluent in Hindi, dressed in shirts and trousers instead of loincloths and turbans,[9] part of the younger generation of adivasis is more confident in bazaaria culture. Although some of those who make it to school come from better-off families, this is not always the case. Sometimes, men with large families will decide to send one son (less frequently, a daughter) to school, to open up the possibility of employment off the land. As they travel in buses to the schools located in local towns, hang out at tea shops and cigarette and *paan* (betel leaf) kiosks, play carom for hours together at the town center, adivasi young men partake of a bazaaria modernity that is cool, but that rarely translates into higher social status beyond more egalitarian treatment in everyday encounters. There are few government jobs for this burgeoning number of formally educated men; most lack the connections or the academic qualifications to be competitive. The bazaaria lifestyle is costly to maintain and the desire for urban comforts is unending.[10] While young men scrounge around for work—driving jeeps, petty trade, brokerage, strenuously avoiding manual, agricultural labor, they are often subsidized by the family that still lives on the land. For those in the village, the urban connection made possible by the "white-collar" child is a source of pride, a potential conduit into a world where they are regarded with contempt. It is an asset to have a town-based kinsman along as a *vaataad* (spokesperson) when negotiating the unfamiliar and intimidating terrain of the bureaucracy at the health clinic or the Block development office.

There are significant differences among adivasis in rural areas too. Bhil, Bhilala, and Tadvi hill adivasis are not a homogenous group but maintain a strict social distance especially with respect to marriage and food-related sociality. In areas where they coexist, Bhilalas tend to have greater economic and political resources than the subordinate Bhils. Bhilalas will not accept water from Bhils who they derogatorily call *padkhadya* ("eaters of beef"). In turn, the circumstances of these adivasis are quite different from those of powerful adivasi groups such as the Chaudhris in Gujarat (Shah 1985) and the Meenas in Rajasthan, all part of a contiguous adivasi landscape.

Adivasis, Indigeneity, and the Hindu Nation

A greater fluency in bazaaria culture among some adivasis coincides with this moment of Hinduization. The articulation between an urban, commercial culture dominated by upper-caste Hindus and the culture of political Hinduism needs to be situated within an older discourse of indigeneity in India. Since its inception, the Sangh Parivar (the family of Hindu fundamentalist organizations) has claimed indigenous status for *all* Hindus and *only* Hindus. Ideologues of Hindutva (the principle of Hindu supremacy) fervently subscribe to the idea of Hindus as indigenous people, historically marginalized by Muslim invaders and rulers.[11] Two hundred years of British rule, and the promotion of Christianity during colonialism, also arouse the same sense of grievance, albeit to a lesser degree. From the Hindutva perspective, Hinduism is the only original religion of the Indian sub-continent; all others are foreign and corrupt. According to Golwalkar, the founder of the RSS, only for Hindus do the boundaries of the Nation (*rashtrabhoomi*) coincide with the Motherland (*matribhoomi*) and Sacred Land (*punyabhoomi*); Muslims look to Mecca and Christians to the Vatican [*sic*], while Buddhists and Sikhs are considered to be lapsed Hindus and, thus, not a problem. These primordial loyalties determine patriotism and the politics of belonging. In claiming "indigeneity" exclusively for Hindus, the Sangh Parivar erases centuries of Muslim presence in the subcontinent, as well as the discomfiting historical fact that the Aryans who high-caste Hindus claim as their forebears were also of foreign origin.[12] Fascism, nationalism and religiosity combine in Hindutva ideology, the criteria of imputed origins and purity determining patterns of inclusion and exclusion. The inside and outside of the Indian nation is neatly conflated with religious identity, such that religious affiliation becomes the primary criterion for recognition as legitimate citizens. To be fully Indian and indigenous is to be Hindu.

Although Muslims and Christians have constituted the hated Other integral to the Sangh Parivar's identity since its formation, the question of adivasi affiliation has only been intermittently in focus over the years, coming into prominence when there have been reports of adivasis converting to Christianity (Xaxa 2000). Hindu fundamentalists have generally assumed that adivasis are default Hindus. They are supported by the Indian state's classification of Scheduled Tribes as Hindus, unless explicitly claimed otherwise.[13] However, state classificatory schemes are also political interventions: in the colonial period, the religion of the Scheduled Tribes was recorded as "animist," to distinguish them from peasant castes who were Hindus. After Independence, nationalist anthropologists argued against attributing a distinctive religious identity to the adivasis, claiming that they were "backward Hindus" (Ghurye 1963). According to this view, differentiating "tribes" from "castes," and claiming an "aboriginal" status for adivasis was a mischievous move, reminiscent of the colonial policy of divide and rule. The unity of Independent India demanded adivasi integration, not difference. And yet the category "Scheduled Tribes" was not dissolved altogether; it was preserved, although with adivasis classified as Hindus.

The contemporary cultural politics of being adivasi is contentious in novel ways, with religious identity taking on an entirely new significance, in opposition to Muslims and Christians. Although adivasis in the Narmada valley have only recently begun to negotiate with political Hinduism, their engagements with the dominant Hindu culture prevalent in local towns have a longer history.[14] In the last century, there have been several waves of Hinduization in the region, when many adivasi families and hamlets have become *bhagat* (lit., "devotees"), joining Hindu sects and worshipping gods from the Hindu pantheon, renouncing adivasi practices, and ostracizing nonbhagat adivasis. A quest for *sudhaar* (improvement or reform)[15] and upward mobility by emulating dominant Hindu values, the bhagat movement has been most influential among adivasis who have closer ties with Hindu townspeople—bazaarias.

Adivasis along the Narmada river have kept their distance from Hinduization though, in particular contexts, their practices display a certain ambivalence in this regard.[16] For instance, as dam construction has flooded parts of the Narmada valley, some adivasis have bought motorboats to negotiate a landscape no longer accessible on foot. I found it curious that the boat men, the same youths who participated wholeheartedly in the rites of indal, singing, dancing and getting possessed, always begin their day by worshipping the boat the Hindu way—with *agarbattis* (incense sticks), an item never used in Bhilala rituals. It reminded me of how nonadivasi bus drivers begin their day at the wheel, and perhaps adivasis echoed that practice as an apt way of propitiating the internal combustion engine. The syncretism that marks such adivasi practices makes them hard to classify. It should also be noted that the religious differentiation of adivasis into bhagat and nonbhagat, those who claim to be Hindu and those who do not, is not a unilinear historical trend; there is evidence of villages reverting to older adivasi ways from time to time.[17] Hinduization's current wave is manifested in the mushrooming of roadside temples all over the Narmada valley in the 1990s. These tall saffron-painted brick and cement structures, usually dedicated to Hanuman, the monkey god who assisted Ram in his battle against evil, and built with donations from local Hindu traders, announce the shared faith of adivasis and caste-Hindus.

Although the adivasis of the Narmada valley did not participate in it, other parts of Jhabua and present-day Rajasthan and Gujarat witnessed a remarkable harnessing of Hinduization for adivasi ends in the 1940s. Led by Mama Baleshwar, the Lal Topi Andolan freed adivasis from the *veth-begaar* (forced labor) imposed by princely rulers by appealing to the Arya Samaj who performed *shuddhi* (purification) and *upanayan* (donning the sacred thread) ceremonies, converting adivasis into twice-born Hindus and, thus, exempt from corvee. Mama Baleshwar enlisted the Arya Samaj to his aid by telling the Kanchi Shankaracharya that oppressed adivasis were converting to Christianity to escape veth-begaar since the British had exempted Christians from forced labor! If the Shankaracharya allowed adivasis to wear the sacred thread, conversions to Christianity would cease. The Hindu leader agreed, on the condition that adivasis become bhagat, giving up meat and liquor. Thousands of adivasis thus donned the sacred thread and circumvented the power of the princely states (Baviskar 1995a: 79–80). In the early 1990s, Mama Baleshwar recalled this initiative as a shrewd ploy calculated to make the most of unequal laws, rather than as a move toward genuine conversion (Amit Bhatnagar, personal communication). One does not know whether adivasis also saw conversion as a purely instrumental step, whether they continued being bhagat or eventually lapsed into more adivasi ways—the varied and complex relations between a hegemonic ideology and subaltern consciousness are hard to interpret across time (Guha 1983).

The multiple spiritual and cultural meanings embodied in the practices of being bhagat now matter less than its potential for recruiting adivasis to political Hinduism. Several bhagat sects are integrated with the Sangh Parivar, local units of which also run village schools where adivasi children are tutored in Hindu nationalism.[18] In areas where state health and education facilities are nonexistent or substandard, Sangh-affiliated organizations like Sewa Bharti (India Service), Vanvasi Kalyan Manch (Forum for the Welfare of Forest dwellers),[19] and Friends of Tribals Society fill the gap.[20] Philanthropic activities provide an easier entry into adivasi villages, where bhagat groups have been mobilized to form village-level *dharma raksha samitis* (religion protection committees). The committees organize religious discourses and *bhajan* (devotional songs) singing sessions. Their members are supplied with calendars adorned with Hindu deities,[21] and are encouraged to celebrate Hindu festivals like Navratri and Ganesh Chaturthi that are unfamiliar to adivasis.[22] Sangh Parivar organizations assist bhagats in performing pilgrimages to important Hindu temples in Gujarat.

Village-level activities are supplemented by larger regional meetings, often addressed by state-level and national Sangh Parivar leaders, who exhort adivasis to assert their Hinduness and defend a religion threatened by missionaries and Muslims. Rituals include giving *deeksha* (religious initiation) by blessing and anointing adivasis, distributing *trishuls* (tridents, the symbol of Lord Shiva), necklaces with Hanuman-icon lockets, and *bhagwa kaapad* (saffron cloth bandanas and scarves), to the chanting of Hindu slogans. An adivasi activist, not a bhagat and a critic of the "saffronization"[23] of adivasis, who attended one of these meetings remarked on their resemblance to the secular social movement events with which he was familiar from the antidam campaign: the same call to action, the expression of collective unity and strength, the rituals of solidarity (K. S. Gavle, personal communication, October 14, 2003). There is a recursivity to such borrowings: Sangh Parivar meetings mimic those of progressive social movements. The latter, in turn, draw on a political repertoire that can be traced to the nationalist struggle that, in its early days, took celebrations of festivals like Ganesh Chaturthi from the home into the streets, a key innovation in fashioning a Hindu, anticolonial public sphere and collective identity in urban western India (Courtright 1985). Campaigns that seek to incorporate adivasis into a Hindu narrative of *jagriti* (awakening), righteous assertion against the encroachments of Muslim and Christian foreign invaders, contain echoes within echoes of older struggles with very different meanings and ends.

The turn to the Sangh Parivar has another political dimension. This region of western MP had for decades voted for the Congress Party, a centrist, secularist formation.[24] The Congress Party, with its image of paternalism, had a long-standing hold over adivasi votes all over the state. Although the entrenched hierarchy of the Congress Party provided few opportunities for people striving to enter electoral politics, the entry of the Sangh Parivar in the region and its rapid expansion offered an alternative, quicker route to a political career. The BJP spoke to more than one adivasi desire—the quest for spiritual reform and social respect combined with individual electoral ambitions. In the elections to the state assembly in 2004, the BJP won all the seats from Jhabua district and went on to form the government in MP state.[25]

The seeds of Hindutva in the adivasi heartland bore fruit in the late 1990s.[26] In 1997–99, Christian adivasis were attacked, and their churches set on fire in south Gujarat and MP. Priests were stripped and beaten. Christian adivasis were forcibly administered *ganga-jal,* water from the sacred Hindu river Ganges in a *shuddhikaran* (purificatory rite) to reclaim their souls. The Sangh Parivar eloquently dubbed this campaign *ghar vaapasi* (returning home), characterizing Christian adivasis as Hindus who had strayed from the fold.[27] Violence against Christian adivasis erupted again in Jhabua in January 2004 when a mission school, several churches, and homes were set on fire.[28] Christians constitute less than 2 percent of Jhabua's population—according to the 1991 census, they were 14,974 in the district's total population of 1.3 million, and they were not particularly well-off compared with other adivasis. Local trade and money-lending is controlled by upper-caste Hindus and Bohra Muslims. But the arrival of Pentecostal Christianity to the area, with meetings that matched the Sangh Parivar in flamboyance if not in size, alarmed the Sangh Parivar (and to some extent, also the Catholic church that has had a localized presence in Jhabua since the 1890s, without many conversions taking place). Episodic violence against Christians, and now Muslims, has become a regular feature of cultural politics in western India over the last decade.

Scholars committed to the struggle for adivasi rights see the participation of adivasis in the anti-Muslim riots in Gujarat in 2002 as a conceptual and political challenge. The standard explanation seeks to deny the agency of adivasis, claiming that they were incited by outsiders. According to Lobo: "In the tribal areas, ... there has been a history of economic exploitation between Bohra Muslim traders and tribal people. This has been exploited by the Hindutva brigade, who gave it a communal color. In many places tribal people had been instigated to loot. The Bhil people in this area are extremely poor. This district has suffered drought conditions. The politicians and Hindutva-vadis with the complicity of government bureaucracy carried out *the entire operation of using adivasis* to loot and arson" (Lobo 2002: 4846–4847, emphasis mine). Another tribal rights activist and scholar commented that "tribals are socially vulnerable and while they would not be bothered much by Hinduism and Islam, liquor would play a role in inciting them to violence" (Devy 2002: 40). These explanations represent adivasis as structural dupes: their economic exploitation and poverty allow them to be cynically manipulated by the Sangh Parivar to target Muslims. As a "socially vulnerable" group, adivasis do not have the luxury of indulging in religious pursuits, of engaging in projects of spiritual reform and social success. But give them a drink, and they revert to a state of savagery.

The Adivasi Struggle for Indigenous Rights

According to tribal rights activists, adivasi participation in anti-Muslim and anti-Christian violence is a tragic aberration from the real historical class struggle for rights to resources. That there are many routes to tribal power, including the path of affiliating with Hindu supremacists, is a political possibility that is hard to accept. Adivasi violence is attributed to false consciousness. "The problems of adivasis are related to *jal* (water), *jungle* (forests) and *jameen* (land). The transfer of their resources to nontribal areas is the question. *Religion is not their problem.* Instead of addressing issues of political economy the Sangh Parivar and the BJP whose social base is among upper castes and middle classes divert the attention of adivasis to misguided targets like Muslims and Christians" (Lobo 2002: 4849, emphasis mine).

The possibility of a united adivasi struggle for rights to natural resources and political power in western India seems far-fetched now. But in 1990, when I first began fieldwork in the area, adivasis in the RSS uniform would have been an incongruous, even impossible, sight. At that time, the Bhil and Bhilala villages along the river were active in the Narmada Bachao Andolan (Save the Narmada Campaign), struggling against displacement by the Sardar Sarovar dam. In the previous decade, they had mobilized through the Khedut Mazdoor Chetna Sangath (Peasants and Workers' Consciousness Union) to secure access to forest land and to government services.[29] The Andolan and the Sangath together defined adivasi identity as informed by a history of dispossession, with their distinctive cultural practices beleaguered by secular and Hindu modernity. Adivasi claims to land and forests, and their opposition to displacement, were legitimized in terms of class and citizenship, as the right of a subordinate people to, at the very least, not suffer further deprivation. But also woven into these claims were ideas of ecological virtue—that, as autochthons, adivasis were better stewards of the land than the government who displaced them in the name of "national development."

Many of the reasons that made a compelling case for adivasis as a category of socially oppressed people are characteristics shared by most members of the Scheduled Castes or *dalits*.[30] If anything, atrocities against dalits are much more violent, the lines of social distance much more entrenched (Shah et al. 2006). If subordination is the criterion, the same claims and entitlements should be applicable in the case of both dalits and adivasis. But there is one crucial difference between adivasis and dalits: most adivasis continue to have some access to land, whereas dalits, as former service castes engaged in "polluting" tasks like sweeping, scavenging, leatherwork, cremation, and prostitution, do not. The link to land, especially to forested lands,[31] gives adivasis a certain cultural cachet that landless dalits cannot claim. Adivasi claims to social justice are made not only on the basis of a shared experience of oppression but also with reference to a special culture. Indigenous rights activists frequently represent adivasis as distinguished by a set of unique values, institutions, and practices that set them apart from other groups. There is a strong spatial dimension to the framing of indigenous culture. Most often, these norms and practices pertain to adivasi relationships with the physical environment that they inhabit, relationships that are described as ecologically wise; but they are also typified as having relatively egalitarian social structures with aspirations and lifestyles that distinguish them from others. Unlike other groups, adivasis are regarded as nonmaterialistic, they respect nature's limits, and their economies are supposed to be based on reciprocity and subsistence, not competition and accumulation. These cultural differences are perceived to be fragile and precious. Not only must adivasis have a right to their culture because it is their own but also because it is a thing of beauty.[32] Such a claim for cultural rights is rarely made in the case of dalits.

The cultural rights argument was a powerful resource for mobilization in the 1980s and early 1990s, when it was frequently used by adivasis themselves to claim that their culture was organically linked to a particular ecology. In the words of Khajan, a key adivasi spokesman in the antidam campaign,

> God made the earth and the forest; then He made us, adivasis, to live
> upon the earth. Ever since we have come out of our mother's womb,

we have lived here. Generation upon generation of our ancestors lived and died here. We are born of the earth and we bring forth grain from it. Governments live in cities and live on our grain. We live in the forest and we keep it alive. Governments and politicians come and go but we have never changed; we have been here from the beginning. The government cannot create the earth or the forest; then how can it take it away from us?[33]

Asserting an indigenous identity by naturalizing the connection between adivasis and their environment was a powerful way of claiming sovereign rights to natural resources. Khajan highlights the ties between blood and soil—this is our ancestral land. At the same time, he distinguishes between those who produce and those who consume—the legitimacy of adivasis against the illegitimacy of the state's claims. To quote Raymond Williams from another context: "We have mixed our labor with the earth, our forces with its forces too deeply to be able to draw back and separate either out" (1980: 83). The landscape of the Narmada valley is produced by adivasi cultural work, cultivating crops as well as cosmologies, not "under circumstances chosen by themselves, but under circumstances directly encountered, given and transmitted from the past" (Marx 1963 [1852]: 15).

The cultural rights claimed by Bhilala adivasis when threatened by displacement resonated with audiences across the world, garnering significant metropolitan support for the antidam movement in India and abroad. Other campaigns of adivasis resisting displacement elsewhere in India were also inspired by the Narmada struggle and strengthened in their staking of similar claims.[34] These claims were received less sympathetically by the Indian government, by the state of Gujarat (the prime beneficiary from the dam), and the majority of newspaper-reading Indians for whom there was nothing in the adivasi predicament that a good rehabilitation package would not solve. The dominant view has been that, as a poor, backward group, adivasis should be content with what they were getting; after all, the government was doing a lot for them, and the dam was needed for national development.[35] Dam supporters received a jolt when the Morse Commission conducted an Independent Review of the Sardar Sarovar dam and advised the World Bank to withdraw its funding from the project on the grounds that it harmed tribal cultures (Morse and Berger 1992). The commission held the bank accountable to its own guidelines and to international conventions on the rights of indigenous peoples. Notably, this discourse of indigenous rights defined adivasis as *global* subjects, kin to aborigines in Australia and indigenous peoples in the Americas, oppressed by the jurisdiction of the nation-state, and not as *national* citizens (also see IWGIA 1995: 33). The commission's report, which ultimately led to the cancellation of the World Bank loan, outraged not only those who supported the project but many social scientists as well (Baviskar 1995b). They charged that the report's conclusion that adivasis were autochthons was wrong; it disregarded the specificities of the Indian case. As a (Brahmin) newspaper columnist declared, "We are all adivasis."

Essentialisms and Exclusions

It is easy to demolish the adivasi claim to indigeneity in "objective" terms. Indigeneity is a hybrid discourse produced through transnational alliances (Conklin and Graham 1995). Anthropologists and NGOs, international law and conventions, have helped to create an ideal type cobbled together from around the world, combining notions of adivasi-as-victim with adivasi-as-exotic Other. Representations of the loincloth wearing adivasi, playing a flute or dancing, circulate more than those of his more prosaic trousers-clad cousin.[36] Such coverage also tends to reinforce essentialist images of adivasis as "ecologically noble savages" (or increasingly, not savages at all, but savants [Redford 1991]), conflating nature and culture.[37] The earlier pejorative quality of being far from Civilization is now glossed positively as being close to Nature. Claims to the physical environment are legitimated by reference to primordial connections of dubious historicity. Ramachandra Guha has criticized such essentialist representations as merely a form of "inverted Orientalism," positively valorizing a mythical Other created by Western environmentalists (Guha 1989). The pervasive presence of such images points to the hegemony of Western forms of knowledge, especially classificatory practices. Akhil Gupta points out the irony that "the effectiveness of 'indigenous' identity depends on its *recognition* by hegemonic discourses of imperialist nostalgia, where poor and marginal people are romanticized at the same time that their way of life is destroyed" (Gupta 1998: 18). However, Gupta and Peter Brosius have subsequently argued that such essentialist representations may be condoned as a strategic necessity (Brosius 1999: 280; Gupta 1998: 19). When adivasis are trapped in dichotomies not of their making, in a world where marginal groups have few political resources at their command, the assertion of rights within an unequal political space compels recourse to creative strategies that are often compromised (Tsing 1999).

This is also the case with the antidam movement in the Narmada valley, where adivasis self-consciously (and sometimes, with irony) perform stereotyped roles, pandering to hegemonic cultural expectations to gain their own ends, usually with some prompting from backstage nonadivasi activists (Baviskar 1995a: 213; 1997b: 59–60). I do not wish to suggest that such representations are "cynical, opportunistic, inauthentic," or that they are ploys chosen by goal-oriented actors, or that they are a form of false consciousness. To quote Tania Li, "a group's self-identification as tribal or indigenous is not natural or inevitable, but neither is it simply invented, adopted, or imposed. It is rather, a *positioning* which draws upon historically sedimented practices, landscapes and repertoires of meaning, and emerges through particular patterns of engagement and struggle" (Li 2000: 150).

This positioning of adivasis in the antidam movement suffered a major blow in September 2000 when the Supreme Court of India ruled that the project should be built because "dams are good for the nation."[38] Adivasi claims about cultural rights to a unique place, the Narmada valley, were dismissed, paving the way for their displacement. At the regional level, too, the bid to form a separate adivasi state faded away. This was the demise of an initiative in the early 1990s that sought to unite all adivasis—Bhil, Bhilala, Tadvi, and Chaudhri, under the common rubric of Bhilkhand, carving out an autonomous territory for adivasis in western India along the lines of Jharkhand and Chhattisgarh in east–central India.[39] At the same time, the Sangh Parivar was expanding its presence in the area, offering to incorporate adivasis into a different community—not an oppositional identity that stressed distinction, but the opportunity to be part of the hegemonic Hindu majority, not to challenge structures of power but to participate in them. Adivasis could now imagine themselves as part of a larger cultural landscape—the Hindu nation, rather than as a subaltern presence incarcerated in a state of nature.

On most counts, the claims to indigeneity made by the Hindu Right are starkly different from the claims to indigeneity made by adivasis fighting against displacement by a large dam. Hindu indigeneity legitimizes the violent *exclusion* and subordination of religious minorities. Adivasi indigeneity is a demand for *inclusion* in the Indian polity, a claim on resources unjustly denied and alienated. This difference is a substantive one and separates a set of fascist organizations from progressive adivasi political organizations and social movements in MP. Yet there is one disturbing common element in these widely divergent invocations of indigeneity. The adivasi claim is made less on the basis of the principle of citizenship—the rights guaranteed to all Indians under the Indian Constitution, and more on the basis of a different culture, tied to nature in a particular place. As I discuss below, this discursive emphasis creates its own exclusions.

Although indigeneity, like all essentialist identities, is a powerful, culturally resonant weapon for political mobilization and one that adivasis are well-positioned to deploy, the language of citizenship rights submerges adivasi difference into a more generalized subaltern subject position. Political groups working on resource rights issues in the Narmada valley who are committed to the adivasi cause within the terms of the Indian Constitution and beyond it, have sought to resolve this tension ideologically and organizationally. Sangath activists argued that adivasis were part of a larger dalit community of oppressed people everywhere (Shankar Tadavla, personal communication, March 15, 1994). The early Andolan protests were joined by the Chhattisgarh Mukti Morcha, cadres of industrial laborers fighting for fair employment making common cause with peasants resisting displacement. At the time of writing, political groups in MP working on the issue of forest-dwellers' rights under the umbrella of Jan Sangharsh Morcha have taken a stand opposing the adivasi–nonadivasi distinction made by the draft forest bill.[40] Such strategic alliances and ideological stands prove that solidarities can be established across cultural difference to forge a more inclusive oppositional politics. Yet the war of attrition waged by the state against the antidam movement took its toll. Those who could stay longer in the movement were those who had land at stake.

The assertion of cultural ties to land, and the ability to mobilize on that basis, leaves out the most vulnerable group—the landless. In the Narmada valley lived Dhankava Naiks, a dalit group that had no land but only legends about how, many generations ago, the adivasis conquered them and captured their forests. Lacking the cultural capital that adivasis could draw on, ignored by an antidam movement that focused on the rights of landed adivasis and Hindu peasants to stress the impossibility of rehabilitation, the Naiks were the first to take the meager compensation offered by the government and fade away into the distance. Their unwitting exclusion is a tiny strand in the antidam saga, an epic struggle that overcame enormous odds to transform conceptions of big dams and displacement across the world, but it is not trivial. Such exclusions remind us of the darker side of the politics of indigeneity and the need to constantly keep alive the possibility of alliances across identities.

When political vocabularies increasingly resort to the "sedentarist metaphysics" (Malkki 1992) of indigeneity, where collective identities are "naturally" tethered to place, they have other unintended consequences too. The majority of the world's poor, rural and urban, live on the margins of subsistence and the most degraded ecological conditions but cannot claim to be indigenous. For instance, recent migrants to Indian cities can establish no authentic genealogies; their resource claims are the most tenuous. The cultural politics of fixing people in place leaves poor migrants vulnerable to physical eviction as authorities declare that they should "go back to where they belong."[41] Movements for adivasi homelands that mobilize around the issue of colonization and exploitation by "outsiders" run a similar risk of turning against migrants, especially religious minorities. Ironically, some of these migrants are likely to be adivasis dispossessed by state projects in the name of the nation, the politics of belonging rendering them "people out of place."

Conclusion

This chapter analyzes one episode in an ongoing series of struggles around indigeneity in India. The particular conjuncture of class and caste, religion, and citizenship that it describes is situated in a regionally limited space and time. In western India, over the last 15 years, the routes to adivasi power have come to coincide with expanding Hindu nationalism in a potent mix of religious faith, cultural aspirations, and electoral opportunity. Adivasis in other parts of India have participated in and created other kinds of cultural politics, from forming political parties based on adivasi identity to joining Naxalite revolutionary groups. This chapter does not claim to represent these and other struggles that inhabit different contexts and yet are similar in that they all address the predicament and promise of being adivasi. I offer a necessarily partial account, but one that I hope will act as a provocation.

There has been a generational shift in the life of the Indian nation-state. National developmentalism has been eroded by economic liberalization; secular-liberal ideologies are threatened by the illiberalism of religious and market-fundamentalisms (Deshpande 1997; Hansen 1999; Ludden 1996; McMichael 1996).[42] Adivasis in western India have experienced a generational shift too. The children of those who struggled against the dam, for rights to the forest, seek other political futures. As they inhabit worlds different from their parents', younger adivasis learn, rebel, and move on. This chapter illuminates one conjuncture in the life of a nation and in the lives of a group of adivasis and, in discussing it, challenges an article of faith for many of us that indigenous action will surely lead to freedom and to a better world. The moment this chapter delineates may well bring social success and greater power to some adivasis who embrace Hinduism. But this is happening at the expense of others, including Christian adivasis and those who continue to practice the religious forms unique to Bhil and Bhilalas. This chapter also records the eclipse of mobilization around resource rights when adivasi activists, even as they asserted entitlements based on autochthonous ties to land, were willing to ally with other groups around questions of displacement. Perhaps this is a temporary phase and the agrarian question will come to the fore once again as the debate around forest-dwellers' rights revives.[43] Yet, however transient, this moment shows that we cannot assume that indigeneity is intrinsically a sign of subalternity or a mode of resistance. Who adivasis are, and what they become, are questions that call for continued engagement and a politics of critical solidarity.

Notes

Acknowledgements. I would like to thank the organizers, Orin Starn, Marisol de la Cadena, and all the others participants at the Wenner-Gren conference for their insights and encouragement. I am also grateful to Ram Reddy, Mihir Shah, Rahul N. Ram, and an anonymous reviewer, for their careful reading and incisive comments.

1. *Adivasi* is the Indian term for social groups designated as "Scheduled Tribes" in the Indian Constitution. I discuss below the contentious social history of this designation, and the difficulties of separating tribes from castes in Indian contexts.

2. Many government and NGO programs seek to educate adivasis to help them emerge out of their "backward" state into the sunshine of development. Some scholars even see being displaced by a dam as an unexpected blessing for adivasis, because it will hasten their movement into the "mainstream" (Joshi 1991). Adivasis are perceived as anachronistic inhabitants of spaces outside modernity.

3. See Baviskar (1995a: 162–4) for a fuller analysis of *indal*.

4. The RSS is a grassroots organization of Hindu supremacists, seeking to replace India's secular polity based on the principle of religious coexistence ("unity with diversity") with the ideology of *Hindutva*—Hindu domination and the subordination of Muslim, Christian and other minorities. Golwalkar, the founder of the RSS founder, was an admirer of Hitler and Nazi Germany. RSS members assassinated Mahatma Gandhi for "appeasing Muslims" by advocating Hindu–Muslim unity. Banned during the 1950s to 1970s, the RSS reemerged in the late 1970s as part of the opposition to the Congress Party government that, led by Indira Gandhi, had imposed a state of Emergency, suspending civil liberties during 1975–77. In the 1980s, the RSS sought to expand its following beyond its upper-caste Hindu base. Although the RSS does not directly participate in electoral politics, it has strong links with the BJP that does; it is also affiliated with a number of other Hindu organizations, such as the Vishwa Hindu Parishad (World Hindu Forum), the Shiv Sena and the Bajrang Dal, together making up the Sangh Parivar (RSS Family). A pivotal event in the Hindu nationalist project was the December 1992 demolition of the Babri Masjid, an obscure mosque in the north Indian state of Uttar Pradesh, which the Sangh Parivar claimed was the birthplace of Lord Ram. The dispute over this site and others has sparked violence in the form of communal riots, incidents that have hardened religious identities. The campaigns of the Sangh Parivar seek to extirpate all aspects of the syncretic Hindu–Muslim culture that marks India. They range from rewriting history textbooks to running neighborhood *shakhas* (branches) where groups of men, women and children imbibe a monolithic Hindu view of the world and a sense of Muslims as the enemy. There is an extensive literature on the RSS and the rise of Hindu nationalism in Indian politics and culture; see Hansen (1999) and Bhatt (2001) for critical reviews.

5. The current Sangh Parivar strategy of claiming autochthonous origins for Aryans is an inversion of this argument, now aimed at emphasizing distance from Muslim "outsiders."

6. Transfers of land to nonadivasis are prohibited in Fifth Schedule areas. Until recently, this was interpreted to apply only to private transfers, with the state empowered to acquire and allocate adivasi land to others, but in 1997 the Supreme Court ruled that even the government could not transfer land to private parties. See the mines, mineral and PEOPLE website (http://www. mmpindia.org, accessed December 30, 2006) for details about the Samata judgment against state lease of adivasi land to mining corporations. The law has usually been implemented in the breach; many adivasis have seen their land pass into the hands of nonadivasi moneylenders and traders. Fifth Schedule areas also receive special funds from the central government toward Tribal Development. All over India, eight percent of all government jobs and

seats in educational institutions are reserved for adivasis (in proportion to their presence in the Indian population). On the success of this policy of protective discrimination, see Xaxa (2001). The Sixth Schedule areas lie in north–east India (see note 8).

7. The PESA empowers village bodies in adivasi areas to manage natural resources, including land, forests, and water. It authorizes the use of customary practices for settling disputes. A far-reaching initiative at decentralizing power, the act has already run into trouble, and has not been implemented in most states. The proposed Scheduled Tribes and Forest Dwellers (Recognition of Forest Rights) Act offers a one-time settlement granting land titles to adivasis who have been cultivating land under the control of the Forest Department. The bill provides a maximum of 2.5 hectares of forest land to each adivasi household if they can prove to a *gram sabha* (village-level body) that they have been farming that land at least since 1980. Although the act promises to undo the historical injustice of forest alienation (Baviskar 1994), it is fiercely opposed by environmentalists who fear that it will result in large-scale conversions of forests to farms and will encourage future encroachments on forests.

8. The situation of Scheduled Tribes in the northeastern hill states of Assam, Meghalaya, Mizoram, Tripura, Manipur, Arunachal Pradesh, and Nagaland differs from the case of peninsular India for a variety of historical, legal and administrative, and cultural reasons.

9. For formally educated adivasi women too, sartorial preferences have shifted, although not to the upper-caste Hindu mode of saree wearing, but to the salwar-kameez and, after marriage, the petticoat and half-saree favored by more prosperous adivasis in the plains of Nimar. On the cultural politics of clothing in Gujarat, see Tarlo (1996).

10. Renting a small room, owning a radio and an electric fan, entertaining friends, visiting relatives, aspiring to buy a television set, and, most coveted, a motorcycle—this lifestyle is difficult to afford for most adivasis.

11. The presence of Muslims (12 percent of the population) in India represents an eternal thorn in the side of the Sangh Parivar, fuelling the imaginary threat of being outnumbered and marginalized. The violence that marked the Partition of British India in 1947, when Pakistan was created by carving out Muslim-dominated areas, and the continuing dispute over Kashmir between the two countries, are two major elements in the narrative of Hindu–Muslim hostilities in India.

12. The RSS has funded ingenious archaeological studies to "prove" that the Aryans did not migrate from central Asia four thousand years ago but were native to the subcontinent (Witzel and Farmer 2000).

13. Most Scheduled Tribes in north–east India are Christian, as are some adivasis in central and south India, and in the Andaman and Nicobar islands. Muslim adivasis are rare.

14. Baviskar 1995a (ch. 4) argues that, despite processes of Hinduization in the region, interaction with Hindu culture in neighboring bazaars and towns has helped produce and sustain a distinctive adivasi identity. Also see Hardiman (1987). Another account of the bhagat movement can be found in Baviskar (1997a).

15. The genealogy of sudhaar or improvement is worth delineating. The notion of Improvement pervaded imperial projects in the colonies. Ideas of improvement, of husbanding resources, controlling lands and peoples for the purpose of conservation, better management for more efficient exploitation, were an intrinsic part of colonial enterprise (Cowen and Shenton 1996; Mehta 1999). Empire was justified as an instrument of development, of "fostering and leading new races of subjects and allies in the career of improvement" (Stamford Raffles, quoted in Drayton 2000: 94). The colonial critique of Oriental religions sparked off soul searching among Hindus and Muslims struggling with the Enlightenment project, contributing to attempts at reformation. The mission to reinvigorate Hinduism by removing the stranglehold of priests and the accretions of ritual and custom resulted in the emergence of sects like the Arya Samaj, dedicated to taking Hinduism back to its Vedic roots. The Brahmo Samaj in Bengal combined Christian values with Hinduism. Contemporary notions of sudhaar draw on this fusion of religious and secular notions of moral and material betterment.

16. See Baviskar (1995a: 97–103) for a description of the *mata* phenomenon.

17. Parkin (2000) describes the revival of adivasi religion among the Santhals in east–central India, and their campaign to not be classified as Hindus in the census. In 1971, 300,000 people in the Chhota Nagpur area reported Sarna as their religion, self-consciously distinguishing themselves from Hindus. In the 1991 census, this number had swollen to 1,800,000. According to B. K. Roy Burman, the doyen of tribal anthropology in India, the number of adivasis reporting a "tribal" religion such as Bhil and Gond has increased dramatically as well (Roy Burman, personal communication, May 8, 2000). Most of the evidence in western Indian points toward greater Hinduization, but perhaps this moment is also marked by the crystallization of a lesser current—the assertion of an autonomous "tribal" culture. This may also result in new electoral formations. In the last five years, a new adivasi political group called the Gondwana Gantantrik Party ([GGP] Gondwana Republican Party) has been formed in the Mahakoshal region of central MP. Operating in a region where 54 percent of the population belongs to the Scheduled Tribes and 22 percent of people identify themselves as of the Gond tribe, the GGP claims 1,700 years of "glorious history," a past when Gond kings and queens ruled large territories. Besides running an antiliquor campaign and organizing banks for rural women, the GGP has successfully contested the state assembly elections.

According to one observer, the GGP has refuted the BJP claim that adivasis are Hindus by burning copies of the religious text Ramayana (M. Prakash Singh, personal communication, October 7, 2005).

18. Sundar (2004) analyzes the pedagogy of Sangh Parivar–run schools in adivasi areas of Chhattisgarh (formerly eastern MP). Benei (2000) argues that even state-run schools promote a soft-Hindutva line on nationalism, indicating the pervasiveness of Hindutva ideology in secular civil society.

19. Hindu nationalists take care to always refer to the Scheduled Tribes as *vanvasis* (forest dwellers) and not as adivasis (original dwellers). Using "adivasi" for the Scheduled Tribes would not be consistent with the Sangh Parivar's contention that *all* Hindus, and not just the Scheduled Tribes, are the original inhabitants of India. The Vanvasi Kalyan Manch (Forum for the Welfare of Forest Dwellers), founded in 1952, claims to have active units in 20,000 villages in the 276 districts that have tribal populations. Its mission is to reestablish and strengthen "the blurred cultural links [between vanvasis and Hindus] and to wean the vanvasi away from the evil influence of foreign missionaries, anti-social, and anti-national forces" (Vanvasi Kalyan Ashram n.d.).

20. In other parts of tribal India, Christian groups have historically stepped into the breach in a similar manner.

21. Calendars with lush oleographs of Indian gods and goddesses have been a popular and inexpensive form of wall art in India since the 1950s.

22. Lobo (2002: 4845) reports that adivasis in Gujarat were involved in the rituals and mobilization leading up the demolition of the Babri mosque as early as 1990.

23. *Saffronization* is a term commonly used to indicate the growing influence of the Sangh Parivar. The color saffron, used to signify renunciation (*sadhus* wear saffron), has now come to connote militant Hinduism.

24. As a district where more than 80 percent of the population is adivasi, electoral seats to the national parliament and to the state legislative assembly are reserved for adivasis.

25. The BJP also defeated the Congress Party in state government elections in the two newly constituted adivasi majority states of Jharkhand and Chhattisgarh.

26. There had been an earlier incident in 1988 in Jhabua, 70 kilometers north of the Narmada valley in the same district. An adivasi mob broke into church premises and raped four Catholic nuns. A government inquiry into the incident faded away inconclusively. The involvement of the Sangh Parivar was not proven.

27. The assumption that adivasis are default Hindus is also reflected in Indian laws against proselytization that target tribal conversions to Christianity, without similarly prohibiting Hindu proselytization (Xaxa 2000: 23).

28. Hartosh Singh Bal, "Faith Seeks a Market" in *Indian Express*. January 25, 2004. The ostensible provocation for the violence was that the body of a nine-year-old girl who had been raped and murdered was found in the Catholic mission school. The girl was Hindu. After a mob had expressed its "anger against Christian depredations on innocent Hindu girls," it was discovered that the culprit was a Hindu man. However, by this time, the BJP was in power in MP and the state government ordered an inquiry into the incident. Narendra Prasad, the retired senior police officer who was appointed investigator, submitted his report in May 2005. Those portions of the report that have been made public indicate that it is a document tailor-made for the Hindutva cause, solidly pushing its communal claims. According to the report, Christian missionaries in Jhabua were forcibly converting adivasis and were therefore attacked by outraged adivasis-Hindus. Independent investigators have found no evidence of forcible conversions. Even local BJP leaders say that they did not know of any forcible conversions. Pintoo Jaiswal, a BJP activist and the vice chairman of the Alirajpur municipal corporation, said, "My children are studying in missionary schools. They have never complained of any attempt to convert them" (*Milli Gazette* 2005). The report also mentions the "worrying" fact that the Christian population of Jhabua has increased more than 80 percent in 1991–2001, a statistic that neglects to mention that Christians are less than 2 percent of Jhabua district's population, and a minuscule 0.28 percent of the population of MP state. The familiar scare-mongering strategies of the Sangh Parivar, the fear of surging Muslim and Christian populations making Hindus a minority in "their own" country, are given the stamp of quasi-judicial authority by this report. In turn, the BJP government in MP is using the report to justify new rules further restricting adivasi conversions to Christianity.

29. See Baviskar 1995a, 2004 (esp. chs. 8, 9, epilogue, and postscript in 2004 edition) for a detailed analysis of Andolan and Sangath politics among Bhilala adivasis.

30. Dalit (lit., "oppressed") is the collective name adopted by the former "untouchable" castes, who make up 16.2 percent of India's population (1991 census).

31. The link to forests is a critical element in distinguishing adivasi claims to land from those of another land-based group—peasants. See Baviskar (1995a: ch. 9) for the different styles of claims making by Bhilala adivasis and Nimari Hindu peasants from the plains in their collective struggle against displacement.

32. The work of anthropologist Verrier Elwin (1964), widely influential in shaping English-educated Indians' attitudes toward adivasis, best exemplifies this perspective. See also his ethnographies of various Indian tribes.

33. Interview on camera with filmmaker Ali Kazimi for his documentary *The Valley Rises*. My translation from the Bhilali. I am grateful to Ali Kazimi for letting me use this material.

34. The Suvarnarekha, Koel Karo, and Netarhat campaigns in east–central India, the campaign against mining in the Gandhamardan hills in Orissa, the Andhra Pradesh antimining campaign led by Samata, are but a few of the movements that stress adivasi cultural rights in the fight against displacement.

35. Such reassurances are self-serving; the actual experience of rehabilitation has been horrific. For evaluations of the rehabilitation experience with the Sardar Sarovar Project, see the Friends of River Narmada website (www.narmada.org, accessed December 30, 2006). Dreze et al. (1997) discuss the conceptual issues underlying the displacement debate. A more recent analysis of the pros and cons of displacement by the SSP can be found in Dwivedi (2006).

36. Beth Conklin (1997) describes similar strategies at work in the Amazonian rainforest.

37. Indigenous struggles are also perceived as struggles for environmental sustainability. See Baviskar (1995a: ch. 6) for an analysis of the constrained and contradictory practices that make it difficult to attribute ecological virtue to Bhilala adivasis. Peter Brosius (1997) describes how, in the context of a movement for indigenous rights to the forests in Borneo, metropolitan environmentalists universalize the complex and diverse practices of the Penan into a homogenous narrative about the sacred wisdom of "forest people."

38. See Baviskar (2004: postscript) for an account of the situation in the Narmada valley since that ruling.

39. Baviskar (1997a). The state of Jharkhand was created from the southern districts of Bihar in 2000 after a century-long movement to create an adivasi homeland in this forested and mineral-rich part of India. The state of Chhattisgarh was formed out of the eastern districts of MP at the same time. Virginius Xaxa (1999: 3594) argues that despite its empirical and conceptual problems, adivasi demands for a homeland adopt a tried-and-tested template for making political claims. Because the Indian system of states is based on linguistic identity mapped to specific regions, the territorial privileges of linguistically dominant communities are recognized whereas those of adivasis are not. The notion of an adivasi homeland is a cultural claim on par with the cultural claims of linguistic communities; whereas the former is disputed, the latter is taken for granted.

40. See note 7.

41. I discuss the predicament of migrants in Delhi in Baviskar (2003), and compare the discourses of rural and urban displacement, arguing that slum

dwellers in Delhi claim rights to land by highlighting not cultural attachment but the investment of labor in making a place habitable (Baviskar in press).

42. These shifts do not signify a *rupture* between two distinct periods as much as certain preexisting countercurrents coming to dominate a particular conjuncture in Indian politics. The resounding defeat of the BJP in the national government elections in 2004 and the subsequent disarray of the party may well signal the beginning of the end of the political dominance of Hindu nationalism. Yet the party continues to be in power in states such as MP, Gujarat, and Rajasthan, and the "tribal" states of Chhattisgarh and Jharkhand.

43. See note 7.

References

Baviskar, Amita. 1994. The fate of the forest: Conservation and tribal rights. *Economic and Political Weekly* 29 (38): 2493–2501.

——. 1995a. *In the belly of the river: Tribal conflicts over development in the Narmada Valley.* Delhi: Oxford University Press.

——. 1995b. The political uses of sociology. *Sociological Bulletin* 44 (1): 89–96.

——. 1997a. Tribal politics and discourses of environmentalism. *Contributions to Indian Sociology* 31 (2): 195–223.

——. 1997b. Who Speaks for the Victims? *Seminar* 451: 59–61.

——. 2001. Written on the body, written on the land: Violence and environmental struggles in central India. In *Violent environments,* edited by Nancy Peluso and Michael Watts, 354–379. Ithaca, NY: Cornell University Press.

——. 2003. Between violence and desire: Space, power and identity in the making of metropolitan Delhi. *International Social Science Journal* 175: 89–98.

——. 2004. *In the belly of the river: Tribal conflicts over development in the Narmada Valley.* 2nd edition. Delhi: Oxford University Press.

——. in press. Breaking homes, making cities: Class and gender in the politics of urban displacement. In *Gender and Displacement,* edited by Lyla Mehta.

Benei, Veronique. 2000. Teaching nationalism in Maharashtra schools. In *The everyday state and society in modern India,* edited by C. J. Fuller and Veronique Benei, 194–221. New Delhi: Social Science Press.

Beteille, Andre. 1986. The concept of tribe with special reference to India. *European Journal of Sociology* 27: 297–318.

——. 1998. The idea of indigenous people. *Current Anthropology* 39 (2): 187–191.

Bhatt, Chetan. 2001. *Hindu nationalism: Origins, ideologies and modern myths.* New York: Berg.

Brosius, J. Peter. 1997. Endangered forest, endangered people: Environmentalist representations of indigenous knowledge. *Human Ecology* 25 (1): 47–69.

——. 1999. Analyses and interventions: Anthropological engagements with environmentalism. *Current Anthropology* 40 (3): 277–288.

Conklin, Beth. 1997. Body paint, feathers, and VCRs: Aesthetics and authenticity in Amazonian activism. *American Ethnologist* 24 (4): 711–737.

Conklin, Beth, and Laura Graham. 1995. The shifting middle ground: Amazonian Indians and eco-politics. *American Anthropologist* 97 (4): 695–710.

Courtright, Paul. 1985. *Ganesa: Lord of obstacles, lord of beginnings.* New York: Oxford University Press.

Cowen, M. P., and R. W. Shenton. 1996. *Doctrines of development.* London: Routledge.

Deshpande, Satish. 1997. From development to adjustment: Economic ideologies, the middle class and 50 years of independence. *Review of Development and Change* 2 (2): 294–318.

Devy, G. N. 2002. Tribal voice and violence. *Seminar* 513: 39–48.

Drayton, Richard. 2000. *Nature's government: Science, imperial Britain, and the "improvement" of the world.* New Haven, CT: Yale University Press.

Dreze, Jean, Meera Samson, and Satyajit Singh, eds. 1997. *The dam and the nation: Displacement and resettlement in the Narmada Valley.* Delhi: Oxford University Press.

Dwivedi, Ranjit. 2006. *Resource conflict and collective action: The Sardar Sarovar Project in India.* New Delhi: Sage Publications.

Elwin, Verrier. 1964. *The tribal world of Verrier Elwin: An autobiography.* New York: Oxford University Press.

Ghurye, G. S. 1963. *The scheduled tribes.* Bombay: Popular Prakashan.

Guha, Ramachandra. 1989. Radical American environmentalism and wilderness preservation: A Third World critique. *Environmental Ethics* 11 (1): 71–83.

Guha, Ranajit. 1983. *Elementary aspects of peasant insurgency in colonial India.* Delhi: Oxford University Press.

Guha, Sumit. 1999. *Environment and ethnicity in India, 1200–1991.* Cambridge: Cambridge University Press.

Gupta, Akhil. 1998. *Postcolonial developments: Agriculture in the making of modern India*. Durham, NC: Duke University Press.

Hansen, Thomas Blom. 1999. *The saffron wave: Hindu nationalism and democracy in modern India*. Princeton: Princeton University Press.

Hardiman, David. 1987. *The coming of the Devi: Adivasi assertion in western India*. Delhi: Oxford University Press.

International Working Group on Indigenous Affairs (IWGIA). 1995. *The indigenous world 1994–95*. Copenhagen: IWGIA.

Joshi, Vidyut. 1991. *Rehabilitation: A promise to keep*. Ahmedabad: Tax Publications.

Li, Tania Murray. 2000. Articulating indigenous identity in Indonesia: Resource politics and the tribal slot. *Comparative Studies in Society and History* 42 (1): 149–179.

Lobo, Lancy. 2002. Adivasis, Hindutva and post-Godhra riots in Gujarat. *Economic and Political Weekly* 37 (48): 4844–4849.

Ludden, David, ed. 1996. *Making India Hindu: Religion, community and the politics of democracy in India*. Delhi: Oxford University Press.

Malkki, Liisa. 1992. National geographic: The rooting of peoples and the territorialisation of national identity among scholars and refugees. *Cultural Anthropology* 7 (1): 24–44.

Marx, Karl. 1963 [1852]. *The eighteenth brumaire of Louis Bonaparte*. New York: International Publishers.

McMichael, Philip. 1996. *Development and social change: A global perspective*. Thousand Oaks, CA: Pine Forge Press.

Mehta, Uday Singh. 1999. *Liberalism and empire: A study in nineteenth-century British liberal thought*. Chicago: University of Chicago Press.

Milli Gazette. 2005. Conversion allegation baseless. Electronic document, http://www.milligazette.com/dailyupdate/2005/20050909-Conversion.htm, accessed January 5, 2007.

Morse, Bradford, and Thomas Berger. 1992. *Sardar Sarovar: The report of the independent review*. Ottawa: Resource Futures International.

Parkin, Robert. 2000. Proving "Indigenity," Exploiting Modernity. *Anthropos* 95: 49–63.

Redford, Kent H. 1991. The ecologically noble savage. *Cultural Survival Quarterly* 15 (1): 46–48.

Shah, Ghanshyam. 1985. Tribal identity and class differentiation: A case study of the Chaudhri tribe. In *Caste, caste conflict and reservations*, edited by Ghanshyam Shah, 44–60. Delhi: Ajanta.

Shah, Ghanshyam, Harsh Mander, Sukhdeo Thorat, Satish Deshpande, and Amita Baviskar. 2006. *Untouchability in rural India*. New Delhi: Sage Publications.

Skaria, Ajay. 1999. *Hybrid histories: Forests, frontiers and wildness in western India*. Delhi: Oxford University Press.

Sundar, Nandini. 1997. *Subalterns and sovereigns: An anthropological history of Bastar, 1854–1996*. Delhi: Oxford University Press.

———. 2004. Teaching to hate: RSS' pedagogical programme. *Economic and Political Weekly* 38 (April 17): 1605–1612.

Tarlo, Emma. 1996. *Clothing matters: Dress and identity in India*. Chicago: University of Chicago Press.

Tsing, Anna L. 1999. Becoming a tribal elder, and other green development fantasies. In *Transforming the Indonesian uplands: Marginality, power and production*, edited by Tania M. Li, 159–202. Amsterdam: Harwood Academic Press.

Vanvasi Kalyan Ashram. n.d. Electronic document, http://hindunet.org/vanvasi, accessed January 5, 2007.

Varadarajan, Siddharth, ed. 2003. *Gujarat: The making of a tragedy*. New Delhi: Penguin India.

Williams, Raymond. 1980. *Problems in materialism and culture*. London: Verso.

Witzel, Michael, and Steve Farmer. 2000. Horseplay in Harappa: The Indus Valley decipherment hoax. *Frontline*, October 13: 23–26.

Xaxa, Virginius. 1999. Tribes as indigenous people of India. *Economic and Political Weekly* 34 (51): 3589–3596.

———. 2000. Tribes, conversion and the Sangh Parivar. *Jnanadeepa* 3 (1): 23–35.

———. 2001. Protective discrimination: Why scheduled tribes lag behind scheduled castes. *Economic and Political Weekly* 36 (29): 2765–2772.

"Ever-Diminishing Circles": The Paradoxes of Belonging in Botswana

Francis B. Nyamnjoh

To define indigenous peoples simply as those who "were there first and are still there, and so have rights to their lands" (Maybury-Lewis 2005) is to incite inquiry about the reality of flexibility of internal and external migration and the political, cultural, economic, and historical factors that have configured competing articulations of being indigenous (Garbutt 2006; Mercer 2003). Although such strategic essentialism may be understandable and indeed useful in the pursuit of common ambitions of dominance or in redressing injustices collectively experienced "as a colonized people," it hardly provides for theorizing pre- and postcolonial identities as complex, negotiated, and relational experiences (Nyamnjoh 2002a). Qualifying to be considered "authentic" is a function of the way race, geography, culture, class, and gender define and prescribe, include and exclude. These hierarchies of humanity assume different forms depending on encounters, power relations, and prevalent notions of personhood, agency, and community. Africa offers fascinating examples of how the term *indigenous* was arbitrarily employed in the service of colonizing forces, of how peoples have had recourse to indigeneity in their struggles against colonialism, and of how groups vying for resources and power amongst themselves have deployed competing claims to indigeneity in relation to one another.

Thus, in Africa, the meaning of "indigenous" has varied tremendously. Here, communities large and small have both accepted and contested arbitrary colonial and postcolonial administrative boundaries and the dynamics of dispossession. Failing to achieve the idealized "nation-state" form and relatively weak vis-à-vis global forces, governments have often sought to capitalize on the contradictory and complementary dimensions of civic, ethnic, and cultural citizenships. In this context, being indigenous socioanthropologically is much more than merely claiming to be or being regarded as the first. Under colonial and apartheid regimes of divide-and-rule, to be called "indigenous" was first to create and impose a proliferation of "native identities" circumscribed by arbitrary physical and cultural geographies; second, it was to make possible not only distinctions between colonized "native" and colonizing Europeans but also between "native citizens" and "native settlers" among ethnic communities within the same colony; and third, it was to be primitive, and therefore a perfect justification for the colonial *mission civilizatrice* (civilizing mission), for dispossession and confinement to officially designated tribal territories, homelands or Bantustans, often in callous disregard to the histories of relationships and interconnections forged with excluded others, or the differences and tensions even among the included. In all, being indigenous was for the majority colonized "native" population to be shunted to the margins. These dynamics of classification and rule conceived of the "natives" through frozen ideas of culture and imagined traditions applied under "decentralized despotisms" in rural areas, while the town and city were reserved for the minority colonial settler population and their purportedly "modernising," "cultured" and "detribalised" African servants and support staff (Mamdani 1996, 1998).

If this negative history still shapes the highly critical stance of African intellectuals and nationalists toward all claims of autochthony, it has also, quite paradoxically, tended to render invisible the everyday reality of postcolonial Africans (including those same intellectuals and nationalists) as straddlers of civic, ethnic, and cultural citizenships, on the one hand, and multiple global and local cosmopolitan identities, on the other hand (Englund 2004a, 2004b; Ferguson 1999; Nyamnjoh 2005). With growing uncertainties and the questioning of the inadequacies of civic citizenship and its illusions of autonomy, rigid and highly exclusionary affirmations of being indigenous have become obsessive among majority and minority communities alike within various states in Africa.

This chapter examines ongoing tensions over entitlements, cultural "purity," and belonging and exclusion among ethnic groups in Botswana. I want to show that in Africa, where the nation-state project has been achieved more in rhetoric than in reality, indigeneity is claimed not only by "first peoples," but by other ethnic (majorities and minorities) communities as well. My examination of the Botswana case leads me to make the case for greater recognition of what I call "flexible indigeneity" in a context of flexible mobility.

Indigeneity in Botswana

Botswana has one of the fastest growing economies in the world, and is relatively better managed than most other economies in Africa (Fombad 1999; Taylor 2002). In spite or perhaps because of this impressive economic record, Botswana has witnessed a resurgence of tensions concerning indigeneity and belonging since the mid-1980s. In the language of the Tswana majority (Setswana), an ethnic group ("tribe") is referred to generally as "morafhe" (pl.: Merafhe), less commonly sechaba. Morafhe also denotes a large public assembly, gathering, or multitude. At independence, Sechaba came to signify nationalism and the forging of an imagined community of citizens of a common fatherland—Botswana. From the national anthem (Pina ya Sechaba) to the national stadium (lebala la sechaba), through other public structures, Sechaba came to symbolize the glue needed to integrate the roughly 20 different ethnic indigeneities into a Botswana nation-state. But this experiment at Sechaba in the image of the big eight Tswana Merafhe only seem to have strengthened the resolve of the smaller merafhe to seek recognition and representation for their language and cultural values, especially since the mid-1980s. Although every Botswana national can claim juridicopolitical citizenship within the framework of the modern nation-state, some are perceived by others as less authentic. Without the right to paramount chiefs of their own and to representation in the national House of Chiefs as "tribes" in their own right, minorities increasingly see themselves more as subjects than citizens, even when clearly more indigenous to the territory. Identity politics and more exclusionary ideas of belonging have become increasingly significant. Minority claims for greater cultural recognition and plurality are countered by majoritarian efforts to maintain the status quo of an inherited colonial hierarchy of ethnic groupings.

This development is paralleled by increased awareness and distinction between "insiders" and "outsiders," with the emphasis on opportunities and economic entitlements (Durham 1993; Nyamnjoh 2002b, 2006). Increasingly, Batswana perceive themselves as the owners of the home (beng gae), and differentiate between those who belong with them (ba ga etsho), and close (Ba tswa kwa) or distant (Makwerekwere) outsiders.

At formal gatherings, speakers often articulate social distance with a view to entitlements by distinguishing between those here present (Ba ga etsho), and outsiders (ba faladi). As the pressures and uncertainties of global consumer capitalism intensify, land allocation has become one of the main arenas where distinction between the truly deserving sons and daughters of the soil (bana ba) and squatters (maipaafela) from elsewhere is played out (Werbner 2004: 109–130). A good case in point is Mogoditshane, a Bakwena periurban village near Gaborone, one of the fastest growing cities in the world that attracts thousands of migrants from elsewhere in Botswana, Africa, and the world (Campbell and Oucho 2003; Nyamnjoh 2002b; Ritsema 2003). For over 20 years, Mogoditshane's proximity to Gaborone has attracted both nationals and foreigners seeking easy access to land. Because land in Mogoditshane is categorized as "tribal," it is allocated freely as opposed to Gaborone where land is "national" and for sale (Werbner 2004: 109–130). Over the last ten years, much of the unrest in Mogoditshane has been about outsiders (Ba tswa kwa) grabbing land at the expense of the morafhe or beng gae. Increasingly, those who consider themselves more indigenous to Mogoditshane village and the Bakwena ethnic area have challenged the land rights of others, regardless of how long the perceived outsiders have lived in the village or how integrated they have become through relationships with "indigenes." Even challenged are Ba tswa kwa who have contested for and been voted into parliament to represent the very same village, beating the "more indigenous" sons and daughters of the village (bana ba Mogoditshane) to it.

The instinct for "ethnic citizens" to feel more entitled to "tribal land" over "ethnic strangers" is not confined to Mogoditshane, as attitudes to decisions by the 12 land boards and their 38 subordinates demonstrate. Even when accepting land boards as arbitrators, Batswana "have often perceived Board actions to be arbitrary—as subject to unreasonably long delays between Land Boards and the Subordinate Boards; contrary to prior understandings of the rule of law; and diverging from expectations of public order that is regular and predictable" (Werbner 2004: 111–112). "Ethnic citizens," especially in periurban tribal land, readily challenge the decisions of land boards that appear to favor "ethnic settlers" or total strangers (immigrants). Recently, for example, residents of Tlokweng, a Batlokwa village just outside of Gaborone, opposed the allocation of a big plot to the Botswana Housing Corporation (BHC), advancing as reason that the "authentic" children of the village community (bana ba Batlokwa) do not have land. This is indeed most telling, at a closer look, because many of the same children of Batlokwa have purchased homes from the same BHC elsewhere in the city and country, sold "tribal" land they were freely allocated in Tlokweng to "outsiders," and acquired land in other parts of the country. Because tribal land does not have the same value everywhere, periurban villages near cities where land is more valuable, want greater protection of their indigeneity than land boards, in their current structure and role, can offer. Paradoxically, the customary Tswana policy of inclusion is being reconfigured by those managing entitlements to the fruit of economic growth in an era of accelerated flows of capital and migrants (Nyamnjoh 2006).

Botswana's linguistic and ethnic structure (see Table 1) represents the hierarchy of indigeneity in cultural and political terms. Although the Bantu languages (headed by Setswana) and the groups to which they are indigenous are the most visible socially, culturally and politically, the Khoesan languages and the Basarwa–Bushman–Khoesan that speak them are the most marginalized, despite the fact they are historically the most autochthonous. In particular, Setswana, the language of the nine Tswana groups ("tribes"), has over the centuries assumed a dominant position, thanks mainly to the prominence of the Tswana under colonial rule: the fact that the Tswana "tribes" as imagined by the European colonizers had, more than all others, lent themselves to "convenient administration" and "convenient evangelization" (MacGaffey 1995: 1031), made the group and their language the most visible to the colonial administration, to the missionaries and ultimately to all the other groups. Today, English and Setswana exclusively enjoy the status of official languages for state institutions and public business, while the languages of the "ethnic minorities" have been relegated to the margins, disallowed even in schools and localities in which such minorities are in the majority. Curiously, although historically the last to migrate to the territory, the splinter Tswana groups variously named after their founder leaders have, thanks to their hegemony, succeeded in legitimating their version of indigeneity and claims of authenticity over all others as the "first" citizens of the Botswana nation-state. This has happened despite the fact that the Tswana are neither a homogeneous unit, nor their language (Setswana) without variants.[1] Historians and anthropologists have documented inter- and intra-Tswana conflicts, ranging from land to succession disputes, without excluding schisms (Comaroff 1978; Comaroff and Roberts 1981; Nyamnjoh 2003; Parsons et al 1995; Ramsay et al. 1996), a clear indication that there is no essential Tswana entity, but, rather, a marriage of convenience where harmony is more assumed than evident.

Table 1. Botswana's Linguistic and Ethnic Structure

Linguistic category	Language Family Group	Associated Ethnic Groups	Administrative District
SeTswana	Bantu, Southern	BaKgatla	Kgatleng
		BaKwena	Kweneng
		BaNgwaketse	Southern: Ngwaketse
		BaNgwato	Central
		BaRolong	Southern: Barolonge
		BaTlokwa	South East
		BaTawana	North West
		BaLete	South East
		BaKhurutshe	Central
Ikalanga	Bantu, Eastern	BaKalanga	North East/ Central
Se-Birwa	Bantu, Southern	BaBirwa	Central
Se-Tswapong	Bantu, Southern	BaTswapong	Central
Se-Kgalagadi	Bantu, Southern	BaKgalagadi	Kgalagadi, Kweneng,
		BaBgologa	North West
		BaBoalongwe	
		BaNgologa	
		BaShaga	
		BaPhaleng	
Shiyeyi	Bantu, Western?	BaYeyi	North West
Otjiherero	Bantu, Western	BaHerero/BaNderu	North West
Thimbukushu	Bantu, Western	Hambukushu	North West
Sesubiya	Bantu, Central	BaSubiya/ Bekuhane	North West
Nama	Khoesan	Nama	Kgalagadi/Ghanzi
!Xoo	Khoesan, Southern	!Xoo	Kgalagadi &others
Ju/'hoan	Khoesan, Northern	Ju/'hoan	North West
Makaukau	Khoesan, Northern	MaKaukau	Ghanzi
Naro	Khoesan, Central	Naro	Ghanzi
/Gwi	Khoesan, Central	/Gwi	Southern/Ghanzi
//Gana	Khoesan Central	//Gana	Central/Ghanzi
Kxoe	Khoesan, Central	Kxoe	North West
Shua	Khoesan, Cenral	Shua	Central
Tshwa	Khoesan, Central	Tshwa	Central/Kwenene
Afrikaans	Indo-European	Afrikaans	Ghanzi

Source: Selolwane 2004.

To make the case for flexible indigeneity, we should examine contested assumptions about liberal democracy, congruence between polity and culture, and individual rights in Botswana closely. Although the rhetoric clearly emphasizes democracy as an individual and civic right, the reality is one that seeks to bridge individual and group rights, civic and cultural citizenship, thereby making Botswana democracy far more complex than is often acknowledged in liberal terms (Comaroff 1978; Comaroff and Roberts 1981; Holm and Molutsi 1989; Kerr 2000; Nyamnjoh 2003; Schapera 1994 [1938]: 53–88; Werbner 2004). Although legal provisions might promise civic citizenship to all in principle, in practice inequalities prevail among individuals and groups, especially along rigid lines of politically constructed indigeneity. Being indigenous thus becomes a matter of degree and power relations, thereby making some less Batswana than others, even as they are armed with the same token Omang (Identity Card) and inspired or protected in principle by the same constitution.

In the past (and still very much today in certain circles), Tswana for example, have to various degrees claimed for themselves the status of landlords, making others tenants, who have earned recognition and entitlements over time. It must be noted, however, that much has been done to liberalize land policies to empower the individual (regardless of ethnic origin) more. Elected land boards now have authority over the land in "tribal" territories. Under state law a citizen may claim and hold land from a land board anywhere in the country, but the past "tribal" order, with subjects holding land under chiefs, still has a hold in everyday attitudes and in the popular imagination (Werbner 2004: 109–130), as noted of Mogoditshane and Tlokweng. Legal pluralism may prove complicated, and in practice being able to get what one is officially entitled is not always easy. As the squatter problem in Mogoditshane demonstrates (Nyamnjoh 2002b: 762–763), in times of crisis, when survival or comfort could imply sacrificing the interests of some, there is a transformation in the politics of indigeneity, one that helps to determine whose interests are to be sacrificed first and whose protected, regardless of provisions for civic citizenship.

Using multiparty elections and other standard indicators, one could make a convincing case for the successful institutionalization of liberal democracy and bureaucratic modernism in Botswana. The country, in fact, is often cited as a rare example of a functioning liberal multiparty democracy in Africa (Holm and Molutsi 1989, 1992; Molomo 2000), even though its ruling Botswana Democratic Party (BDP) has held power continuously since independence in 1966. There is little doubt that liberal democracy in Botswana has contributed greatly to the questioning of the customary patriarchy that has tended to allow for recognition of descent exclusively through the male line. Nor is there doubt about how much the position of women has been enhanced by women's movements (Dow 1995; Emang 1994; Selolwane 1997, 1998).

As for ethnic differences and overt conflicts, these were largely masked or rechanneled until the 1980s, as the state sought to negotiate conviviality by emphasizing consensus and unity. The prevalent Eurocentric rhetoric on nation-building demanded a congruence between polity and culture that tended to be blindly, deafly, and rigidly prescriptive about nationality and indigeneity.

However, a closer look at Botswana reveals a liberal democracy not as uncontested as is often claimed. Kenneth Good argues that over 35 years of multiparty politics has resulted in little more than "elite democracy" (1999a; 2002), and a booming economy has not necessarily yielded better opportunities and higher standards of living for the masses in general, and the destitute Basarwa–Khoesan–Bushman minority in particular (1999b). It is obvious that structures alone cannot provide the economic well-being and strategic mobilization needed to guarantee civic rights beyond rhetoric and hierarchies. Democracy, like indigeneity, is an unending project, an aspiration subject to renegotiation with changing circumstances, growing and competing claims by individuals and groups (Nyamnjoh 2005: 1–39).

Whether or not in the past Botswana actually enjoyed a national consensus, free of ethnic tensions, that is not the case now. Long-standing assumptions of citizenship and nationhood are being questioned in ways very similar to what has been observed elsewhere in Africa during this era of accelerated globalization (Akindès 2004; Alubo 2004; Bayart et al. 2001; Geschiere and Nyamnjoh 1998, 2000; Halisi et al. 1998; Harnischfeger 2004; International Crisis Group [ICG] 2004; Mamdani 2001; Nnoli 1998). Minorities in Botswana are employing a variety of methods to seek better "political representation, material entitlements, and cultural recognition" for themselves as groups (Solway 2002). Recently, the focus has been the provisions of sections 77, 78, and 79 of Botswana's constitution, criticized by minority "tribes" for mentioning only the eight principal Tswana "tribes," arguing that such discrimination is contrary to the spirit of democracy, as it assumes a rigid hierarchy of indigeneity that is counter to the ideal of equality of citizenship (Mazonde 2002; Selolwane 2000: 13; Werbner 2002a, 2002b, 2004). The Balopi Commission appointed to investigate on the discriminatory articles of the constitution made public its report in March 2001 (Republic of Botswana 2000: 93–110). The commission contained both radical and conservative elements, but endorsement of any of its more dramatic recommendations was more likely to be hailed by minority groups than by Tswana with vested interests in the status quo.

Unsurprisingly, an initial government draft white paper informed by the Balopi Commission Report met with approbation from the minority "tribes" and resistance from the Tswana majority. The situation pushed President Mogae, himself from a minority "tribe"—Batalaote, to embark on a nationwide "explanation tour" of different kgotla. The initial white paper was criticized by the major "tribes," who believed it might erode chieftaincy in Botswana by emphasizing territoriality over birthright, and viewed it as dividing the nation by "placating minority tribes to the detriment of the rights of tribes that are mentioned in the Botswana Constitution."[2] Especially problematic for the major "tribes" was the amendment of certain sections of the constitution, and membership of the House of Chiefs. On the latter, the draft white paper had argued that, "it makes sense to remove the ex-officio status in the membership of the House and subject each member of the House to a process of designation by morafe [tribe]. The same individual may be redesignated for another term if morafe so wishes." In drafting the white paper, a central concern was to ensure that "territoriality rather than actual or perceived membership of a tribal or ethnic group should form the fundamental basis for representation in the House of Chiefs." Sections 77, 78, and 79 of the constitution were to be replaced with new sections "cast in terms calculated to ensure that no—'reasonable'—interpretation can be made that they discriminate against any citizen or tribe in Botswana." The draft white paper also endorsed creating new regional constituencies, "which are neutral and bear no tribal or ethnic sounding names." Regions were to have electoral colleges of Headmen of Record up to Head of Tribal Administration to designated members, and each region was to be entitled to one member of the House. The President would appoint three special members, "for the purpose of injecting special skills and obtaining a balance in representation."

However, under pressure from the major (Tswana) "tribes," President Mogae reportedly "backtracked" on some key aspects of the draft white paper such as more equal representation in the House of Chiefs and change of names of some regions. He appointed a panel to redraft the relevant sections in time for submission to parliament. In a "war of words" meeting with Bangwato (the leading Tswana "tribe") in Serowe, the President was told, among other things: "It is of course fair that some [minor] tribes should be represented at the House of Chiefs, but their chiefs should still take orders from Sediegeng Kgamane [acting paramount chief of Bangwato]. We do not want chiefs who will disobey the paramount chief and even oppose him while there [in the House of Chiefs]."[3] In his retraction statement, President Mogae stressed that as a democracy, it was only proper for his government to draft "the white paper in good faith with the intention of telling the nation what we as government thought was the best way to implement the motion passed by parliament."[4] The revised white paper, which reintroduced ex officio as "permanent" members and raised the number from eight to 12 and that increased the total membership of the House to 35, was finally adopted by parliament in May 2002. The four additional ex officio members were to be chiefs from the districts of Chobe, Gantsi, North East, and Kgalagadi, elevated to paramount status, while the traditional eight from the Tswana "tribes" were maintained.[5]

The adopted revised white paper was rejected by most minority "tribes," some of whom claimed the changes were "cosmetic" and accused the government of having succumbed to pressure from Tswana "tribes." Petitioning President Mogae, a coalition of minority elite mostly prominent academics in Gaborone, argued the revised and adopted white paper had merely entrenched Tswana domination over other tribes by translating from English into Setswana words such as "House of Chiefs" [Ntlo Ya Dikgosi] and "Chief" [Kgosi], oblivious of the fact that minority "tribes" have different appellations for the same realities (e.g., "chief": She for Bakalanga, Shikati for Bayei). The petition accused the government of betraying its original intention to move from ethnicity to territoriality as a basis for representation, by yielding to Tswana pressure to maintain processes of representation tied to birth. "While the Tswana chiefs will participate on the basis of their birth right as chiefs of their tribes, the non-Tswana groups will be elected to the House as sub-chiefs, that is, of an inferior status." On the contrary, "territoriality as a basis of representation is only applicable to the non-Tswana-speaking tribes" as "their dominant ethnicities remain unrecognised," even for the four regions, which will henceforth have the option to elect representatives or paramount chiefs. And what is worse, non-Tswana "tribes" will not even participate in the election of their chiefs to the Ntlo Ya Dikgosi, because the chiefs "will be elected by government employees serving as subchiefs and chiefs and by the Minister." They considered this process "undemocratic as it takes away the people's rights to participate in the selection of those who should represent them in the House of Chiefs." Also, while it is possible for homogenous Tswana speaking regions to have more than one paramount chief (e.g., Balete and Batlokwa for the southeast district, and Barolong and Bangwaketse for the southern district), this was not possible for other regions shared by Tswana and other tribes (e.g., Tawana and Bayei of the northwest district), a situation that spoke of a hierarchy of ethnic groups, indigeneity and ultimately of citizenship.

The petition also called for "the repeal of tribalistic names of land-boards, which promote the entrenchment of Tswana domination over the rest of the tribes," and insisted that the so-called lack of land of the minorities must not "stand in the way of the recognition of our paramount chiefs, as we the tribes have and live on our own land."[6] Clearly, they argued, "the discrimination complained of has not been addressed," as "The White paper fails to make a constitutional commitment to the liberty and recognition of, and the development and preservation of the languages and cultures of the non-Tswana speaking tribes in the country." Instead, it has entrenched Tswanadom; but "the Tswana speakers will not enjoy their superiority at the expense of our justice under discriminatory laws."[7] Other critics claimed the revised white paper had left unresolved the fundamental issue of tribal inequality, instead bring things "back to square one," thereby making it difficult for the minority tribes to "trust a government like this one."[8] Werbner (2002c; 2004: 86–108) situates the significance of this petition not only in its content, but also as a landmark in alliance politics. The petition demonstrates, as well, the contested nature of democracy and nation-building, and assumptions of indigeneity that have informed and challenged these processes in Botswana.

Although every Botswana national (sing., Motswana; pl., Batswana) can legally claim to be a civic citizen or an ethnic citizen, some, such as BaKalanga, are perceived in certain Tswana circles as less authentic citizens. Indeed, they are presented as having more in common with "total outsiders," Makwerekwere from Zimbabwe and further north. The term *Makwerekwere* is generally employed in a derogatory manner to refer to African immigrants from countries suffering economic downturns. Stereotypically the more dark skinned a local is, the more likely she or he is to pass for Makwerekwere, especially if she or he is not fluent in Setswana (Nyamnjoh 2006: chs. 1 and 2). BaKalanga, who tend to be more dark skinned than the rest, whose articulation of Setswana is less fluent, are also more at risk of being labeled Makwerekwere, at having their indigeneity put to question. In general, the "le-/ma-" (sing., pl., respectively) prefix in Setswana usually designates someone as foreign, different or outside the community, and is often employed to refer to all others whom Tswana consider beneath them. It is not used just for ethnic groups but for any group or profession that seems to be set apart from average folks (Volz 2003).

The fact that BaKalanga are relatively more successful in education and business, and in creating cosmopolitan links with foreigners (Selolwane 2000; Werbner 2002b, 2004: 63–85), only makes their indigeneity more problematic to their Tswana "hosts," who do not hesitate to talk derogatorily of "MaKalaka" instead of the implied tribal equality and familiarity in the use of "BaKalanga." As Selolwane observes, the early access to education by BaKalanga "gave them certain advantages that the other ethnic minorities did not initially have." For instance, not only have they, in real terms, "enjoyed representation as substantive as that of the larger ethnic Tswana groups," their share of seats in parliament increased from 11 percent in 1965 to 17 percent in 2000, making them one of three groups with the largest share of members in parliament and government. This notwithstanding, the Tswana in general, and the BaNgwato in particular, continue to dominate elected office and representation in parliament, even in constituencies where their overlordship has ended, and to have the lion's share of cabinet positions (70 percent average) in government (Selolwane 2004: 24–27).

The most underrepresented of all ethnic minorities are the Ma-(Ba)Sarwa–Bushman (Khoesan). Although the most indigenous in terms of longevity in the territory, they are dismissed as less rightful owners of the country because of their "inability" to indigenize (domesticate) the land through agriculture and permanent settlements. By giving priority to rigid agropastoral and residential usages of land as key determinants of the definition of land rights, policy makers have denied BaSarwa the right to land where they have hunted, gathered, and kept some livestock for centuries if not millennia (Madzwamuse 1998; Wilmsen 1989: 158–194). This denies the BaSarwa the right to determine who they are, where they are, how they are and why they are, thereby stunting both their ethnic and civic citizenships (Saugestad 2001). They are thus rendered invisible and inarticulate by rigid hierarchies of indigeneity designed and imposed by those with ambitions of dominance.

Some frustrated BaSarwa have taken the government of Botswana to court over its claim of ownership of the Central Kgalagadi Game Reserve, created in 1961 by a colonial administration with mixed versions of what the intention was. One version is that the reserve was intended to "settle" the "nomadic" BaSarwa, whose land had been encroached by big cattle ranches, into a parcel of land that could keep them from "trespassing" in the now privately owned encircling land. Another version is that the reserve was created to preserve the hunter-gatherer livelihood of the BaSarwa. For many years, the lives of the peoples in the reserve have become more sedentary, and now the government is using their adaptability as a case against their continued occupation of the reserve. They have, since 2002, been forced to relocate just outside the reserve. Without significant educated elite of their own, BaSarwa opposed to relocation have drawn on international support to rekindle their dreams of indigeneity and entitlements as "the first people of the Kalahari." However, they have received little sympathy from other ethnic groups in Botswana, despite the fact that all of these other groups, are preoccupied with their own politics of recognition, representation, and entitlements. Other Batswana are quick to point to the nomadic livelihood of the BaSarwa as the cause of their poverty, rather than a measure of their indigeneity.

One consequence of the stereotypes and attitudes of superiority displayed by other Batswana is that the BaSarwa have never been directly represented in parliament nor in most other public structures. They have had minimal access and representation and have been treated instead as barbarians at the fringes, capable of little more than servitude and subjection. In this way, they epitomize in a postcolonial setting what Africans as "natives" or "indigenes" collectively represented to the civilizing mission of the colonial gaze. The BaKalanga, by contrast, have regained some lost recognition through civic citizenship thanks to their modern education and cosmopolitan connections. The BaSarwa "position contrasts sharply with the situation of other ethnic groups who, though excluded over time, have been able to establish a parliamentary presence." On the contrary, with the exception of the BaLete, "all ethnic Tswana groups have consistently enjoyed some representation for most of the period since the advent of Parliament" in 1965 (Selolwane 2004: 21–22), thereby circumscribing structural power to politically constructed notions of indigeneity that have little bearing with the history of mobility and effective presence on the territory that is Botswana.

The fact that the name of the country and its citizens derives directly from the dominant Tswana tribe, is revealing in itself. The elite of an ethnic minority such as BaKalanga, although perceived to be dominant economically and in the state bureaucracy, seem convinced these other indicators are more significant signs of success and belonging (Werbner 2004). This explains, in part, why the BaKalanga and other elite members of some minority ethnic groups, opted for an ethnic submission to the Balopi Commission, with some arguing for a change of name from "Botswana" to "Kgalagadi" to honor the very first occupants of the territory.[9] As Andrew Murray notes, the definition of the "nation" has been "manipulated to provide Tswana culture with a monopoly of political legitimacy in Tswanadom's new guise, the Republic of Botswana" (Murray 1990: 35). Although all may be Batswana (indigenes) in relation to present-day immigrants and to the outside world, not everyone is a Motswana in terms of ethnic (cultural) identity and national politics, even though they may have a longer ancestry in the territory than those now policing indigeneity. Some have maintained cultural and political advantages and privileges inherited from the colonial era, and even greatly magnified in the postcolonial politics of nation-building (Comaroff and Comaroff 1997; Parsons et al. 1995; Ramsay et al. 1996; Volz 2003). Others are yet to enjoy the cultural and political citizenship they believe they deserve in a democracy, even when that same democracy has favored them economically and professionally, as is largely the case with the BaKalanga elite (Selolwane 2004; Werbner 2004). Indigeneity is a matter of power and degree, even for nationals of the same country, as they are selectively drawn on to claim liberation or to justify exclusion.

Challenging Democracy, Negotiating Indigeneity

Postindependence nation-building has meant the privileging of large-scale over small-scale indigeneity. The quest for congruence between culture and polity has resulted in the undue essentialization and oppression or celebration of identities while overlooking ongoing contradictions, contestations, and clamors for rights and entitlements. However, as the pursuit of nation-building increasingly fails to justify the sacrifices made in its name, individuals and communities become more vociferous about the inequalities such sacrifices have engendered or exacerbated. The upsurge in tension around ethnic belonging and access to power and resources in Botswana, speaks for the continuous relevance of group and cultural solidarities in the face of the uncertainties of neoliberal possibilities. "Decentralised despotism" constructed or appropriated by the colonial state (Mamdani 1996) is being drawn on in postcolonial Botswana either to fight against inherited discrimination or to protect a heritage of privileges. Batswana, even the most modernized, seem reluctant to be identified solely as nationals. Few of them, it seems, are too cosmopolitan to be indigenous as well: it is fascinating to watch elites distribute their time between their modern workplaces in the cities on the one hand, and their home villages and cattle posts in the lands on the other hand (Werbner 2002b, 2004: 63–85). That cultural citizenship remains of utmost importance to Batswana elite, regardless of their subscription to the "modern" civic regime of rights, is further evidenced by the widespread reluctance to bargain away their indigeneities. Despite over 500 years of interethnic marriages and relationships, the patriarchal customs of cultural communities have ensured the illusion of ethnic purity by stubbornly adhering to traditions of descent defined so narrowly. This juridicopolitical or structural rigidity emphasizes cultural essentialism despite a reality of flexible indigeneity.

Liberal democracy, especially as exported to Africa, has not been too keen to acknowledge and provide adequately for such social nuances in its articulation of citizenship (Nyamnjoh 2005). Yet in parts of the continent not only does indigeneity matter, struggles for cultural rights are rife and include cases of disenfranchised majorities seeking redress against a state controlled by a minority. Thus, for example, in South Africa the white minority still effectively controls virtually all "modern" cultural industries and institutions of cultural reproduction. The fact is that liberal democracy promises political, economic, and cultural enrichment for all, but is able to provide only for a few, and in uncertain ways. Its rhetoric of opening up, of cosmopolitanism and abundance, is sharply contradicted by the structural reality of closures, rigid indigeneity, and want for most of its disciples within and between cultural communities and states. An emphasis on winner-takes-all politics has tended to downplay the reality of migratory flows that challenge rigid claims of indigeneity, while blindly yielding to the dictates of those powerful enough to override even the legitimate claims of relatively more.

In July 2000, *Mmegi Monitor* published an open letter by a "Concerned Motswana Citizen" accusing "Makalaka" (BaKalanga) of being from Zimbabwe, of using their tribalism to monopolize economic opportunities and public service jobs, and of being hungry for power over "real Batswana."[10] Although historically more indigenous to the territory, BaKalanga, according to the "concerned Mostwana" were considered as not quite belonging, as being less indigenous than their Tswana counterparts, "real Batswana." Although this letter pointed to evidence of cracks in the national consensus, which supposedly had kept Botswana in one piece for 34 years, Mmegi Monitor's publication of it was criticized in certain circles as divisive and xenophobic. Two months later, another opinion piece was featured in the Mmegi, accusing BaKalanga of hypocrisy by screaming oppression and constitutional discrimination, while "in things that matter most to individual's daily lives they are the most intolerable, tribalistic and frustrating group of people." BaKalanga, according to this opinion, were frustrating the ambitions of the very Tswana whom they accused of dominance, by monopolizing positions in the state bureaucracy, and organizing clandestine nocturnal meetings to frustrate them even further (Nyamnjoh 2002b).

These concerns in the media were preceded by the conference on Challenging Minorities, Difference and Tribal Citizenship in Botswana in May 2000, at which BaKalanga were the most prominent and the most vocal minority. As conference organizer and long-standing researcher on the BaKalanga, Richard Werbner devoted his keynote address to how BaKalanga elite employ cosmopolitan ethnicity as a coping mechanism to foster interethnic partnerships without sacrificing difference entirely (Werbner 2002b, 2004: 63–85). By "cosmopolitan ethnicity," Werbner means a sort of ethnic indigeneity that is at once inward and outward looking, and that "builds inter-ethnic alliances from intra-ethnic ones, and constructs difference while transcending it." Being cosmopolitan, in this sense, "does not mean turning one's back on the countryside, abandoning rural allies or rejecting ethnic bonds" (Werbner 2002a: 731–732). The conference reportedly "raised a storm" in Tswana circles, and newspapers singled out a paper by Anderson Chebanne (a Kalanga senior lecturer and vice dean at the University of Botswana), which pointed out that language rights were human rights, and lamented the fact that in a country of at least 21 indigenous languages, "only one language, Setswana, has a status which has made it to benefit from the developments of the last three decades" (Chebanne 2002: 47).[11]

Over time, especially since the arrival of the Tswana groups approximately 500 years after the Kalanga and the Kgalagadi had settled in the territory, "a process of social hierarchization of … languages has emerged in tandem with the social ranking of the speakers of these languages," to the effect that today all Khoesan languages, despite having the longest roots in the territory, "occupy the lowest social ranking nationally as well as within district communities," thanks mainly to the systematic displacement, subjugation and absorption of Khoesan by successive groups of Bantu migrants. Tswana were particularly centralizing and subjugating, as they sought domestication of the territory and competing claims of indigeneity (Selolwane 2004: 7–10). Setswana, although initially a minority language, has over three centuries risen to majority status; today, it is Botswana's most dominant language, with at least 70 percent of the population identifying it as the primary language and another 20 percent as the secondary language. Setswana is followed by Ikalanga, which is identified by 11 percent as a primary and secondary language (Selolwane 2004: 4–9). Despite being relatively the most well-placed minority group politically and economically, BaKalanga are particularly aggrieved having both lost their land to a British company in colonial times and endured cultural and political subjugation by BaNgwato, whom the British had favored (Selolwane 2004: 10). For being very vociferous about the need for restitution and cultural recognition, BaKalanga, although not "the only ethnic group who could claim to have sacrificed their language and culture for the greater ideal of nation-building," have been singled out in particular for attacks by others who perceive them to have benefited disproportionately in material and economic terms (Selolwane 2000: 17–18).

This is a point shared by Methaetsile Leepile (former editor of Mmegi, proprietor of a new Setswana language newspaper—*Mokgosi* (the *Echo*), and a staunch Tswana critic of "doublespeak among Bakalanga intellectual spokespersons"). Leepile considers the BaKalanga elite as not only having the lion's share of opportunities, but of being dishonest about their power and influence. This elite, contrary to what they claim, "are not working for national unity, peace and development." To him, "they are in fact in a position to dictate the tempo and direction of change and to make strategic interventions when it suits their peculiar interests." In this regard, although "the Kalanga elite has always been resentful of other people," of recent "they have attempted to embrace other ethnic groups in their fight against what they perceive to be majoritarian over-rule." BaKalanga rhetoric of marginalization, he argues, conceals the fact of their dominance and elite status in various spheres of life in Botswana. He singles out the ethnic composition of the public service and uses the judiciary (in which allegedly 7 of the 13 Batswana judges are Kalanga and only two come from "the so-called principal eight merafhe [tribes])" to show how dominant BaKalanga really are. The BaKalanga struggle, like that of the Bayei spearheaded by Lydia Nyathi Ramahobo (Nyati-Ramahobo 2002)[12] is not so much "for linguistic and cultural recognition, but the quest for power and control of the resources of this country by those people who already possess or have a measure of control of these things."[13] In general, he argues that "the Bakalanga are very well placed in positions of power and influence" and that "It is the Bakalanga who are marginalizing other ethnic groups not the other way round" (Leepile n.d.).

Batshani Ndaba is editor of the *Sunday Tribune,* a paper he started publishing on April 16, 2000.[14] He is Kalanga and has served as president of the Society for the Promotion of Ikalanga Language (SPIL). He was a signatory both to a BaKalanga submission to the Balopi Commission, and also to another document to President Mogae by some BaKalanga challenging the conclusions of the Balopi Commission.[15] Asked to situate growing anti-Kalanga sentiments in certain circles, Ndaba pointed to several factors that include "a longstanding war between BaKalanga and Setswana speaking stock." According to him, BaKalanga have never forgotten nor forgiven the humiliation of a chief of theirs—She John Madawo Nswazwi—by chief Tshekedi Khama of the BaNgwato, "because he had refused to be made a second-class citizen in his country of birth."[16] A second factor is the fact that "BaKalanga are hardworking." According to Ndaba, BaKalanga have invested a lot in schooling, which explains much of their achievements under the postcolonial state. In his words, unlike their Tswana counterparts who had land and cattle to tend, BaKalanga "are people who have had no land, no opportunity to tribal land of their own, where you could look after your father's cattle as a heritage; and the only way you could survive in future was to get an education and get a job."

Having invested in education it is hardly surprising, Ndaba argues, that BaKalanga should qualify for various levels of expertise as "civic" citizens in the Botswana nation-state, and as civic citizens, take advantage of the authority accorded land boards over the land in "tribal" territories, that makes it possible for all citizens to claim and hold land from a land board anywhere in the country. "A lot of BaKalanga are now occupying fairly influential positions, not because they are BaKalanga but because of merit, qualification, experience and those are some of the basis for appointing people to positions of responsibility" (see also Werbner 2004: 146–187; Selolwane 2004) A final factor, according to Ndaba, is the fact that: "BaKalanga, unlike other so-called minority groups, have refused to be ruled over and subjugated to inferiority status by other so-called majority, and therefore that is why we are hated. We have refused." From this and other accounts (cf. Mazonde 2002; Selolwane 2004; Werbner 2004), it is evident that while the BaKalanga have, relatively speaking, benefited significantly from their civic citizenship, they sorely miss the benefits of ethnic citizenship, and, as "reasonable radicals" (Werbner 2004) their well-educated, well-connected, and well-placed elite are determined to do all it takes to affirm and legitimate their indigeneity.

Although BaKalanga may have an influential elite, other non-Tswana minority groups (with perhaps the exception of the Wayeyi—Nyati-Ramahobo 2002), do not enjoy the same quality elite, and are thus easily maneuvered and manipulated by the state, on the one hand, and external agents, on the other hand. The BaSarwa–Khoesan are a good case in point, as they must depend largely on forces external to their communities (e.g., Survival International, Ditshwanelo, mass media, anthropologists, and other human rights advocacy groups)—who, sometimes worse than the state, are often insensitive to the nuances and creative dynamism of local identity configurations—to make their case for recognition and representation as a cultural community with a right to indigeneity.

Flexible Indigeneity

It should be evident that indigeneity is a process subject to renegotiation with rising expectations by individuals and groups. For one thing, political, cultural, historical, and, above all, economic realities, determine what form and meaning the articulation of indigeneity assumes in any given context. The possession of rights is something individuals and communities may be entitled to, but who actually enjoys rights does not merely depend on what individuals and groups may wish, are entitled to under the law, by birth, or in a universal declaration of one kind or another. Increasingly and quite paradoxically in Botswana and elsewhere, globalization and the accelerated flow of capital, goods, electronic information and migration it occasions, is exacerbating insecurities, uncertainties and anxieties, bringing about an even greater obsession with autochthony, and the building or reactualization of rigid indigeneity (Geschiere and Nyamnjoh 2000; Comaroff and Comaroff 2000).

Productively addressing surging uncertainties and anxieties is hardly to be accomplished through a narrow and abstract definition of indigeneity much less in any politics of exclusion and difference within and between groups, indigenous or foreign. The answer is not simply to shift from a state-based to a more individual-based universal conception of citizenship, as some have suggested (Basok 2004), because this fails to provide for the rights of collectivities, however construed. The answer to the impermanence of present-day achievements, lies in incorporating "outsiders" without stifling difference, and in the building of new partnerships across those differences. The answer, in other words, is in a cosmopolitan life informed by allegiances to cultural meanings drawn from different sources in the rich repertoire of multiple, kaleidoscopic encounters by individuals and groups (Waldon 1995; Werbner 2002b, 2004: 63–85). Englund talks of a cosmopolitanism informed by relationships that stress "a deterritorialized mode of belonging," that makes it possible to feel at home away from home (Englund 2004a).

President Mogae of Botswana shares this vision: "I expect all people—men and women—of tribally or regionally or racially mixed parentage to be the glue that holds this nation together."[17] Ethnic communities in Botswana have hardly if ever, been of highly exclusive membership. Within each so-called tribe, are multiplicities of "tribal identities," often expressing their variety by the different myths of origin and symbolic orders they identify themselves by (Selolwane 2004). Even the wards (makgotla) or clusters of homesteads in a village sharing a common root are many and diverse, each with a family tree that hardly ever points to a common ancestry between all that can unite solidly the entire village. This speaks of a patchwork and multiple layers that the rigid indigeneity implicit in the distinction between "ethnic citizens" and "ethnic settlers" hides, and appeals to a sort of flexible indigeneity, which Botswana can attest to historically (Murray 1990: 34). Indeed, African communities are historically renowned for their flexibility of mobility and indigeneity (de Bruijn et al. 2001; MacGraffey 1995), a reality only enhanced by the arbitrary nature of colonial boundaries, on the one hand, and a mainstream philosophy of life, agency, and responsibility that privileges people over profit, on the other hand. The history of Botswana demonstrates such flexible modes of belonging that make it difficult to claim identities in essentialist terms. Over the years, the real sociology and anthropology of Botswana's constituent communities suggest far more contradiction, contestation, negotiation, interdependence and conviviality in the identities of ordinary people and communities than is often acknowledged or provided for politically, culturally or in scholarship.

The tendency especially in Africa has been for scholars to deemphasize small-scale "ethnic" in favor of large-scale "civic" citizenship, whose juridicopolitical basis is uncritically assumed to be more inclusive than the cultural basis of ethnic citizenship (Mamdani 1996, 2000). The mistake has been to focus analysis almost exclusively on institutional and constitutional arrangements, thereby downplaying the hierarchies and relationships of inclusion and exclusion informed by race, ethnicity, class, gender, and geography that determine indigeneity in real terms (Alubo 2004; An-Na'im 2002; Englund and Nyamnjoh 2004; Harnischfeger 2004; Nyamnjoh 2005). There has been too much focus on "rights talk" and its "emancipatory rhetoric," and too little attention accorded the contexts, meanings, and practices that make indigeneity possible for some but an aspiration relentlessly deferred for most (Englund 2000, 2004b). The concept of cultural citizenship has actually won itself more disciples recently, not least from among scholars, who are no longer simply keen on juridicopolitical citizenship but also on claiming indigeneity over and beyond the essentialist identities the state has to offer (Halsteen 2004; Nnoli 1998; Nyamnjoh and Rowlands 1998; Werbner 2004; Werbner and Gaitskell 2002).

The history of difficulty at implementing rigid notions of the "nation-state," "indigeneity" and "citizenship" in Africa attests to the gross inadequacy of a narrow and inflexible juridicopolitical regime of rights and entitlements in a context where individuals and communities are questioning the Western monopoly over "freedom of imagination" and challenging themselves to think of "new forms of the modern community" and "new forms of the modern state" (Chatterjee 1993: 13). The challenge is clearly to hearken to the reality of Africans and their communities at work in laboratories that experiment with different configurations, as they seek broader, more flexible regimes of indigeneity. Here meaningful cultural, political, economic recognition, and representation could be negotiated for individuals and groups to counter the ever-diminishing circles of inclusion imposed by race, ethnicity, class, gender, and geography.

Throughout the world civic citizenship is facing hard times, as multitudes clamor for inclusion by challenging the myopia implicit in the conservative juridicopolitical rhetoric and practices of nation-states (Antrobus 2004; Imam et al. 1997; Kabeer 2005; Kerr et al. 2004; Yuval-Davis and Werbner 1999). Just as cultural, economic, and social citizenship are as valid as juridicopolitical citizenship, collective, group or community citizenship is as valid as individual citizenship, to be claimed at every level, from the most small-scale local to the most megascale global level. The emphasis should be on the freedom of individuals and communities to negotiate inclusion, opt out and opt in with flexibility of belonging in consonance with their realities as straddlers of a kaleidoscope of identity margins.

Obviously, such flexible indigeneity is incompatible with the prevalent illusion that the nation-state is the only political unit permitted to confer citizenship in the modern world. Neither is it compatible with a regime of rights and entitlements that is narrowly focused on yet another chimera—"the autonomous individual." Everywhere the price of perpetuating these illusions has been the proliferation of ultranationalism, chauvinism, racism, tribalism, and xenophobia that have consciously denied the fragmented, multinational, and heterogeneous cultural realities of most so-called nation-states. The tendency has been for indigeneity thus inspired to assume the stature of a giant compressor of, especially, cultural differences. Almost everywhere, this narrow model has cherished hierarchies based on race, ethnicity, class, gender, and geography, that have tended to impose on perceived inferior others decisions made by those who see themselves as more authentic or more deserving of citizenship. Indigeneity that hails from such a celebration of insensitivities is clearly not a model for a future of increased mobility and increased claims for rights, recognition, and representation by its individual and collective victims.

Notes

1. The fact of writing, printing, and teaching Setswana in schools, has helped toward the crystallization of a standardized version, against which all others can be measured as deviations.

2. The *Botswana Gazette,* April 2, 2002 and April 10, 2002; see also *Mmegi Monitor,* March 26, 2002.

3. The *Midweek Sun,* May 1, 2002; *Mmegi Monitor,* April 2, 2002.

4. See the *Botswana Gazette,* April 10, 2002; see also *Mmegi Monitor,* March 26, 2002.

5. See the *Botswana Guardian,* May 3, 2002.

6. The *Midweek Sun,* May 22, 2002, "Minorities Petition President Mogae."

7. *Mmegi Monitor,* May 21, 2002, "Minorities Petition Mogae."

8. *Mmegi,* May 24, 2002, "Politicians Criticise Mogae."

9. Interview with Sechele Sechele, editor of the *Mmegi.*

10. *Mmegi Monitor,* July 11–17, 2000, an open letter by a "Concerned Motswana Citizen."

11. See also *Mmegi,* June 2, 2000, on "Minorities conference raises a storm."

12. See the *Botswana Guardian,* August 10, 2001, "Leepile Forces Tribalism on the Table," for an example of press representation of Lydia Nyathi Ramahobo's position.

13. See the *Botswana Gazette,* August 29, 2001, for Methaetsile Leepile's reply to Edward Maganu, "Dealing with the Ethnic Cutworm."

14. Interview with Batshani Ndaba, July 30, 2001.

15. See the *Midweek Sun,* July 18, 2001, for "BaKalanga Challenge Balopi Commission"; see also Werbner 2004: 48–62.

16. For more on this version of history, see the *Sunday Tribune,* September 9, 2001, for "Clearing Cobwebs off Leepile's mind," by Eric Moseja. See also Werbner 2004: 66–85.

17. See the *Sunday Tribune,* August 12, 2001.

References

Akindès, F. 2004. Les Racines de la crise militaro-politique en Côte d'Ivoire. Dakar: CODESRIA.

Alubo, O. 2004. Citizenship and nation-building in Nigeria: New challenges and contestations. *Identity, Culture and Politics* 5 (1): 135–161.

An-Naim, A. A., ed. 2002. *Cultural transformation and human rights in Africa*. London: Zed Books.

Antrobus, P. 2004. *The global women's movement: Origins, issues and strategies*. London: Zed Books.

Basok, T. 2004. Post-national citizenship, social exclusion and migrants rights: Mexican seasonal workers in Canada. *Citizenship Studies* 8 (1): 47–64.

Bayart, J.-F., P. Geschiere, and F. Nyamnjoh. 2001. Autochtonie, Démocratie et Citoyenneté en Afrique. *Critique Internationale* 10: 177–194.

Campbell, E. K., and J. O. Oucho. 2003. *Changing attitudes to immigration and refugee policy in Botswana*. SAMP Migration Policy Series, 28. Cape Town: Idasa.

Chatterjee, P. 1993. *The nation and its fragments: Colonial and postcolonial histories, Princeton*. Princeton: Princeton University Press.

Chebanne, A. 2002. Minority languages and minority peoples: Issues on linguistic, cultural and ethnic death in Botswana. In *Minorities in the millennium: Perspectives from Botswana*, edited by Isaac N. Mazonde, 47–56. Gaborone: Light Books.

Comaroff, J. L. 1978. Rules and rulers: Political processes in a Tswana chiefdom. Man *(n.s.)* 13: 1–20.

Comaroff, J., and J. Comaroff. 1997. Of revelation and revolution: The dialectics of modernity on a South African frontier, vol. 2. Chicago: Chicago University Press.

———. 2000. Millennial capitalism and the culture of neoliberalism. *Public Culture* 12 (2): 291–343.

Comaroff, J. L., and S. Roberts. 1981. *Rules and processes: The cultural logic of dispute in an African context*. Chicago: University of Chicago Press.

de Bruijn, M., R. van Dijk, and D. Foeken, eds. 2001. *Mobile Africa: Changing patterns of movement in Africa and beyond*. Leiden, the Netherlands: Brill.

Dow, U., ed. 1995. *The citizenship case: The attorney general of the Republic of Botswana vs. Unity Dow, court documents, judgements, cases and material*. Gaborone: Lentswe l a Lesedi.

Durham, D. 1993. *Images of culture: Being Herero in a liberal democracy.* Ph.D. dissertation, Department of Anthropology, University of Chicago.

Emang, Basadi. 1994. *The women's manifesto: A summary of Botswana women's issues and demands.* Gaborone: Lentswe la Lesedi.

Englund, H. 2000. The dead hand of human rights: Contrasting Christianities in post-transition Malawi. *Journal of Modern African Studies* 38 (4): 579–603.

——. 2004a. Cosmopolitanism and the Devil in Malawi. *Ethnos* 69 (3): 293–316.

——. 2004b. Towards a critique of rights talk in new democracies: The case of legal aid in Malawi. *Discourse and Society* 15 (5): 527–551.

Englund, H., and F. B. Nyamnjoh, eds. 2004. *Rights and the politics of recognition in Africa.* London: Zed Books.

Fombad, C. M. 1999. Curbing corruption in Africa: Some lessons from Botswana's experience. *International Social Science Journal* 52 (160): 241–254.

Ferguson, J. 1999. *Expectations of modernity: Myths and meanings of urban life on the Zambian Copperbelt.* Berkeley: University of California Press.

Garbutt, R. 2006. White "Autochthony." *ACRAWSA e-journal* 2 (1): 1–16.

Geschiere, P., and F. B. Nyamnjoh. 1998. Witchcraft as an issue in the "politics of belonging": Democratization and urban migrants' involvement with the home village African Studies Review 41 (3): 69–92.

——. 2000. Capitalism and autochthony: The seesaw of mobility and belonging. *Public Culture* 12 (2): 423–452.

Good, K. 1999a. Enduring elite democracy in Botswana. *Democratization* 6 (1): 50–66.

——. 1999b. The state and extreme poverty in Botswana: The San and the destitutes. *Journal of Modern African Studies* 27 (2).

——. 2002. *The liberal model and Africa: Elites against Democracy.* Basingstoke: Palgrave.

Halisi, C. R. D., P. J. Kaiser, and S. N. Ndegwa, eds. 1998. Rethinking citizenship in Africa. *Africa Today* 45: 3–4.

Halsteen, U. 2004. Taking rights talk seriously: Reflections on Ugandan political discourse. In *Rights and the politics of recognition in Africa,* edited by H. Englund, and F. B. Nyamnjoh, 103–124. London: Zed Books.

Harnischfeger, J. 2004. Sharia and control over territory: Conflicts between "settlers" and "indigenes" in Nigeria. *African Affairs* 103 (412): 431–452.

Holm, J. D., and P. Molutsi, eds. 1989. *Democracy in Botswana*. Gaborone: Macmillan Botswana.

———. 1992. State-Society relations in Botswana: Beginning liberalization. In *Governance and politics in Africa*, edited by Goran Hyden and Michael Bratton, 75–98. Boulder, CO: Lynne Rienner.

Imam, A., A. Mama, and F. Sow, eds. 1997. *Engendering African Social Sciences*. Dakar: CODESRIA.

International Crisis Group (ICG). 2004. Côte d'Ivoire: No peace in sight. Africa Report, 82, July 12, Dakar–Brussels: ICG.

Kabeer, N., ed. 2005. *Inclusive citizenship: Meanings and expressions*. London: Zed Books.

Kerr, D. 2000. *Media democracy in Botswana: The Kgotla as myth, practice and post-colonial communication paradigm*. Paper presented at the International Seminar on the Political Economy of the Media in Southern Africa, University of Natal, Durban, South Africa, April 25–29.

Kerr, J., E. Sprenger, and A. Symington, eds. 2004. *The future of women's rights: Global visions and strategies*. London: Zed Books.

Leepile, M. n.d. *The ethnic composition of the public service: The case of the administration of justice and the attorney general's chambers*. Unpublished MS.

MacGaffey, W. 1995. Kongo identity, 1483–1993. *South Atlantic Quarterly* 94 (4): 1025–1037.

Madzwamuse, M. S. 1998. *Basarwa and the land issue: Perceptions of land rights held by the Basarwa*. B.A. Research Project, Department of Sociology, FSS, University of Botswana.

Mamdani, M. 1996. *Citizen and subject: Contemporary Africa and the legacy of late colonialism*. Cape Town: David Philip.

———. 1998. *When does a settler become a Native? Reflections of the colonial roots of citizenship in Equatorial and South Africa*, 208 (n.s.). Cape Town: University of Cape Town

———. 2000. *Beyond rights talk and culture talk*. Cape Town: David Philip.

———. 2001. *When victims become killers: Colonialism, nativism, and the genocide in Rwanda*. Kampala: Fountain Publishers.

Maybury-Lewis, D. 2005. Defining indigenous. *Cultural Survival Quarterly* 29: 1.

Mazonde, I., ed. 2002. *Minorities in the millennium: Perspectives from Botswana*. Gaborone: Lightbooks.

Mercer, D. 2003. "Citizen Minus"?: Indigenous Australians and the Citizenship Question. *Citizenship Studies* 7 (4): 421–445.

Molomo, M. G., guest ed. 2000. Special issue: "Elections and Democracy in Botswana." *Pula* 14 (4).

Murray, A. 1990. *Peoples' rights: The case of BaYei Separatism*. Human and Peoples' Rights Project Monograph, 9. Maseru: National University of Lesotho.

Nnoli, O., ed. 1998. *Ethnic conflicts in Africa*. Dakar: CODESRIA.

Nyamnjoh, F. B. 2002a. "A child is one person's only in the womb": Domestication, agency and subjectivity in the Cameroonian grass-fields. In *Postcolonial subjectivities in Africa*, edited by Richard Werbner, 111–138. London: Zed Books.

——. 2002b. Local attitudes towards citizenship and foreigners in Botswana: An appraisal of recent press stories. *Journal of Southern African Studies* 28 (4): 755–775.

——. 2003. Might and right: Chieftaincy and democracy in Cameroon and Botswana. In *The dynamics of power and the rule of law: Essays on Africa and beyond*, edited by W. van Binsbergen, 121–149. Leiden: Lit Verlag Hamburg–African Studies Centre.

——. 2005. *Africa's media, democracy and the politics of belonging*. London: Zed Books.

——. 2006. *Insiders and outsiders: Citizenship and xenophobia in contemporary southern Africa*. London: CODESRIA–Zed Books.

Nyamnjoh, F. B., and M. Rowlands. 1998. Elite associations and the politics of belonging in Cameroon. *Africa* 68 (3): 320–337.

Nyati-Ramahobo, L. 2002. From a phone call to the high court: Wayeyi visibility and the Kamanakao Asssociation's campaign for linguistic and cultural rights in Botswana. *Journal of Southern African Studies* 28 (4): 685–710.

Parsons, N., W. Henderson, and T. Tlou. 1995. *Seretse Khama 1921–1980*. Gaborone: Macmillan.

Ramsay, J., B. Morton, and T. Mgadla. 1996. *Building a nation: A history of Botswana from 1800 to 1910*. Gaborone: Longman Botswana.

Republic of Botswana. 2000. *Report of the presidential commission of inquiry into sections 77, 78 and 79 of the constitution of Botswana*. Gaborone: Government Printer.

Ritsema, M. 2003. Gaborone, Botswana. In *Encyclopedia of twentieth-century African history*, edited by P. T. Y. Zeleza and D. Eyoh, 231–232. New York: Routledge.

Saugestad, S. 2001. *The inconvenient indigenous: Remote area development in Botswana, donor assistance, and the first people of the Kalahari*. Uppsala: Nordic Africa Institute.

Schapera, I. 1994 [1938]. *A handbook of Tswana law and custom: Compiled for the Bechuanaland Protectorate Administration*. Hamburg: International African Institute and Lit Verlag.

Selolwane, O. D. 1997. Gender and democracy in Botswana: Women's struggle for equality and political participation. In *The state and democracy in Africa*, edited by Georges Nzongola-Ntalaja and Margaret C. Lee, 25–41. Harare: AAPS Books.

——. 1998. Equality of citizenship and the gendering of democracy in Botswana. In *Botswana politics and society*, edited by W. A. Edge and M. H. Lekorwe, 397–411. Pretoria: J. L. van Schaik.

——. 2000. *Botswana: The challenges of consolidating good governance and plural politics*. Paper presented at the OSSREA sponsored Workshop on Promoting Good Governance and Wider Civil Society Participation in Eastern and Southern Africa, Addis Ababa, November 6–8.

——. 2004. *Ethnic structure, inequality and governance of the public sector: Botswana case study*. Paper presented at the UNRISD International Conference on Ethnic Inequality and Public Sector Governance, March 25–27, Riga Latvia. Geneva: UNRISD.

Solway, J. 2002. Navigating the "neutral" state: "Minority" rights in Botswana. *Journal of Southern African Studies* 28 (4): 711–729.

Taylor, I. 2002. The New Africa initiative and the global political economy: Towards the African century or another false start? *Third World Quarterly* 23 (1).

Volz, S. 2003. European missionaries and Tswana identity in the 19th century. *Pula: Botswana Journal of African Studies* 17 (1): 3–19.

Waldon, J. 1995. Minority cultures and the cosmopolitan alternative. In *The rights of minority culture*, edited by W. Kymlicka, 93–119. Oxford: Oxford University Press.

Werbner, R. 2002a. Conclusion: Citizenship and the politics of recognition in Botswana. In *Minorities in the millennium: Perspectives from Botswana*, edited by I. Mazonde, 117–135. Gaborone: Lightbooks.

——. 2002b. Cosmopolitan ethnicity, entrepreneurship and the nation: Minority elites in Botswana. *Journal of Southern African Studies* 28 (4): 632–753.

——. 2002c. Introduction: Challenging Minorities, Difference and Tribal Citizenship in Botswana. *Journal of Southern African Studies* 28 (4): 671–684.

——. 2004. Reasonable radicals and citizenship in Botswana: The public anthropology of Kalanga Elites. Bloomington: Indiana University Press.

Werbner, R., and D. Gaitskell, guest eds. 2002. Special Issue: "Minorities and Citizenship in Botswana." *Journal of Southern African Studies* 28 (4).

Wilmsen, E. N. 1989. *Land filled with flies: A political economy of the Kalahari*. Chicago: University of Chicago Press.

Yuval-Davis, N., and P. Werbner. eds. 1999. *Women, citizenship and difference*. London: Zed Books.

The Native and the Neoliberal Down Under: Neoliberalism and "Endangered Authenticities"

Linda Tuhiwai Smith

This chapter draws on the postcolonial position of "speaking back" to examine the impact of neoliberal policies as developed in New Zealand from 1984 and throughout the 1990s on indigenous Maori communities and their responses to the process of reform and the changed environment. Maori people are the indigenous people of New Zealand whose representatives from different groups, (referred to as "hapu," "iwi," or "tribes") signed the Treaty of Waitangi in 1840 with the British Crown that facilitated British settlement of New Zealand as a colony of the British Empire. Within 15 years of the Treaty of Waitangi, Maori people became a minority within their own lands and were at war with settler groups. After the land wars from the 1850s to the 1870s, the New Zealand Government enacted a range of legislative initiatives that ultimately led to Maori people becoming colonized and marginalized in a settler-controlled society. As has happened in other colonial contexts the Maori population declined and it was thought that Maori people would eventually "die out" (Pool 1991). But in 2006 Maori represent approximately 14 percent of the total New Zealand population and are a highly visible indigenous minority group with a growing rate of participation in New Zealand society.

The term *Maori communities* rather than Maori *tribes* is used in a deliberately loose sense in this chapter to encompass the wide-ranging and dynamic social and political groupings and organizations through which Maori as the indigenous peoples of New Zealand have come to be constituted in the latter part of the 20th century. Government discourse, as expressed in legislation and public policy, has tended to define these groupings as whanau (extended families), hapu ("subtribes") and iwi ("tribes") and apply the terms as fixed and rigid categories. Although the terms are indeed Maori terms and are used by Maori to describe both the way they were traditionally organized and the ways they are currently organized, Maori understandings of them are as flexible and dynamic social institutions. Government legislation and public policy has a tendency to create narrow and rigid definitions that are used as criteria for belonging or for one's identity. In the neoliberal moment of the late 20th century many of these groupings came to be recontested, reconfigured and redefined, and new groupings were constituted such as "urban Maori," or "rangatahi or young Maori." Differing notions of indigeneity have been accorded more legitimacy by the state, such as iwi or tribal structures "mandated" to negotiate settlements with the British Crown, over small groupings of Maori viewed as unofficial or troublesome minorities. The terms such as, whanau, hapu and iwi, may have remained the same but their meanings have been subtly transformed such that while some terms such as *iwi* have been "empowered" by legislative definition such that its legislated meanings have been upheld in the British Court system, others such as "pan-Maori" organizations became marginalized and excluded.

The neoliberal project of the late 20th century produced a challenging and contentious program of economic and social reform that has had far-reaching impacts within states, across regions and across the globe. The fundamental thesis of neoliberal economics has been well documented by its architects such as Milton Friedman, Fredrich Hayek, and James Buchanan, its advocates, for example, Margaret Thatcher, and by its adversaries and critics. Neoliberalism presented an economic theory for addressing issues of social inequality and disadvantage and offered a promise for social inclusion and participation to various marginalized and disadvantaged communities that differed from the models of welfarism that had become a feature of post–WWII social programs. Dismantling the Welfare State alongside major reforms in health and education were key platforms for delivering the promise of inclusion and greater equality. The New Zealand version of Neoliberal reform has been referred to by one of its ardent critics, Jane Kelsey (1993), as "The New Zealand Experiment" partly because New Zealand's isolation constituted a small laboratory to test strategies that could then be applied in structural adjustment programs elsewhere. This experiment seemed to crystallize and bring forth the economic and social ideals that came to be summed up in Britain as Thatcherism, named after Prime Minister Margaret Thatcher, and in the United States as Reaganomics, named after President Ronald Reagan. In New Zealand, the reform process is still referred to popularly as Rogernomics named after a Labour Government Minister of Finance Roger Douglas, who was its initial chief political architect. Neoliberal reform is known for its powerful use of rhetoric and discourse that in 1980s New Zealand undermined leftist critiques of the state by first appropriating them and then applying them as justification for a far reaching reform program that attempted to hollow out the state, reregulate the economy, and privatize many government functions.

The economic reform program began in 1984 under a Labour or center-left Government and continued through the 1990s with a center-right National Government and again under the current Labour Government. Neoliberal economic philosophy has become the dominant and common sense approach to development. The concern of this chapter is not so much the reform agenda itself, but the interaction between this agenda and indigenous Maori communities and the struggles by Maori to sustain a momentum of cultural regeneration, that had been reignited many years earlier, through the darkest periods of reform and the accelerated widening of socioeconomic disparities between Maori and non-Maori that appeared during the height of the reforms. It is important to acknowledge that, because of the history of colonialism, Maori as a group were not deeply wedded to notions of the Welfare State or to the existing models of education and health care for which New Zealand was highly regarded internationally as they had been systematically excluded from the benefits of such systems. The old system was often viewed as patronizing, paternalistic, and racist. A new approach that promised less dependency on a welfare system and more opportunity for choice and for the devolution of the state was viewed with hopeful anticipation by many Maori, especially as it was initially to be delivered by a Labour Government with whom Maori felt they had some kind of compact based on a historic agreement between the Labour Party and a large pan-Maori movement known as the Ratana Church.

Part of what I argue in this chapter is that the neoliberal vision of society and the power by its proponents to implement much of that vision through the political process sought to sever and then reformulate and privatize the relationships between the British Crown and state and Maori people as individuals. Maori communities, tribal entities, and political activists have long argued that the British Crown and Maori have a relationship as equal partners is embodied in the *Te Tiriti o Waitangi* or the Treaty of Waitangi. A second part of the argument is that Maori resisted in quite complicated ways that included co-opting the promises of the reform—for example, the promise of public choice or the devolution of the government bureaucracy—and making them at least mediate what were in fact quite hostile agendas. A third part of the argument is that neoliberalism is not just a little New Zealand experiment, but part of an ambitious agenda that has restructured the global economy through such strategies as free trade agreements and enforced structural adjustment programs in developing countries. In this sense, the impact on Maori communities resonates with other indigenous and minority communities across the world.

At a broader level, the New Zealand Maori example illustrates the ways in which ideas about the "Native" and the lived realities of native or indigenous communities are bound up in and "endangered" by the shifts in the "Settler" and the changes in relations created by the neoliberal global project. The terms *Native* and *Settler* are employed as markers and vestiges of early-20th-century colonial relations or as the "images" of colonized and colonizer that still inform popular discourses and define understandings about race and empire. As postcolonial scholars have argued, however, the oppositional category of settler or native was complicated through systems of power, sex and intermarriage, religion and opportunity, warfare and education, and lived and regulated identities. Even when there were wars between settlers and native Maori communities, there were also complex alliances within and between differing settler and Maori interests with some tribal groups fighting for the British Crown and some missionaries speaking for the rights of Maori. By the end of the 19th century, however, British settlers had established themselves in power and had taken control of all the instruments of colonialism from Great Britain. In the late 20th century, Maori identities have been shaped by deeply constituted precolonial relationships and understandings, by the conditions of colonialism, by what was lost and gained in struggles of resistance and efforts of engagement, and by the opportunities, resources, and discourses that were available at key historical moments. It would be naïve to assume that the "past" either in its precolonial or 19th- and 20th-century colonial formations is not also always present in the way identities, subjectivities, discourses, and social formations are deployed and contested in contemporary relations of indigeneity, of settler societies and native communities.

New Zealand—The Emergence of the Neoliberal Project

In 1984 with the election of a Labour Government, New Zealand began a significant neoliberal program of reform, of deregulation and reregulation of the economy and of a restructuring of the education, health, and welfare systems. As various writers have pointed out, neoliberalism is not a unitary stable ideology but an idea that encompasses various theories and positions that share some features of classical liberal thought about the nature of the individual, the role of the state, and the mechanisms through which individual needs and interests are best met. As Olssen has argued, the market is a key feature of the neoliberal agenda. Olssen lists some of the features of neoliberalism as the notion of economically self-interested individuals, of competition as the major driver for efficiency and quality, of a reduced state, of flexible and deregulated labor markets and free trade and open economies. These doctrines have informed the major political discourse in New Zealand for the last two decades and have framed the lives of a generation who are now adults (Codd 1990; Kearns and Joseph 1997; Kelsey 1993; Moran 1999).

Neoliberal doctrine and the continuous process of reform and institutional restructuring that New Zealand has undergone in the last two decades, and its effects, has had a cumulative and deeply profound effect on New Zealand society. New Zealand has become a more open economy, its international reach has moved from its colonial heritage with Great Britain to Asia, the Pacific, and North America. New Zealand institutions have all been transformed by neoliberal reform and by their own responses to the reforms. In education neoliberalism has been marked by a discourse of education as a marketplace with parents and students as consumers and clients, teachers and schools as self-managing providers of services, and curriculum knowledge as a commodity that can be traded in or traded up for social goodies such as well being and social status (Apple 2001; Olssen 1996). The reform process redesigned the way schools were administered so that they become more competitive and efficient and more accountable to parents and students for outcomes. The reform process redesigned the role of the principal government agency that was responsible for education as a policy ministry with minimal operational capacity in areas such as curriculum. A new agency to review and assess school performance was created. A new curriculum framework was established and implemented. A new agency to accredit qualifications and institutions was established. A user pays system for postsecondary education was instituted with universities and polytechnics having to charge fees that recovered the costs for delivering courses. A highly competitive environment was constituted to keep the system perpetually responsive, efficient, and excellent. Private providers of postsecondary education and training were until very recently able to compete with public institutions for public funding and aspire to attain accreditation to grant degrees. By any measure this represents a major restructuring of the public education system in terms of a new hegemony embedded in the disruption of organizational change.

Maori Cultural Regeneration Going into the 1980s

Maori people have experienced the devastating impacts of British colonization since the 18th century. Education played a significant role in the colonizing process offering the possibility of both civilization on earth and salvation in heaven in the 19th century. The possibilities changed to those of assimilation and integration into the New Zealand society that had been created by the colonizers in the 20th century. Arguably, education until the late 20th century was designed to create and maintain social disparities between *Maori* and *Pakeha* (the Maori-language term for the dominant settler population), and between rich and poor (Simon and Smith 2001). University education, for example, was only ever conceived of as being available to the very few. The school curriculum as another example was organized around the separation of academic and technical subjects. By the mid–20th Century Maori people had begun a more concerted resistance to structural inequality (Walker 1990). The process of resistance produced a political and cultural renaissance in the 1970s that eventually coalesced around two organizing symbols, the Treaty of Waitangi and the Maori language (Walker 1990). Focusing on either or both of these two symbols exposed education as a significant site of contestation.

In 1982 the beginnings of a Maori educational revolution (Smith 1999) was taking place with the development and rapid growth of Te Kohanga Reo (the Maori-language nests) and the rising Maori expectations that education would deliver on its promise of equality of opportunity. Parallel to these developments was the establishment of the Treaty of Waitangi Tribunal and a settlement process for addressing historic and contemporary grievances committed by the British Crown. The settlement process has started to deliver a series of treaty settlements between iwi (nations or tribes) and the British Crown and the development of partnerships of various kinds between the British

Crown, government agencies, and iwi. It is not my intention in this chapter to examine the complex arrangements and dynamic nature of iwi or Maori communities but, rather, to focus on the points at which Maori developments and neoliberal reform intersected and the results that were produced as a consequence.

The development of Te Kohanga Reo, the Maori immersion-language nests, in the early 1980s sparked and continues to inspire the development of a range of Maori initiatives in education that have developed as alternative models within and outside the current system from early childhood to postsecondary tertiary education (Jones et al. 1990). The alternative models include Kura Kaupapa Maori, Maori-language immersion schools, which developed independently of the state but were included as a separate category of state education in the Education Amendment Act 1989 and Wananga or tribal degree granting institutions of higher learning that were also included as a category of the Education Amendment Act 1989. These alternatives were Maori-initiated institutions based on different conceptions of the purpose of education. They were community efforts that challenged the taken for granted hegemony of schooling and, as argued by Graham Smith (2000), revolutionized Maori thinking by demonstrating that Maori people could free their minds from the colonizer and exercise agency in a purposeful, tactical, and constructive way.

These educational alternatives did not begin with state support and, even after they were included in legislation, there was no supportive infrastructure to ensure their sustainability. There was an implicit expectation that in the competitive environment such schools would ultimately fail because according to the neoliberal theory self interested parents would choose to send their children to "quality" schools over schools that taught in the Maori language. In the case of the Wananga the three institutions took a claim to the Waitangi Tribunal related to the disadvantages that were faced by Wananga when the New Zealand Ministry of Education rules regarding capital expenditure were changed. The rule change that was part of the reform process for education meant that existing institutions such as universities, some of which had over a hundred years of state support to build, furnish, and equip their institutions, were able to own their capital infrastructure. Meanwhile, new institutions such as the Wananga were denied state support for buildings and capital and were expected to finance their infrastructure out of income derived on the basis of student numbers (Waitangi Tribunal 1999). The tribunal recommended in favor of the Wananga and the three institutions have almost completed settlement negotiations.

As mentioned earlier, there was little reason prior to 1984 for Maori to support the status quo. The Maori development momentum was already in progress when the neoliberal reform process began. This meant that Maori had already established a cultural and political platform leading into the 1980s for challenging those aspects of the reform process that seemed to threaten Maori development as well as a platform for engaging with the process to influence change. That platform was based on several decades of political protest and some successful use of the legal system to resist government changes. This is not to say that the reform process was welcoming of Maori participation; in fact Maori had to make serious demands to be included or to be heard. At times overseas experts were often brought in by the Business Roundtable, a neoliberal think tank, to dismiss Maori concerns or show how those concerns would be addressed by the new structures (Marshall, Peters, and Smith 1991). Neither can it be claimed that Maori were particularly well organized or mobilized, in fact, the early reforms that privatized the state industries such as forestry created massive Maori unemployment and a high degree of community stress. At its worst period the unemployment rate for Maori males was 24 percent of the available workforce. The significance of the transformation in thinking created by the development of Te Kohanga Reo was that in the absence of organized resistance there was enough critique to provide a counter hegemonic possibility and to have it voiced at every opportunity available. The point is that if Maori had been in disarray without any alternative models, the reform process would have run a different and a likely more devastating course. The reform process has had a disproportionately negative impact on Maori communities widening disparities between Maori and non-Maori in educational achievement, health, and economic status.

Some might argue that Maori educational initiatives since the 1980s have been produced because of the reform process. However, many of these initiatives were created prior to the reforms—this is the case for Te Kohanga Reo, the early childhood language immersion nests (1982), Kura Kaupapa Maori the alternative Maori-language immersion schools (1986), and Wananga (1981). Other initiatives were established in the 1980s as work programs for the growing number of unemployed and "unskilled" that accelerated as a consequence of reforms and continued growing throughout the 1990s. More recently, there have been initiatives that have come about as responses to the impact of reforms such as the high rate of Maori participation in tertiary education. Tertiary education includes bridging courses, basic skills, and literacy programs as well as higher education. A disproportionately high rate of Maori compared to non-Maori participate at subdegree level of the tertiary system. So, although the general rate of participation is high, it is only because the tertiary education system has had to absorb people who are not in the labor market. Similarly, the growing number of "partnerships" between schools, tribal authorities, and the Ministry of Education has occurred in regions where the "pure" version of the self-managing school model actually failed and schools needed support, capacity development, and intermediary agencies to self-manage.

There are a number of lessons learned by communities as they attempted to make sense of, genuinely attempt to comply with, the model that they saw as a self-determination strategy, and then react to the looming crisis. In one sense they were left to their own devices, since communities were viewed as undermining of parents, parents as undermining of professionals, and professionals of failing to understand the radical changes in the system. Some communities subsequently found strength and social cohesion in working together while other communities attempted to create fragmented units within a single school that would cater for their particular "choice" of education. These units included bilingual or immersion classrooms within English-medium schools.

Maori educational institutions continue to face inequities in the system. Te Whare Wananga o Awanuiarangi has been accredited to offer doctoral degrees and offers degrees in environmental studies, indigenous studies, visual arts and culture, and media studies, and also provides community-based programs. In schools there have been a number of educational partnerships between the Ministry of Education and Maori communities that have sought to facilitate a range of interventions that focus on improving Maori achievement and reengage communities in learning and achievement (Ministry of Education 2004). In Maori-language education there are a range of options available to parents who want either partial or full immersion in a Maori medium environment (Ministry of Education 2004). In the curriculum there is a Maori-language curriculum for the core learning areas and there are new curricula for students that draw on aspects of Maori culture such as the visual and performing arts. In the governance and management of education there is an increasing demand for institutions to be more accountable for Maori participation and achievement. In the broader social area there are more Maori organizations providing social services for Maori communities. More broadly there has been some recognition that communities need help to build capacity. Maori engagement with education during the reforms has created new educational pathways and institutions that were not there prior to the reform—the question then is whether the reforms enabled such opportunities to occur or whether the momentum of Maori initiatives provided the capacity by Maori to exploit the moment and insert an alternative agenda.

Maori Responses to Neoliberal Reforms

The neoliberal agenda is held together by a powerful alliance of different interest groups that include fundamentalist Christian groups, neoconservatives, probusiness interests, and libertarians all working in a coalition to *"change our common sense, altering the meanings of the most basic categories, the key words, we employ to understand the social and educational world and our place in it"* (Apple 2001: 9; emphasis mine). Apple, points out that the coalition has its own tensions and contradictions and argues that by understanding these tensions we may find some useful strategies for disrupting the slide to the right. Olssen (2004) argues that these conservative alliances do configure differently in each country and such alliances cannot be read as cohesive or monolithic. In this section of the chapter, I argue that Maori people as one example of a marginalized community have also gained an insight into the contradictions and tensions of the neoliberal agenda and have found ways to either subvert or disrupt the reform agenda or to compromise and accommodate the reform process in ways that may actually have improved the proposed reform model for education.

Over the course of the reforms Maori communities have acquired some critical understandings of the reform agenda and process, of policymaking and the role of Maori as minority voices in the policy process (Durie 2004; Smith 1999; Smith and Smith 1996). There has been a willingness to engage with the state, although always a struggle over the terms of engagement and the outcomes of engagement. There is a thin layer of capacity to do this work while sustaining other programs and there is some recognition by Maori that individuals in the process get "burned out." Maori aspirations continue to be perceived as a threat by non-Maori and the struggle for other developments such as Maori television, customary rights to the foreshore and seabed and a large number of treaty claims rages on with heightened political and media attention. Over time, however, the Maori vision of society has not really wavered from being conceived of as a relationship that is based on the Treaty of Waitangi and on a principle of partnership.

Maori have deployed a range of tactics for engaging with or resisting neoliberal reform. Rather than focus on what the state has learned about reform, I focus on what Maori communities have learned partly because community resistances offer hope to others and partly also because the lessons reveal those aspects of neoliberal reform with which communities can engage and can find ground to shift the agenda. In the New Zealand context Maori communities view themselves as active partners to the British Crown and therefore engage with the state and with policy in quite proactive and often intimate ways, for example Ministers of Government attend Maori gatherings and are told in direct terms what people and communities expect from them. New Zealand is a small country so public figures such as politicians can be contacted directly, one can quite literally email or phone them at work and expect a response from them. Maori gatherings are frequently used as forums for political discussions and if politicians want to engage with Maori then one of the more effective ways to meet Maori is during these major gatherings.

Competing Understandings of the Individual and Community

Neoliberalism views the individual as an entrepreneurial, self-interested, and competitive entity who best understands his or her own interests and needs. This conception of an individual is coupled with a view that the role of the state is as a mediator of the marketplace keeping it open as a place in which individuals can compete. This assumes the idea of a "level playing field." The state is distant from the individual and is not there to take care of individuals. Olssen argues that the neoliberal individual is a slightly different conception from the "old" liberal view as the neoliberal individual is one who is "continually encouraged by the state to be perpetually responsive" (2004: 137). Furthermore, Olssen argues that the role of the state is exercise "new forms of vigilance, surveillance, performance appraisal and control." In this conception there is only limited space for passive "victims" and no room for those who are seen as choosing to remain outside the ideological framework. The reforms displaced individuals from psychiatric institutions to be cared for by their families, from the workforce, from entitlements to universal child subsidies, from welfare benefits, and from communities that "died" because industries closed down.

What many communities have learned from these processes is that the neoliberal emphasis on the individual cuts against any conception that an individual is accountable to, often dependent on, and works in relation to social groups. The strength of many Maori communities is their strong sense of collective identities; that is, that individuals are members of different kinds of social collectives from small families, to complex intergenerational and extended families, from marae or community places, and through genealogical networks that are connected to specific lands and histories. These connections provide the glue of community cohesion as they work through value systems and practices that ensure reciprocal relationships are honored over time and over succeeding generations, and that recognize the process of gifting to ensure that no one goes without. Such social practices are more available to communities that have remained connected to a place and to each other over extended periods of time. In the 1960s and 1970s urban Maori communities had established cultural institutions that represented their "pan-Maori" needs and aspirations well before the reforms were implemented but the reforms positioned some urban Maori communities as delivery agencies for devolved social services. Two of the largest organizations became powerful voices for Maori not living in their tribal areas and these organizations challenged the tribal authority and mandate of tribes who were seeking settlements from the Waitangi Tribunal process for historic grievances. Of course, this competitive model was exactly what neoliberalism fosters, but it was divisive for communities and individuals who felt torn by a debate about definitions of Maori terms that were being contested in non-Maori contexts such as the British Parliament and Court system. The definition of an *iwi* for example was taken to the Privy Council in England to adjudicate with the decision ultimately reinforcing the definition of an iwi as imposed by government legislation.

Both urban- and tribally based social service organizations were contracted to government to deliver services that governments had previously monopolized, but without the infrastructure of government, they were seen as more efficient and less bureaucratic operations for dealing with the vulnerable members of community. Many Maori, however, interpreted the devolution of social service delivery to Maori "providers" as an example of self determination with greater decision making autonomy over how services were to be delivered. It was seen by some Maori commentators as a better way to demonstrate Maori capacity to self-manage and by other Maori as a risky proposition that would lead to devolution of responsibility and accountability without real devolution of power. This was especially noticeable in the educational reforms where self-managing schools in socially disadvantaged areas occupied by mostly Maori and Pacific Islands communities struggled to meet the accountability demands for educational achievement that all Western governments struggle with themselves in terms of socially disadvantaged groups. In other words, they were made responsible for their own oppression and freedom.

As mentioned earlier, the notion of the perpetually responsive individual and organization is a significant aspect of neoliberal institutional reform. It is connected to the competitive and contestable nature by which the state mediates the market. Social service providers were expected to compete for government contracts to deliver services more efficiently than government agencies. In the initial reform phase when attempts were made to keep the model "pure," community agencies were discouraged from building in costs for infrastructure or community capacity. The "perpetually responsive" community provider of services was viewed as an efficient way to deliver programs through contestable processes and a regime of surveillance put in place by the contracting government agency on the provider.

Many of the above lessons are very specific to the neoliberal project. They are strategies used to contest key elements of neoliberal reform such as the market competition model of education, the use of discursive strategies for gaining legitimacy for the reforms such as "school choice" and more "parental control," the neoliberal policy of "targeting" groups that qualify for limited support because universal benefits are removed, and the assertion of the "level playing field" as a determinant of social justice and equity (Smith 2000). There is also the cycle of perpetual reform that sustains the neoliberal project and keeps marginalized groups and schools alike in the mode of perpetual responsiveness (Apple 2001). In New Zealand, neoliberal reform is 20 years old and still going. The lessons however are also an attempt to capture a sense of the resources and capacities that marginalized communities can bring to bear in a struggle that is not equal. These resources and capacities are uneven, vulnerable, and often unreliable. Engaging in educational reform processes was one of many engagements that communities were embroiled within as the neoliberal reforms penetrated all aspects of economic and social reform.

Educational reform is a political process that is often fraught with contradictions and assumptions about social change that do not quite connect with social realities. Garnering public support through both reconstituting and appealing to common sense is an important discursive strategy that neoliberal reform has been particularly effective at employing. However, the process itself is messy even if the ideological message seems clear, simple, and unambiguous. In the New Zealand context, the messiness related in large part to the disestablishment of one set of agencies and the reestablishment of a new one. These changes were accompanied by media campaigns that invited parent participation while also blaming teachers and professionals for declining educational standards. Even when there was clear evidence that New Zealand's educational standards had not fallen but remained high in the western world the evidence was dismissed. The processes of reform required people to create something new while simultaneously destroying institutional memory of the old regime.

Maori participation in the working parties that discussed the reform implementation was crucial even though the overall changes may have seemed to be inevitable. One small victory for Maori in the early part of the reform was that an additional working party was formed to address the establishment of Kura Kaupapa Maori and the inclusion of Kura Kaupapa Maori in the Education Act Amendment 1989. This came about because Maori representatives argued that the implementation process had failed to include an initiative in Maori education that was offering "choice" to Maori and had been operating outside the state system for a number of years. The outcome was that Kura Kaupapa Maori was included in the Education Amendment Act 1989 as a distinct category of state schooling. The lesson here is that it is important for communities to act even when the odds seem to be against any compromise. It was also important that an alternative vision was able to be articulated in such a way that aspects of the vision could connect with the reform agenda. The Maori educational crisis was a key justification for reform and so there was a meeting ground in terms of contesting the legitimacy of the overall reform agenda. However, Maori were also able to engage in the rhetoric of school choice by arguing that the choices available to Maori were limited and therefore disadvantageous or "unfair."

Another key lesson for Maori was the need to build something together in the face of what seemed to be a deliberate fragmentation and exclusion of communities. Neoliberalism views competition as an important strategy for gaining efficiency and quality. In small marginalized communities with one or two schools competition can also be destructive and groups wanting to pursue one type of education, for example in Maori language, were pitted against other parents who wanted the status quo. There was a period in the 1990s in which whole communities and their school systems seemed to be unraveling in their struggle to survive. This context helped lead to a series of Ministry of Education interventions ostensibly to improve educational achievements but also to strengthen schools capacity to educate their own communities. These initiatives were, not surprisingly, in areas where there were significant socioeconomic disadvantages and where there are large populations of Maori and Pacific islands communities. Initially Maori communities were caught up in trying to compete with each other for school resources in terms of options around Maori-language education but have over time have settled into a gradation of options that attempt to balance parental desires and schooling capacities.

As Apple also points out, much of the neoliberal agenda is also about identity politics and is organized around "*conscious and unconscious racial dynamics*" (2001: 17; emphasis mine). For Maori, the racial dynamics are played out in complex ways with attempts to accommodate certain kinds of engagements by Maori as a legitimation of reform, and yet, with a larger agenda of reforms that has had the effect of increasing the marginalization of Maori in the actual outcomes of education (Ministry of Maori Development 2000). It is important to the reform promise that Maori "rise" to the middle class, but an assumption of such a rise is that Maori will take on the interests and values of the dominant white middle class and erase those aspects of their identity that are fundamentally different. This has not happened for two reasons: not enough Maori have "risen" into the middle class and even where they have there is still a strong desire by well educated Maori to protect Maori language, knowledge, culture, and identity.

Another series of lessons learned is that communities need their activists, their translators, negotiators, and problem solvers. This is a kind of leadership that draws on a range of skills and understandings for working as minority group leaders in a political environment. Indigenous leadership is often regarded as being in crisis because of the perception of things going terribly wrong in indigenous governance and economic development. However, governments and government agencies have a long tradition of dividing the leadership of minority communities by selecting to hear only those leaders that are seen as palatable to the dominant group in society. Community activists are often viewed by the media, by politicians and officials as troublemakers intent on being destructive. There are also active attempts to silence the voice of activists in favor of those seen as more "moderate" and more accommodating. In the New Zealand context, being perceived as an activist is not difficult, one just has to exercise concern, provide a critique, or express an alternative opinion that is pro-Maori for the perception to take hold that one is an activist. Community activists are important because they do lead opinion, frequently have a different interpretation of official policies, and have the kinds of networks that reveal the wider ramifications of policies. But activists are also needed to help interpret and negotiate official policies for communities in a context in which the quality of information required by them to make informed decisions is often not present.

In the end, solutions posed either by neoliberal reformers or communities themselves are never going to be really perfect on the ground even if the model is perfect on a drawing board. Educational reform is a sensitive process involving systems and people in an ongoing series of change processes. What Maori communities have learned is that engagement in these processes can influence some of what happens and more about how it happens. They have also learned that their own good ideas are actually needed by policy because policy makers do not have all the answers themselves and actually struggle with many aspects of implementation. In regards to Maori, many policy makers tended to have very little idea about who Maori people were and hence worked off their own stereotypes, where and how they lived and what challenges they faced on a daily basis. Many policy makers would have little ideas as to the levels of disadvantage experienced by many Maori in New Zealand society. Maori engagement in education has been important to the reform process and has provided New Zealand with a unique set of solutions to educational diversity and issues of social inclusion that would not have come about without participation by Maori in the process. New Zealand's Maori-language provision in schools for example is well known internationally, as is the early childhood curriculum that is infused with Maori concepts and values. Most tertiary institutions and many secondary schools have their own marae and meeting houses. Most schools with strong Maori communities can perform basic cultural ceremonies of welcome. These changes have not come about by good will or an unexpected gift; they have been argued for, protested over, and ultimately established by Maori people.

Endangering Authenticities and New Subjectivities

What are the implications of this experience for other indigenous peoples? Rey Chow (1993) reminds us that that the native did exist before the "gaze" of the settler and before the image of native came to be constituted by imperialism. Chow refers to the "fascination" with the native as a "labor with endangered authenticities." The identity of "the native" is regarded as a complicated, ambiguous and therefore troubling term even for those who live the realities and contradictions of being native, and a member of a colonized and minority community that still remembers other ways of being, of knowing and of relating to the world. What is troubling to the dominant cultural group about the definition of "native" is not what necessarily troubles the "native" community. The desires for "pure," uncontaminated and simple definitions of the native by the settler is often a desire to continue to know and define the Other whereas the desires by the native to be self-defining and self-naming can be read as a desire to be free, to escape definition, to be complicated, to develop and change and be regarded as fully human. In between such desires, however, are multiple and shifting identities and hybridities with much more nuanced positions about what constitutes native identities, native communities and native knowledge in anti- and postcolonial times. Does the shift to a neoliberal global order alter the relationships between the Native and the Settler? Does neoliberalism endanger the authenticities of native or indigenous peoples? Does neoliberalism constitute new subjectivities of native and indigeneity?

The notion of authenticity is one that is open to critique and claims by indigenous peoples to having and living an authentic life as a native person or culture is often seen as romantic or politically motivated. In reality, most Maori people and communities do not claim to live the same life their ancestors lived and question the idealization and the "image" of the native held by non-native people. They are often expected to make such claims in contexts where their rights as indigenous peoples are not recognized or are under threat. As an example in New Zealand, the Treaty of Waitangi Tribunal processes require claimants to establish a grievance and then to substantiate that grievance by reciting their genealogies and providing evidence that they are who they say they are. This very process constitutes specific Maori subjectivities: as people with a grievance, as people who need a treaty and to some extent as "victims." The victim position is one that many Maori reject preferring instead the indigenous term, *tangata whenua* or "people of the land," as a term that assumes colonization has taken place but also encapsulates an alternative set of world views, relationships and future. The occasional non-Maori public figure also echoes the common sense belief that Maori people should "look" Maori. In one recent speech the leader of the main opposition party referred to Maori as no longer a real indigenous people as their blood was watered down by intermarriage. When they do "look" Maori with a moko or facial tattoo they are denied jobs or told that they are "making up" their culture. Neoliberalism has helped constitute new subjectivities through discourse and through a theory of the competitive entrepreneurial individual, but that view has not entirely replaced the range of subjectivities available, rather resistant subjectivities are also created to counter the hegemony of neoliberalism.

Through a series of national gatherings in 2004–06 that discussed Maori aspirations, it would seem that most Maori who attended the gatherings wanted to be able to choose to "live as Maori" and also be able to live as citizens of New Zealand, as citizens of the world and enjoy the benefits of good health and well-being (Durie 2004). Most Maori also accept that Maori culture is a dynamic culture that changes in response to structural and cultural conditions. Indeed many of the debates held within the Maori community are often about social and cultural change. Neoliberalism has been the ideology that has shaped the New Zealand economy and society. Neoliberalism has been influential in creating the market place as the site where native and indigenous peoples, communities, knowledges, and identities are contested as if they are simply commodities of culture and legacies of the past. Charles Hale similarly suggests that neoliberalism has included limited recognition for indigenous cultural "rights" in other places such as Latin America, but this recognition has had unexpected effects that have included greater capacity by the state to manage and control political dissent. Hale argues that neoliberalism has constituted it own version of multiculturalism that awaits disruptions from groups that do not fit the neat neoliberal multicultural identities.

Hale's examples from Latin America have some resonance with the wider context of multiculturalism in New Zealand. New identities of indigenous have been re-formed, formed, and articulated in the era of neoliberalism. Some identities have been created by legislation and confirmed by the British Courts for example the current definitions of *iwi* or *tribe* in New Zealand. Other identities have been created by the British Courts and over turned by legislation for example native title holders to the foreshore and seabed. Yet another political phenomenon known as the Maori Party emerged in direct response to the government's stance on abrogating native title to the foreshore and seabed and after entering the parliamentary elections has four members of parliament (Smith 2006). Some identities established in responses to 19th-century colonial practices such as the Kingitanga movement that saw Maori chiefs at the time elect a "King" have become institutionalized in the 21st century as an almost traditional institution with legitimation coming from different Maori groupings as well as from politicians and the British Crown. The recent deaths and funeral ceremonies of the Maori "Queen" Dame Te Atairangikaahu and the King of Tonga demonstrate the infusing of culture with all kinds of influences: traditional, colonial, and contemporary; western and Polynesian Pacific; New Zealand; and media news broadcasts for both ceremonies in the English and Maori languages by Maori television. When examined against a longer and wider historical frame, it is possible to see the formation of new indigenous identities over time as creations of the state in the case of regulated identities, reactions to the state such as indigenous political resistances and sometimes creative almost tangential occurrences driven by events happening in the indigenous communities themselves. In this chapter, I have attempted to stand partly inside Maori perspectives to argue that communities of different kinds engaged in the reform processes by drawing on a range of cultural indigenous aspirations and resources and that the capacity to do this in a sustained although not highly organized manner—through different avenues such as education, the Waitangi Tribunal, the British Court system and the political system—has disrupted some aspects of the New Zealand version of neo liberalism.

References

Apple, Michael. 2001. *Educating the "right" way: Markets, standards, God, and inequality.* New York: Routledge Falmer.

Chow, R. 1993. *Writing diaspora: Tactics of intervention in contemporary cultural studies.* Bloomington: Indiana University Press.

Codd, J. 1990. Educational policy and the crisis of the New Zealand state. In *New Zealand educational policy today: Critical perspectives,* edited by S. Middleton, J. Codd, and A. Jones, 191–205. Wellington: Allen and Unwin.

Durie, M. 2004. *Progress and platforms for Maori educational achievement.* Paper presented to Hui Taumata Mautauranga Maori Education Summit. Electronic document, http://www.minedu.govt.nz/index. cfm?layout=document&documentid=6491&indexid=6506&indexp arentid=8734, accessed January 18, 2007.

Hale, Charles. 2005. Neoliberal multiculturalism: The remaking of cultural rights and racial dominance in Central America. *PoLAR* 28 (1): 10–28.

Jones, A., J. Marshall, G. McCulloch, G. H. Smith, and L. T. Smith. 1990. *Myths and realities.* Palmerston North: Dunmore Press.

Kearns, R. A., and A. Joseph. 1997. Restructuring health and rural communities in New Zealand. *Progress in Human Geography* 21: 18–32.

Kelsey, Jane. 1993. *Rolling back the state: Privatisation of power in Aotearoa/ New Zealand*. Wellington: Bridget Williams Books.

Marshall, J., M. Peters, and G. H. Smith. 1991. The business roundtable and the privatisation of education: Individualism and the attack on Maori. In *Education policy and the changing role of the state*, edited by L. Gordon and J. Codd, 99–106. Delta, Palmerston North: Massey University.

Ministry of Education. 2004. *Maori education*. Electronic document, http://www.minedu.govt.nz/index.cfm?layout=index&indexid=10 63&indexparentid=2107, accessed January 18, 2007.

Ministry of Maori Development. 2000. *Closing the gaps* (June). Wellington: New Zealand Government Publication.

Moran, W. 1999. Democracy and geography in the reregulation of New Zealand. In *Restructuring societies: Insights from the social sciences*, edited by D. B. Knight and A. E. Joseph, 33–58. Ottawa: Carleton University Press.

Olssen, M. 1996. Neoliberalism and the welfare state: Prospects for the Year 2000. *ACCESS Critical perspectives on Cultural and Policy Studies in Education* 15 (1): 1–33.

——. 2004. Neoliberalism, globalisation, democracy: Challenges for education. *Globalisation, Societies and Education* 2 (2): 231–276.

Pool, I. 1991. *Te Iwi Maori. A New Zealand population past, present and projected*. Auckland: Auckland University Press.

Simon, Judith, and L. T. Smith, eds. 2001. *A civilising mission? Perceptions and representations of the New Zealand Native schools system*. Auckland: Auckland University Press.

Smith, G. H. 1999. Reform of the New Zealand education system and responses by the indigenous Maori of New Zealand. *Directions: Journal of Educational Studies, Institute of Education, USP* 21 (1): 60–72.

——. 2000. Maori education: Revolution and transformative action. *Canadian Journal of Native Education* 24 (1): 57–72.

Smith, G. H., and L. T. Smith. 1996. New Maori mythologies. In *Nga Patai*, edited by P. Spoonley, D. Pearson, and C. McPherson, 217–234. Palmerston North: Dunmore Press.

Smith, K. T. 2006. The Maori party. In *New Zealand government and politics*, edited by Raymond Miller, 507–516. Auckland: Oxford University Press.

Waitangi Tribunal. 1999. *Wananga Capital Establishment Report*. Electronic document, http://www.waitangitribunal.govt.nz/publications/ published_reports.asp, accessed January 18, 2007.

Walker, Ranginui. 1990. *Ka Whawhai Tonu Matou: Struggle without end*. Auckland: Penguin Books.

Part 5

Indigenous Self-Representation, Non-Indigenous Collaborators and the Politics of Knowledge

thirteen

Melting Glaciers and Emerging Histories in the Saint Elias Mountains

Julie Cruikshank

Concepts travel, Andre Beteille (1998) reminds us, carrying and accumulating baggage that may gain unexpected ideological weight. He targets the casual use of "indigenous," an idea with layered historical meanings that accrued initially during expanding European colonialism and proliferated more recently in postcolonial discourses. Indigenous is a concept now lodged worldwide, Beteille suggests, applied indiscriminately to peoples anthropologists formerly called "tribes." He addresses the ironies of exporting this term from classic settler societies (North America, Australia, New Zealand, etc.) to geographical settings where complex populations movements defy such shorthand.

The concept "indigenous," though, has rhetorically expanded from an exogenous, category to one of self-designation signifying cultural recognition, defense of human rights, and protection under international law (Stavenhagen 1996).[1] In a world now abstractly universalized as postcolonial, ethnographic investigation of emerging indigenous identities may contribute to social analysis in settings where land rights and the legal, economic and social status of minority rights remain controversial. Anthropological investigations of indigenism's twin traveler, the equally essentialized term *nationalism,* have demonstrated that nationalism is not one thing, and that what may appear superficially to be a European category is frequently embedded in radically differing ideologies.

In everyday practice, the term indigenous is now more often used in relational contexts than as a primary category of self-ascription. In Canada, for instance, the terms *Aboriginal* and *First Nation* emerged as preferred forms for self-reference during the 1980s and 1990s. *First*

355

Nation replaces the administrative term *Indian band* long used by the Government of Canada, whereas *Aboriginal,* the more inclusive term, encompasses Inuit and Métis. In northern Canada, self-designations in local languages are in frequent use. *Indigenous,* however, is becoming the term of choice for some young urban activists who describe Aboriginal and First Nation as too enmeshed with official state discourses. Invoked with reference to emerging international alliances, indigeneity high-lights similarities with other populations who share histories of dis-possession, impoverishment, and enforced schooling. Increasingly authorized by UN working committees, indigenism has been identified as a new kind of global entity currently gaining momentum (Niezen 2000: 119). Yet its expanding usage, as chapters in this volume attest, highlights tensions.

If the new indigenism is increasingly a relational and constructed process in Canada, it emerges from a history of distinct encounters and builds on diverse connections. Early treaty-making processes in British North America suggest that colonial powers tacitly acknowledged local sovereignty. Subsequent emplacement of an international border across North America in 1867 partitioned Canada from the United States and arbitrarily allocated aboriginal populations to one nation state or the other. A century on, a new generation of young activists, emboldened by social protest and radical activism that characterized the 1960s began rebuilding cross-border alliances. On the Canada's Pacific west coast, First Nations forged connections with New Zealand Maori during the 1970s (Tsing this volume). Further north, circumpolar networks have drawn arctic and subarctic peoples into common causes (Minority Rights Group 1994; Smith and McCarter 1997). Ongoing encounters with postcolonial states, with science, and with international organizations are themes explored in this chapter.

Postcolonial theory forces us to look critically at how Enlightenment categories were exported from Europe through expansion of empire to places like northwestern North America once deemed to be "on the verge of the world" and how those categories have become sedimented in contemporary practice. In this chapter, I look at concepts of indigeneity through the lens of local knowledge, in a setting where such knowledge is seemingly gaining ground yet still received and adjudicated largely within scientific norms of universalism. I trace some of the continuities or similarities in the ways that concepts of knowledge—variously deemed to be "local," "indigenous," "Western," or "universal"—are deployed, arguing that the coloniality of indigeneity is sometimes reinforced by hierarchies even in seemingly progressive contexts.

My chapter originates in a puzzle from my ethnographic research—
the appearance of glaciers in life stories told by elderly indigenous
women who were born in the late 19th century and lived their entire
lives just inland from the Saint Elias Mountains. I spent the 1970s and
early 1980s in the Yukon Territory working with several women eager to
document memories for younger generations. Among the accounts they
recorded were some about a desperately cold year during the mid–19th
century when summer failed to arrive, and about glaciers that damned
lakes and eventually burst with catastrophic consequences. Their stories
also chronicled voyages made by inland Athapaskan and coastal Tlingit
ancestors who traded, traveled, and intermarried between the Yukon
plateau and the Gulf of Alaska. Sometimes protagonists crossed over
glaciers on foot and other times traveled in hand-hewn cottonwood
boats, racing under glacier bridges that periodically spanned major rivers
draining to the Pacific from the high-country interior. Other narratives
recounted how strangers, *k'och'en,* (the colorless "cloud people") first
came inland from the coast, traversing glaciers, and the transformations
their arrival heralded.

Initially, I was perplexed by references to glaciers in these life stories.
By the 1970s, the women I knew were living well inland from the Saint
Elias Icefields, yet insisted on including glacier narratives to explain
regional human history. Following connections they made initially led
me to literature centered on three seemingly distinct themes that I use
to frame this discussion: histories of environmental change; analyses
of colonial encounters; and debates about local knowledge.

First, glacier stories directed me to accounts about *environmental change*
that occurred in northwestern North America during the lifetimes of
these women's parents and grandparents. Stories of geophysical risks
that dominate these accounts are associated with late stages of a period
some scientists call the "Little Ice Age." Jean Grove, the physical geographer who coined this term for an interval of global cooling between
the Middle Ages and the early 20th century, traces some of its slip-
periness in her classic volume *The Little Ice Age* (1988), and notes that
chronologies vary from region to region. Archaeologist Brian Fagan's
recent book of the same title (2000) suggests C.E. 1300–C.E. 1850 for
western Europe, but also notes that scientists disagree about dates. In
the Pacific Northwest, the years between C.E. 1500 and C.E. 1900 are
commonly cited.

Second, I argue that glacier stories also depict *human encounters* that
coincided with late stages of this Little Ice Age. In the Gulf of Alaska, two
fundamental processes that are often discussed independently coincided:

geophysical changes (the turf of natural sciences) and European colonial incursions (a sphere of social sciences and humanities). By the late 1700s, when icefields were especially active, so was commerce in furs transported from America's far northwest to London, Paris, and Moscow. Both oral and written accounts depict encounters with changing landscapes, but also with Europeans who were crossing glaciers from the Pacific to reach the interior by the late 1800s. Notably, another kind of encounter follows from those meetings—between stories written and told about such events and their subsequent readers and listeners as they get taken up in different knowledge traditions. Glacier stories move through time, connect with others, and are being reinvigorated as global climate change influences local glacier conditions.

Third, I use the term *local knowledge* to refer to tacit knowledge embodied in life experiences and reproduced in everyday behavior and speech. Variously characterized as "primitive superstition," as "ancestral wisdom," or as "indigenous science," it has long been framed as a foil for concepts of Western rationality. Local knowledge, then, is a concept often used selectively and in ways that reveal more about histories of Western ideology than about ways of apprehending the world. Its late-20th-century incarnation as "indigenous" or as "ecological" knowledge continues to present local knowledge as an object for science—as potential data—rather than as a kind of knowledge that might inform science. I argue that local knowledge is not something waiting to be "discovered" but, rather, is continuously made in situations of human encounter: between coastal and interior neighbors, between colonial visitors and residents, and among contemporary scientists, managers, environmentalists and First Nations.

I begin with a few words about the physical dimensions of the mountains and glaciers in this place. I next outline some old and some new stories that show how themes of environmental change, human encounters, and local knowledge are still central to struggles in places depicted as "remote" despite long entanglements with world markets. I conclude with reference to conflicting stories circulating in these mountains and their ongoing connections to memory, history, and indigenous rights. Not surprisingly, interpretive frameworks seem to be continually recast on all sides to meet contemporary specifications. Insights from current work on memory and forgetting clarify just how profoundly these three strands—changing environment, transformative human encounters, and local knowledge debates—are entangled as they circulate in transnational contexts under new rubrics like environmentalism, postcolonialism, and "traditional ecological knowledge" in its many acronyms.

America's Northwest Glaciers

The Saint Elias Mountains include some of North America's highest peaks and support the world's largest nonpolar icefields (see fig. 1). These glaciers were created by ice ages, maintained by climate, and have been in place for thousands of years. This region fascinates me for several reasons. First, in my ethnographic research in the Yukon Territory and Alaska I have heard vivid accounts of glacier travel transmitted in indigenous oral traditions. Second, a sustained record of scientific research here, at high altitude and high latitude, makes it a key site for contemporary climate change studies. Third, this region has recently become the world's largest UNESCO-designated World Heritage Site spanning the Alaska–Canada border and encompassing four parks: Kluane National Park and Tatshenshini-Alsek Provincial Park on the Canadian side, Wrangell-Saint Elias and Glacier Bay National Parks in the United States. The far northwest, once the source of a fabulously lucrative sea otter trade has re-merged as a site for new global narratives, this time with strong environmental themes.

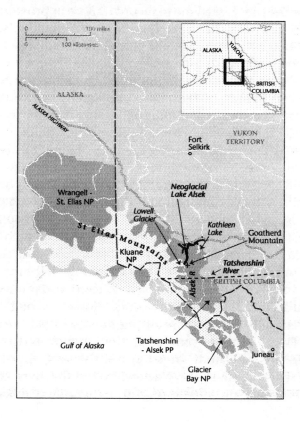

Significantly, Icefield Ranges includes glaciers that surge—of great interest to geophysical sciences. Surging glaciers may advance without warning after years of stability, sometimes several kilometers, and they frequently create ice-dammed lakes that build up and burst out when the ice thins and the dam breaks. Surging glaciers also occur in Greenland and the Antarctic, but issues of scale and accessibility make them easier to study in the Saint Elias Mountains. Of some 4,000 glaciers on these icefields, a relatively large number—at least 200—have this characteristic. In this place, we now see nature represented in many ways—as "primordial wilderness," as a "climate change laboratory," or as a giant "jungle gym" for ecotourists. In northwestern Canada, such depictions now compete with views by local indigenous residents who lived and hunted in these lands until 1943, when they were relocated east of the Alaska Highway after the Kluane Game Sanctuary (and, later, Kluane National Park and Reserve) was set aside as the Yukon's first "protected area."

I begin with one story about a glacier now officially named Lowell Glacier that I first heard in November 1978 when Mrs. Kitty Smith, almost 90 at the time, asked me to record it. Born approximately 1890, she grew up in the Tatshenshini River valley. As a child, she became well acquainted with unpredictable glacial surges and the interpretive challenges of living with glaciers. Lowell Glacier, for instance, has crossed the Alsek River more than once. Mrs. Kitty Smith identified it by the name Nàlùdi, or "Fish Stop" because it interrupted salmon migrations up that river to the interior, leaving land-locked salmon in Kathleen Lake.

Her narrative demonstrates consequences of hubris, a classic theme in stories told here. Nàlùdi, she says, was provoked to surge when a reckless child traveling to the interior with coastal Tlingit traders joked about a balding Athapaskan shaman. "Ah, that old man," he reportedly said, "the top of his head is just like the place where gophers play, a bare stump!" To punish this transgression, the shaman withdrew to the top of a high bluff facing the glacier and began to dream, summoning the glacier to advance across the Alsek River valley. It surged, reached this bluff, and built an immense wall of ice that dammed the river and created an upstream lake a hundred kilometers long. When that ice dam eventually burst, the resulting flood scoured the landscape, drowning Tlingit families camped at the junction of the Alsek and Tatshenshini rivers. Nàlùdi surged again, she says, shortly after her own birth. That summer, the glacier blocked the river and flooded the valley basin for just a few days before draining (Cruikshank with

Sidney, Smith, and Ned 1990: 205–208, 332–333; McClellan 2001 [1975]: 71–72).

These events are preserved in the geoscience record, although scientists provide different causal explanations for surges (Clague and Rampton 1982). They estimate that the advancing Lowell Glacier created a two hundred meter high ice dam after it came to rest against Goatherd Mountain and impounded Neoglacial Lake Alsek in the mid–19th century, as it had several times during the previous 2800 years. When the dam broke, it discharged water through the Alsek valley in an enormous flow, emptying the lake in one or two days. Giant ripple marks left in its wake are still visible from the air and on the ground. Scientists now refer to oral histories, tied to genealogies of named persons that suggest 1852 as a possible date for the last major outburst flood (De Laguna 1972: 276).

At issue here are diverging notions of agency and interpretation. One key difference between Athapaskan oral traditions and scientific discourse is that elders' narratives merge natural and social history, whereas scientists assessing environmental change describe one of their objectives as disentangling natural from cultural factors. Elders, for instance, cite the folly of "cooking with grease" near glaciers, lest this excite either the glacier or the being living within such a glacier den. Food should be boiled, never fried, in the presence of glaciers and no grease should ever be allowed to escape from the cooking vessel. Inevitably, such explanations fall out of most contemporary studies of "local knowledge," because they neither fit easily with contemporary scientific understandings of causality nor contribute to databases.

Other stories about glaciers are harder to understand, like those depicting glaciers emitting heat so intense that people were driven to submerge in glacial rivers to avoid being consumed. We know the terrible consequences of epidemics, particularly smallpox, that raged north up the North Pacific coast during the 19th century, and that alternating sweating and submersion in water was a strategy used by coastal victims seeking relief (Gibson 1983). But few details are known about epidemics that traveled up the Alsek. Public health physician Robert Fortuine (1989) identifies the coastal smallpox epidemic that occurred between 1835 and 1840 as one of the most significant events in Alaska history. Starting at Sitka, it spread northward to Lynn Canal. Anthropologist Catharine McClellan estimates that it swept up the Alsek in 1838, and that another smallpox epidemic followed in 1862 (McClellan 2001 [1975]: 24, 223). Two epidemics and an outburst flood must have coincided within one generation, but the extent of losses seems to have prevented transmission of firsthand accounts to the present.

Historian Mike Davis has documented how imperial expansion through Asia was enabled when it coincided with El Niño induced droughts and famines in the late 19th century (Davis 2001). In north-western North America's far northwest, Tlingit traders encountered similar intrusions during late stages of the Little Ice Age. They traveled inland in 1852 and destroyed Fort Selkirk, a trading post that Hudson Bay Company trader Robert Campbell had established three years earlier to divert trade away from long-established Aboriginal networks and into British hands.

Anthropologists, geographers, and historians have demonstrated the enduring power of landscape features to act as points of reference anchoring memories, values, and tacit knowledge. A growing body of research about social memory suggests that landscapes are places of remembrance and sites of transmission, and that culturally significant landforms often provide a kind of archive in which memories are can be mentally stored (Boyarin 1994). In the Saint Elias Mountains, though, we can see also how changing landscape features like fluctuating glaciers have also provided imaginative grist for comprehending *changing* social circumstances affecting human affairs. Orally narrated stories indeed provide empirical observations about geophysical changes and their consequences, but also demonstrate how glaciers provide material for evaluating changes wrought by colonial histories.

Such overlapping and conflicting interpretations of glaciers have 21st-century consequences. They seem to typify or even model classic and continuing struggles over cultural meanings replicated in contemporary debates. Implications of what Bruno Latour calls this "Great Divide" differentiating nature from culture continue to cascade internationally through debates about environmentalism, biodiversity, global climate change, and indigenous rights (Latour 1993; see also Franklin 2002; Hornberg and Pálsson 2000; Macnaghten and Urry 1998).

I now turn to some contemporary narratives that provide further points of overlap and contrast.

New Stories from Melting Glaciers

In the 1990s, the Saint Elias Icefields began to reveal fresh surprises. Three recent "discoveries" show just how slippery our views of nature and society can be. In 1991, biologist David Hik spotted a rectangular piece of hide roughly one meter in length and half a meter wide melting from a glacier near the center of what is now Kluane National Park. It had been modified by humans—with slits around the edge and a possible fragment of thong—and looked old. As required by Canadian law, Hik informed Kluane Park staff, who took charge of the hide and then sent it to park headquarters in Winnipeg where it has remained in a freezer. It appears to have been left in the central icefields by a traveler approximately 1,000 years ago (1,110 BP +/- 50, calibrated to account for fluctuations of carbon in the atmosphere). After it was identified as bear hide, parks scientists hoped that it might reveal information about genetic relationships and diversity in the Kluane grizzly bear population over time; however, no genetic information has been salvageable because of repeated thawing and freezing (personal communications from David Hik, University of Alberta, 1992; and David Arthurs, Parks Canada, 2003).

Six years later, in 1997, a wildlife biologist hiking near a north facing alpine basin some 1,830 meters above sea level stumbled on a square-kilometer concentration of caribou droppings melting from an alpine snow patch. Artifacts were literally pouring out of melting ice. Subsequent research revealed evidence of ancient caribou harvesting on the mountain named Thandlät in Southern Tutchone language.

Scientists describe this as a rare opportunity to explore questions about the prehistoric ecology of large caribou populations, implications of climate change for caribou, and human use of high-elevation hunting sites. The droppings contain mitochondrial and nuclear DNA that biologists intend to compare with that of living caribou populations as well as ancient pollen that may help to reconstruct past climates (Kuzyk et al. 1999). By 2003, 72 ancient alpine ice patches, usually no more than a square kilometer and 50 meters deep, had been identified in southwest Yukon. Eighteen of these have yielded tools and the work continues. Radio-carbon dates for rare wooden tools and other organic material melting from these patches demonstrate an enduring relationship between caribou and human hunters at high altitude and latitude for at least 8,000 years, right up until the late 19th century (Farnell et al. 2004; Hare et al. 2004; Krajick 2002).

Archaeologists working in Athapaskan territories are accustomed to making their inferences from a sparse material record. Subarctic hunters made their tools largely from perishable materials—skin, wood, sinew— used them, left them behind and remade them as needed, a technology constructed from ingenious principles and carried in the head rather than on the back. Understandably, then, perfectly preserved tools made from organic materials melting from glaciers are spectacularly interesting to scientists as well as to local people, if for different reasons. In their subsequent investigations of Yukon ice patches, archaeologists and Yukon First Nations have formed partnerships and community members have participated in archaeological field research. Culture camps organized by Champagne-Aishihik First Nation around the theme of ice patches have included visiting scientists who meet with local students. In Alaska, archaeologists are now using global positioning system (GPS) models to "prospect" for potential melting sites that may be releasing similar evidence on the other side of the Saint Elias Range.

More widely publicized was the accidental discovery, by sheep hunters in August 1999, of a young hunter's remains, a man in his late teens or early twenties. He was melting from a glacier in the traditional territories of Champagne-Aishihik First Nation (also within Alsek–Tatshenshini Provincial Park). His death was probably accidental. His woven spruce root hat, part of his squirrel fur robe, some tools (including a bone knife with iron stains), and a piece of fish he was carrying were preserved with him. His robe, radiocarbon dated at 550 BP, carried traces of spruce and pine pollen and some fish scales. Local elders named him Kwäday Dän Ts'ínchi or "Long Ago Person Found" in Southern Tutchone language.

From the beginning, there was close cooperation among scientists and members of the relevant Champagne-Aishihik First Nation, without which the scientific research could not have proceeded. If the Native American Graves and Repatriation Act structures such relationships in the United States (see Brown 2003; Starn 2004; Thomas 2000), partnerships are being carefully negotiated as part of implementing recent land claims agreements in Canada. Members of this First Nation were interested in learning more about this potential ancestor and how his travels overlap with their oral histories. They agreed to allow scientific investigations that included First Nation representatives on the management team and to let the materials travel for scientific analysis. Scientists are especially interested in how this rare evidence—flesh and hair and as well as bones—might contribute to understandings of health, nutrition, and disease, but also what his perfectly preserved hat, tools, and fragments of robe may reveal about everyday life from that time (Beattie et al. 2000). As agreed, his remains were returned to the community within a specified time frame. The First Nation held a funeral potlatch for him on July 21, 2001, and his cremated remains were returned to the location where he was found. Radiocarbon and DNA testing continue, but so far DNA indicates only that the young man had closer connections with other Native Americans than with populations in Asia or Greenland (Monsalve et al. 2002). Botanists have determined more about his early diet from bone samples (Dickson et al. 2004). Cross-border connections between coastal Tlingit and inland Champagne-Aishihik First Nations have been strengthened during community negotiations surrounding this research and the funerary arrangements for Kwäday Dän Ts'ínchi.

These events all received wide publicity for a short time—locally, nationally, and internationally, and in sources ranging from news media to scientific journals. In such circumstances, scientists and Aboriginal people are encountering concrete, material evidence of the past but they are also encountering each other at close range. Contemporary encounters fall into new transnational contexts—global climate change, environmentalism, social justice, and scientific studies of human remains—and we see how the same evidence produces different interpretations. The piece of bearskin presents scientists with possibilities of learning about ancient grizzly populations and provides local residents with possible evidence of an early ancestor who traveled in the central icefields. Tools pouring from glaciers suggest that high-latitude, high-altitude landscapes were intensely shared by humans and caribou for thousands of years. Elders born before the turn of the last century, with whom I worked, still remembered large herds at the beginning of the 20th century before they disappeared, and biologists cannot pinpoint the cause of their disappearance. Tellers do not separate the tools from the toolmakers: women, for instance, speculate about the coastal woman who may have made Kwäday Dän Ts'ínchi's coastal hat or the grandmother who might have knitted his inland robe. So his arrival both confirms oral traditions in the minds of local people and authenticates the antiquity of such travel by ancestors. Melting glaciers are revealing material evidence of interest to scientists but they are also reinvigorating longstanding oral histories about travel and trade near the Saint Elias Mountains. Again, questions arise about where stories told by scientists and elders connect and where they slide apart.

Crucially, Athapaskan and Tlingit oral traditions attribute to glaciers characteristics rather different from those discovered through science. Glaciers long provided travel routes or "highways" that enabled human connections between coast and interior. Glaciers are described in many narratives as characterized by sentience. They listen, pay attention, and they are quick to take offense when humans demonstrate hubris or behave indiscreetly. I have been struck by how people who speak knowledgeably about glaciers refer to listening, observing, and participating in ritualized respect relations (see also Anderson 2004). Such visions originate in intense engagement with environment maintained through millennia, creating what anthropologist Tim Ingold calls a "dwelling perspective" so profoundly relational that everyone understands how humans and nature coproduce the world they share (Ingold 2000: esp. 153–156; see also Basso 1996). Glacial landscapes described in oral traditions, then, are intensely *social spaces* that include relationships with nonhuman beings (like glaciers and features of landscape) sharing characteristics of personhood.

In this place, memories of the Little Ice Age are sedimented both in physical processes studied by scientists (bands of grit, layers of ice and rock, etc.) and in memories of long-term residents. Both kinds of knowledge are acquired through close engagement with a physical environment. During the last century, one discourse (science) has gained authority and park managers, ecotourists, and the general public have adopted conceptions of glaciers as places of "raw nature." Once again, glaciers seem to be playing an active role in negotiating the modern terrain of science, history, and politics in these mountains.

Narratives about melting glaciers echo the three interpretive frameworks identified earlier, but also incorporate contemporary concerns. New narratives of *environmental change* associated with melting glaciers now address global climate change rather than Little Ice Age advances. Stories about *human encounters* that once depicted Euro-American incursions across glaciers now speak to implementation of land claims in the context of social justice. *Local knowledge* is again being produced in new contexts and is assuming an expanding role in the rhetorics of comanagement policies. In the remainder of this chapter, then, I offer snapshots of these rapidly changing contexts.

Environmental Change

From the Andes to the Arctic, the environmental change of concern at the beginning of the 20th century is global climate, symbolized by visibly melting glaciers. Evidence mounts that warming will be extreme at Arctic and Subarctic latitudes. Scientists may disagree about the magnitude of globally averaged temperature changes or about the role of humans in the process, but they agree that extreme values are being experienced in arctic regions and that that this will continue. Climate change is a global process, but has profoundly local consequences. Yukon First Nations, now completing land claims negotiations and engaged in economic planning as part of self-governance agreements, are raising questions about regional consequences for water levels, forest yield, permafrost, wildlife, and human activities. Their past experience with climate variability evokes risky times and territories (Cruikshank 2001).

There is growing interest in how Aboriginal people and policymakers can work together on questions surrounding climate change and acknowledgement that some solutions must come from local levels. Up close, though, consultations can lead to awkward exchanges. Scientists, for instance, make a distinction between weather and climate. By definition, they tell us, climate is the statistics of weather, including measurement of means (mean temperature, or mean precipitation) and variance. Climate scientists talk about precise and measurable data—temperature, air pressure, precipitation, and wind speed (Weaver 2003). As anthropologists report from one collaborative study in northern Finland, oral traditions are unlikely to provide transferable "data" to climate change scientists, partly because local people are often referring to weather when they talk about environmental change. Memories passed on in the Yukon, for instance, attend to summer warmth from sun-drenched days or biting cold of deep river valleys in winter. People recall chilling boreal winds and nasty hailstorms. "Climate is recorded," Ingold and Kurttila note succinctly, "weather is experienced" (2000: 187). Knowledge about weather, they point out, cannot be transmitted as a set of customary prescriptions or formulae; it accumulates from a lifetime of experience traversing and inhabiting well-known places and is embodied in tacit knowledge.

Climate science presents a more comprehensive picture than weather. But similarly, oral traditions convey understandings that are more comprehensive than data. The two cannot always be conflated, but both reveal a great deal about the human experience of environmental change. One primary value of local traditions about weather is to deploy authoritative local traditions in problem solving during unexpected weather events (McIntosh et al. 2000). A dominant theme in the Yukon concerns living with uncertainty surrounding behavior of glaciers—unexpected advances, violent surges, catastrophic floods, and accompanying weather variations. Another concerns travel: glacier-filled passes between coast and interior provided ancient travel routes. In one well-known story about two trading partners crossing glaciers to reach the coast, one coastal Tlingit and the other interior Athapaskan, the dramatic consequences center on an accident as the coastal Tlingit man slides into a crevasse and his partner, knowing that he will be held responsible, must make choices and construct a rescue plan. Narratives that are useful in times of crisis concern proper relations with land and crystallize quick and timely social responses. Kwäday Dän Ts'ínchi' probably lost his way in an unexpected storm, archaeologists speculate. Stories now associated with his appearance, his contribution to science, his ceremonial cremation, and his return to the glacier where he was found also point to practices crucial to maintaining balance in a moral world. Scientists may necessarily distinguish environmental data from social history, but Aboriginal storytellers are just as likely to equate disastrous effects of environmental change (specifically pollution) with history of colonialism and its imbalances, rather than viewing these as isolatable physical problems that science might help "fix."

Human Encounters

My larger project traces the role glaciers play in social imagination—in Aboriginal traditions but also in accounts left by Russian, Spanish, French, British, and U.S. and Canadian visitors to the far northwest in the 18th and 19th centuries (Cruikshank 2005). The idea of encounter seems especially useful because of what it reveals about scale and subjectivity. Initially, actors in this region were relatively few and their motives, intentions, and imaginings can be traced partially in diaries and reports, but also in orally narrated stories still told. As national dreams flared in this corner of northwest North America, power shifted decisively.

More than half a century ago, Canadian economic historian Harold Innis (1950) identified arctic and subarctic regions as furnishing a classic illustration of the modernist tendency to conceptualize time as spatially laid out, mechanically segmented, and linear. Colonial projects, he observed, move forward by devising and reinforcing categories—such as objectivity, subjectivity, space, and time. Once normalized as "common sense," these classifications provide a visual template for the annexation of territories and the subjugation of former inhabitants. Innis's analysis is especially apt here. Ironically, a location that gathers much of its imaginative force as a place where boundaries were always being negotiated (between trading partners, between coast and interior, between glaciers and humans, and among residents and strangers) has now become a place festooned with boundaries rather than stories. The international boundary was almost a century in the making, mapping, adjudication, and production (from 1825–1915). Like layers of an onion, successive tribunals and commissions struck to resolve the thorny issue of why, how, and where this boundary would be drawn, demonstrate how an imagined "Nature" can become swept into the formation of nations, and how dreams of nationhood become embedded in borders. As others have noted, these national boundaries were more formidable to negotiate than glaciers.

Boundaries propagate. Fundamental to recent human–environmental histories in this region is the transformation of hunting territories to a nature preserve in linked steps that disenfranchised indigenous hunters at the stroke of a pen. During WWII, the United States became concerned about a possible invasion by Japan through Alaska. They conceived the idea of a military highway connecting their distant northwesterly territories with the national core, an enormous operation that brought 34,000 workers north between April 1942 and December 1943. Following overhunting attributed to U.S. military personnel and Canadian civilians during this Alaska Highway's construction, the Kluane Game Sanctuary was established in 1943. New regulations prohibiting hunting within the sanctuary, including subsistence hunting, meant that a hunter who killed a sheep just east of the boundary was deemed a good provider whereas someone who took a sheep a few feet west was subject to prosecution. When those boundaries were modified to create Kluane National Park in 1979, the region joined a national administrative parks network. The subsequent layering of a UNESCO-designated World Heritage Site across the U.S.–Canadian border drew the region into an international agenda. An international boundary severs people in Alaska from relatives in Canada; provincial and territorial boundaries separate families in British Columbia from those in the Yukon; and boundaries placed around Protected Areas in 1943, and a National Park in 1979, locked ancestral territories *in* behind a boundary, or locked people *out* beyond a boundary, depending on point of view. A crucial problem for those separated by boundaries is how to pass on knowledge about places to those who never experienced them—hence, their appearance in life histories.

Local Knowledge

Melting glaciers have generated partnerships among scientists and First Nations that inevitably enliven local debates about knowledge. Internationally, there has been an explosion of interest in indigenous knowledge or "traditional ecological knowledge" during the last decade. Yet the "locality" of such knowledge sometimes disappears as prescriptive methodologies become enshrined. "Local knowledge" has become a commonsense term in early-21st-century rhetoric. Acronyms like TEK are ubiquitous in research management plans on topics as diverse as fisheries, wildlife management, and forestry, yet often depict local knowledge as static, timeless, and hermetically sealed within categories like "indigenous" in ways that reinforce the coloniality of that concept.

The implication is that oral sources are somehow stable, like archival documents, and that once spoken and recorded, they are simply there, waiting for interpretation. Yet ethnographic research clearly demonstrates that the content of oral sources depends largely on what goes into the discussions, the dialogue, and the personal relationship in which it is communicated. Oral testimony is never the same twice, even when the same words are used, because, as Allesandro Portelli (1997: 54–55) reminds us, the relationship—the dialogue—is always shifting. Oral traditions are not "natural products." They have social histories and *acquire* meanings in the situations where they are used, in interactions between narrators and listeners. Meanings shift depending on the extent to which cultural understandings are shared by teller and listener. If we think of oral tradition as a social activity rather than as some reified product, we come to view it as part of the equipment for living rather than a set of meanings embedded within texts and waiting to be discovered. One of anthropology's most trenchant observations is that meaning is not fixed, but must be studied in practice—in the small interactions of everyday life.

A growing critique of the uses and abuses of traditional knowledge identifies several problems associated with uses of TEK. One is the underlying premise that different cultural perspectives are bridgeable by concepts in English language (like "sustainable development" or "comanagement") and within scientific discourse (Morrow and Hensel 1992). Another is the idea that statements by knowledgeable people can somehow be "captured," codified, labeled, and recorded in databases. Third is the growing evidence that concepts of "local knowledge" or "tradition" most likely to be selected in management-science studies usually reflect ideas compatible with state administration rather than those understood by local people (Ingold and Kurttila 2000; Nadasdy 1999). Scientists working on TEK projects have not been shy about naturalizing culture as an endangered object, then selecting data that effectively conflates environmental and social agendas (See Raffles 2002: 152).

Gender also plays a significant role in local narratives, a theme I have explored elsewhere at greater length (Cruikshank with Sidney, Smith, and Ned 1990). I heard these glaciers stories from elderly local women who incorporated them into accounts of life experience and made them reference points for interpreting and explaining life transitions and gendered family histories. Their interests and perspectives contrasted sharply with masculine narratives of science and empire that characterize so much of the historical literature from this part of the world. Kitty Smith and her peers paid attention to the specificities of everyday life and made glaciers central images in stories that ground social histories in well-known landscapes. Nineteenth-century narratives of imperial science, by contrast, rarely mention residents of inhabited landscapes other than fellow scientists and sponsors, and they virtually ignore local history. These female storytellers claim agency and embed their knowledge in narrative rather than presenting it as locatable "data." In arctic global cultural flows, though, such storied knowledge tends to be displaced and to slide out of grander narratives (see Bravo and Sörlin 2002).

Crucially, stories transmitted in northern oral traditions make no sharp distinction between environmental and social change and indeed take as axiomatic the connections between biophysical and social worlds. The modernist wedge partitioning nature from culture (reflected in TEK studies and databases) severs important connections that Athapaskan narratives explicitly affirm. The overall effect of segregating environmental snippets from their social context inevitably submerges some memories and recasts others to fit dominant transnational narratives. Once again "indigenous data" is subsumed within universalizing hierarchies. What is included and what is left out is not random (see Cooke and Kothari 2001; Cruikshank 2004; Fienup-Riordan 1990: 167–191; Nadasdy 2003: 114–146; Scott 1996).

Modern science, as Sheila Jasanoff explains so concisely, achieves its accomplishments by abstraction. Scientific observations gain authority by being removed from local contexts and recombined in larger wholes—framed as "universal"—that both travel and frequently transgress boundaries of custom and tradition (Jasanoff 2004) Walter Benjamin's famous essay "The Storyteller" eloquently captures this same distinction between knowledge embedded in stories and disembodied information: "Information," he says, "lays claim to prompt verifiability. The prime requirement is that it appear 'understandable in itself.' ... A story is different. It does not expend itself. It preserves and concentrates its strength and is capable of releasing it after a long time" (Benjamin 1969: 89–90; see also Cruikshank 1998).

A historical approach to memory reveals how socially situated but also how porous knowledge practices are. The field of science studies demonstrates that all knowledge is ultimately local knowledge and has a history. The idea that a measurable world can be pried from its cultural moorings also originated in local knowledge traditions that expanded within Enlightenment Europe. In the space now called Kluane Park, science and oral tradition are both kinds of local knowledge that share a common history. That history includes authoritative gains for one kind of formulation—science—at the expense of another. Since 1960, when the Icefield Ranges Research Project was established under the institutional sponsorship of the Arctic Institute of North America and the American Geophysical Society, the Saint Elias mountain ranges have provided research sites for natural and physical sciences, and now for climate change studies. One ironic consequence is that as part of current comanagement agreements, mandated by land claims and self-governance agreements in Canada, indigenous people living near park boundaries are now being asked to document their "traditional knowledge" about places from which they were evicted 60 years ago. In such instances, it would seem, "our flattery of 'primal peoples' and their knowledge, inevitably deemed to be timeless and ahistorical can be viewed as an act of immense condescension" (White 1998: 218).

Entangled Narratives

Stories about glaciers in the Saint Elias Mountains, in constant and uneasy interplay, contribute to a two-century debate about humanity's relationship with the natural world. Regional political and economic practices involved in setting aside protected areas (e.g., parks) now intersect with global practices (e.g., scientific research) that make claims from these spaces. The mountains and glaciers are again being reinvented for new purposes—this time as a hybrid comprising management techniques and measurement practices, sometimes circulating on Internet spaces. Just as narratives of Euro-American national dreams once normalized practices of mapping and measuring, global environmental narratives now fill that role. They help to bring primordial wilderness under the human protection of international committees, like Geneva-based UNESCO, in which morally tinged stories of rational use and protection allow global committees to soberly adjudicate local concerns (see Anderson 2004). The United Nations, centrally positioned within international debates about indigeneity, appears in many guises.

The UNESCO World Heritage List categorizes sites given this status into one of three categories: "natural," "cultural," or "mixed properties," reasserting modernist opposition between nature and lived experience. As of April 6, 2007, the 830 properties inscribed on the World Heritage

List included 644 sites deemed cultural, 162 classified as natural, and 24 as having mixed properties. The awkwardly named "Kluane/Wrangell-Saint Elias/Glacier Bay/Tatshenshini-Alsek" World Heritage Site, the first to cross an international boundary, has been allocated to the "natural" World Heritage Site category, to the consternation of local First Nations. Breaking the bond between people and place along lines so arbitrary as one imagined between cultural heritage and natural environment marks a decisive rift (Giles-Vernick 2002; Ingold 2000).

The nature we are most likely to hear about in the early 21st century is increasingly represented as marvelous but endangered, pristine or biodiverse. Such depictions tend to exclude other ways of seeing and make it more difficult to hear or appreciate unfamiliar points of view (Franklin 2002; Slater 2002). Environmental politics have so normalized our understandings of what "nature" means that we can no longer imagine how other stories might be significant. As claims and counterclaims made in nature's name proliferate, areas deemed to be primordial wilderness are reimagined as uncontaminated by humans. Such views largely exclude other practices, memories, conceptions, and beliefs of people that do not match this vision. Ever-narrowing subsets of nature push humans out except as subjects for management-science to regulate.

Indigenous visions passed on in narratives about glaciers (like those about caribou, forests, or rivers) seem uniquely important because they position nature and culture in a single social field and graft colonial and environmental histories onto older stories. They draw connections between relationships and activities on the land and proper social comportment. They provide rich, complex alternatives to normalized values that now conventionally frame nature as a redeemable object to be "saved." Always in motion even when they appear static, surging glaciers encompass both the materiality of the biophysical world and the agency of the nonhuman, and draw on traditions of thought quite different from those of academic materialism (see Raffles 2002: 38, 181 for a differently situated discussion of this). They *are* grounded in material circumstances but also carry a multitude of historical, cultural, and social values that slide away when they are relegated uncritically to "nature."

Narrative recollections about history, tradition, and life experience represent distinct and powerful bodies of local knowledge that have to be appreciated in their totality, rather than fragmented into data, if we are to learn anything from them. Rarely do either management-driven studies of TEK or environmentalist parables tap into the range of human engagements with nature—diverse beliefs, practices, knowledge and everyday histories of nature that might expand the often crisis-ridden focus of environmental politics. What looks similar on the surface often turns out to have different meanings and different aims. Codified as TEK, and engulfed by frameworks of North American management science, local knowledge shifts its shape, with sentient and social spaces transformed to measurable commodities called "lands" and "resources." Indigenous peoples then continue to face double exclusion, initially by colonial processes that expropriate the land and ultimately from neocolonial discourses that appropriate and reformulate their ideas. Environmentalist values may now shape our understandings of nature (much as science or survey did in the past) but they, too, become entangled with questions of justice working their way through local debates in northwestern North America.

Successive visions of Saint Elias Mountains, continuously recast to serve present purposes, become entangled with those of contemporary First Nations whose visions deserve more space in such schema. In the Gulf of Alaska where European and indigenous forms of internationalism have been enmeshed for two centuries, physical places and people have always been entangled, and in the future they are likely to be more entangled than ever before. Local knowledge in northern narratives is *about* unique entanglements of culture and nature, humans and landscapes, objects and their makers. Material evidence of human history—from Kwäday Dän Ts'ìnchi, caribou pellets, or from the modified bear hide, may be naturalized as probable genetic evidence of natural history. But memories covered by appliquéd layers of sanctuary, park, and World Heritage Site are also being reenergized as human history emerges. The glacier stories I began hearing more than two decades ago may originate in the past but they continue to resonate with current struggles surrounding environmentalism, indigenous rights, land claims, nationhood, and national parks. Such narratives will undoubtedly continue to lead entangled social lives.

Note

1. The *Oxford English Dictionary* defines *indigenous* as "born or produced naturally in a land or region; native to [the soil or region]" and traces its earliest use to 1646.

References

Anderson, David G. 2004. Reindeer, caribou and "fairy stories" of state power. In *Cultivating arctic landscapes: Knowing and managing animals in the circumpolar North*, edited by David G. Anderson and Mark Nuttall, 1–16. Oxford: Berghahn.

Basso, Keith. 1996. *Wisdom sits in places: Landscape and language among the Western Apache*. Albuquerque: University of New Mexico Press.

Beattie, Owen, Brian Apland, Eric W. Blake, James A. Cosgrove, Sarah Gaunt, Sheila Greer, Alexander P. Mackie, Kjerstin E. Mackie, Dan Straathof, Valerie Thorp, and Peter M. Troffe. 2000. The Kwäday Dän Ts'ínchi discovery from a glacier in British Columbia. *Canadian Journal of Archaeology* 24: 129–147.

Benjamin, Walter. 1969. The Storyteller. In *Illuminations*, edited by Hannah Arendt, 83–109. New York: Schocken.

Beteille, Andre. 1998. The idea of indigenous people. *Current Anthropology* 39 (2): 187–91.

Boyarin, Jonathan. 1994. *Remapping memory: The politics of timespace*, edited by Jonathan Boyarin, 1–37. Minneapolis: University of Minnesota Press.

Bravo, Michael, and Sverker Sörlin, eds. 2002. *Narrating the arctic: A cultural history of Nordic scientific practices*. Canton, MA: Watson Publishing International.

Brown, Michael F. 2003. *Who owns Native culture?* Cambridge, MA: Harvard University Press.

Clague, John J., and V. N. Rampton. 1982. Neoglacial Lake Alsek. *Canadian Journal of Earth Sciences* 19: 94–117.

Cooke, Bill, and Uma Kothari, eds. 2001. *Participation: The new tyranny?* London: Zed Books.

Cruikshank, Julie. 1998. *The social life of stories: Narrative and knowledge in the Yukon territory*. Lincoln: University of Nebraska Press.

——. 2001. Glaciers and climate change: Perspectives from oral tradition. *Arctic* 54 (4): 377–393.

——. 2004. Uses and abuses of "traditional" knowledge: Perspectives from the Yukon Territory. In *Cultivating arctic landscapes: Knowing and managing animals in the circumpolar North*, edited by David G. Anderson and Mark Nuttall, 1–16. Oxford: Berghahn.

——. 2005. *Do glaciers listen? Local knowledge, colonial encounters and social imagination*. Vancouver: UBC Press.

Cruikshank, Julie, with Angela Sidney, Kitty Smith, and Annie Ned. 1990. *Life lived like a story: Life stories of three Yukon elders*. Lincoln: University of Nebraska Press.

Davis, Mike. 2001. *Late Victorian holocausts: El Niño amines and the making of the Third World*. London: Verso Press.

De Laguna, Frederica. 1972. *Under Mount Saint Elias: The history and culture of the Yakutat Tlingit*. 3 vols. Smithsonian Contributions to Anthropology, 7. Washington, DC: Smithsonian Institution Press.

Dickson, James H., Michael P. Richards, Richard J. Hebda, Petra J. Mudie, Owen Beattie, Susan Ramsay, Nancy J. Turner, Bruce J. Leighton, John M. Webster, Niki R. Hobischak, Gail S. Anderson, Peter M. Troffe, and Rebecca J. Wigen. 2004. Kwäday Dän Ts'ìnchí. *The Holocene* 14 (4): 481–486.

Fagan, Brian. 2000. *The little ice age: How climate made history, 1300–1850*. New York: Basic Books.

Farnell, Richard, P. Gregory Hare, Erik Blake, Vandy Bower, Charles Schweger, Sheila Greer, and Ruth Gotthardt. 2004. Multidisciplinary investigations of alpine ice patches in Southwest Yukon, Canada: Paleoenviromental and paleobiological investigations. *Arctic* 57 (3): 247–259.

Fienup-Riordan, Ann. 1990. *Eskimo essays: Yu'pik lives and how we see them*. New Brunswick, NJ: Rutgers University Press.

Fortuine, Robert. 1989. *Chills and fevers: Health and disease in the early history of Alaska*. Fairbanks: University of Alaska Press.

Franklin, Adrian. 2002. *Nature and social theory*. London: Sage.

Gibson, James R. 1983. Smallpox on the Northwest Coast, 1835–38. *BC Studies* 56: 61–81.

Giles-Vernick, Tamara. 2002. *Cutting the vines of the past: Environmental histories of the Central African rain forest*. Charlottesville: University Press of Virginia.

Grove, Jean. 1988. *The little ice age*. London: Methuen.

Hare, P. Gregory, Sheila Greer, Ruth Gotthardt, Richard Farnell, Vandy Bower, Charley Schweger, and Diane Strand. 2004. Ethnographic and archaeological investigations of alpine ice patches in Southwest Yukon, Canada. *Arctic* 57 (3): 260–272.

Hornborg, Alf, and Gísli Pálsson, eds. 2000. *Negotiating nature: Culture, power and environmental argument*. Lund, Sweden: Lund University Press.

Ingold, Tim. 2000. *The perception of the environment*. London: Routledge.

Ingold, Tim, and Terhi Kurttila. 2000. Perceiving the environment in Finnish Lapland. *Body and Society* 6 (3–4): 183–196.

Innis, Harold. 1950. *Empire and communications*. Oxford: Clarendon.

Jasanoff, Sheila, ed. 2004. *States of knowledge: The co-production of science and social order*. London: Routledge.

Krajick, Kevin. 2002. Melting glaciers release ancient relics. *Science* 296 (April 19): 454–456.

Kuzyk, Gerald W., Donald, E. Russell, Richard S. Farnell, Ruth M. Gotthardt, P. Gregory Hare, and Erik Blake. 1999. In pursuit of prehistoric caribou on Thandlät, Southern Yukon. *Arctic* 52 (2): 214–219.

Latour, Bruno. 1993. *We have never been modern*. Cambridge, MA: Harvard University Press.

McClellan, Catharine. 2001 [1975]. *My old people say: An ethnographic survey of southern Yukon Territory*. 2 vols. Mercury Series, Canadian Ethnology Service Paper, 137. Ottawa: Canadian Museum of Civilization.

McIntosh, Roderick J., Joseph A. Tainter, and Susan Keech McIntosh, eds. 2000. *The way the wind blows: Climate, history and human action*. New York: Columbia University Press.

Macnaghten, Phil, and John Urry. 1998. *Contested natures*. London: Sage.

Minority Rights Group. 1994. *Polar peoples: Self-determination and development*. London: Minority Rights Publications.

Monsalve, M. Victoria, Anne C. Stone, Cecil M. Lewis, Allan Rempel, Michael Richards, Dan Straathof, and Dana V. Devine. 2002. Brief communication: Molecular analysis of the Kwäday Dän Ts'ìnchi ancient remains found in a glacier in Canada. *American Journal of Physical Anthropology* 119: 288–291.

Morrow, Phyllis, and Chase Hensel. 1992. Hidden dissension: Minority-majority relationships and the uses of contested terminology. *Arctic Anthropology* 29 (1): 38–53.

Nadasdy, Paul. 1999. The politics of TEK: Power and the "integration" of knowledge. *Arctic Anthropology* 36 (1–2): 1–18.

——. 2003. *Hunters and bureaucrats: Power, knowledge, and Aboriginal-state relations in the Southwest Yukon*. Vancouver: University of British Columbia Press.

Niezen, Ronald. 2000. Recognizing indigenism: Canadian unity and the international movement of indigenous peoples. *Comparative Studies in Society and History* 42 (1): 119–148.

Portelli, Alessandro. 1997. *The battle of Valle Giulia: Oral history and the art of dialogue*. Madison: University of Wisconsin Press.

Raffles, Hugh. 2002. *In Amazonia: A natural history*. Princeton: Princeton University Press.

Scott, Colin. 1996. Science for the West, myth for the rest? The case of James Bay Cree knowledge construction. In *Naked science:*

Anthropological inquiry into boundaries, power and knowledge, edited by Laura Nader, 69–86. London: Routledge.

Slater, Candace. 2002. *Entangled Edens: Visions of the Amazon.* Berkeley: University of California Press.

Smith, Eric Alden, and Joan McCarter, eds. 1997. *Contested arctic: Indigenous peoples, industrial states, and the circumpolar environment.* Seattle: University of Washington Press.

Starn, Orin. 2004. *Ishi's brain: In search of America's last "wild" Indian.* New York: W. W. Norton.

Stavenhagen, Rudolfo. 1996. Indigenous rights: Some conceptual problems. In *Constructing democracy: Human rights, citizenship, and society in Latin America,* edited by Elizabeth Jelin and Eric Hershberg, 141–160. Westview Press, CO: Boulder.

Thomas, David Hurst. 2000. *Skull wars: Kennewick Man, archaeology and the battle for Native American identity.* New York: Basic Books.

Weaver, Andrew J. 2003. The science of climate change. *Geoscience Canada* 30 (3): 91–109.

White Richard. 1998. "Using the past: History and Native American studies. In *Studying Native America,* edited by Russell Thornton, 217–243. Madison: University of Wisconsin Press.

The Terrible Nearness of Distant Places: Making History at the National Museum of the American Indian

Paul Chaat Smith

On September 21, 2004, 20 thousand red people, and scores of dignitaries including the president of Peru, celebrated the opening of the National Museum of the American Indian (NMAI). It occupies the last open space on the National Mall in Washington, D.C., that boulevard of broken dreams that serves as the main street of the United States, and is just a stone's throw from the U.S. Capitol. The project cost nearly a quarter of a billion dollars and took 14 years to complete.

It is unlikely that there will ever be anything like it again. It is hard to imagine where the dollars, resources, and attention would come from to build a comparable museum. And if such a museum is built someday (and God knows I hope it is, and soon), it's a safe bet it will never achieve the popularity of the NMAI. During its first three months, the museum had more than 800,00 visitors, and if that pace continues, more than 4 million people will visit in the first year. If only half that show up, it will still make NMAI one of the most popular museums in the world, and its location, between the Capitol and the Air and Space Museum would seem to guarantee those kind of numbers no matter what people find inside.

NMAI is going to influence how indigenous experience is understood on a massive and profound level with audiences of all kinds, and perhaps most importantly, how indigenous people ourselves view our present circumstances. I also believe it is incumbent for curators at public institutions to share information about their work and how it was assembled. For that reason, I offer this account of how one relatively small piece of the NMAI project came together. I am still coming to terms myself with this experience, and this account, obviously a subjective one, is limited in many important ways. For example, most of the crucial decisions had been made years before my arrival, and NMAI's corporate culture is somewhat secretive. However, I was at the center of the thing that I felt—and continue to believe—was the raison d'être for the museum's very existence.

I've decided to tell this history through a narrative focusing on key documents written (mostly by me) during the construction of the exhibit. I think this will be more useful than if this entire chapter were just about what I thought now, or how I remembered events from today's perspective. It'll help keep things honest. A central theme of the exhibit is about the nature of history itself, so I think it appropriate that I apply those standards to this document as well. It's a story of extraordinary possibilities, brilliant mistakes, realized dreams, and ultimately failed revolution. It's a story about the agitprop opportunity of a lifetime.

Dr. Bruce Bernstein phoned me up in April, 2001, and asked me to come in for an interview. He said they had some projects they'd like me to consider working on. I had met Bruce in November 1999 at the Native American Art Studies Association in Victoria, British Columbia. He knew my work, and made clear he was shopping for Native talent, and even talked about building an Indian dream team. I was all ears. Though I had not heard from since that time, it didn't surprise me to get his call. I knew Gerald McMaster, an artist turned big time bureaucrat in Canada was working at NMAI, and broadly speaking we were in the same camp. I had also come in for a two day "vetting session" in December 2000 to help the curatorial staff think about contemporary issues for one of the permanent galleries. I figured I was on their radar, and they'd call me one of these days.

The interview was at the Museum's Cultural Resources Center in Suitland, Maryland, seven miles outside Washington, D.C., and was with Bruce, Gerald, and Dr. Ann McMullen, who would become, and still is, my boss. It was casual and friendly, and they all said nice things about my work. They offered me a vague job that had to do with helping out Cynthia Chavez, the curator for "Our Lives," the contemporary issues gallery, and possibly serving as an editor for the exhibition scripts. I told them I would be delighted, and said I considered doing whatever one could for NMAI as nothing less than a patriotic obligation.

The federal government's hiring process takes forever, so I didn't actually start until late August, 2001. In the meantime, I continued working as an office temp.

I had followed NMAI since the 1980s, when I lived in New York and visited the Museum of the American Indian in upper Manhattan, and also followed the battle over whether the Smithsonian Institution (SI) or Ross Perot or the American Museum of Natural History would take over the collection. I moved to the D.C. area in 1991 and got updates on NMAI from friends who would be in town to speak at an NMAI event or hear the latest on who had been hired or fired. I wasn't that connected; it was just part of the landscape. After the opening of the New York facility in 1994, and especially after the opening of the CRC in 1998, I heard more about the direction things were taking. It didn't sound that good, or that unexpected. For those reasons, I was pleasantly surprised at what I found when I finally began working in Suitland, until I started looking at the exhibition plans.

The plan for me to work with Cynthia Chavez had never actually been seriously discussed with Cynthia, who felt she didn't need another curator but, instead, more research assistants. We tried it out for a month and a half, and took one trip together to the Kahnawake reserve in Canada, but parted amicably after that. Ann and Bruce didn't know what to do with me, so I had lots of time to read exhibition planning documents and think about the museum. This was during the days and weeks following September 11, 2001 (9/11), a sorrowful time for all of us living in Washington. I began putting my thoughts into a lengthy critique, addressed to Ann, Bruce, and Gerald. It was called *Love and Theft: Notes on Sixteen Weeks at the National Museum of the American Indian.* I wrote about how impressed I was at what had been accomplished, especially with the unprecedented move of the collection from New York to Maryland. And I wrote about my reaction to one of the key documents that guided the exhibitions, the *National Mall Museum Exhibition Plan* (Smithsonian Institution internal document, 1997). It featured images of ancient duck decoys, one of the treasures of the museum, and for that reason everyone called it *The Duck Book.* After reading that, and an exhibition narrative that imagined majestic doors opening into an indigenous United Nations, I wrote about being so depressed that I went home and medicated myself with gin. From *Love and Theft*:

Anyway, I dragged myself back to Suitland the next morning and kept reading, and as I did my view of this journey to the land of tears and gin gradually changed. I've started to think of these documents as our version of the Pentagon Papers. Those were an internal history of the Vietnam War ordered by the top brass in the midst of the war, who, like everybody else wanted to know how the hell we got to this point. Before, I thought a handful of essentialist Indian gatekeepers had set the major policies and intellectual boundaries of NMAI, and that it reflected a narrow and partisan point of view. (Prior to 9/11 I routinely referred to them as the "Taliban.") I don't think I had grand illusions about the broader points of view out there, understand, but I thought it was a lot better than this.

Now I've come to believe what the Duck Book and related documents, as well as the current exhibit plans for NMAI, constitute nothing less than a detailed mapping of the North American Indian intellectual world at this moment; call it "The Way We Think Now."

Here's the way I read the map: Essentialism is the coin of the realm; Indian intellectuals have largely abdicated their role of providing critical perspective and building an environment that encourages debate and rigorous scholarship; and we've failed to provide direction to this new and troublesome idea of the Native Voice. At the same time, we should remember it's really just a snapshot of a moment in time, and new editions come out frequently. In truth, this map is unfinished and its borders contested. This is good news, sort of. The problem is NMAI's mandate is broad and insanely ambitious, and furthermore we are instructed to carry out this work "in consultation, collaboration, and cooperation" with Indian people. To me, this means, among other things, we must be really good at reading a really, really bad map.

Why is all this so hard? Partly because Indian intellectuals have not constructed a framework with defined meanings for terms like sovereignty, or nation, or built a consensus on historical narratives or on any of the broad themes the NMAI's exhibits must engage. Compare this to African Americans and you can see what I mean. There are a million controversies in African American studies, but there is also broad agreement on at least the facts and usually much consensus on the narratives of the slave trade, the middle passage, Reconstruction, and the civil rights movement. That blacks have an intellectual infrastructure and we don't shouldn't be a surprise: there are 30 million blacks and 1 or 2 million Indians. African Americans have much more of a shared experience that Indians.

And the story of Indians and the continent is much, much harder. It's the elephant in the American living room. Harder not simply because it is unpopular and in contradiction to what the United States wants to believe about itself, but because the story is so fantastically complex and largely unknown. Slavery in the Americas and the Holocaust in Europe are hardly simple events and processes to describe, but NMAI is addressing events pre-contact to the present day in Indian societies throughout the hemisphere. The best non-Indian historians know instinctively to stay away from this topic. Indian intellectuals for the most part remain endlessly fascinated in what anthropologists think of Indians, romanticism, and stereotypes and less interested in taking on the larger questions. This is changing, I think, and I was encouraged at the recent AAA panel of Indian anthropologists. But I still maintain this infrastructure does not yet exist, and this goes a long way in explaining why the NMAI is using the tools, language, and methodology of anthropology to design exhibits of social history. It's all we know how to do.

Because I am arguing we don't have a common language yet for this discussion, I think it's imperative to be as specific as possible, so I will now turn to the Apache and the Seminole and how I fear the NMAI is about to embarrass them in front of millions of people, day after day, for ten, possibly fifteen years.

I discussed how naïve the tribal histories read to someone familiar with how ferocious contemporary tribal politics are, and what it would mean to allow our Apache collaborators to deify their late tribal chairman, who stood accused of skimming large amounts from the tribe's casino and achieved national attention for seeking permission to store nuclear waste on the reservation. I thought Wendell Chino was a great story, but it couldn't be presented in a one-sided way, curated by his relatives, without voices from other Apaches. About the Seminole, I argued that to have no reference to Africans being central to the existence of the Seminole was untenable and would get us in trouble.

I also felt the museum was locked in a moment of *Dances with Wolves* (1990, Orion Pictures, 181 min) and post-Quincentennial triumphalism: "As bad luck would have it, the discussions that led to the Duck Book took place during the early 1990s, a period that future historians will not regard as our finest hour. We knew everything back then. It was all very we talk, you listen, only problem being nobody was listening except a bunch of New Age freaks, which actually was a blessing when you look at the kind of things we were saying. Like similar manifestos, say the Chicago Indian Conference of 1961, the Indians of All Tribes Alcatraz in 1969 declaration, the Port Huron statement of 1962 or President Reagan's 1984 'Morning in America' TV ads, they are instructive as snapshots of a moment. Yes, they are artifacts who will be studied for generations, but they are anything but timeless in their message" (*Love and Theft*).

I continued in this vein:

Things change. During the late 1960s Negroes ceased being Negro and in the space of just a few years became black. By 1970 Negroes had disappeared, they were history. In 1965 Clyde Warrior was bound for glory: He was our Malcolm X, our shining red prince, smart and bold and fearless who will forever be remembered kicking back in the Oklahoma sun on a chaise lounge, wearing that tacky Hawaiian shirt and leafing through *The New Republic*. He knew more songs and dances than perhaps any Indian of his generation, none of which he was inclined to share with white folks. He didn't hate white people, he just thought it wasn't really anyone else's business. Clyde Warrior never lived to see 1969 so we'll never know how he might regard our project. It's possible, who knows, maybe he would have come around to the idea of a Smithsonian museum run by Indians (well, kinda sorta) featuring dances performed for tourists, excuse me, visitors. But if you had to guess, based on what we know of him, a prediction that Indians at the dawn of the next century would choose this path more likely would have provoked disbelieving laughter or disgust. After all, he once worked at Disneyland, dressed in buckskin and feathers, paddling a canoe through the manmade rivers of Anaheim. Probably not the best of memories. In 1972 the Oglala Sioux Tribe sponsored a sun dance. They charged admission and sold beer. Five years later things had changed, and any Sioux suggesting such a thing likely would have been beaten, jailed, or dispatched to the South Dakota insane asylum.

Let me be clear. I do not think the term *Negro* will make a comeback. I don't expect that Indians en masse are going to adopt the ideas of Clyde Warrior or that despite my best efforts, "jukebox spiritualism" will suddenly be the new catch phrase in Window Rock. And I don't think NMAI hosting dances in 2004 is the same as Disneyland paying Clyde Warrior to paddle canoes. My point is that ideas go in and out of fashion in the Indian world like anywhere else. If a vote were taken today, Indians in North America would approve dances at NMAI by a landslide. If a vote were taken ten years from now, who knows? And in any case, a sizable minority of Indians have always been uncomfortable with dancing for visitors. I think we're on stronger ground to look for ways to reflect this ambivalence in our practice. We should anticipate that Indian opinions will change over time. In the early 90s I remember hearing stories of things like mandatory attendance at morning religious ceremonies for people whose only crime was attending a two-week performing arts workshop in British Columbia. Individuals got carried away sometimes, and their zeal to restore balance earned them derisive nicknames like "Smudgasaurus." You don't hear stories like that so much these days. We can laugh about it now. It's no big deal, no worse than white people in bell bottoms or black people in dashikis. Humans get carried away sometimes, it's one of our great charms. The thing is, we eventually put the mood rings and pet rocks in a drawer someplace and don't enshrine them as guiding principles for the rest of our lives.

This is the dilemma. We want to tell our stories, but we don't always know our stories. This is among the most challenging issue facing the museum. David Penney talks of four archetypal types of stories: comedy, tragedy, romance, and ironic satire and how they apply to historical narratives. "It seems to me that when non-Native Americans consider their nation's history in relation to Indians, they tend to tell stories of comedy and tragedy. ... Native American people often speak in terms of irony and romantic transcendence. Are there other ways to structure narratives from a Native American perspective? I am not qualified to say, though I sense that Indian curators and artists are struggling to find them."[1]

How do we explain why the first thing most tribal museums do is build precisely the kind of exhibits the NMAI stands in opposition to? Do we think the people on these reservations are morons? That they don't know how to involve their tribal historians? My theory is they are smart people who know exactly what they are doing. They build dioramas because people in their community want to know how they lived long ago. The dioramas are tacky because they can't afford to hire Industrial Light and Magic.

If our job is to present the Native Voice *unfiltered,* I believe is the word Bruce used in one memo, the Natives are naturally going to say, okay, well which Natives are we talking about? Who chose them? Or, often, it will be who chose *them?!* The first OL meeting in Kahnawake took place before the Mohawk Council of Kahnawake. The second one took place at the cultural center, and all but one or two of the people at this meeting refused, on principle, to even vote in the elections for the MCK. The unstated NMAI fieldwork protocol is always going to say let's talk to the regular folks, the traditionals, which is okay. But we can't hide behind the process and say we did no choosing of our own. And we better not say it doesn't make much difference which Kahnawake Mohawks we talk to, because which Kahnawake Mohawks you talk to makes all the difference in the world. Here's the thing: as David Penney has pointed out, "identity, by itself, does not bestow knowledge or wisdom." Knowledge and wisdom and culture and history don't come standard with any particular territory or anyone's particular DNA. They just don't.

And I expressed my dismay at the lack of any broad historical narrative:

> There has to be a substantial piece of the museum devoted to the disaster of contact. Not guilt trips, not just first-person accounts, but a factual, narrative overview. No matter how excellent the *OP* gallery might turn out, that won't be enough. If we don't directly address this in a straightforward and serious way, well I don't know how to end that sentence, because I don't see it as even a choice. I think people would be amazed and baffled to know that at this point this presentation simply doesn't exist in the exhibition plan. I guarantee you that just will not fly. It also makes no sense to have glancing references to boarding schools and loss of language without a broader context. Talking about boarding schools without straightforwardly addressing contact is like complaining about the lunch menu at Auschwitz.
>
> We should provide basic information on disease and warfare settlement, and a timeline. It should be factual. It should talk about all that we don't know. It is the most important exhibit in the entire building and it has to be really, really good. What happened? This is the main thing people want to know. Because people intuitively understand that what they've read and heard and seen is not true. Because people know this is the great untold story of the Americas.

I had not told anyone I was writing the critique, and I delivered it to Bruce, Ann, and Gerald on December 12, 2001. The timing coincided with the increasing dissatisfaction by curatorial and others about the history gallery. Several months earlier, NMAI had rejected the design for the gallery, believing the designers just didn't get Indians or the content. Now, it was becoming apparent that the problem wasn't with the design, but with the exhibition content itself. Partly based on *Love and Theft,* Bruce invited me to join a group he was putting together to review everything. In addition to Bruce, it included Gerald, Ann, and Patsy Phillips, the Cherokee project manager.

We met over the holidays, often for entire mornings and afternoons. The focus was almost exclusively on the tribal histories, which were a dense collection of accounts that were somehow to be turned into exhibits in an area the size of a large bedroom. At this point, there were going to be 12 tribes in the history space (which had the terrible working title of *Our Peoples,* which tragically became the final name for the exhibit). As a writer, I felt it was nearly impossible to make these accounts coherent because they required so much exposition, and that's before considering the problem of making them visually compelling.

This resulted on something Ann and I, who led during the discussions, would label a revolution, and a document (authored by the two of us) remarkable for its candor and self-criticism. The cover memo from Bruce said "we conclude that *Our Peoples* is broken, and if work continues on its present course the gallery cannot succeed. As you will see, we believe this is not a matter of anything as simple as individual failings: they are instead collective and institutional. They pose hard questions that strike at the very core of our work: How is our Museum different? Is it different? Who are we accountable to? Whose stories will we tell? Who decides? What is history? The attached document is the product of those discussions, and I ask you to read it carefully." It was called "Looking for a Showcase for Indian History," after a headline from a *New York Daily News* article taped on Ann's office door from the 1980s, when the museum itself was up for grabs. We distributed our manifesto on January 11, 2002.

About the tribal histories:

What we may have now as events and stories about them are in the nature of epigrams: brief, potentially pithy excerpts drawn from much larger texts. Epigrams are a form of shorthand and we know that epigrams can sometimes work to convey much larger stories or texts. But other things which we might think of as epigrammatic are instead too short and too densely embedded in their larger texts to be comprehensible without a mountain of context and explanation. They may be truisms, but who can read their truth? If "Our Peoples" or any other exhibition included as an exhibit text the quote "I will fight no more forever," who would get it? How much would have to be added in terms of culture and history to make this make sense? How much Nez Perce culture, how much Nez Perce history, how much Indian history, how much Chief Joseph biography, and how much U.S. military policy would have to be added to make this make sense to our museum visitors? Does this or any other epigram do justice to the story it abbreviates, to history, or to culture? When we strip it all away and let a quote speak for an event, depriving it if its temporal and spatial context and its ideological framework, what's left?

And:

Now, we face a choice. Do we force these tribal histories to become the result we wished for, to make connections where none really existed, to edit them not for coherence or clarity but in order to tell a story the communities did not actually tell? We could do it. We could privilege the stories we like, the ones that fit our idea of what we expected to hear (of what they *should* have told us) and drop the other ones, to shoehorn the Kiowa story so it complements the Cherokee story and fits into the guns and horses theme and becomes the pleasing narrative we expected.

Or do we let the stories stand as they are? In their spare literalness, they allow any person to create their own *Rashomon* of Indian history, and, perhaps, this is a good thing. However, in reviewing the framers' intent we never saw anyone calling for that level of inscrutability. It is one thing to say it's okay for some stories to be mysterious and clear to a certain Indian audience and confusing to others, but to accept this as the rule rather than the exception would represent a radical shift and doom the gallery's effort to speak clearly to visitors. Within the scores of "epitomizing events" are tales of wonder and heroism and epic tragedy but they compete with many more that are likely to appear baffling, dense, incomplete, and boring to both Indian and non-Indian visitors. If we think the baffling and dull tales will turn into diamonds with the right context, we are back to the very recontextualizing we've tried to avoid.

In retrospect, we believe a central mistake was the failure to sufficiently interrogate the idea of history itself. It's there, in the earliest documents through the latest ones, including Dave Warren's 1997 mentor statement, but like other key theoretical guideposts history has been lost along the way. Even if we could find a way to do justice to the stories in the tribal histories, to somehow give them the meaning to our visitors they presumably have to those communities, we still face big problems.

For example, although we often use the word *multivocality,* in practice the tribal histories are speaking for all tribal members. Part of the NMAI dissertation outline included an assumption that tribes had a consensus, a shared view of their history. In some cases this is true, in other cases it is not. If the OP team had met with a different group of Kiowas two years earlier, or even the same group, it seems unlikely they would have come up with an identical list of key events or that they would have spun them in the ways they have. It is probable many of the events would be different, told differently, and meant different things. After all, each story is spun out of the ideology of the moment—and the event—of its telling. If the consensus actually exists, that is, if there is a widely shared view of history, that's okay. But what if it isn't? And how do we tell the difference? The way it is currently constructed is as if all tribal members have the same way of telling history and the same understanding of what it is about. The imagined "Kiowa-ness" we keep talking about represents some presumed consensual fabric of history and culture against which we place singular, individual narratives which are made to fit into that consensus. Often, though, they are individual voices crying for context. We could include text that makes clear who we met with, when, and say these opinions don't necessarily reflect all Kiowas, but would that really work? We think it would do just what the NMAI has always wanted not to do, which is have the museum mediating the exhibit instead of giving Indian communities their chance to finally speak for themselves.

We think by making the gallery about history itself, to foreground the message that histories have agendas, histories change, histories lie, histories can lie but be true to their tellers, to even specifically point out this very gallery has an agenda, the visitor will be able to look at the tribal histories in more complex ways—beyond the frame of the mirror—and not simply see them as "true" or not. So the visitor would think about the ideas of consensus, and see that understanding the process of how the stories were gathered is crucial to understanding the stories themselves. In a word, transparency. We propose an introduction that explores the issues of history in a general way, discusses how "Indian history" only came together after European contact, and touch on the myriad of issues that involve "tribal history."

And about the biggest missing piece of all:

What about the missing narratives of a broader Indian history? It is clear that from the very earliest discussions about the museum there has been a consensus (a real one) that it must include the broad narratives of contact: colonialism, disease, warfare, and so forth. We have looked at adding a kind of "metanarrative" to go on top of, or around, or through the tribal histories as one solution. In truth, we very much wanted this to be the answer, to keep the tribal histories more or less as originally envisioned and add a new component. In the end, however, we felt it would be an overlay that would not help illuminate the tribal histories. We think it would be a quick fix that would not really fix anything.

We propose something else. We have yet to name this beast. It isn't a metanarrative, or narrative, or timeline, or history, or filter, but it is partly all those things. At present this organizing core is made up of five themes: Origins, Destruction, Resistance, Accommodation, Revital-ization. Within those themes will be the missing narratives and the key events from the tribal histories. Events from tribal histories might fit in several categories at once. The themes explicitly include precontact events, so that the "destruction" might be one tribe against another in 1100, or "resistance" might be one tribe fighting another in 1750. The connections between objects, tribal stories, and broader narratives will be infused with the notion of that making sense of history requires interrogation of history. We don't know what that looks like exactly, but we have some ideas. What we do know is that we need to become complete—and active—partners in assisting Indian people in telling their histories, and to bring to bear all of our experience in museums, exhibits, interpretation, cultural presentation, and representation. *Our Peoples* will still include tribal histories, but these must change. Because the whole of the exhibition will be different, the interconnections of the parts will also be different.

The paper ended on a note of optimism that captured how this group I would name the Gang of Five felt at this time. Bruce would call it the best work he'd been part of all year.

It is important to recall that the original framers of *Our Peoples* believed the broader narratives that touch every Native person would flow out of the tribal histories. It seems to us very unlikely any concept would have been approved that focused exclusively on 18 communities and did not produce the "Indian history" that has been at the core of NMAI from its very beginning. Creating a gallery that met the approval of 60 Indians (that would be 12 communities times five people each) but had limited relevance to the broader Indian community that NMAI is accountable to would mean failing to meet one of our main objectives. That imagined exhibition is still a dream, but we are closer to achieving it than ever before.

We believe the lessons from *Our Peoples* merit additional study and reflection and have major implications for work throughout Curatorial and the entire museum. We look forward to sharing and deepening our understanding of these lessons with our colleagues.

Well, life being what it is, the people who had so painstakingly assembled the accounts that we trashed with such eloquence weren't too keen on sharing and deepening an understanding of anything except their own defensiveness. I can't really blame them: The mostly young, mostly white research assistants had worked extremely hard for years on this and felt they were the heart and soul of NMAI because of their relationship with "the communities."

A few meetings took place in which we tried to persuade them of our way of looking at history and so forth, but that didn't really go anywhere. One really good thing did happen, however. Bruce gave me permission to recruit someone from outside to work with me on developing the central core, and I knew just the right person.

I had met Jolene Rickard in Thunder Bay at a conference in 1994, and we had been comrades ever since. She came from a family of Tuscarora patriots, and we disagreed nearly as much as we agreed on things. We had never actually collaborated on a project before, but I knew she wasn't just brilliant, and not just an exceptional conceptual artist and photographer, but had also spent the 1980s at major Madison Avenue advertising firms working as a creative director. For the first time in several years, she had no major projects lined up, having just completed a major exhibition called *Across Borders: Beadwork in Iroquois Life*. She signed on in February, and I brought her down a few weeks later to talk to Bruce, Ann, Gerald, and Patsy about that exhibit. I believed it was an important model because it included Indian scholarship, leading non-Indian scholars (she had four cocurators, all white, and all experts in the topic) and people from the so-called communities.

On February 19, 2002, I issued a "statement of intent" that declared what we thought the revamped gallery would look like.

What really happened?
For the Americas, this question has never been satisfactorily answered. The usual replies are punch lines and cartoons, amnesia and denial, or not quite believable tales of paradise and conquest, generals and natives. It is not a question serious adults ask out loud, because asking it is proof of naiveté or bad manners, yet it preoccupies Americans—north and south—all the same. The continent is filled with Indian-named streets and rivers, corporations and sports teams, and mountains and cities. This untold past is everywhere, in the landscape and the air we breathe, and it's not even past, and we all know it. Confusingly, millions of Indians are still here too, living all over the place: in cities, jungles, suburbs, in the shadow of pyramids and shopping malls. Everywhere you look, there it is, asking the same question few ask but everyone still wonders about. What happened here? What really happened, and why?
For NMAI, this simple, devastating question is the key reason for the museum's existence. It may have taken 12 years, but with the reimagined

Our Peoples gallery NMAI finally accepts the challenge of the most profound, most ignored, and most urgent question of the hemisphere.

In the past five weeks, like the NMAI itself and amnesiac, conflict-averse Americans everywhere, we have danced around the issue of what those larger narratives actually are. Our five discourses (origins, destruction, resistance, accommodation, revitalization) offered a way to think about the narratives but didn't tell us what they are. Time ran out, and eventually the question was called. What exactly are those narratives everyone, including us, talks so knowingly about but never quite describe?

We conclude they are the biggest story never told: the rise and fall and rise of the Americas, the ways America changed Europe, Europe changed America, a story featuring Indians as actors on the world stage and not merely victims. It is a story of changing worlds and how people managed that change in dreadful, surprising, ingenious ways. How the Black Death in Europe led to a desperate search for cod that, even more than gold, explains Columbus. How his journey led to the greatest mass human extinction in history, and the countless ways Indians survived and triumphed in the face of adversity. It is a story where Indians are partners in global markets, savvy diplomats, and eager consumers of new technology. It brings into focus a hemisphere that before contact was outrageously diverse, deliciously complex, endlessly fascinating, and one that would become only more so with every passing century.

It is a story with Indians at the center but also, by definition, relevant to every visitor, whose identity and personal history is shaped by those events. We argue understanding this hemisphere and your place in it is impossible without investigating the centrality of the Indian experience. We argue it changed everything, *it changed you*. Further, we advise visitors that just about everything you know about this story is wrong. That goes for red people, too.

We will privilege beautiful stories and objects and ruthlessly edit out the mediocre ones. We conspire to dazzle and amaze, and not dazzle and amaze some mythical Iowa family but the toughest, most jaded critics we can find: each other. This story is so extraordinary, so important, so different than what people expect and think and, yet, at the same time precisely what our visitors, especially our Indian visitors are hoping for; finally, to learn a bit about what really did happen.

We're going to tell them. To do so *Our Peoples* must become the most exciting, the most controversial, the most moving and talked about exhibition in Washington. The United States Holocaust Memorial Museum currently holds that position, and we pay them our highest compliment by declaring today our ambition to put them in second place.

Sigh. I was so much older then, I'm younger than that now ... anyway, it was still a time of great promise. During the spring and summer, Jolene made frequent trips to Washington. We met with Ann McMullen and Dr. Gabrielle Tayac most often, sometimes with Bruce and Gerald although they were not usually available.

I was beginning to have doubts about the five discourses, and wanted to find a way to avoid labeling any particular piece of the content as one thing or another. For example, gaming: For some people it is resistance, for some it is destruction. And, anyway, I had always felt there was something false about them anyway. We thought about hanging big banners over the gallery, naming each discourse, and letting visitors decide what to call the stories they encountered.

Also during this time, Ann had been formally named curator for the gallery, and most of her time was taken up with fixing the tribal histories. She had not been very involved before, so it was a massive task to determine what had been done already, what the work was based on, and what to do about it.

Mainly we just talked a lot. By now I had developed two principles for what we had started calling "The Big Story": (1) Most Indians don't know their own history; and (2) Most Indians have bad taste. The first seemed obvious to me, the second even more so. I wanted to introduce the idea of history itself as something we had to fight for; it was never just there for us to know, and the notion that we all carried on these wonderful intact deep narratives of our past seemed to be like so much colonial bullshit. And, second, of course most people have bad taste. I was taking aim at the idea you go out into one of "the communities" and ask people who'd never thought twice about museum exhibitry to design exhibits. My other principles included *The Simpsons* as an appropriate model for The Big Story's epistemological approach because they successfully entertained our SI demographic (everybody from kids who can't talk or read to the very old, all races, and very smart people and very dumb people). Who else, I asked, had punch lines involving Eubie Blake or Adlai Stevenson or Noam Chomsky? This was part of a theme that arose from a Jimmie Durham line about how you always have to make work for people smarter than yourself. I felt SI had elitist ideas about audience, and they kept telling me the average visitor had a seventh grade education. This meant, to SI, that all the content had to be understood by this average visitor, rather than the Simpsons model that had something for everyone. And I never got an answer when I asked why can't our audience be like the Holocaust Museum's, which was always packed with visitors willing to read long labels and spend entire afternoons there.

One part of NMAI's design process ruled that you couldn't begin thinking about what it would look like until you had an abstract, conceptual model of the exhibit. Jolene and I already knew we wanted an art installation aesthetic and felt hamstrung by this approach. She would sneak in ideas about a hundred buffalo robes, or a wall of treaties.

Firing the design firm in 2001 meant there was no money left for an outside designer, so we waited until the new designer came on board. When Verena Pierik did begin work, all of her time was taken on the tribal exhibits for most of 2002. Lynn Emi Kawaratani, on loan from another branch of SI, helped out. These two would prove to be the perfect designers for what Jolene and I had in mind.

The physical design for the gallery came together over the space of just a few months in late 2002 and early 2003. In December 2002, I made a presentation to Jolene about how we might show visitors the ways that contact changed everything, and I put this on a whiteboard. It was really boring. She erased it, and said what about a wall of gold. That turned things around, and we used this approach, what Verena called "repetition with difference," throughout the gallery to emphasize how unique the particular experiences of red people were depending on time and place. We chose hundreds of precontact figurines, favoring the ones that looked African and Asian, to emphasize how diverse the place we called "1491" actually was. The gold crystallized our belief that the gallery had to focus on dispossession. Massive diversity. Massive wealth. Red gold turning into money, then into dozens of swords. A column of fire. A wall that argued you could not speak about colonialism in the Americas without speaking in the same breath about disease, showing how the biological catastrophe was the greatest tragedy in history and changed everything that followed. A wall of guns. A wall of bibles in Indian languages. And a wall of treaties. Jolene Rickard's contributions cannot be overstated: She was more responsible than anyone else for the way the gallery looks, and equally responsible with me for what it says.

Just weeks after finally resolving all the components, I presented the work to the museum director in March 2003. He approved it. The following 18 months were mostly a nightmare because we didn't have enough time or staff or talent to select or acquire nearly a thousand objects, design the space, and write the script. The museum had become a physical reality, and every delay became a crisis. Jolene began working on the central core of the "Our Lives" gallery, so she wasn't as available as before. In November 2003 I lost control of the "Church and State" walls, partly because I was never sure myself what we should actually say in the labels.

For all that, we achieved most of our vision. At the same time, the installations were crammed into a space half the size of one of the museum's two gift shops. It got lost. There wasn't room to stage it correctly. Worse, big chunks of it weren't ready at opening, so the press wrote stories about how we ignored genocide. The final pieces weren't completed until just before Christmas.

We failed to displace the Holocaust Museum as the most powerful and emotionally compelling museum in Washington. We actually never even came close to the experience I imagined in a piece I wrote in early 2003 called *Not Dark Yet*:

> Up past the curved walls and their beautiful weapons and books you can see the wall of names, this too changes, one name morphing into another, others never quite coming into view, others with only part of the name readable. It's like they're floating off into heaven, although do Indians believe in Heaven? Anyway, that's what's watching over us as stumble through five centuries of this history almost nobody knows.
>
> Silver, blue, and gold. You get up from the evidence thingy so this very intense guy can ask it something or other, and swing by for one last look at that cool Eskimo gun with the walrus bone trigger, and finally step inside the glow.
>
> It's not what you expect at all. The air feels charged, and inside the mother ship is a storm, and you're standing in the middle of it. The storm moves across the walls in front of you and you remember that time in Nebraska back in 1975 when you stood on Interstate 80 and nobody would give you a ride, and on that hot afternoon you could see thunderheads rolling across the sky from approximately forever, thunderbolts exploding inside clouds taller than mountains; thunder and rain, fury and chaos. You almost feel the rain on your tongue, and imagine a cool, almost cold breeze sweeping past you, so welcome but promising far more than just relief from the hot Nebraska sun.
>
> The storm is so beautiful. And so dangerous. Things that are beautiful and dangerous: storms, Eskimo guns, life, beaded Bibles, faded treaties.
>
> But you are not in Nebraska, you're in this Indian museum. And above the storm all around you are flashing images that dance with the changing weather and walls that are color itself, a dance of silver, blue,

and gold. The images are all from now, and from all over the globe. The storm has its own soundtrack, rhythmic, propulsive, industrial, like something dreamed up by one of those old guys from the Native American Church and Dr. Dre. They images appear and disappear as the storm does its terrifying thing. It's all Indians, all the time, right here right now in 2004, in the biggest cities and smallest towns, living large, pickups next to tipis, guerillas in a jungle with AK-47s, businessmen in three piece suits, doublewide trailers on a back road, strip mines in the desert, bank tellers and TV weather girls, tour guides at the pyramids in Mexico, a hundred kids running for the gold in an all-Indian Olympics, scenes of power lost and won, wealth, poverty, and life. Silver, blue, and gold. Rays of hope, shafts of sunlight, bolts of lighting, revealing images of struggle and loss, and survival.

To be Indian is to live in a hurricane, 24/7. To be Indian is to know the past really does live in the present, and that 2004 is maybe not so different than 1804. They're both good years to be Indian, and a good time to be alive in a world that is always beautiful, and always dangerous.

When you leave the gallery, at the end of a short hall, you see a window. Outside the window, close enough to touch, is the white dome of the U.S. Capitol.

Two hours before the opening on September 21, I spent an hour alone in the space, so flawed, so beautiful, so powerful, and felt humbled and proud. But I also remembered an e-mail from Ann McMullen during one of the many trying moments over the past three years that quoted Bruce Springsteen: "Is a dream a lie if it don't come true/or is it something worse?"

Note

1. See Penney's *The Changing Presentation of the American Indian: Museums and Native Cultures,* 59. Seattle: The National Museum of the American Indian and the University of Washington Press, 2000.

Afterword: Indigeneity Today

Mary Louise Pratt

As I wrote these words, in the first days of the year 2006, Evo Morales, an Aymara coca farmer, trade unionist, and political leader, had just been inaugurated as Bolivia's first indigenous president. In Mexico, the Zapatistas had launched "La Otra Campaña" ("the other campaign"), an alternative to a three-party presidential campaign that, they said, offered no real choices. In the United States, front pages reveled in the breaking scandal of corrupt Washington, D.C., lobbyist Jack Abramoff defrauding Indian tribes of tens of millions in casino profits by posing as their advocate. Weeks before, a young Mapuche professor at Harvard had organized a conference in Chile on indigenous media, bringing together Mapuche cultural workers from Chile and Argentina with indigenous scholars from the United States and Canada. The event was a first; meanwhile, lawyers in Chile were trying to liberate 20 Mapuche leaders imprisoned for years without trial for their role in land claims. Around the same time, the United States, Australia, and New Zealand demanded revisions of the UN Declaration on the Rights of Indigenous Peoples so that the principle of self-determination would specifically exclude the right to territorial secession or full independence.[1] Since 1990, half-a-dozen Latin American states have rewritten their constitutions to define themselves as multicultural and pluriethnic societies. None have made good on the promises of such recognition; the language is there.

Evidence abounds that the historical agencies of indigenous peoples all over the planet are expanding and evolving in new directions, posing new challenges and leaving older coordinates behind. In many places indigenous and tribal peoples are experiencing accelerated encroachment as checks on profit-driven corporate activities dissolve, and pressures on space, ecology, and resources bear down with an intensified ruthlessness

397

and aggression. Many collectivities find themselves more vulnerable now than they were 30 years ago. At the same time, the communications revolution has brought new ways of claiming agency and joining forces. The *Declaración de Quito* in 1991 was a watershed in this regard. Produced by a convention of indigenous leaders held in connection with the 1992 Columbus Quincentennial, it was one of the first documents produced by a coalition of indigenous peoples from across the hemisphere. The Quincentennial catalyzed indigenous peoples and indigenous issues on a new hemispheric and planetary scale.

The chapters in this volume bear witness to old relationships undergoing permutations, and new agents and theaters of action taking form. If they demonstrate nothing else, the chapters confirm, for better or worse, the generative power of the category indigenous in contemporary geopolitical theaters. As an analytical instrument, the chapters also show, indigeneity brings into focus key relationships, conflicts, and forms of collectivity at work in the world today, whether or not these are identified as indigenous. Indeed, the term illuminates situations in which it applies awkwardly or badly (Tibet, India, Minnesota, Botswana, etc.) as well as situations in which it has always "belonged" (Chile, Oklahoma, Washington, New Zealand, Nunavut, Australia, Bolivia, etc.).

On Prior-ity

In English, the cluster of generic descriptors used to refer to indigenous peoples—indigenous, native, aboriginal, first nations—all refer etymologically to prior-ity in time and place.[2] They denote those who were "here (or there) first," that is, before someone else who came "after." This of course makes the terms relational and retrospective: social groups become indigenous or aboriginal or native by virtue of the recognition that someone else arrived in a place and found them or their ancestors "already" there. Ironies abound here. Although party A (the indigenous) are marked as having "prior-ity" in relation to party B (the invaders), what in fact has priority is B's (the invader's) temporality. It is only with reference to B's temporality that A was "already" there. Until B arrived bearing a different temporal frame, A was most likely not the first subject on the scene, but the "last," that is, the most recently arrived. Certainly, until that moment, A was living a temporal narrative whose projection into the future did not include B. Yet A's relational status as "indigenous" depends on the perdurance of that prior, nonrelational self-identity. This perdurance is commonly encoded as "survival," the failure to die off or dissolve. The process of becoming indigenous, as Linda Tuhiwai Smith eloquently explains, does not end when one acquires the label. It begins there. Indigeneity for her names an ongoing, nonteleological process of becoming, self-creation and self-determination, the living out of a collective's being in time and place.

The relational nucleus of indigeneity explains the fact that "indigenous" is rarely if ever the primary identity of indigenous people. One is first Maori, Cree, Hmong, Aymara, Dayak, Kung, Quiché, or Adivasi, and one claims indigeneity by virtue of that (temporally and socially) prior self-identification.[3] In this sense, the fact of being who one is has semantic priority over the relational link between A and B. At the same time, as an umbrella category, indigeneity enables historically and geographically separated peoples to recognize each other and collaborate. Precisely because it references B's temporality, it generates agencies and interests that B must recognize, and must recognize as separate and distinct. These complexities were already apparent in 1562, some 30 years after Pizarro's landing in Cajamarca, Peru, when several hundred Andean indigenous leaders met and addressed a petition to the Spanish crown. Their long list of demands included this one:

> "Que se nos guarde nuestras buenas costumbres y leyes que entre nosotros ha habido y hay, justas para nuestro gobierno y justicia y otras cosas que solíamos tener en tiempo de nuestra infidelidad."
>
> (May our good customs and laws be retained that among us have existed and exist suitable for our government and justice and other things that we were accustomed to having in our time of as infidels).[4]

The "us" in this passage is a collective Amerindian subject brought into being by the Spanish invasion. That subject here assert its prior-ness: we "have existed and exist." That sequence of verb tenses marks the historical watershed of the European invasion, from the point of view of the invaded (albeit in the invader's language, perhaps already seized as a lingua franca among the newly constituted "indigenous"). The emergent Amerindian "us" asserts itself as a subject specifically of culture, law, history, and the future: "May we keep the good laws and customs from our time as infidels." This demand for continuity with the past is made in a moral universe already acknowledged to be radically altered. Two words in particular specify the alteration: *buenas*, (good), and *infidelidad* (the status of infidel). The Andean speakers deploy the bifurcated axes of Christianity—good–evil, Christian–infidel—inserting themselves, perhaps only strategically, into the Christian moral universe. So it is that in the very act of demanding continuity with the preconquest world, they constitute themselves as "other" to their prior, preconquest selves. At the same time, by calling for retaining prior customs and laws, they situate themselves outside the Spanish legal, political, and social universe. The sentence claims, for instance, that in them, for them, "infidelity" can coexist with goodness.

The Complexity Problem

Although our conference title named indigenous experience as its object of study, we tended to gravitate away from experience, toward the question of whether "indigenous" was a coherent or useful analytical category. The more skeptical papers (Nyamnjoh, Baviskar, and Yeh) that questioned the self-privileging power of indigeneity at times were sidelined. The liminal cases (like the Hmong studied by Schein, or the Bolivian musicians Bigenho accompanied), in which the logic of indigeneity worked only to a point remained intriguing. Some important and painful aspects of contemporary indigenous experience remained on the edges of our field of vision, or outside it: trauma, addiction, suicide and invitation to suicide, criminalization, religion and religious violence, gender, and sex, sex—the unrelenting transgressiveness of the erotic that leaves no boundary uncrossed.

It was overdetermined that our deliberations would begin and end with the claim that indigeneity today is much more complicated than people think. We performed the always legitimating scholarly gesture of presenting complicated truth against ignorance and reductive ideology. This gesture informs, often enchants, but it also leaves things pretty much in their place. Demonstrating complexity does not require or demand new ways of thinking. It seems unbearable that this should be the most scholars are able to do. Where else might we end up? Is there a way to grasp indigeneity not as a condition but a force? How might the fertility or potency of thinking and knowing through (i.e., by means of) the indigenous be apprehended?

Generalization

As the Peruvian example cited above reminds us, the concept of the "indigenous" has a privileged historical link to European expansionism of the 16th through the 19th centuries. This expansion produced what one might call a template or schema of indigeneity, a set of narrative elements that are seen as having widespread applicability. They account for the habitual conjugation of the term *indigenous* with the term *plight*. It seems possible to identify the salient elements of this template or schema:

1. Unsolicited encounter. The collective indigenous subject comes into being on the receiving end of an encounter it did not seek. Pizarro was looking for the Incas, but they were not looking for him. Cook was looking for lands in the South Seas, but no one there was looking for England. There is, thus, not a reciprocal crossing of paths but, instead, an encounterer and an encounteree. The idea of "prior-ness" or "ab-originality" is produced at the moment of encounter. It cannot preexist it.
2. Dispossession. In the schema, the dispossession takes the form of conquest and settler colonialism. More generically, becoming indigenous means losing control of one's land base and being obliged to sell one's labor. The acts of conquest and dispossession mean that equivalence between encounterer and encounteree is impossible. This becomes all the more obvious when exploitation is brought into the picture. In the schema, the encounterers conscript the surplus labor of the encounterees and exploit it for their own enrichment. These relations are sustained by co-optation and violence. Dispossession does not always succeed, of course. Groups are sometimes able to fight it off or escape to higher ground as in western Guatemala or the Lacandon forest. These circumstances, if anything, make one even more indigenous. The indigeneity, in other words, lies in the script rather than in what actually happens.
3. Perdurance. Exploitation, like indigeneity itself, is only possible when the encounteree perdures and continues to reproduce as a self-identifying collectivity. Being indigenous means not being eradicated or assimilated. Relations of exploitation, ironically, generate support for this perdurance, since the exploitation is justified by marking off the exploited as a distinct, nonequivalent group.
4. Proselytization. Indigeneity is also the product of religious encounter, again not a reciprocal crossing of paths (you worship your deities and I worship mine), but an asymmetrical engagement in which the encounterer condemns the encounteree's religion and claims entitlement to convert. It is not the case, however, that indigeneity evaporates if conversion succeeds. This is possible, but not in the least inevitable.[5]
5. Unpayable debt. Over time, the combination of unsolicited encounter, dispossession, and perdurance produce a relation of indebtedness

between the ex-dispossessors and the ex-dispossessed, and in-digeneity becomes the unfolding of that relationship. In other words, at the heart of the social formations that develop out of this historical genesis lies a debt, a wrong that—and this is important—can be addressed but never righted. Racist paradigms affirming the invader's superiority may deny or justify the wrong, but they cannot, I think, make it go away. Even when there is denial, the debt resurfaces in the subjunctive mode: "If we were to recognize a wrong, there would be no end to their demands."

Generativity

This schema is a given that permits generalization, characterizes a wide range of instances, and illuminates the divergences in other instances. It is also an obstacle, however. It generates a picture of indigeneity that non-indigenous moderns have learned to find satisfying, even as the lived experience of indigenous peoples remains largely beyond their grasp. It has the power, as schema do, to forestall further questions, to kill curiosity. The idea of generativity offers an antidote, perhaps. The historical relationships that underwrite claims or recognitions of indigeneity have many potential sources of historical energy. Willfully setting aside the satisfaction of the schema, one can imagine indigeneity as a bundle of generative possibilities, some of which will be activated or apparent at a given time and place while others will not. Different settings and historical junctures will activate different sources of energy, with effects that are unpredictable beforehand but decipherable in retrospect. This is one way of describing what Tuhiwai Smith calls becoming indigenous or indigenous becoming. In the terms introduced recently by Anna Tsing (2005), indigeneity is produced by particular points of friction in specific settings. Remoteness—geographical marginality with reference to a centralized state—for example, is a powerful generator of indigeneity. Remoteness, when activated as a force, almost inevitably translates into difference and a perceived absence of assimilation. It can also generate a narrative of refusal of a presumed invitation to assimilate. Territoriality, that is a claim to territory by virtue of long-term habitation, is another key generator of indigeneity. As Tsing and others show, the decontrolled plunder of lumber and mineral industries unleashed in the last decades of the 20th century activated this claim to habitus in forested regions. Indigeneity in these contexts generates authority for making claims on institutions and forging alliances. Subsistence lifeways also generate indigeneity—that is, these lifeways become indigenous at the moment they are threatened, at the moment they become a point of friction.

Indigeneity has destructive potentials, as several of the chapters point out. Intersecting with religious intolerances, Baviskar argues, indigeneity acquires a fascistic, misogynist force. Nyamnjoh finds similarly that the relation of nonequivalence between indigenous–nonindigenous has the power to obstruct the working out of differences on an equal footing. At our conference, we were most at home reflecting on the variable, mutable, negotiated, unpredictable character of agencies and possibilities that arise today from the relation of indigeneity, and the accidental, contingent, circumscribed character of what indigeneity today can and cannot achieve. The idea of generativity perhaps takes one small step past jaded pragmatism. It conceives of indigeneity not as a configuration or a state, but as a force that enables, that makes things happen.

This generativity, I would suggest, lies not only in what indigeneity actually makes happen in a given instance, but also in the unrealized possibilities that it creates in every situation, and that remain as potentialities that can be activated in the future.[6] One imagines indigeneity, then, as an unfolding in space–time that generates realized and unrealized possibilities. Unrealized possibilities of the past remain available to the present, and unrealized possibilities in the present remain available to the future; they are part of the fertility or potency of thinking and knowing through (i.e., by means of) the indigenous.

How might one think with this idea? Can one usefully reflect on the unrealized (and, perhaps, unrealizable) potentialities of indigeneity? What could this enable? Could thinking through indigeneity bring into clarity the unrealized rewriting of knowledge called for by the postprogress, posthumanist, postexpansionist predicament the planet and its inhabitants now share? Were such a rewriting achieved, the category of the indigenous would probably disappear. To enable the imagining of such a rewriting, however, it has rather to bloom.[7]

Notes

1. I thank Tove Skutnabb-Kangas for relaying me this information, and professor Aroha Te Pareake Mead of Victoria University of Wellington (New Zealand) for sending it out with insightful analysis.

2. Etymologically, *native* derives from *born* (here); *aboriginal* means (here) "from the beginning"; *indigenous* means "begotten within" (here).

3. Generic "tribal" names are also often secondary to clan identity, place of habitation, language, or other parameters.

4. For a detailed discussion of this passage, see M. L. Pratt 1994.

5. Renato Rosaldo argues that in the Philippines the main difference between highland "tribal" groups and lowlanders was that the latter converted to Christianity and the former did not.

6. I am indebted here to the thought of Elizabeth Grosz 2004.

7. I draw here on remarks made at the conference by Frances Nyamnjoh, whose wish for indigeneity was that it would be allowed to blossom, ripen, and then die.

References

Grosz, Elizabeth. 2004. *The nick of time: Politics, evolution and the untimely.* Durham, NC: Duke University Press.

Pratt, M. L. 1994. Autoethnography and transculturation: Peru 1615–1980. In *Colonial discourse/postcolonial theory*, edited by F. Barker, P. Hulme, and M. Iverson, 24–46. Manchester: Manchester University Press.

Tsing, Anna. 2005. *Friction: Ethnography of global connection.* Princeton: Princeton University Press.

Index